Women's Employment in

One of the most profound changes in European societies in recent decades is the increased involvement of women in waged work. This feminisation of employment has accompanied service sector expansion, occupational change and a general reorganisation of employment and working-time. Moreover, family life is changing: the male breadwinner supporting non-employed wives and children is increasingly rare.

This book examines these far-reaching changes in all fifteen member states of the European Union during the 1990s. Women's employment can no longer be neglected by anyone interested in the development of the new Europe; it is central to the changing face of European labour markets and social systems. Jill Rubery, Mark Smith and Colette Fagan also point out the significance of social and economic conditions and policy, both at European and national level, in shaping trends in gender relations.

Looking at women's progress to labour market equality over the last decade, the book highlights four major dimensions of inequality: care and wage work, occupational segregation, pay and working-time. The authors identify significant national differences in terms of gender relations, employment regimes and forms of gender inequality, and reveal how different national policies influence the labour market and welfare system. Finally, the book considers women's future prospects in a context in which equal opportunities has been identified as one of the pillars of Europe's new employment policy. Women will be a key source of labour in the new millennium, and their position now and in the future should be fundamental to policy-making. This book is a comprehensive, up-to-date key text in the fields of economics, gender studies, policy-making and European studies.

Jill Rubery is Professor of Comparative Employment Systems and Director of the European Work and Employment Research Centre (EWERC) at the Manchester School of Management, UMIST. From 1991–96 she was the co-ordinator of the European Commission's Network of Experts on the Situation of Women in the Labour Market. **Mark Smith** is a Research Associate in EWERC and Honorary Lecturer at the Manchester School of Management, UMIST. **Colette Fagan** is a lecturer in sociology at the University of Manchester and an Honorary Research Fellow at EWERC, UMIST. All three (with Damian Grimshaw) wrote *Women in European Employment* (Routledge, 1998) and contributed to *Part-Time Prospects: An International Comparison of Part-Time Work in Europe, North America and the Pacific Rim* (edited by J. O'Reilly and C. Fagan), also published by Routledge.

Women's Employment in Europe

Trends and Prospects

Jill Rubery, Mark Smith and Colette Fagan

London and New York

First published 1999
by Routledge
11 New Fetter Lane, London EC4P 4EE

Simultaneously published in the USA and Canada
by Routledge
29 West 35th Street, New York, NY 10001

Routledge is an imprint of the Taylor & Francis Group

Typeset in Times by
The Florence Group, Stoodleigh, Devon
Printed and bound in Great Britain by
TJ International Ltd, Padstow, Cornwall

British Library Cataloguing in Publication Data
A catalogue record for this book is available
from the British Library.

Library of Congress Cataloging in Publication Data
Rubery, Jill.
   Women's employment in Europe : trends and prospects / Jill Rubery, Mark Smith and
   Colette Fagan.
   p. cm.
   Includes bibliographical references and index.
   1. Women—Employment—European Union countries. 2. Labor market—European
   Union countries. 3. Manpower policy—European Union countries. 4. Employment
   forecasting—European Union countries. I. Smith, Mark, 1971– . II. Fagan, Colette.
   III. Title.
   HD6134.R83   1999
   331.4′094—dc21
                                                                    98–47473
                                                                      CIP

ISBN 0-415-19853-4 (hbk)
ISBN 0-415-19854-2 (pbk)

Contents

Figures

Tables

Appendix Tables

Boxes

Acknowledgements

This book is based upon research carried out when the authors acted as the co-ordinating team for the European Commission's Network of Experts on the Situation of Women in the Labour Market. Much of the information in this book is derived either from the European Labour Force Surveys or from the national reports provided by the Network of Experts. These national reports have in turn been based on national data sources and national studies. Many of the references in this text refer to the national reports for the network; details of the national sources are only provided in the national reports. Part II of the book provides an update and summary of previous reports by the Network, some of which were produced by national experts and assistants not mentioned in the list below. However, full details of the relevant national reports are to be found in the first section of the bibliography of this book. The authors of the national reports are as follows: Belgium: D. Meulders and C. Hecq; Denmark: T. Boje; Germany: F. Maier, S. Quack, A. Martschink, Z. Rapp; Spain: M.-L. Moltó; Greece: M. Cavouriaris and H. Symeonidou; France: R. Silvera, C. Granie, A. Gauvin and A. Eydoux; Ireland: U. Barry; Italy: F. Bettio and P. Villa; Luxembourg: R. Plasman; Netherlands: J. Plantenga, E. Koch and M. Sloep; Portugal: M. Chagas Lopes and H. Perista; United Kingdom: J. Rubery; Austria: U. Pastner; Finland: P. Keinänen; and Sweden: L. Gonäs and A. Spånt.

We are grateful to the following people for assistance in the preparation of this book: Damian Grimshaw, who worked on the previous reports of the Network on which this book draws heavily; Phil Almond, who contributed to Chapter 6; Jane Parker for general research assistance, Ana Franco, Didier Lesnicki and Laurent Freysson from Eurostat, who provided the special tabulations upon which much of the analysis presented here is based; Peter Elias of the Insitute for Employment Research, Warwick University, UK and Shirley Seal, Alphametrics (UK) Ltd who provided additional data; Eloise Turner for the detailed work on the preparation of the EC report and for her efficient administration of the project in general; Helen Dean and Jackie Dunn for assistance in the final stages of the preparation of the book; and Els van Winckel, Odile Quintin, Maria Stratigaki and Agnes Hubert of the Equal Opportunities Unit at the European

Commission for their help and support throughout the study. We would also like to acknowledge the help and support provided by UMIST, in particular by Manchester School of Management and by UMIST Ventures, in the administration of the Network.

Abbreviations

A	Austria
B	Belgium
CCT	Compulsory competitive tendering
CEC	Commission of the European Communities
D	Unified Germany
De	East Germany
DK	Denmark
Dw	West Germany
E	Spain
ELFS	European Labour Force Survey
EMU	European monetary union
ERM	Exchange Rate Mechanism
EU	European Union
F	France
GDP	Gross domestic product
Germany (e)	East Germany
Germany (u)	Unified Germany
Germany (w)	West Germany
GR	Greece
I	Italy
ID	Index of dissimilarity
IFO	Institute for Economic Research (Munich)
ILO	International Labour Office
IRL	Ireland
IS	Index of segregation
ISCED	International Standard Classification of Education
ISCO	International Standard Classification of Occupations
L	Luxembourg
NOW	New Opportunities for Women
OECD	Organisation for Economic Co-operation and Development
P	Portugal

S	Sweden
SF	Finland
UK	United Kingdom
UN	United Nations
USA	United States of America
USSR	Union of Soviet Socialist Republics

Introduction

Women's employment in Europe: trends and prospects

One of the most sustained and widespread changes within European societies over recent decades has been the growth of women's employment. There
is increasing recognition that this integration of women into the wage labour
market is related to a permanent and largely irreversible change in economic
and social life. Women's employment, far from constituting a marginal
segment of European labour markets, has come to be a key force in the
restructuring of work and employment within Europe. There has been an
increasing recognition of the significance of gender in the shaping of
European labour markets, such that equal opportunities issues have begun
to be integrated into European employment policy. In 1997 the European
Union agreed, first through the Amsterdam Treaty and second through the
approval of common employment guidelines at the Luxembourg Jobs
Summit, both to act collectively to draw up common action plans on employment, and to include equal opportunities as the fourth pillar of employment
policy, along with employability, entrepreneurship and adaptability. European governments are now committed to develop and to monitor policies
designed to promote the employment of women. Equal opportunities has
moved up the agenda, from being solely an issue of social justice, to an
integral part of the changing employment map in Europe. Integration of
women into employment is an essential part of the European employment
strategy of boosting the overall share of the population in work in Europe.
Moreover, women's employment growth has been integral to the development of more flexible labour markets, associated with the growth of part-time
and non-standard employment and with the expansion of the service sector
labour market.

The inclusion of equal opportunities within the framework of European
employment policy represents the logical conclusion of the policy adopted
by the European Commission, following on from the recommendations of
the 1995 Beijing Fourth UN World Conference on Women, to 'mainstream'
gender into all areas of its policies and practices. This commitment requires
the impact on gender equality to be taken into account in the design of

policies and within the decision-making and implementation process, as well as in the monitoring of the effects of policies. The focus on equal opportunities within the European employment guidelines is primarily on employment targets and objectives and does not explicitly embrace the objective of equal treatment in all its aspects. Equal treatment can be considered a much longer standing commitment from the European Union, incorporated into the Treaty of Rome and made manifest in the two directives in the 1970s requiring equal pay and equal treatment. Although in the 1998 agreed employment guidelines there was no commitment to make progress towards the goal of equal pay for women and men, this was added in 1999. This change was necessary as it cannot be assumed that gender equality will be achieved simply through an expansion of women's employment. Thus at a time when the European Union is perhaps congratulating itself for paying more direct attention to the issue of gender within its employment policy programmes, it is timely to revisit the whole issue of women's employment in Europe and to identify not only trends in access to the labour market, but also trends in the form and level of equality that women are experiencing within the labour market.

The objective of this book is twofold. The first is to assess recent trends, to determine the areas where there has been genuine progress towards gender equality and the areas where there was little change or even reinforcement of gender inequality during the first half of the 1990s. This assessment is set within an analysis of change, focused both on the changes in labour markets and organisations and on the broader political, economic and social changes which have shaped women's experience of employment over recent years. Particular attention is paid to the variations in women's position within European labour markets, and their relationship to differences in European employment and societal systems. From this perspective, gender is an important structuring influence in all labour markets, but the degree and form of gender inequality reflects, on the one hand, the different systems of labour market organisation found within European labour markets and, on the other hand, the system of gender relations in the broader society (Connell 1987; Crompton *et al.* 1990; Duncan 1995; Esping-Andersen 1990; Lane 1993; O'Reilly and Fagan 1998; Rubery 1988; Rubery *et al.* 1998a; Walby 1998). For example, the position of women within the labour market depends not only on the level of part-time work opportunities, but also on the form of part-time working across societies, whether it is organised as a marginalised and casual employment form or as an integrated and protected employment form. Moreover, whether part-time work is critical for women's integration will depend, *inter alia*, upon whether women are still expected to be only second or marginal income-earners, or to act as the prime or only care-providers. While no European society has moved fully towards dual-breadwinner households or to dual care-providers, the expectations relating to women's labour market and family roles still take on very different forms across the 15 European states.

The second objective is to provide some indicators of future prospects for women's employment in Europe, in the light of current trends in the restructuring of labour markets and current expectations relating to the development of European labour supply. This analysis of future scenarios for women's employment seeks to identify the significance of women's labour supply for the overall employment objectives of the European Union, while keeping in mind the policy and institutional developments necessary if the quantitative trends are to be associated with genuine progress towards equal opportunities for women and men (Rubery and Smith 1997; IFO 1994, 1995).

It might be considered that the growing centrality of women's employment to European labour markets reduces the need to consider women's participation and employment patterns separately from male or 'standard' employment. Not only have women been narrowing the gap with men on a number of key labour market trends including, for example, participation rates and levels of qualifications, but there is also evidence of much greater heterogeneity in the experience of women within the labour market, and indeed an increasing overlap in opportunities between the male and the female working populations. Nevertheless, there are several reasons for continuing to assess the position of women within the European labour market. First, despite the universal trend towards an increase in women's participation, there is still considerable variation in the pattern and pace of female integration into European labour markets (Rubery *et al.* 1998a). This means that differences in the current position of women within European labour markets may be one of the major reasons for differences in future trends in labour market developments within Europe. Second, the integration of women into the wage labour market has been associated as much with the maintenance and reinforcement of difference – difference between European societies and difference between men and women – as with processes of convergence and equality. Women's employment thus still merits separate and specific treatment, to identify the ways in which gender is influencing the organisation and restructuring of labour markets.

The argument for maintaining the interest in the growth of women's employment goes beyond even the pattern of labour market restructuring. Women's employment is associated with a process of major social and economic change. European societies are all moving, albeit slowly and at different speeds along varying trajectories, away from the deeply embedded male breadwinner system of family and welfare organisation to a more diverse system of household formation and provisioning. This restructuring of social organisation is taking place alongside fundamental reviews of welfare systems within Europe. These reviews are not, however, primarily motivated by the need to reform the welfare system in line with changing gender and household roles but by the objective of cutting costs. As a consequence these reforms put in jeopardy the systems developed in the less traditional or 'weak male breadwinner' states (Lewis 1992) which have underpinned the move towards a dual-earner and dual-carer society. These problems experienced within the more developed welfare states suggest that, as with any process of major social and economic change, no smooth transition towards a more gender-equal society can be expected. Trends in women's employment opportunities cannot be considered as separable or independent from general social and economic policies. In particular, progress towards equal treatment in the labour market may be determined more by overall trends in employment opportunities and in labour market policies than by specific equal treatment policies. Unless these general labour market policies and employment trends are acting in favour of equal opportunities, gender equality policies face an uphill struggle and may at best be able to protect women's existing employment position against further deterioration.

It is against this social and economic climate that this book assesses the progress made towards the achievement of equal opportunities in European labour markets during the first half of the 1990s and the likely prospects for women into the millennium and beyond. Although we find women to have made some progress over this period, the results are patchy and uneven, an unsurprising result perhaps, given the background of significant – and indeed often dramatic – social, economic and political change in this first part of the decade. Nevertheless, as the conclusions make clear, women are destined to continue to play an ever more significant role in the reshaping of European labour markets. As such Europe will need to take seriously its new-found commitment to make equal opportunities a fourth pillar of its employment policy. A broader approach to employment policy, embracing social as well as labour market change, is needed if the objectives of European employment policy to both raise the employment rate and move towards equal opportunities are to be achieved.

The plan of the book

To set the development in context, the first part of the book situates the evolution in women's employment position during the first half of the 1990s within an analysis of the key changes that have taken place in European economy and society. The first chapter explores change in the political and economic context at the level of the international and national economies. Many of these changes can be regarded as quite unexpected and unforeseen during the 1980s. The collapse of the former USSR and the Eastern European economic area, the movement into severe recession in the early 1990s and the rising tide of unemployment, changes to political regimes, the near bankruptcies of some welfare state regimes and the massive realignments of exchange rates and exchange regimes, all constitute events which have shaped the experiences of EU member states over this period, but which were either invisible or only just surfacing even at the beginning of the 1990s. By the late 1990s Europe appeared to be moving into another

new era, as the uncertainties over whether the proposed European monetary union (EMU) would actually be realised disappeared. Yet it would be
premature to predict a long-term move towards both stability and convergence within the EU; the impact of EMU on employment in general and
equal opportunities in particular will provide a subject for analysis in future
years.

The second chapter looks at change within enterprises. During the 1990s
there was a strong momentum to the restructuring of enterprises, including
moves towards decentralisation, privatisation and flexibilisation, accentu-
ating trends already evident in the 1980s. The implications of these new
systems of working, flatter organisational hierarchies and new employment
relations for gender relations are explored.

The third chapter considers the implications of changes in the behaviour
and aspirations of individuals and households. Changes in the European
context to the pursuit of equal treatment for women and men do not necessarily result solely from changes in external factors or factors beyond the
control and influence of the citizens of the Community. Women and men
are active social agents and the early 1990s have reinforced the finding,
already evident in earlier decades, that changes in social and economic
behaviour, and in women's roles in both the private and the public sphere
cannot be regarded as dictated by economic factors and structural conditions alone. The apparent irreversibility of trends towards greater integration
of women in the economy takes away the option from policy-makers of
solving the unemployment problem by excluding women from the labour
market.

This analysis of the changing context and the changing behaviour of social
actors in Part I of the book provides the backcloth for Part II. Here we
assess the progress made towards equal treatment across four key dimensions of the labour market, which can be regarded as the defining features
of gender difference or gender inequality. Chapter 4 looks at the organisation of *wage work, care work* and *welfare*, Chapter 5 looks at *segregation*;
Chapter 6 at *pay*; and Chapter 7 at *work* and *working-time patterns*. These
four areas are examined for evidence of both change and continuity in the
form and intensity of gender inequality, and for evidence of differences both
between member states and between groups of women. It is not only the
case that recent progress in closing the gender gap across these various
dimensions has been slow, but also that in some cases progress in the 1970s
and 1980s began to be reversed in the 1990s. However, alongside this
uneven and sometimes regressive pattern of change, we also find evidence
of widening dispersion of the experience of women within European societies, related to both education and age.

From this analysis of change and continuity in the key dimensions of
gender difference in the labour market we attempt in the third and final part
of the book to consider the future prospects for women's employment
into the millennium. Chapters 8 and 9 explore four main dimensions to

this analysis of future prospects. First, there is women's potential role in the future labour supply for European labour markets, related both to likely future trends in women's aspirations and behaviour, and the significance of female labour supply in comparison to alternative potential sources of future labour supply. Second, there are the implications for the quality and quantity of jobs available to women of the restructuring of organisations, technology, work and labour market regulation. Third, there are the variations in evolution towards gender equality both among countries and among different groups of women. Fourth, there are the implications of the commitment to raise employment and promote equal opportunities embedded in the new employment agenda for Europe and in the commitment to mainstream gender into all areas of policy. The ramifications of this double commitment for change within European society and economy are explored, together with a discussion of the policy approach which may be necessary to establish genuine opportunities for gender equality in the European Union.

Sources of information

This book is based on research undertaken for the European Commission by the Network of Experts on the Situation of Women in the Labour Market during the European Commission's Third Action Programme for equality of opportunity between women and men (1991–1995). The Network consisted of an academic expert appointed for each member state, each of whom was charged with drawing up a national report on a specific research topic on an annual basis, according to a research plan devised by the co-ordinating team, the authors of this book. This book is based on the last year of the work of the Network during the Third Action Programme, but effectively represents a summary of all the work undertaken by the network during the five-year programme. During the final year of work the experts were asked first to assess developments with respect to equal opportunities in their countries during the period of the Third Action Programme, focusing specifically on the period from 1989 to 1994, to pick up from the previous assessment by the Network on the Position of Women in the Labour Market, which had ended in 1989 (Meulders *et al*. 1993). This period also covered the movement of the European economy from relative boom to severe depression, to the beginnings of a recovery. Much of the statistical analysis in the book covers this time.

The second task of the experts was to update and summarise the position with respect to the four topics the Network had studied in the first four years of work: namely segregation (see Rubery and Fagan 1993); pay (see Rubery and Fagan 1994; 1995a); working-time patterns (see Rubery *et al*. 1995, 1997a; Rubery *et al*. 1998b); and the relationship between wage work, care work and welfare (see Rubery *et al*. 1998a; Grimshaw and Rubery 1997a). The book thus draws upon, summarises and extends the previous analyses of the Network with respect to these four key dimensions of gender equality.

All the national reports covering the full five years of the Network's research are listed for reference in the first section of the bibliography. It should be noted that over this five-year period a large number of people were actively involved in the work which has contributed to the final outcome. In some cases the membership of the Network changed and in other cases Network members collaborated with other academic experts in their own country. This book would not have been possible without the input of the Network members, and much of the information on the institutional and social structures and on the specific characteristics of European labour markets is derived from these national reports. While the authors accept responsibility for the views expressed in the book, the volume should be seen as arriving out of a truly collective effort between the Network experts and the co-ordinating team. The composition of the co-ordinating team has also changed during the five-year period; the current authors of this book are indebted to the contributions of other team members, particularly Damian Grimshaw who owing to pressures of a doctoral thesis did not contribute directly to this volume but assisted in all the previous four reports, and Philip Almond and Jane Parker who joined the team to assist in the preparation of the fifth report. Eloise Turner as the project secretary over four years was central to the collective effort. The co-ordinating team was also able to draw upon assistance and information from the staff of Equal Opportunities Unit of the European Commission and from the European Statistical Office. Use of the harmonised European Labour Force Survey data is an essential part of any comparative analysis of European labour force trends and this book draws heavily on both published and unpublished data from this source, supplemented by other internationally harmonised data sources such as the OECD reports and other Eurostat publications. The 'data box' provides further information on the statistical sources and definitions used throughout this book.

Information on the data used in the book

Most of the data referring to the 12 member states used in this book are from special tabulations of the European Labour Force Survey (ELFS) provided by Eurostat, Luxembourg. Additional European Labour Force Survey data were provided by Alphametrics (UK) Ltd and the Institute for Employment Research at Warwick University, UK.

Eurostat implements basic guidelines based upon the sample size and design of the European Labour Force Surveys in various member states in order to avoid the publication of figures which are statistically unreliable. Using the conventions from the published European Labour Force Survey, figures that appear between parentheses, '( )', are published with a warning concerning their reliability and '..' indicates that no reliable data are available. '—' indicates that no data are available.

The European Labour Force Survey uses internationally recognised definitions for the variables used. Here we briefly outline the key variables used in this book.

Unemployment: the European Labour Force Survey uses the International Labour Office (ILO) definition that someone is unemployed who has looked for work in the past four weeks, is able to start work within a week and does not currently have a job.

Employment: to be defined as employed in the European Labour Force Survey, an individual has to have done at least one hours' paid work in the reference week or be away from work.

Inactivity: includes all those who do not qualify under the definitions of employment or unemployment.

Part-time work: a self-definition of part-time work is used, to avoid variations resulting from different standard hours between countries or enterprises.

Temporary work: jobs are regarded as temporary if the end of the employment relationship is related to objective conditions, for example reaching a certain date, the completion of a task or assignment, or the return of another employee.

Full details of the definitions used in this book can be found in *Labour Force Survey: Methods and Definitions* (1988, 1992) published by Eurostat, Luxembourg.

Data on Austria, Finland and Sweden

The data used for Austria, Finland and Sweden in this book have been taken from a range of sources. Where possible we have tried to include data from the 1995 European Labour Force Survey, the first year that

Austria, Finland and Sweden were required to submit data to Eurostat for inclusion in the Survey. We have also used data from *Employment in Europe* (Alphametrics), the OECD and the national reports of the Network of Experts on the Situation of Women in the Labour Market. Tabulations from the National Labour Force Surveys in Sweden and Finland provided by Lena Gonäs and Päivi Keinänen were particularly helpful in the preparation of Chapters 6 and 7. Until 1995 there was no Labour Force Survey in Austria and this has limited the availability of quantitative information comparable to other member states throughout the book.

Data for Germany

Data prior to 1991 are not available for the former East Germany, so in this book we provide information for the former West Germany for time series prior to 1991 and for the former East Germany from 1991 to 1994 whenever possible. The convention used in this book for the former East Germany is 'De' and 'Germany (e)'; for the former West Germany 'Dw' and 'Germany (w)'; and the Unified Germany is referred to as 'D' and 'Germany (u)'.

Data on motherhood and households

In the European Labour Force Survey respondents are not asked directly whether they are parents and the only information available is derived from the presence of children in the household. Because of the way the data are collected this information is only available for women who defined themselves as spouse of household heads or household heads. This limitation has the greatest effect in Southern Europe, Ireland, the Netherlands and Luxembourg, partly due to the higher incidence of extended families living within one household (Rubery *et al.* 1995:22). Household data for Denmark were not available for 1994 so we have used data for 1993.

To define mothers with current responsibilities for a dependent child we take all women who are heads of household or spouse of household heads in a household with a child under 15. For most analyses we use the age group 20–39 for mothers to reduce the impact of generational effects. Moreover, when we compare mothers to non-mothers in this age bracket this will usually be with women who have never had children and not with women who have had children who are no longer of an age to be dependent.

Occupational data

The occupational data used in Chapter 4 for the 12 member states in 1994 is based on the new ISCO 88 (COM) occupational classification. Some of the data from the European Labour Force Survey was provided by Peter Elias of the Institute of Employment Research at Warwick University, UK and by Eurostat in Luxembourg. For full details of the occupational classification please refer to Eurostat (1992), Elias (1995) and Elias and Birch (1995).

Educational Data

Most of the educational information used in this book is based on the European Labour Force Survey question relating to the highest level of general education completed. The categories used are based on widely accepted principles and expressed in terms of the standard internal terminology of ISCED (International Standard Classification of Education). Respondents to the European Labour Force Survey are asked for the highest level of general education actually completed. Therefore if an individual is undertaking a course of education but it is not yet completed, they are regarded as having attained the level of education for which they have completed rather than none at all. The levels of general education have been classified as follows: **low** refers to individuals who have completed the first stage of the general second-level education but have not completed the second stage of the second level, and those who have not completed the first stage of general second-level education; **medium** refers to persons who have completed the second stage of the general second-level education but have not completed a recognised third-level education; and **high** refers to individuals who have completed a recognised third-level education. A small share of qualifications in some countries are not classifiable into this grouping.

Part I

Women's employment in a changing Europe

Introduction

The integration of women into the wage economy over the past decades has represented one of the most profound social and economic changes within European economy and society. This integration has been associated with a restructuring of employment and a reorganisation of work, involving the growth of service employment, more diversified working-time arrangements and new patterns of industrial relations. At the same time women's integration into wage work has involved a restructuring of household and family life, based on different and more complex patterns of household formation, fertility and social reproduction and with changing patterns of consumption and lifestyles. Too often the study of women's employment is treated as an area of marginal interest to the core issues of European employment and European social policy, and the linkages between changes in gender relations and changes in economic and social structures are not made. These relationships are two-way: the integration of women into employment shapes the wider economy and society, and changes in women's employment position is contingent upon the evolving patterns of economic and social conditions.

This two-way relationship can be considered to have both a long-term and a short-term dimension; the long-term considers the evolving role of women in the economy and society, which may develop a dynamic that is relatively independent or autonomous from short-term disruptions or changes in economic conditions (Humphries and Rubery 1984). Thus changes in women's role in the labour market might initially have been instigated by changing patterns of labour demand, but over time the dynamic towards women's integration has become less dependent upon the level of labour demand or on the prevalence of state policies designed to help women into the labour market. High levels of unemployment and even the dismantling of childcare provision would not be sufficient to send women back to the home. From the short-term perspective, changes to policies and to economic conditions may accelerate or stall these longer-term trends or transformations, but may not affect the underlying direction or shape of the trajectory of transformation.

The analysis presented in this section spans both the short and the long term; on the one hand we are concerned with a relatively short-term

perspective, namely the trends and developments in the political and economic (Chapter 1), organisational (Chapter 2) and household (Chapter 3)
environments during the first half of the 1990s. These developments had
clear impacts upon the short-term prospects for women within European
economies and both reinforced and, in some cases, even partially reversed
the changes to women's employment evident in previous decades. The
longer-term transformation of gender roles has still been evident, however,
as women have taken action to protect and reinforce their position in the
labour market and have failed to respond to recessionary conditions by
giving way in favour of the young or the long-term unemployed. Women
participated more in education, married later or not at all, reduced their
fertility and became more continuous participants in the labour market,
almost in spite of changes to the economic and social climate that were
reducing employment opportunities and putting pressure on childcare provision and social welfare.

Yet before we can conclude that the long-term trends are triumphing
over the short-term setbacks we also have to consider whether the 1990s
marked the beginning of a transformation in the organisation of European
societies and economies which may place under threat some of the gains
that women have made over recent decades and which we now almost take
for granted. Short-term trends or cycles can only be separated from the
longer-term transformation if the short-term variations do not become prolonged and deep, involving new transformations of underlying institutions
and structures (see Rubery 1988 for a discussion of the link between cycles
and trends in the development of women's employment). For some the recessionary experiences of the early 1990s were not simply a phase of a business
cycle but symptoms of the instability in and changes to the global economy
and, in particular, of the incompatibility between the emerging economic
conditions and the system of strong welfare states and regulated labour
markets characteristic of many parts of Europe. This recession, in short, could
be considered as marking the death knell for the European model, a sentence
reaffirmed by the decision of all European states to adopt conservative macroeconomic policies to meet the Maastricht convergence criteria. If these
developments were to spell the end of the welfare state as we know it and to
herald the full adoption of a deregulated approach to labour market organisation, these changes might be sufficiently significant to mark a new phase
in women's relationship to the labour market. They might mean, for example, that the conditions under which women will become more fully integrated
into the labour market might be based even more on unstable jobs within a
deregulated environment than has been the case over past decades and that
progress towards gender equality, where this is made, might be achieved more
by a levelling down of men's employment opportunities and position than
through a levelling up of women's position.

As to the verdict on the longer-term consequences of the changes to both
economic conditions and economic and social policy identified in the 1990s,

the jury is still out. There is little evidence from women's own behaviour of any major change or rupture to their continued integration into wage work and their conversion into more permanent and continuously committed employees. Yet this continuity of behaviour is to some extent at odds with the major shocks experienced within some key economies in Europe, from Sweden with its new-found doubts over its capacity to maintain its welfare state system, to Germany, yet to come fully to terms with the implications of unification for the German model. A lagged adjustment may still be possible, but on the balance of probabilities the next phase of European employment development will still be based around an increasing share of women within the labour market.

However, whatever the eventual pattern of development, it is clear that gender will continue to play an important role in shaping the future European evolution. Women's employment trends and prospects need to be situated within the context of a changing Europe, but changes in Europe will continue to be shaped on the one hand by the influence of gender on the organisation of labour markets and economic and social institutions more generally and, on the other hand, by the actions of both women and men in changing and shaping these gender roles.

1 Political and economic change

At the end of the 1980s Europe was preparing for 1992 and the creation of the single European market; the forecasts were upbeat (Cecchini 1988) with predictions of large-scale job creation, enhanced international competitiveness and a smooth development towards monetary union based upon the European Exchange Rate Mechanism (ERM). The changes in regimes in Eastern Europe and the former USSR were already underway but the impact on the world economy and on specific countries and regions of the EU was not yet apparent. The Community seemed poised on the brink of a major push to extend the benefits of the market to European citizens through the implementation of the European charter of fundamental social rights. With the commitment to equal treatment firmly established in the 1959 Treaty of Rome and reaffirmed in the 1992 Maastricht Treaty, the prospects for equality appeared propitious.

However, the 1990s did not live up to their anticipated promise. At the beginning of the decade the European Union experienced one of its worst recessionary periods, and faced crisis within the ERM. The record unemployment levels led to a change in priority, in principle towards more employment-intensive growth, but this objective was adopted against a prospect of yet higher unemployment as the economies struggled to meet the conditions for the next stage of European integration. The Union expanded to absorb three new member states, two of them – Finland and Sweden – having faced major problems of restructuring to meet changing internal and external conditions from the start of the decade. Further expansion plans, this time towards Eastern European countries, provided a backcloth to debates on prospects for political, monetary and economic integration. By the late 1990s, the turbulence in the exchange rates had settled down and most countries had been deemed to have met the Maastricht conditions for European monetary union, perhaps in some cases revealing the greater importance of political will and political agendas over bureaucratic rules in determining the development of Europe. However, the problems of unemployment appeared to be even more intractable as the two economies that are perhaps most central to the European project, France and Germany, have continued to face record levels of unemployment.

These problems led to the agreement in the 1997 Amsterdam Treaty to establish employment as an area of common concern, for member states to develop employment action plans according to an agreed set of guidelines, and for the action plans to be monitored and evaluated at a European Union level.

While the macroeconomic and political conditions for progress towards equality have deteriorated, the equality agenda has apparently moved more to centre stage within the Community, accorded equal priority with employment, and bolstered by the adoption, following on from the 1995 Beijing UN World Conference on Women, of a Communication on mainstreaming. Yet while there is a greater public recognition of the need for equality policy, at least at European level, the early 1990s perhaps saw the re-emergence of a view that equality had perhaps been taken not only far enough, but even perhaps too far (National reports, Italy: Bettio and Villa 1996), such that it was now men who faced the most severe problems of coming to terms with their changing economic and social roles. This potential backlash against equality has coincided with a general disenchantment with social legislation. There thus now seems little prospect that the implementation of the European charter of fundamental social rights through the social chapter to the Maastricht Treaty will lead to a major expansion of new social legislation. While in the 1970s and 1980s the Commission played a leading role in initiating and developing major areas of social legislation, such as the equality directives, the 1990s saw a shift in practice, supported by the member states and the social protocol of the 1992 Maastricht Treaty, towards an increased role for the social partners in negotiating social policy through framework agreements (see Box 1.1 for a summary of the main measures taken by the European Union in the area of social policy directly or indirectly relevant to gender equality). That procedure necessarily limits the likely development of social legislation to that felt appropriate by European employers and clearly places a limit on the extent to which the social chapter could be used to develop a new platform of rights for citizens of Europe.

How have these changing economic and political conditions impacted on the development of women's position in the labour market in Europe and in the individual member states? To consider these issues further we look first in more detail at the changing world and European economic conditions, followed by an analysis of recent trends in growth, productivity, employment and unemployment. This provides the background for an assessment, from a gender perspective, of the current policy agendas within the EU at European and national level, towards the macroeconomy, the labour market and the welfare state.

Box 1.1 EC directives, memoranda, recommendations, resolutions and programmes to promote equality of opportunity

Council Directives

Directive 75/117/EEC. Equal pay for men and women for the same work or for work of equal value.

Directive 76/207/EEC. Equal treatment for men and women in relation to access to employment, vocational training, promotion, and working conditions.

Directive 79/7/EEC. Equal treatment for men and women in matters of statutory social security.

Directive 86/378/EEC. Equal treatment for men and women in occupational social security schemes.

Directive 86/613/EEC. Equal treatment between men and women engaged in a self-employed capacity, including agriculture, and on the protection of self-employed women during pregnancy and motherhood.

Directive 92/85/EEC. The protection of pregnant workers and workers who have recently given birth or are breastfeeding.

Directive 93/104/EC. The Working Time Directive establishes limits to weekly hours, night work and provides basic entitlements to rest periods and annual leave.

Directive 96/34/EC. Grants male and female workers the right to unpaid parental leave of at least three months.

Directive 96/97/EC. Amends Directive 86/378/EEC (Post-Barber Directive)

Directive 97/80/EC. Shifts burden of proof in sex discrimination cases except in social security cases. Plaintiff no longer bears the full burden of proving her case and a clear definition of indirect discrimination is also provided.

Directive 97/81/EC. To remove discrimination against part-time workers, to improve the quality of part-time work, to facilitate part-time work on a voluntary basis to contribute to flexible working-time arrangements which take into account employer and worker needs.

Memoranda

Memorandum of 23.6.1994 on equal pay for work of equal value COM(94). Defined the scope and concept of equal pay for work of equal value and provided guidance on the criteria to be taken into account in job evaluation and job classification.

Follow-up Code of Practice for use by employers, employees and trade unions adopted by the Commission on 17.7.1996.

Council recommendations

Recommendation of 13.12.1984 on the promotion of positive action for women (84/635/EEC).

Recommendations of 27.11.91 on the protection of the dignity of women and men at work (92/131/EEC). Supported by a Code of Practice on measures to combat sexual harassment in 1991.

Council recommendation of 31.3.1992 on childcare (92/241/EEC).

Commission recommendation of 27.5.1998 on the ratification of ILO Convention no. 177 on homework of 20.6.1998.

Council resolutions

Resolution of 12.7.1982 on the promotion of equal opportunities for women.

Resolution of 7.6.1984 on action to combat unemployment amongst women.

Resolution of the Council and of the Ministers of Education, meeting within the Council of 3.6.1985, containing an action programme on equal opportunities for girls and boys in education.

Second Council resolution of 24.7.1986 on the promotion of equal opportunities for women.

Resolution of 16.12.1988 on the reintegration and late integration of women into working life.

Resolution of 22.6.1994 on the promotion of equal opportunities for women and men through action by the European structural funds.

Resolution of 27.3.1995 on the balanced participation of women and men in decision making.

The equality action programmes

The First Community Programme on the Promotion of Equal Opportunities for Women (1982–1985) recognised that while legal measures were important, there was a need for additional and complementary measures in the form of 'positive action' in various fields.

The Second Medium-Term Community Programme for Women (1986–1990) continued to develop the implementation of the directives in an enlarged Community of 12 member states. It widened the scope of equal opportunities to new spheres of positive action in training, in new technology, in the reconciliation of working and family life and in local development.

The Third Medium-Term Community Action Programme on Equal Opportunities for Women and Men (1991–1995) proposed a new, more comprehensive, strategy for action.

The Fourth Medium-Term Community Action Programme on Equal Opportunities for Women and Men (1996–2000) focuses on the principle of mainstreaming. It proposes that methods, strategies, models and studies aimed at integrating the equal opportunities dimension into policies and activities be developed and promoted in the member states.

The first three programmes were implemented on the initiative of the Commission via Council resolutions. The fourth programme was proposed by the Commission to the Council and established by Council decision.

A changing world and a changing European economy: the implications for women and men in the European Union

There are two main competing perspectives on the changes in the world economy in the 1990s. For some it marked a watershed when the impossibility of regaining full employment or maintaining a strong welfare state within an integrated and globalised world economy became clear even to the most interventionist nation states. These beliefs have been bolstered by the collapse of the Communist bloc which for so long tried, but eventually failed, to buck the need to succumb to the discipline of the market. For others the increasing debate over globalisation hides instead a political change, whereby governments have effectively abdicated their responsibility for policy and for ameliorating the impact of economic change on citizens. Whatever the relative merit of the two arguments, the outcome has been a downplaying of the possibility of using macro policy to influence growth and employment and a re-emphasis instead on supply-side measures, aimed at increasing competitiveness of firms and the employability of people.

Changing patterns of international competition and women's employment

Changing patterns of international competition and increasing globalisation have been invoked as the main factors explaining, for example:

- high levels of unemployment;
- the relocation of activities and the restructuring towards services;
- the increasing impact of technological change on employment patterns and distribution;
- the widening of earnings dispersion;
- the decentralisation of collective bargaining and abandonment of wage indexation;
- the increase in flexible and unsocial hours working;
- the pressure to reduce public expenditure and public sector deficits.

All of these developments have implications for gender equality. The emergence of *high and persistent levels of unemployment* has affected both sexes but overall in Europe women have higher unemployment rates and account for a disproportionate share of the long-term unemployed. Moreover, progress towards equality is unlikely to be made rapidly in a period of sluggish employment growth or decline; desegregation of the labour market is likely to be much easier to achieve under conditions of expansion and full employment.

Yet while women face greater risks of unemployment than men they have also, up to now, tended to benefit from the *relocation of manufacturing activities and the restructuring towards service sector employment*, both because of gender segregation by job task and because the often lower pay and more flexible contracts found particularly in private services favour women's employment. While some women have benefited from restructuring, others have also faced displacement through the processes of competition, including the effects of opening up of the Eastern European economies, which has provided opportunities for displacement to low-cost production areas within Europe itself. Moreover, the rapid *diffusion of new technologies*, exacerbated through globalisation, may further destabilise prospects within many service and clerical areas, as opportunities increase for new forms of employment and for relocation of employment through, for example, teleworking. Thus it is not the case that economic restructuring can be relied upon to continue to favour the increasing employment of women.

Widening earnings distributions have also been attributed to the impact of world trade, as those parts of production involving less skilled work lose comparative advantage relative to production requiring skilled workers (Wood 1994). The reasons for these developments remain subject to controversy, with many casting doubt on the role of world trade in changing patterns of earnings (Freeman 1995). Nevertheless, widening income distribution and a declining value of the minimum wage (OECD 1997a) have clear negative impacts on those women concentrated at the bottom of the hierarchy. Moreover, wide earnings differentials are often found to be a more important factor in explaining differences between countries in gender pay inequality than the relative position of women within the pay structure (Blau and Kahn 1992).

This move towards greater earnings dispersion can be expected to be at least in part the outcome of the *decentralisation of pay determination* (Katz 1993; Traxler 1996). The devolution of pay determination to companies, and within companies to individual establishments, is often seen as a requirement of new competitive conditions, where more scope is apparently needed at the level of the organisation to adapt systems of work organisation and structures of costs to changing demands. Decentralisation of pay determination has also gone hand in hand with *moves away from the indexation of wages*, and a requirement that pay should be linked more closely to the profitability of the organisation. These developments are, however, as we document below, likely to have removed more women than men from the protection of wage regulation and to have allowed wages for the less advantaged to fall, relative to the average.

The 1990s have renewed interest in the *development of flexible employment forms*, seen as offering the advantages of both allowing more competitive systems of work organisation and being a means of work sharing. Increased unsocial hours working is often argued to be necessary both to meet changing consumer demands for services and to allow the development of lean production systems based on just-in-time systems of production, together with a more intensive utilisation of capital equipment (Bosch 1995). The spread of flexible employment contracts and unsocial hours working affects both men and women, but the form of flexibility tends to be gendered; men are more frequently involved in annualised hours working or in unsocial hours or shift working as part of full-time contracts, while women tend to be concentrated in flexible part-time work (Rubery *et al.* 1997a, 1998b; Bettio *et al.* 1998a). Nevertheless, differences between countries in the extent and nature of flexible work contracts may call into question the assumption that these working arrangements are a requirement of modern competitive conditions.

Even the *pressures to reduce public expenditure and public sector deficits* are often attributed to new competitive conditions. These are said to require first of all exchange rate stability and monetary union, which brings with it convergence criteria; but this argument is bolstered by a belief that neither employers nor citizens are able or willing to pay for a large welfare state without this impacting seriously on the capacity of the economy to create and maintain employment. Thus pressures to reduce non-wage labour costs, in the belief that this will promote employment, complement arguments that the welfare state is no longer sustainable. Women's interests are at stake in these developments from a range of perspectives: public sector services are being cut back, placing more burdens on women's domestic labour and at the same time reducing job opportunities in the public sector; cutting non-wage labour costs, particularly on low-paid jobs, could boost employment of women, but women will be disadvantaged if the result is an expansion in the number of jobs outside protection or greater reliance on private welfare provision (Maier 1995).

Thus, to summarise, many of the changes in the economies of Europe have been attributed to changing competitive conditions, even though questions may be raised in many cases regarding the validity of the argument. Nevertheless, there is little doubt that changes have taken place within the world economy and domestic economies which have destabilised relationships and placed in doubt the pattern of future developments. One universal or common feature of the 1990s recession was a loss of consumer and employee confidence with respect to future income and job prospects, fuelled by the ever-increasing search for flexibility and by the collapse in some countries of key markets such as the housing market. The long-term impact of this increased instability on both the labour market and the markets for commodities is not yet clear, but it must be recognised that short-term boosts to the economy will not necessarily be sufficient to rebuild confidence among labour market participants in the stability and security of their jobs and careers.

Under these conditions it is arguable that the effectiveness of macro-economic policy in providing conditions for stable growth has been eroded. The destabilisation of the labour market in the 1990s particularly affected demand for male labour. Yet while the demand for female labour has remained more robust, closer inspection reveals that this high level of demand for female labour was at least in part associated with the emphasis on flexibility and low labour costs, characteristics associated more with female than male labour. Moreover, even the female labour market is facing destabilisation in the face of new technologies and the cutbacks to public expenditure being made again in the name of international competitive pressures. Where globalisation and international competition are implicated in changing patterns of production and changing labour market systems, there is again a clear gender impact; women are the most vulnerable to pressures towards wider earnings dispersion, more flexible working-time and decentralisation and fragmentation of forms of labour market regulation and protection. These issues will be explored in more detail below.

Convergence and divergence within European member states

While recession has been a feature of all advanced countries during the 1990s, the intensity of the recession experienced within the European Union compared to that of Japan and the USA is shown clearly in Figure 1.1. However, it is primarily on the employment and unemployment indicators that the European Union performed worse than its competitors. In Japan employment, output and productivity moved downwards in parallel through the early 1990s, giving rise to a slight increase in unemployment; the USA moved into steep recession in 1990, with employment falling faster than output, but after 1992 employment growth resumed, outstripping output growth. In contrast, in the European Union output growth began to decelerate in 1989 and declined consistently until reaching a negative figure in 1993, before moving fairly strongly upwards again into positive growth in 1994. The decline in employment which followed the output decline with a lag was much steeper and more prolonged than in the USA. Although employment growth has been positive since 1995, it has remained at a very low level, insufficient to make a major impact on unemployment rates. The EU unemployment rate moved steeply upwards in the early 1990s, from a low of 7.6 in 1990 to a high of 11.1 in 1994, and subsequent declines have still left rates well above those in the 1980s. The impact of the slow growth of output on employment was contained during the first part of the 1990s by a relatively slow growth of productivity, well below the long-term average of 2 per cent per annum, thereby increasing the employment intensity of growth over this period. However, indications that this pattern is more cyclical than long term are found in the rapid increase in productivity in 1994, which modified, at least in the short term, the impact of output recovery on employment.

The problems that these macroeconomic conditions caused countries in meeting the Maastricht convergence criteria are indicated in Table 1.1. Despite the commitment at the end of 1992 to move towards a maximum public sector debt of 60 per cent of GDP (gross domestic product),

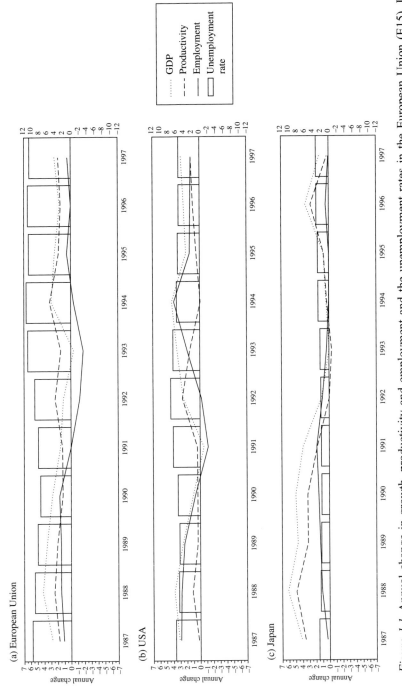

Figure 1.1 Annual change in growth, productivity and employment and the unemployment rates in the European Union (E15), USA and Japan, 1987–1997

Source: CEC (1997a).

Table 1.1 General government deficit and general government gross debt

	Government deficit[a]					Government debt[b]				
	1993	1994	1995	1996[c]	1997[c]	1993	1994	1995	1996[c]	1997[c]
Belgium	7.4	5.1	4.1	3.4	2.7	136.8	134.8	133.5	130.0	126.7
Denmark	3.9	3.4	1.9	1.6	0.3	80.2	76.2	72.1	70.2	67.2
Germany (u)	3.5	2.4	3.5	3.8	3.0	48.2	50.4	58.1	60.7	61.8
Greece	14.2	12.1	9.2	7.4	4.9	111.8	110.4	111.8	111.8	108.3
Spain	6.8	6.3	6.6	4.4	3.0	60.5	63.0	65.7	69.6	68.1
France	5.6	5.6	4.8	4.1	3.0	45.6	48.4	52.8	56.2	57.9
Ireland	2.4	1.7	2.0	0.9	1.0	94.5	87.9	81.5	72.8	68.3
Italy	10.0	9.6	7.0	6.7	3.2	119.1	125.1	124.4	123.7	122.4
Luxembourg	-1.7	-2.9	-1.7	-2.7	-1.1	6.1	5.7	5.9	6.4	6.7
Netherlands	3.2	3.4	4.0	2.4	2.3	80.5	77.3	79.6	78.5	76.2
Austria	4.2	4.4	5.9	4.3	3.0	63.9	67.0	69.3	70.0	68.8
Portugal	6.9	5.8	5.1	4.0	2.9	64.3	66.7	66.4	65.6	64.1
Finland	8.0	6.2	5.2	3.3	2.2	58.0	59.6	58.8	58.7	59.2
Sweden	12.3	10.8	8.1	3.9	2.9	76.0	79.0	78.2	77.7	76.5
UK	7.8	6.8	5.8	4.6	3.5	48.5	50.5	54.2	54.8	54.7
E15	6.2	5.4	5.0	4.4	3.0	66.1	68.1	71.2	73.2	72.9

Source: CEC (1997a: Tables 76, 78).

Notes
a Net lending as a share of gross domestic product at market prices.
b General government consolidated gross debt as a share of gross domestic product (market prices).
c Figures for 1996 (except Italy, Germany and Finland) and 1997 are estimates.

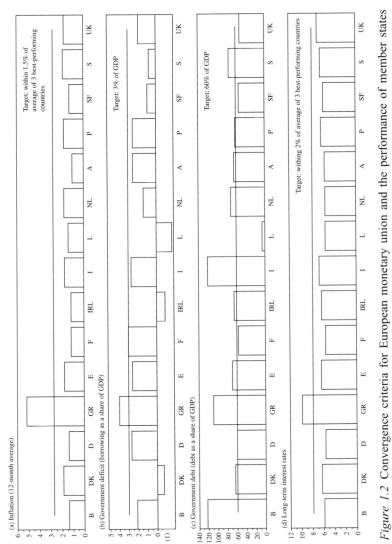

Figure 1.2 Convergence criteria for European monetary union and the performance of member states

Source: CEC (1998).

Notes
Data for inflation: January 1998.
Data for government deficit: 1997.
Data for government debt: 1997.
Data for interest rates: January 1998.

indebtedness continued to rise, from 60 per cent of E15 GDP (including unified Germany) in 1992 to 73.2 per cent in 1996, with a predicted marginal decline in 1997. Of the 11 countries joining the EMU in the first wave, 8 had cumulated government debt to GDP ratios above permitted levels and required the European Council to abrogate an excessive debt decision to allow them to proceed (see Figure 1.2). The basis for this decision was that by 1997 most countries' cumulated debt was beginning to fall as a percentage of GDP. European countries were more successful in meeting the target of reducing current public sector deficits as a share of GDP to 3 per cent. These reached a high of 6.3 per cent on average in 1993, but fell consistently over subsequent years, with 13 out of 15 countries estimated to hit the 3 per cent target or below in 1997 (see Table 1.1 and Figure 1.2), with Italy slightly above and Greece the major exception with a 4.9 per cent debt ratio. The longer-term impact of these efforts to meet these criteria on the macroeconomic stability and employment creating capacity of the European Union have yet to be assessed.

These economic trends need to be considered in the context of the prospects for resolving the need both for employment and for sustainable development. There is little evidence that Europe has moved from employment creating to employment displacing growth, but the problem still remains of generating sufficient growth to do more than keep pace with productivity increases and thereby satisfy the increasing demand for work. However, if 'sustainable development' requires a slower rate of growth than in the past, then there may be a need to increase the employment intensity of growth to higher levels than before (CEC 1994). This policy needs to be squared with the general view that Europe's comparative advantage in the world economy lies in the direction of creating high-value-added production based on skilled labour, a view now incorporated into the employment guidelines. These apparently conflicting policy objectives might require both a reconsideration of issues such as work sharing, and a reconsideration of whether high-skill production systems can be based upon high utilisation of skills and labour, and not on minimum staffing ratios (see Chapter 8 for further discussion of the need for employment- and skill-intensive growth).

While there is a high degree of similarity in the experience of EU member states over this period, significant differences can still be identified with respect to the level and intensity of the recession, the timing of the recession and recovery, the change in employment and unemployment levels associated with the output changes, and the trends in convergence towards the Maastricht public sector debt and deficit requirements (see Table 1.1). These differences between member states (see Figure 1.3), as we explore further below, have provided different contexts for the evolution of women's employment position between member states. Two countries stand out as having maintained a relatively buoyant output growth during this recessionary period, although their impact on the E15 is limited, as both countries concerned – Ireland and Luxembourg – are small states. Ireland's output and productivity growth was particularly robust, while its employment performance was much more modest. Luxembourg has fared better in employment terms while productivity growth has stagnated.

Denmark also differs from the remaining E15 in having a poor output and employment performance in the late 1980s, such that the experience of the 1990s has been relatively similar to, and in output and productivity terms even somewhat better than, the late 1980s. In Denmark unemployment rose steadily since the mid- to late 1980s but stabilised around 1993 and subsequently started to decline. Four countries – Greece, the UK, Sweden and Finland – also stand out as having experienced a somewhat earlier move into recession than that of the EU as a whole, although the reasons for this and their subsequent experience have all been somewhat diverse. Greece, for example, experienced negative growth in both output and employment at the turn of the decade, recovered somewhat between 1991 and 1992, only for output to slump again between 1992 and 1993 (but with employment continuing to rise). Growth in both the UK and Sweden decelerated at the end of the 1980s, only moving into positive growth in the UK between 1992 and 1993 and in Sweden in 1993–1994. Sweden's employment fell consistently from 1990 to 1997, except for a slight rise in 1995. The UK also suffered significant decreases in employment between 1990 and 1993, but employment, along with output, started to rise from 1994 onwards. Undoubtedly the most exceptional experience is found in Finland, where output and employment collapsed at the turn of the 1990s following a period of very rapid growth in the 1980s, as a consequence of the disintegration of trade with the former USSR and Eastern Europe and the ending of the domestic credit boom. Output fell by over 7 per cent between 1990 and 1991 and employment fell by over 12 per cent between 1990 and 1992 and continued to fall until 1994. From 1995 onwards there has been a modest recovery in employment, but by no means sufficient to compensate for the earlier falls.

Even among those remaining countries which largely followed the cyclical pattern of the E15 level there are considerable differences in the intensity of the recession. The Netherlands, for example, experienced only a relatively gentle recession with output and employment stagnating rather than declining and unemployment hovering around 6 per cent to 7 per cent over the time period. In contrast, in Spain employment fell every year from 1991 to 1994 and by 4 per cent in 1992–1993, while unemployment rose steadily from 16.2 per cent in 1990 to 24.1 per cent in 1994, before falling slightly up to 1997. This poor employment performance reflects a relatively strong growth in productivity in Spain over this period. Differences in productivity performance are associated with differences in the outcome of the recession on employment and unemployment. Greece's poor output performance did not result in even greater employment falls and rises in unemployment only because of a slow growth of productivity.

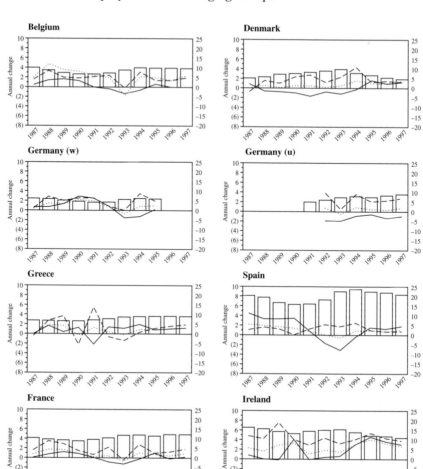

Figure 1.3 Annual change in growth, productivity and employment and the unemployment rate, 1987–1997

Source: CEC (1995b, 1997a).

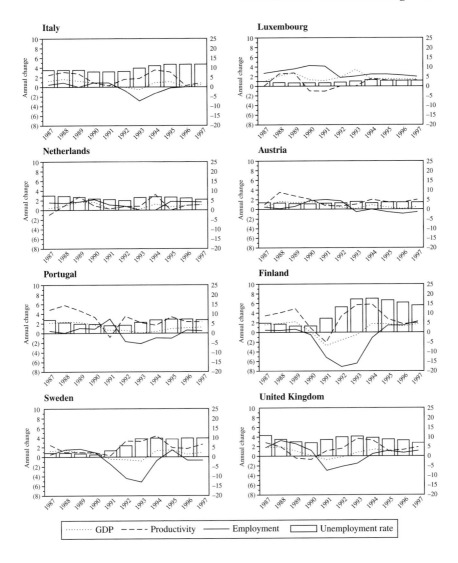

The changing political and policy context for women's employment

Although there are strong similarities in the overall pattern of growth, employment and unemployment to emerge from this investigation of EU member states, there is also considerable evidence of diversity in the context of the development of women's employment position over the 1990s. When the factors behind the diversity in main economic indicators are considered, some quite different structural and political conditions facing member states are revealed. These range from specific economic conditions, such as differences in the size and structure of labour supply (see Box 1.2) and differences in the stage of economic development (see Box 1.3), to more politically- and policy-related variables, discussed in more detail below.

Impact of political change

One of the major factors differentiating the experience of European member states during the 1990s has been the impact of the collapse of the former USSR and the Eastern European trading bloc on the economies of the member states. Two countries in which these developments have had a dominant impact on their internal evolution can be singled out, namely Germany and Finland, with Austria also experiencing a significant but less dramatic restructuring of its economy as a consequence of the opening of its borders with Eastern European economies.

For Finland and Germany, the internal transformations associated with this development are both radical and extensive. It is in fact more by chance

---

Box 1.2 Population change and migration flows

Four countries stand out as having faced notable changes to their labour supply conditions due to changes in migration flows.

Germany faced a rising population and labour supply due to immigration from Eastern Europe, and within Germany due to immigration to the West from East Germany, with flows in the opposite direction primarily related to West Germans taking up higher level jobs in the East. Thus within East Germany there was competition with West Germans for key jobs. **Austria** also experienced an inflow of migrants with the opening of its borders to Eastern Europe.

In contrast **Ireland** experienced a rise in its population and labour supply due to decreased rates of out-migration and the impact of the high birth rate of the 1970s and early 1980s. Thus the rising Irish employment rates were achieved against the background of an increasing labour supply. Finally, **Luxembourg** continued to increase its use of foreign labour during the period, involving both inward migration and the use of trans-border employment flows.

Box 1.3 Economic development and EU transfers and structural funds

Divergent experience between member states is in part related to differences in stage of development and structural adjustment, including the degree of integration of women into the economy. For example, countries such as **Spain** entered the 1990s with a very low level of female participation, and faced the problems of adjusting to world recession against a background of a rapidly increasing demand for employment from its female population.

Some of the small countries of the EU in fact experienced better growth and employment prospects than their larger and wealthier counterparts as a result of the flow of funds into the economies through structural funds and other income transfer policies of the EU. The most important example of this pattern is **Ireland**, but **Portugal** and **Greece** have also benefited from these transfers. Irish per capita income has been forecast to rise from 72 per cent of the European average in 1990 to around 83 per cent in the year 2000, to some extent as the result of these EU transfers (National reports, Ireland: Barry 1996:3). Much of Ireland's growth has been stimulated by a major public investment programme, funded through EU structural and cohesion funds.

---

that Germany does not appear as a country with a non-standard pattern of evolution in output and employment over this time period, rather than evidence of underlying stability in the system. The former East German GDP fell by more than a third over two years to a trough in 1991, although much of the subsequent recovery has been brought about by direct transfers from West to East and the employment losses have been underestimated because of the high share of the East German workforce on employment schemes (National reports, Germany: Maier *et al.* 1996:10). The integration of East Germany into the old Federal Republic of Germany has dominated the development of the whole German economy in the 1990s. In the first instance the unification resulted in an employment stimulus in the West but the impact of transfer payments plus the transfer of production to the East has turned a boom into historically high unemployment rates for the postwar period in both the East and the West. Men and women in the East have experienced a fundamental transformation of their economic and social lives, with women in the East facing particular problems of being expected to adapt to the participation patterns of their West German counterparts. These changes have involved not only a cutback in employment opportunities but also changes in childcare facilities, the growth of part-time employment and a change to women's legal rights, for example over abortion. What was perhaps most significant about the experience of the early 1990s, however, was the resistance shown by East German women to adjustment to West German norms and values. Whatever the resistance in terms of attitudes, though, there was still a real change in economic conditions, with less than a quarter of East Germans in 1994 (National reports, Germany: Maier *et al.* 1996:23) still in the same job they held at the time of unification. Likewise, the West Germans have been profoundly affected by the unification process, which has challenged the survival of many elements of the German economic and welfare model. Within the former West Germany the impact of unification was found in the continuing depressed levels of domestic demand, in part the consequence of the higher tax regime imposed to fund the unification process.

Finland has faced a loss of its main trading relationships, and a loss of its political position as a neutral state within the Cold War framework. Although other Nordic countries have faced similar problems to Finland in maintaining its high employment level and strong welfare state, the actual cause of the threats to the Finnish model must be regarded as rather different in origin from, for example, the problems faced by Sweden in the early 1990s, although Finland also suffered from an overexpanded domestic economy relative to its international strength.

Destabilisation was not only related to the collapse of the Soviet bloc. In Italy, political corruption scandals led to the apparent overthrow of the main parties by new political forces, only for those to be engulfed again in corruption charges and to be replaced, after a period of government by 'technical experts', by a new left coalition. However, the impact of this period of political upheaval in Italy was felt in the economic sphere through a variety of effects, most notably the massive devaluation of the lira, and the deflationary impact of delays to public tenders and the virtual ending of aid to the south which had been a vehicle for much of the corruption. These changes had significant effects on employment patterns in the south, where most unemployed women are located.

Macroeconomic and fiscal policy

Macroeconomic and fiscal policy debates have been dominated by the agreement to meet the Maastricht convergence criteria. The significance of Maastricht increased as the date for monetary union approached and as governments increasingly used the criteria to justify a restrictive economic policy. Policy in the earlier part of the decade to some extent seemed to have been conducted relatively independently of convergence criteria, with, for example, some member states accepting or even encouraging the loosening of the ERM arrangement. However, while all currencies became in principle free to float, some economies geared their policies around maintaining a strong currency: for example, much of France's unemployment problem has been attributed to its *franc fort* policy.

Table 1.1 and Figure 1.2 indicate the tightening policy environment implied by the criteria; these show that many countries were required to reduce significantly their public sector deficit as a share of GDP. One of

Table 1.2 Annual variation in wages and inflation in the European Union, 1992–1997

	Annual wage variation[a]						Inflation[b]					
	1992	1993	1994	1995	1996	1997	1992	1993	1994	1995	1996	1997
Belgium	2.9	3.8	4.6	2.3	1.8	2.6	2.1	3.0	3.2	1.6	2.0	1.9
Denmark	3.8	1.6	3.8	3.6	3.1	3.4	2.0	0.4	1.8	2.1	2.1	2.3
Germany (u)	10.6	4.3	3.4	3.6	2.5	2.3	4.8	3.9	2.7	1.9	1.8	1.9
Greece	10.7	8.1	12.2	12.5	11.7	9.4	15.0	13.8	10.8	9.3	8.3	6.0
Spain	10.4	6.7	2.2	2.2	4.6	2.6	6.4	5.6	4.8	4.7	3.6	2.4
France	4.2	2.8	2.2	2.3	2.6	2.5	2.4	2.2	2.1	1.7	1.8	1.6
Ireland	6.8	6.9	2.6	0.7	2.7	4.1	2.5	2.0	2.6	2.0	1.7	2.0
Italy	5.8	3.7	2.9	4.8	5.5	4.9	5.6	5.4	4.6	5.8	4.3	2.7
Luxembourg	5.3	5.1	4.0	2.2	1.6	3.3	3.4	4.1	2.3	0.7	1.9	1.7
Netherlands	4.7	3.3	2.4	2.0	1.2	2.7	3.1	2.1	2.7	0.9	2.0	2.4
Austria	5.8	4.4	3.4	3.7	1.9	1.8	3.9	3.3	2.9	1.3	2.0	2.1
Portugal	15.9	6.2	10.7	2.5	6.5	5.0	9.1	6.6	4.8	4.2	3.1	2.5
Finland	1.9	1.0	3.5	4.3	3.2	3.0	4.1	4.2	1.4	0.2	1.2	0.9
Sweden	3.9	4.4	4.8	2.9	7.5	4.8	2.2	5.7	3.0	2.4	1.2	1.6
UK	5.0	4.4	3.6	2.4	3.6	4.2	5.0	3.4	2.5	2.6	2.8	2.3
E15	7.0	4.1	3.3	3.1	3.5	3.2	4.7	4.0	3.3	3.0	2.7	2.2

Source: CEC (1997a:Tables 29, 25).

Notes
a Nominal compensation per employee; total economy.
b Price deflator – private consumption.

the most significant aspects of the Maastricht convergence criteria was that they imposed a convergence of financial criteria independently of levels of development or levels of public sector service. Thus all countries, whether they have a well-developed or only an embryonic welfare state, have been under pressure to reduce public sector services and expenditure. While Maastricht may inhibit the long-term convergence upwards of levels of public service provision within Europe, those with high levels of service provision also faced problems in cutting back on these activities to meet the criteria. For example, in Scandinavia the economy is now based on dual-earner families reliant on public sector services for employment and for facilitating care work, so that cutbacks to welfare threatened to destabilise the whole Scandinavian labour market and gender model.

Within this general macroeconomic framework, member states have changed their welfare state and public sector employment policies (see

---

Box 1.4 Wage moderation has been achieved by a range of different policies, with different implications for women

In **Greece** there was severe pressure applied on real wage levels in order to maintain competitiveness and meet the Maastricht convergence criteria. The consumer price index rose from 100 to 217 between 1988 and 1993, but wage levels only rose to 183. The statutory wage-indexing system was abolished in 1991. The policy of wage restraint was applied particularly to the public sector with significant implications for women (CEC 1996a).

In **Italy** the long-standing policy of wage indexation was abolished, leaving those workers outside strongly organised sectors vulnerable to real wage falls as minimum wage rates could now be adjusted only every two years through sectoral collective agreements. Wage gaps widened, including the gender pay gap (National reports, Italy: Bettio and Villa 1996:4).

In **France** the real value of the minimum wage was maintained (National reports, France: Silvera *et al.* 1996:73), and policies to introduce a lower minimum wage for young people, in addition to the lower rates already allowed for young people on training contracts, were successfully resisted.

In **Denmark** the ending of indexation in the early 1980s led to a widening of the gender gap between men and women, albeit from a relatively low level. This widening was the result of two factors; the move to decentralised bargaining and the policy of wage moderation in the public sector (National reports, Denmark: Boje 1996:42).

Wage increases in **Ireland** were regulated in the mid-1990s by a three-year Programme for Competitiveness and Work, an agreement negotiated between the social partners and the government (National reports, Ireland: Barry 1996:5). This agreement set a target increase of 6 per cent over three years, but with higher increases for low-paid workers, of potential pp. 38–45) and changed their fiscal regimes, often with a view to meeting other EU objectives such as reducing non-wage costs of employment, as well as to meet macroeconomic targets.

The macroeconomic and political environment has led to two main policy directions with respect to wage policy in the 1990s: wage moderation and decentralisation of pay determination. Both policies may not necessarily be compatible; while it has been argued that only a high level of centralisation or alternatively a high level of decentralisation can control wage inflation, this position is not universally accepted. Examples of countries where wage moderation policies were enacted through relatively centralised systems of wage determination include Belgium, Ireland, Finland and Germany, where wage freezes or wage growth below inflation have been associated with below average EU inflation rates in the 1990s (see Table 1.2 and Box 1.4). However, other countries sought to bring about wage

---

benefit for women. However, local productivity increases were allowed up to 3 per cent, and women are likely to have benefited less than men from local deals.

In **Spain**, perhaps the main contribution to reductions in wage costs in the 1990s came from changes in the structure of costs, rather than from reform of collective bargaining. The growth of temporary jobs contributed to control of unit labour costs, although with significant negative effects on the women and young people trapped in this form of employment (National reports, Spain: Moltó 1996:13).

In **Belgium** a wage freeze was imposed in 1995/6 and a new system of wage indexation was introduced which provided less complete protection against inflation as it excluded changes in prices of petrol, cigarettes and alcohol (National reports, Belgium: Meulders and Hecq 1996:3).

Sweden moved to a more decentralised system of wage determination from its traditional centralised system based on the principle of wage solidarity and narrow wage dispersion. The result of decentralisation and the movement away from a commitment to narrow wage dispersion was an increase the gender pay gap (National reports, Sweden: Gonäs and Spånt 1996:16).

In **Finland** centralised wage determination was maintained, and in fact used to achieve wage moderation during the recession. There was an equality supplement negotiated in both 1991 and 1995, but wage freezes in the public sector offset these benefits for women to some extent (National reports, Finland: Keinänen 1996:29–30).

In the **UK** the policy of deregulation of wages and decentralisation of collective bargaining was taken to further extremes, to include not just the private organised sector but also the low-paid unorganised sectors and the public sector. The wages councils which set legal minimum wages in a range of private sector low-paying sectors were abolished in 1993 and in the public sector moves were made to encourage local pay determination (National reports, UK: Rubery 1996:99–101).

moderation by encouraging decentralisation – or in the case of Italy by drastically reforming collective bargaining in order to impose wage freezes and
by ending the indexing of minimum wages in line with inflation. In contrast,
France maintained the real and relative value of the national minimum wage
(OECD 1997b:13) at the same time as encouraging decentralisation of collective bargaining.

While we are not in a position to assess fully the impact of 1990s wage
policies on gender pay differentials, it does appear that different methods of
implementing wage moderation polices are likely to have diverse gender
effects. Thus policies which result in a proportional real reduction in all wages
are less likely to protect women than policies which maintain the real value
of the minimum wage while attempting to moderate collectively negotiated
rates. Thus those countries that attempted to control wages through dismantling national or industry-level collective bargaining – or in the case of Italy
weakening the capacity of collective bargaining to protect real wages by

---

Box 1.5. Pension reforms and gender equality

Sweden provides a universal pension to all citizens but it also has a national
supplementary pension based on contributions. The contribution record for
a full pension has been extended from 30 to 40 years, a measure which
will disadvantage more women than men particularly as no credits are given
for home duties in this supplementary pension (National reports, Sweden:
Gonäs and Spånt 1996:9–10).

The process of bringing about pension reform in **Italy** was long and con-
tentious. The new system announced in 1995 will probably reduce gender
inequalities but through a process of levelling down rather than levelling up;
men suffer more than women but women do not benefit directly. Women
with short employment histories or in part-time jobs will find it difficult to
meet the requirements for 14–15 years of full-time equivalent contributions,
but not many women are in part-time work in Italy. On a more positive level,
self-employed women will now be compulsorily insured (National reports,
Italy: Bettio and Villa 1996:6).

Pension coverage was extended in **Ireland** to the self-employed and to
30,000 part-timers under a 1991 act. Most of the part-timers covered were
women, but a substantial number (approximately 12,000) still remained outside the scope of the pension system as they earned below the earnings
threshold of IR£30 per week. About 90,000 atypical workers were still outside the system, including low-paid self-employed and unpaid family
helpers, many of whom are also female. Those on 'home duties', the
majority of whom are, of course, women, were also still excluded from social
protection except as dependants (National reports, Ireland: Barry 1996:7).

Portugal spends the lowest share of GDP on social protection but in
order to meet the Maastricht criteria introduced reforms to the welfare state
in 1994, including an increase in contribution years for a pension from 10

removing the automatic indexation mechanism – might be expected to have had negative implications for gender pay equity, as more women were likely to find themselves outside the protective collective bargaining net. Those countries that targeted control of public sector wages, either as an end in itself or as an example to private sector employees, are also likely to have widened the gender pay gap, although the inadequate coverage of the public sector within wage data sets prevents a full analysis.

Crisis in welfare state regimes

Reform of the welfare state came to be regarded in the 1990s as an essential element of adjustment to changing competitive and demographic conditions. The country whose economic problems have been identified most closely to a crisis in its welfare state regime is Sweden. The basis of the Scandinavian model involved the provision of high levels of benefits coupled

to 15 and equalising the female and male retirement age at 65, compared to the 62 years previously set for women. Both these changes may disadvantage women more than men, even though women have a high participation rate. Moreover, one element of the reform, the introduction of a new system of index linking the pension should benefit all recipients (National reports, Portugal: Lopes and Perista 1996:6).

In **Spain** there is a need for more people to make contributions to pensions, but Spain has a low employment rate due to a low participation rate of women. Thus the entry of women into the formal economy is seen as an essential element in welfare state reform (National reports, Spain: Moltó 1996:5).

In **Austria** childcare in 1993 became recognised for the first time in accumulation of credits for pension entitlement, although the credits offered were still very low (National reports, Austria: Pastner 1996:94). Women's retirement age is to be equalised with men's at 65 in 2019, and as part of the negotiations over this change some improvements in the situation of women were agreed upon, including reforms to equal rights laws and improvement in legislation for atypical workers (National reports, Austria: Pastner 1996:5, 17).

Germany decided in 1996 to end its generous early retirement scheme as this was being used by large employers as a means of adjusting their labour forces (National reports, Germany: Maier *et al.* 1996:12).

To some extent the **UK** avoided the need to bring in pension reforms, as the measures it took in the early 1980s ensured that the basic pension will have no more than 'nugatory value', even according to government sources, by the time most of the present workforce retire. Reliance has increasingly been placed on private pensions, an area where women tend to be strongly disadvantaged because of their low wages and less continuous careers (National reports, UK: Rubery 1996:31)

Box 1.6 Policies to increase means-testing reduce women's access to benefits; but policies to extend coverage tend to bring more women within the social security net

Ireland has a welfare system strongly based around the concept of a male breadwinner, with many benefits means-tested, and some restricted to one claimant per household. Changes in the 1990s have reinforced these characteristics, thereby reducing women's access to independent benefits. Tighter restrictions were also imposed on the earnings of the spouse in households claiming benefits, thus trapping more women into dependency (National reports, Ireland: Barry 1996:7–8).

Reforms to the unemployment benefit system in **Belgium** in the first half of the 1990s were particularly likely to have a negative impact for women. First, the value of the flat-rate benefit paid to those unemployed forced to withdraw temporarily from the labour market due to social and family circumstances was seriously eroded. Almost all the unemployed in this position were women (98 per cent in 1994). Second, those deemed to be on unemployment benefit for an abnormally long period faced possible withdrawal of benefit. The definition of 'abnormally long' was changed from twice to one and a half times the average for the district and gender. However, heads of households and single people were not subject to having benefit withdrawn; this measure applied mainly to those cohabiting but who were not heads of households, i.e. women (National reports, Belgium: Meulders and Hecq 1996:18).

In **Portugal** the coverage of social security provided to freelance workers was strengthened. These changes were aimed at increasing revenues while at the same time extending benefits such as health care, maternity

with active labour market policies which were designed to reduce the extent to which the benefit payments would be activated. When the Swedish economy was no longer able to maintain its commitment to full employment, its capacity to meet its benefit payments bill was called into question. While these problems affected Sweden before joining the EU, its problems of reforming its welfare state have continued since, for although it is not joining EMU in the first phase, it has adopted a public expenditure policy in line with the convergence criteria.

Other economies have also faced problems with funding the welfare regime, but in some cases more as a result of other stronger economic factors – for example, the collapse of trade in Finland and the costs of unification in Germany. Yet other economies have faced problems with their welfare regime triggered, at least to some extent, by the timetable of the Maastricht Treaty. These problems, for example, led to a prolonged period of industrial unrest in France in December 1995 and fuelled the political problems in Italy, with proposed reforms to pension entitlements providing the stimulus to protests in both countries. Changes of government in both countries over the protection and insurance for old age to a larger share of the population (National reports, Portugal: Lopes and Perista 1996:5).

In **Sweden** the approach to financial crisis was not to increase means-testing for unemployment benefits but to decrease the level of benefit, from 90 per cent to 75 per cent of earnings between 1995 and 1996. However, more persons became reliant on means-tested benefits as more ran out of entitlements as a consequence of persistent high unemployment (National reports, Sweden: Gonäs and Spånt 1996:55).

In 1994 **Finland** stopped means-testing the basic unemployment allowances payable after income-related benefits were exhausted. However, after 1994 fewer persons received the allowance as eligibility had become dependent upon the person being in employment at least 6 months out of the previous 24. Those who failed to qualify were eligible for the labour market support benefit, which remained means-tested. The extension of the child homecare allowance, coupled with other means-tested household benefits, also served to trap some married women with children into inactivity until their children reached the age of 3 because of the high effective marginal tax rate if they tried to return to the labour market (National reports, Finland: Keinänen 1996:19).

In the **UK** the introduction of the Jobseeker's Allowance in autumn 1996 reduced access to non-means-tested benefits from 12 to 6 months, and also required jobseekers to be available for full-time work unless they were deemed to have significant care responsibilities. The extension during the 1990s of the Family Credit system, which provides benefits to those in low-paid work, also trapped many women into dependency, owing to the high marginal tax rates on the second income earner (National reports, UK: Rubery 1996:163).

period 1996 to 1997 were also influenced by debates on how to cope with the adjustment to the European convergence criteria.

Changes in the welfare state over the 1990s have involved changes to the levels of benefit provision, to access rules, to the taxation of benefits and to methods of financing provision. The dual concerns over meeting public expenditure targets and coping with changing demographics meant that most countries considered and many implemented pension reforms (see Box 1.5). Where these involved extending the period of employment required for full pension rights, or reduced the relative value of guaranteed state pension, the impact is likely to be particularly negative for women. However, these reforms were also undertaken in a context of increasing awareness of a demand for enhanced rights for women, and many countries at the same time introduced or extended pension credits for those taking a career break to look after children. These reforms, while on the one hand recognising women's domestic labour, also tended to reinforce sex roles within the family.

Another tendency was to increase the importance of means-testing in benefit provision. Where insurance principles were maintained, conditions

Box 1.7 Family policy changes extend leaves but lower benefits or increase means testing

In **France** child allowances were not uprated in 1996, thus reducing their value in real terms, and family allowances were in future to be classed as taxable income. Earlier reforms extended subsidies to women staying at home with a second child, instead of the previous system which only paid with the third child (National reports, France: Silvera *et al.* 1996:13, Gauvin *et al* 1994:5).

Denmark introduced a wide range of leave arrangements or schemes in the early 1990s, primarily to improve work sharing, but providing increased opportunities for parental leave without loss of labour market position. Most leave-takers were women, and most leave has been taken for family reasons. The scheme clearly has helped to reconcile work and family life, but risks reinforcing women's responsibility for the family, and could encourage the cutback of childcare provision (National reports, Denmark: Boje 1994, 1995).

Most support for children in **Ireland** has been provided in means-tested benefits to unemployed households. This policy has trapped many households, and women in particular, in inactivity and benefit dependency. Concern about poverty led to a slight shift in policy, with the non-means-tested child benefits uprated significantly and more than other benefits in 1995 (National reports, Ireland: Barry 1996:8).

Part of the Global Plan of 1993 in **Belgium** involved the further promotion of career breaks in the private sector, such schemes having been well established in the public sector for some time. This promotion was part of the policy of work redistribution, which was formulated in apparently sex-neutral terms but which in practice mainly affected women. In 1994 87.5 per cent of those taking a career break were women (National reports, Belgium: Meulders and Hecq 1996:16).

In 1991 in **Austria** childcare leave, which is paid but at a low level, was extended from one to two years. This resulted in a high take-up rate among women, and in practice few returned to work at the end of the two years. The high take-up brought about a debate in Austria over the expense and in 1996 there was a reduction to 18 months unless the father took at least 6 months' leave (National reports, Austria: Pastner 1996:97).

Sweden still has perhaps the most generous family policies, but these were undergoing significant change in the first half of the 1990s. Parental

of eligibility for insurance payments were tightened or the duration of benefits reduced, thus forcing a higher share of claimants onto means-tested benefits (see Box 1.6). Moreover, increasing shares of benefit recipients were without insurance cover, either because cover had been exhausted or because of the increased difficulty of building up eligibility in the first place. Women tend to benefit less than men from insurance-based benefits as they are less able to fulfil the eligibility requirements, and the tightening allowances were reduced to 75 per cent of previous earnings and child allowances were cut by 15 per cent from January 1996. The cost of childcare services was being increasingly passed on to parents but this was in part offset by a new requirement that local authorities had to provide child-care for children aged 1 to 12 if parents were working or studying (National reports, Sweden: Gonäs and Spånt 1996:9–10).

In **Finland** the first half of the decade saw the introduction of the child homecare allowance which allowed all parents, even those without a job, to have paid leave up until the child was 3. However, the parental allowance was reduced from a maximum of 80 per cent to a maximum of 66 per cent. Child allowances were first increased in the early 1990s but from July 1995 were again reduced (National reports, Finland: Keinänen 1996:16).

Germany withdrew parental leave allowances for high-income house-holds in 1994 and reduced child benefits for third and fourth children for higher income households. Families were required to choose between child benefits or child tax allowances. In principle the government was commit-ted to providing childcare for children aged 3 to 6 by the deal struck when abortion laws were harmonised between East and West. However, the *Länder* postponed meeting this commitment until 1996 and instead of increasing resources to childcare, planned to reallocate funds and reduce the quality of care. Thus there was no real reorientation of the German welfare state away from transfers towards services. Moreover, the East German system of providing social welfare, from cheap family holidays to hot meals in canteens, was disbanded and access to childcare reduced (National reports, Germany: Maier *et al.* 1996:14, 18).

The **UK** introduced new legislation providing maternity leave rights to all employees, a change in policy forced upon the UK Conservative govern-ment by the passing of the EC directive on maternity leave (National reports, UK: Rubery 1996:24). The government also tried to reduce state support for lone mothers by requiring fathers to provide support instead of the state. This policy initiative was both inept in its implementation and extremely unpopular, particularly with men. In the area of childcare the Conservative government agreed to extend provision for pre-school children, but its proposed method of delivery – through a voucher system – threatened to undermine the viability of the limited state provision for the most needy families (National reports, UK: Rubery 1996:31). The incoming Labour government abandoned the voucher scheme but announced plans to expand nursery and after-school provision.

of eligibility rules are likely to increase these problems. However, while women may be more often forced to fall back on social assistance measures even under systems where main benefits are insurance-based, fewer women are eligible for means-tested benefits as they are more frequently living in households with an employed spouse. Some countries' benefit reforms were particularly likely to affect women: for example in Belgium, heads of house-holds were explicitly excluded from some of the benefit reforms, and in the

UK benefit entitlements were restricted to those available for 40 hours of work (see Box 1.6). Against these trends there were some moves to extend the coverage of benefit systems, to bring a wider section of the population within the social security net, and indeed thereby to widen the tax basis for contributions to old age and other forms of social protection.

Policy changes related to the provision of support for families and for women's domestic role tended to involve reductions in benefit levels, or more targeted benefits through use of means-testing or taxation, coupled with longer leave entitlements (see Box 1.7). In some countries, notably the Scandinavian countries, there were cutbacks in the level of benefits for those on maternity leave, although in common with other countries such as Austria and France, increased opportunities were provided to prolong leaves or to enjoy family support with the second instead of previously with the third child (see Box 1.7). Policies such as extensions of leave could, however, be considered as a means of reinforcing gender roles, while the cutback in benefit levels reduced women's independent income and thus again served to increase dependency on men.

Box 1.8 Cutbacks in public sector employment threaten women's jobs, but in some countries the public sector has still provided more stable employment than the private sector

In the mid-1990s **Greece** was engaged in a major privatisation programme which threatened to increase gender inequality in both pay and promotion prospects. The public sector in Greece traditionally operated a policy of narrow wage dispersion and women also made more progress in moving up the career ladder in the public than in the private sphere (National reports, Greece: Cavouriaris and Symeonidou 1996:7).

In **Denmark**, public sector employment proved to be more stable over the cycle than private sector employment. Women have tended to become over-represented in unemployment when the private sector expands relative to the public sector: This occurred in the mid-1980s and again in 1994, although the expanded leave programmes could disguise these trends to some extent if unemployed women participate in the schemes (National reports, Denmark: Boje 1996:9).

In **Spain** public sector employment has traditionally proved more stable than private sector employment but in 1994 private sector employment started to expand while public sector employment continued to fall. Further cutbacks were threatened and although private services have increased in importance, the quality of job opportunities in the private service sector has not compared with that in the public sector (National reports, Spain: Moltó 1996: 7–8, 22).

Up until even the end of the 1980s much of the **Austrian** industry and finance sector was in public ownership. Since that time there has been a major privatisation programme. Meeting the Maastricht criteria led to further

Yet perhaps the most notable characteristic of the reforms was the absence of any radical transforming policies to bring welfare state systems up to date with the new complexities of household and family organisation and with the changing role of women in particular. There were some minor modifications to those conservative welfare state models based on the insurance principle, to accommodate increased access for women to benefits, but there has been no rethink of the fundamental bases of policies. Moreover, in those welfare states where progress had previously been made towards a fully individualised system – that is, where there was little or no expectation that women would be economically dependent upon men – there was some modification and in part a reversal of this policy approach.

The impact of the increasing concern to control the costs of the welfare state was felt not only in benefit provision and transfer payments but also in the provision of services, and in the level and quality of employment within the public sector (see Box 1.8). Recent employment trends have not all pointed in the direction of a declining public sector, in part because any

---

cutbacks in the state's involvement in the economy, in particular restricting its ability to use publicly funded construction projects to offset recessions. This policy change in the first instance primarily affected men (National reports, Austria: Pastner 1996:4).

Around half of **Swedish** women work in the public sector. Employment fell in the public sector by 7 per cent for women and by 2 per cent for men between 1991 and 1995, and while private sector employment started to rise in 1995, that in the public sector remained static or continued to fall. Public sector employment has been of double importance for women in Sweden as it has facilitated the high participation of women in the labour market – through the provision of care services – as well as boosting demand for female labour (National reports, Sweden: Gonäs and Spånt 1996: Appendix Tables 4, 5).

By the mid-1990s public sector employment in **Finland**, at least in the municipalities sector, had remained more stable than that in the private sector. However, new systems of budget management within the public sector, which allow municipalities more freedom as to how to organise the provision of services, might yet herald major cutbacks in employment (National reports, Finland: Keinänen 1996:9, 25).

In the **UK** major changes were made in the organisation of public sector employment. Large areas of the public sector were subject to competitive tendering and although most tenders were won by public sector employees, the result was a deterioration in pay and conditions, especially for female manual workers. The EC directive on the transfer of undertakings reduced the opportunities to use poor terms and conditions of employment as part of the competitive tendering process (National reports, UK: Rubery 1996:119).

downturn in the public sector may have been masked by the even poorer employment performance in the private sector. However, while the public sector has been an agent of female employment growth in most of the post-war period, there are signs emerging of major cutbacks in employment growth or even employment levels, with significant consequences for women. These trends have been most evident so far in Sweden, which had in any case the largest share of public sector employees within Europe, but in line with the common impact of the convergence criteria, countries such as Spain also registered relative falls in public sector employment. Even more common is the tendency for pressure on public sector expenditure to lead to efforts to contain costs, either through wage control policies or through privatisation of public services and activities (Box 1.8).

Labour market flexibility, employment creation and work sharing

Government labour market policy can be argued to have been directed at three rather different objectives: increased competitiveness, employment creation and redistribution of work (Box 1.9). While policies to meet these three objectives may at times all pull in the same direction, there can be no necessary presumption that this is the case. Indeed, similar policy measures may be enacted in one member state primarily with one or other objective in mind, while in another member state the policy has quite a different primary focus or objective.

This likelihood can be illustrated with respect to a range of policies, including for example non-wage labour costs. In some countries there were moves to reduce these costs across the board in the interests of both competitiveness and general job creation, but in other cases the reductions were targeted at those employers actually creating jobs or offering jobs to hard to place groups (see Box 1.10). Deregulation of the labour market, through weakening of controls on hirings and dismissals, can similarly be presented as either a policy to enhance competitiveness by reducing bureaucracy and removing unworkable regulations (e.g. in Italy) or a policy to redistribute access to work by, for example, reducing segmentation between permanent and temporary workers, as has been the case in Spain. Neither the motives for such policies nor their effects on women can be considered clear or unambiguous. While policies to reduce non-wage labour costs may be expected to stimulate demand most in low-wage jobs, often dominated by women, these cutbacks in contributions often go hand in hand with reforms to the welfare state, as we saw above, which often act against the interests of women.

Promotion of flexibility not only has different objectives but is also pursued through very different types of policies (see Box 1.9). In some cases the emphasis was on extending rights, thereby making flexible employment contracts more acceptable to employees and ensuring more equal treatment. Such policies can be regarded as beneficial to women, except to the extent that they have led to a growth of part-time work and a reinforcement of gender roles in the labour market and in the household. In other cases the emphasis was on deregulation or on the simplification of the framework of regulations to promote the use of flexible employment among employers. Sometimes policies were more specifically targeted at employment-creation and work-sharing policies in which subsidies were available if flexible employment policies led to work sharing or to the hiring of 'hard to place' workers.

Flexible employment includes not only part-time and temporary contracts, but also an increasing range of leave arrangements or partial employment contracts which allow flexibility over the life cycle or staged entry into retirement, and other non-standard contracts such as training contracts which may facilitate initial entry or re-entry into the labour market. Many of these measures are more likely to involve women than men, although one of the notable features of recent years has been an increasing involvement of men within flexible employment schemes. In some cases this male involvement reflected declines in male job opportunities, especially among young people; the increased precariousness of the youth labour market has been a constant theme of the 1990s. However, in other cases men's involvement – for example in partial early retirement schemes and the like – also demonstrates gender divisions even within flexible employment. Men may still enjoy better rights and benefits – for example continued full-time insurance – if they move into flexible jobs from full-time employment or unemployment than is the case for women, who often enter into flexible employment directly from inactivity (Rubery 1998a).

A more positive approach to flexible labour markets is to focus on creating a skilled and flexible workforce through expanded education and training provision. The 1990s saw the reinforcement of trends toward universal upper secondary level education, with the raising of school leaving ages in some of the Southern European countries: in Portugal from 14 to 15 and in Italy and Spain from 14 to 16. These changes have tended to equalise the basic system of educational provision throughout the EU. However, major differences in vocational education and training remain. Some countries, such as Austria and Germany, still have very well developed and extensive vocational training systems, known as the dual training system, while other countries still place greater emphasis on educational qualifications than on vocational skills. Nevertheless, vocational training was also expanded in some countries in part as a response to unemployment, and in part as a direct result of EU aid for training, particularly in Southern European countries.

A strong system of vocational training based on the dual system of work experience and education, as in the Austrian and German models, seems to be associated with a relatively low unemployment rate among young people, which may be particularly beneficial to young women, as in most countries their unemployment rate tends to exceed that of young men. These training systems still, however, act to segment the labour market by gender and also often reinforce men's position as skilled workers as many female-type skills

Box 1.9 Flexibility policies take different forms and fulfil different objectives

In **Spain** there was a major reform of labour market regulation away from the system of legal regulation. The new policy did not fully embrace dereg- ulation, as the principle of universal coverage for collective bargaining continued to be accepted. But collective bargaining was in practice uneven, leaving scope for some sectors to be relatively unregulated. The aim of reducing divisions between those in permanent and those in temporary jobs was not fully realised. Employers, still unclear as to the exact implications of the changes, continued to prefer to use temporary contracts rather than risk the decisions of the Labour Courts. The labour market reform also aimed to increase part-time jobs, an objective which appeared to be being realised, as 38 per cent of the new jobs in the third quarter of 1995 were part-time (National reports, Spain: Moltó 1996:2).

The **Netherlands** had the highest ratio of employed persons to full-time equivalent labour years, at 1.19 compared to a European average of 1.04, in 1991. Short working hours may be an indication of labour under- utilisation or evidence of a successful work redistribution policy. However, most of the redistribution is among women, where the employed persons to full-time equivalent labour years is 1.49, against a European average of 1.14. (National reports, Netherlands: Plantenga *et al.* 1996:5). The policy used to promote part-time work and work sharing was through legislation designed to prevent or reduce any distinctions between part-time and full- time employees. In this respect redistribution policy took precedence over policies to reduce labour costs and increase flexibility (National reports, Netherlands: Plantenga *et al.* 1996:8).

Luxembourg stood out against any policy of deregulation, and even strengthened regulations against collective dismissals and provided new rights for part-timers, such as overtime pay for hours above contractual hours (National reports, Luxembourg: Plasman 1996:9,14).

In **Italy** there was a growth of work sharing through solidarity contracts, in the early 1990s, in part as an unplanned response to the rising problem of threatened redundancy. Other policies to promote new working-time and flexibility arrangements were more haphazardly applied (National reports, Italy: Bettio and Villa 1996:4). However, in 1998 there was evidence of a renewed interest by the government in using reductions in working-time as a means of improving worksharing as a new law was introduced to promote a 35-hour week, despite widespread opposition from employers.

In **France** public policy in the first half of the 1990s promoted external flexibility by weakening dismissal laws and allowing new forms of less binding employment contracts, together with work sharing through subsidies for part-time and short-time working where these prevented redundancy or created new jobs, and job creation through subsidies to take on the unemployed (National reports, France: Silvera *et al.* 1996:20). The use of reduced working-time to help to create and protect jobs took on a new momentum after the election of the Jospin government in 1996 and the development of the new legislation to introduce a 35-hour week in France.

Employment protection, covering a range of issues from holiday entitlement to unfair dismissal protection, was extended to part-timers in **Ireland** under a 1991 act (National reports, Ireland: Barry 1996:9).

In **Belgium** the encouragement of part-time employment, career breaks and temporary employment contracts was embedded in a range of measures included within the 1993 Global Plan and the multi-annual employment plans. Companies were encouraged to draw up plans to redistribute work which in practice concentrated strongly on part-time and career break options. Although in principle these measures promoted work sharing in general, in practice both part-time and career breaks primarily concern women. More women are also employed on temporary contracts and the Global Plan allowed the issuing of up to four temporary contracts, provided the total duration does not exceed two years (National reports, Belgium: Meulders and Hecq 1996:25). However, the Belgium government, along with French, Italian and Portuguese governments, has in the late 1990s renewed its interest in using reduced working-time to fight unemployment (IDS 1998a:2)

In **Germany** there has been consistent pressure from the unions for a shorter working week in the interests of work sharing. Both the government and employers sought to combine this change in number of working hours with greater working-time flexibility. In May 1994 a new act was passed allowing more flexibility in scheduling and abolishing special protections for women. Labour market policy has tended to be discussed as a tripartite policy between the government, employers and unions, a forum in which the interests of women have rarely been taken explicitly into account. (National reports, Germany: Maier *et al.* 1996:39, 43).

In the **UK** the thrust of Conservative government policy in the 1990s was to deregulate the labour market in the interests of flexibility and the maintenance of competitiveness. There was no commitment on the part of the Conservative government to stimulate work sharing and to date the incoming Labour government has not departed from this policy (National reports, UK: Rubery 1996:128).

The **Portuguese** socialist government, elected in 1996, has joined with other European governments in seeking to reduce working hours to help with the unemployment problem, but in the Portuguese case the hours were cut from 44 hours, the longest standard hours in Europe, to 40 hours, a level achieved many years ago in other parts of Europe (IDS 1998b).

Box 1.10 Towards lower non-wage labour costs: a female friendly policy?

In the **Netherlands** debates over employment policy have been conducted without reference to their potential impact on the female segment of the labour market (National reports, Netherlands: Plantenga *et al.* 1996:8). For example, there was no debate on the gender consequences of a measure to reduce employers' labour costs on jobs with wages up to 115 per cent of the minimum wage or of a proposal to allow low wage jobs to be created for the long-term unemployed.

Employers' costs have been reduced in **Luxembourg** by exempting them from contributions to family allowances (previously 1.75 per cent of the gross wage) (National reports, Luxembourg: Plasman 1996:10).

In **Italy** some reductions were applied to social security contributions on part-time jobs, as strict proportionality is believed to result in higher wage costs for part-timers (National reports, Italy: Bettio and Villa 1996:5).

In **France** contributions still accounted for 78 per cent of social security expenditure in 1993 but the trend in policy was to begin to switch taxation away from employers towards employees and general taxation, notably through the introduction of the General Social Security Contribution levied on earnings. Employers were also allowed to pay lower child benefit contributions on low-wage jobs. In addition they were given full or partial exemption from non-wage costs when participating in various employment-creation or work-sharing initiatives, including creating part-time jobs in the interests of work sharing, thereby reversing previous discrimination against low-wage jobs (National reports, France: Silvera *et al.* 1996:8–10).

Belgium, as part of the Global Plan of 1993, reduced employers' contributions on low-paid jobs by up to 50 per cent, dependent upon the level of remuneration. Although a large number of jobs were subject to reductions, the impact on job creation is unclear. Significant reductions in non-wage labour costs were also made available to employers for hiring the young unemployed (National reports, Belgium: Meulders and Hecq 1996:6).

Spain introduced a general reduction in employers' contributions in 1995 as a means of trying to stimulate job creation. It also pledged to move further towards the principle of proportionality in social security contributions, away from a system based on maximum ceilings which had the effect of penalising employers of workers in low-paid jobs more than employers of those in high-paid jobs (National reports, Spain: Moltó 1996:4).

In **Finland** some of the cost of social security contributions was redistributed from employers to employees in the 1990s in an effort to stimulate job creation (National reports, Finland: Keinänen 1996:9).

In **Germany** some steps were taken to reduce non-wage costs such as the cancellation of the early retirement programme and the introduction of a long-term care insurance, the first scheme to involve only contributions from employees (National reports, Germany: Maier *et al.* 1996:18).

Table 1.3 Gender composition of participants in initial vocational education and training by gender, 1993–1994

	Men	*Women*
Austria	56.6	43.4
Belgium	50.9	49.1
Denmark	55.8	44.2
Germany	54.3	45.7
Spain	53.4	46.6
Finland	43.9	56.1
France	54.7	45.3
Greece	57.3	42.7
Ireland	49.0	51.0
Italy	56.6	43.4
Luxembourg	56.0	44.0
Netherlands	58.0	42.0
Portugal	54.0	46.0
Sweden	56.0	44.0
UK	55.5	44.5
E15	55.2	44.8

Source: CEC (1997b).

may not be included (see Chapter 5). Indeed, Table 1.3 gives the percentage of participants in initial vocational education and training by gender and reveals a systematic gender gap in favour of men, except in Finland and Ireland. Some countries have been enacting policies to try to redress these gender inequalities. Austria has extended its apprenticeship system to cover service sector areas and in Denmark there has been a marked equalisation upwards of the share of women who are now vocationally qualified, compared to earlier generations. Some other countries which have been attempting to follow the German model by developing and strengthening apprenticeships have not necessarily been so successful in extending these opportunities to women. For example, women hold only one-third of places in the new French apprenticeship system, and in the UK the recently introduced modern apprenticeship system appears to be focused on male-dominated job areas.

Young women have, however, been taking action to counter discrimination in both the labour market and the education and training system (see Chapter 3). Not only are they participating more in higher education, they are also becoming more 'efficient' at completing their education than their male counterparts, for example in Italy where the time taken to complete is highly variable.

One type of policy which largely remained off the agenda of member states in the first half of the 1990s, with the possible exception of Germany, was that of reductions in full-time working weeks (see Box 1.9). The absence of a significant debate around moving towards a shorter working week reflected not only the dominance of competitiveness objectives over work-sharing objectives but the continuation of policies designed to shore up the male breadwinner model of household organisation. Part-time work was seen as a more acceptable method of income and work sharing – as it normally impacted on women and young people – than any policy which, if the cuts in working hours were not fully funded, might further undermine the earning capacities of men and reinforce a dual-earner model of household organisation. However, the second half of the 1990s has seen a revival of debate, and indeed an enactment of new laws and measures to reduce standard working-time in France, Belgium, Portugal, Sweden and the Netherlands (see Box 1.9). This renewed interest in the use of working-time policy for reducing unemployment reflects both the persistence of unemployment and the changed political landscape, with governments of the left elected in France, Portugal and Italy in 1995 and 1996.

Equal opportunities policy

In the first half of the 1990s there were relatively few initiatives in most European member states in the field of equal opportunities, with the exception primarily of the Scandinavian countries, and where action was proposed or taken the results were weak or even non-existent. This lack of attention to equal opportunities in national policies was revealed in the multi-annual plans which the member states drew up on employment policy following the Essen summit agreement, and in which equal opportunities issues were hardly referenced (Meulders 1996; Bettio *et al.* 1998b).

Several examples can be found of countries which started the decade with good intentions but in practice failed to take the necessary action to implement their policies once they became distracted by the impact of the recession and other policy priorities. For example, Italy in 1991 passed a law not only sanctioning but also providing incentives for positive action, redefined the role and status of equal opportunity agencies and expanded the definition of discrimination to include statistical discrimination. But it is perhaps symptomatic of the 1990s that the act proved to be largely ineffective, as attention focused on the problem faced by men during the recession and on the dramatic declines in fertility (see Chapter 3). Ireland established a new government department in 1993 under a Minister for Equality and Law Reform, with responsibility for monitoring, co-ordinating and evaluating all policy proposals with reference to their impact on women and minority groups. However, commitments in the early 1990s to amend existing employment law legislation and to introduce equal status legislation to outlaw discrimination in non-employment areas had still not been fully implemented by 1998.

Germany has introduced more measures related to equal opportunities but this activity was related to the consequences of unification. The changes to its equal opportunities legislation were made in order to reduce, to some extent, the gap between West and East Germany in its approach to equality. However, the impact so far has been relatively slight and the main effect of unification has been to impose the West German legal situation on East Germany. Some positive advances were made, including for example a requirement on works councils to include equal opportunities in their agenda and a blanket law banning sexual harassment in the workplace. Positive action plans, including rights to part-time work at all levels of the hierarchy, were, however, confined to the public sector (National reports, Germany: Maier *et al.* 1996:44–45).

One of the main areas of activity in equal opportunities has been initiatives which require organisations to carry out equality audits and/or develop equality action plans. Scandinavia has been at the forefront of these developments. From 1991 onwards public institutions in Denmark have been effectively required to develop annual plans for equality and although an evaluation in 1993 found these actions still to be less than satisfactory, in 1995 parliament responded by strengthening the requirement to draw up action plans, with targets for women in managerial jobs and with proposals for reconciliation between work and family life. In Sweden and Finland the requirement for plans extended to the private sector: for firms with more than 10 employees in Sweden and with more than 30 employees in Finland. In Sweden the plans mainly focused on reducing pay differentials, while in Finland they covered recruitment and selection, pay and sexual harassment. Belgium too enacted legislation requiring reports on equality issues to be presented to works councils and positive action plans to be drawn up in the public sector, and permitting such plans in the private sector. In the UK there was the launch of a major voluntary initiative to monitor and improve women's position within organisations but this is a purely voluntary system, albeit receiving the backing of the government (see Chapter 2). The impact of these initiatives has yet to be assessed but it should be remembered that France has had legislation since 1983 allowing for equality plans and for equality audits, but the number of companies developing such plans has been very small, affecting only around 30 companies (Chalude *et al.* 1994; de Jong and Bock 1995).

There are two other areas in which equal opportunities initiatives at member state level were evident in the early 1990s: as regards wages and job classifications and with respect to helping unemployed women (see Box 1.9 for measures with respect to rights of part-timers, for example in the Netherlands). In Spain and Portugal there were efforts to remove gender from job titles in job classification schemes (CEC 1996a). In Finland a joint working group was set up to investigate ways in which work can be evaluated under the principle of equal value. In Sweden wage plans were required to be approved by the local Equal Opportunities Ombudsman. Measures to help unemployed women were also taken in a number of countries, but these were either part of general programmes to help vulnerable groups or were intended to offset the discrimination faced by women in gaining access to active labour market programmes because such schemes tended to be targeted on the registered unemployed in receipt of benefits. Some of the measures involved help with childcare, some gave help to train in non-traditional areas, others simply offered training opportunities, on a full or sometimes part-time basis.

While a range of measures can be identified which were adopted at the nation state level to develop equal opportunities, the European Union has been responsible for many of the measures implemented, or changes made to legislation within member states. The European Union provided direct assistance to equal opportunities through its NOW (New Opportunities for Women) programmes[1] which provided for structural funds to be targeted specifically on equal opportunities (Rees 1995a, 1995b,1998). In addition, the European Union legislative framework has been a significant influence on the direction of equal opportunities policy in member states. The new legislation or initiatives have included the directive on maternity leave, the directive on the reconciliation of work and family life providing for parental leave, the memorandum on equal value and the memorandum on sexual harassment. More recently still, the European Union in December 1997 adopted two directives, one to give equal rights to part-timers and one to shift the burden of proof in sex equality cases (see Box 1.1). Furthermore, the EU has adopted equal opportunities as its fourth pillar of employment policy under the new employment guidelines, and this decision may help to stimulate member states at least to assess and identify their equal opportunities employment policy agenda.

However, not all interventions from Europe were positive for equal opportunity within member states in the 1990s. The European Court considered that the laws on positive action in Bremen were incompatible with European law by granting women automatic preference if they had equal qualifications with a man. Most of the German state laws do allow for individual circumstances to be taken into account and thus might not be found illegal. However, the potential damage that this decision could have had on member states' positive action programmes has been reduced by the inclusion in the Amsterdam Treaty agreed in June 1997 of a provision for positive action. This change in European law through the Amsterdam Treaty was facilitated by the change in government in the UK just immediately prior to the Amsterdam Summit, as the previous government had been hostile to any amendment which would allow for positive action. There have been other examples, again involving German cases, in which the European court has found against women's interests, for example in the 1995 ruling that it was acceptable for part-timers to be excluded from social protection when working under 15 hours a week, or to be excluded from overtime payments when working more than their normal hours (CEC 1997d:98; IDS 1996a:3). Another example of a case which went against women's interests was the Barber case on pensions, which has led to many member states equalising women's pension ages upwards to those of men, an unwelcome overspill

Table 1.4 Employment rates by gender in the European Union, 1989–1996

	Men								Women							
	1989	1990	1991	1992	1993	1994	1995	1996	1989	1990	1991	1992	1993	1994	1995	1996
Belgium	67.9	68.1	68.7	68.4	67.0	66.5	66.9	66.8	39.7	40.8	43.0	44.6	44.9	44.8	45.4	45.5
Denmark	80.9	80.1	79.0	78.5	75.9	77.6	80.8	80.5	69.5	70.7	70.1	70.4	68.7	67.1	67.0	67.4
Germany (w)	77.8	78.7	78.4	78.3	76.5	75.3	—	73.3	50.3	54.0	54.5	55.6	54.8	54.7	—	55.3
Germany (u)	—	—	78.6	71.2	68.3	69.1	73.9	72.7	—	—	67.7	57.9	55.7	56.2	55.3	55.4
Spain	67.0	68.2	67.9	65.7	61.3	60.1	60.8	61.3	29.5	30.7	31.2	31.3	30.3	30.2	31.2	32.2
France	71.4	71.0	69.9	69.3	67.8	66.6	67.3	67.3	50.6	50.9	51.4	51.3	51.6	51.3	52.0	52.3
Greece	74.1	73.4	72.3	72.3	71.7	72.2	72.2	72.6	37.6	37.5	34.9	36.2	36.4	37.1	38.0	38.5
Ireland	66.4	67.8	66.3	64.7	64.1	65.3	66.8	66.8	33.9	35.5	35.5	36.8	38.2	39.8	41.3	42.8
Italy	71.4	72.0	71.5	68.9	68.3	66.5	65.7	65.3	35.8	36.4	37.2	36.1	35.7	35.6	35.6	36.1
Luxembourg	77.0	76.5	77.3	76.4	76.7	74.9	74.3	74.3	41.3	41.4	43.6	46.2	44.7	44.9	42.2	43.8
Netherlands	73.5	75.2	75.6	76.1	75.1	74.5	75.0	75.8	44.4	46.7	48.3	50.9	51.7	52.7	53.2	54.8
Austria	—	82.9	82.3	81.3	82.1	80.8	80.4	78.9	—	56.7	57.3	60.1	59.6	60.2	61.3	60.7
Portugal	78.9	78.6	79.8	77.2	74.6	72.5	71.2	71.0	52.4	53.3	56.4	55.7	54.9	54.1	54.3	54.2
Finland	—	78.2	72.8	66.8	63.0	62.1	63.5	63.8	—	71.5	68.2	63.8	59.3	58.8	59.9	59.5
Sweden	—	84.9	82.6	78.3	72.9	72.4	73.7	71.6	—	80.7	79.1	76.1	72.0	70.3	70.5	69.0
UK	80.2	80.5	78.1	75.3	73.7	74.1	74.8	75.0	60.9	61.7	61.1	61.0	60.9	61.1	61.4	62.3
E12 (w)	74.1	74.6	73.8	72.4	70.7	69.8	—	69.7	46.3	47.6	48.1	48.3	48.0	48.0	—	49.0
E12 (u)	—	—	74.0	72.4	70.6	69.8	69.9	69.7	—	—	49.0	48.7	48.4	48.4	48.8	49.3
E15 (u)	—	—	75.1	73.5	71.4	70.6	70.8	70.4	—	—	50.4	50.2	49.5	49.6	49.9	50.2

Sources: European Labour Force Survey (1989–1996); data for Sweden, Austria, Finland and E15 are from CEC (1996b, 1997c).

Notes
(u) data include the New German Länder.
(w) data exclude the New German Länder.
— indicates no data available.

Table 1.5 Unemployment rates by gender in the European Union, 1989–1996

	Men								Women							
	1989	*1990*	*1991*	*1992*	*1993*	*1994*	*1995*	*1996*	*1989*	*1990*	*1991*	*1992*	*1993*	*1994*	*1995*	*1996*
Belgium	5.3	4.6	4.6	4.9	6.2	7.8	7.3	7.4	12.9	11.5	10.6	9.5	10.9	12.5	12.3	12.4
Denmark	7.6	8.0	8.5	8.5	10.6	7.3	5.7	5.6	9.0	9.0	10.1	10.0	11.1	9.1	8.7	8.4
Germany (w)	4.5	4.0	3.6	3.8	5.6	6.8	—	7.8	7.5	6.3	4.9	4.8	6.2	7.3	—	7.9
Germany (u)	—	—	7.7	10.0	11.0	11.3	7.1	8.3	—	—	11.6	19.9	20.7	21.1	9.7	9.7
Spain	13.2	12.1	12.0	13.7	18.7	20.2	18.2	17.8	25.5	24.4	23.3	25.3	28.9	31.7	30.5	29.7
France	7.4	7.2	7.3	8.2	9.7	11.2	10.1	10.7	12.6	12.2	11.7	12.9	13.6	14.6	14.2	14.6
Greece	4.8	4.3	4.9	5.0	5.8	6.2	6.4	6.2	12.6	12.0	13.2	13.2	13.9	13.9	14.1	15.8
Ireland	16.4	14.0	15.8	15.3	15.9	14.9	12.3	12.0	16.7	15.1	16.9	15.4	15.9	14.8	12.2	11.8
Italy	7.5	6.5	6.9	6.9	7.8	9.0	9.3	9.7	17.5	15.7	15.8	14.0	15.0	15.6	16.3	16.6
Luxembourg	1.2	1.2	1.2	1.5	1.9	3.0	1.9	2.8	2.4	2.4	2.2	2.7	3.0	4.3	5.0	4.8
Netherlands	6.8	5.6	5.6	4.0	5.4	6.6	6.2	5.3	11.9	10.9	9.9	7.8	7.7	8.0	8.7	8.1
Austria	—	2.9	2.4	2.7	3.0	2.9	3.1	3.7	—	3.4	4.9	4.7	5.1	4.9	5.0	5.3
Portugal	3.7	3.4	2.7	3.5	4.7	6.1	6.8	6.7	7.6	6.7	5.8	4.9	6.5	8.0	8.1	8.8
Finland	—	3.7	8.6	15.5	18.5	18.5	16.4	15.0	—	2.8	5.6	10.5	15.3	16.1	16.2	15.8
Sweden	—	1.8	3.6	6.9	11.1	11.2	10.1	10.5	—	1.8	2.9	4.7	7.7	8.2	8.3	9.4
UK	7.6	7.3	9.5	11.7	12.5	11.6	10.2	9.8	7.2	6.7	7.4	7.4	7.7	7.4	7.0	6.4
E12 (w)	7.3	6.7	7.1	7.8	9.4	10.2	—	9.8	12.0	11.0	10.7	10.6	11.6	12.5	—	12.5
E12 (u)	—	—	7.1	7.9	9.5	10.2	9.6	9.9	—	—	10.7	11.2	12.2	13.0	12.8	12.8
E15 (u)	—	—	7.0	8.1	9.7	10.0	9.4	9.6	—	—	10.0	10.9	12.2	12.7	12.5	12.5

Sources: European Labour Force Survey (1989–1996); data for Sweden, Austria, Finland and E15 are from CEC (1996b, 1997c).

Notes
(u) data include the New German *Länder*.
(w) data exclude the New German *Länder*.
— indicates no data available.

from the principle of equal treatment. However, other cases did much to strengthen and clarify the meaning of equal opportunities. For example, the Danfoss case established the need for transparency in equal pay claims (CEC 1997d:104), and cases taken against the British Conservative government established that unequal rights for part-timers could be considered a form of indirect discrimination (Dickens 1995). Moreover, these decisions have led to actual changes in national law; for example in the UK part-timers are now covered by unfair dismissal and redundancy protection whereas previously most of those working less than 16 hours were excluded.

The impact of the changing economic and political conditions on men and women: gender and country differences

On average men suffered somewhat more than women from the recession of the early 1990s. In most countries the employment rate for men fell faster than that for women, and their unemployment rates rose faster in absolute and proportional terms. Men's employment fell by well over 4 percentage points between 1989 to 1994 at the E12 level (using ELFS (European Labour Force Survey) data both including and excluding East Germany), and by nearly 5 percentage points if we consider the fall from the peak in 1990 to the trough in 1994 (see Tables 1.4 and 1.5). Since 1994 the employment rate has stabilised but not shown an upward trend. A similar picture emerges if we look at *Employment in Europe* data for the E15 level (CEC 1996b; 1997c). Between 1991 and 1996, the male employment rate fell by nearly 5 percentage points. Including the new member states thus tends to worsen the male employment performance for Europe as a whole. In contrast, the female employment rate rose by 1.7 percentage points between 1989 and 1994, and even from its peak in 1992 only registered a fall of just over a quarter of a percentage point before rising again to a new high of 49 per cent in 1996. If the former East Germany is included there is a larger fall between 1991 and 1994, but the average female employment rate is also higher, as it is at the E15 level with the new member states. For the E15, the female employment rate fell by 0.8 percentage points between 1991 and 1994 but recovered to just 0.2 percentage points below the 1991 peak by 1996.

There was also some convergence of female employment rates during the 1990s, as falls tended to occur in those countries with the highest female employment rates, in particular Sweden, Finland, Denmark and the UK. In some countries there was also a marked convergence of male and female employment rates, as a consequence either of very poor employment performance for men or of rising female employment in the face of the recession. The gender gap in employment rates narrowed by more than 5 percentage points between 1990 and 1996 in Belgium, the former West Germany, Spain, France, Ireland, Italy, the Netherlands, Portugal, Austria and the UK. We also find some narrowing of the gender gap in unemployment rates, but less

Table 1.6 Youth unemployment rates by gender in the European Union, 1989–1996

	Women								Male–female differential							
	1989	1990	1991	1992	1993	1994	1995	1996	1989	1990	1991	1992	1993	1994	1995	1996
Belgium	20.1	19.1	17.2	15.1	19.6	23.3	23.8	24.5	-8.9	-9.1	-6.3	-3.7	-2.1	-2.7	-4.0	-7.2
Denmark	12.3	11.6	12.3	12.5	14.7	10.2	12.3	12.4	-1.6	-0.3	-1.5	-0.3	-0.2	-0.1	-4.5	-3.4
Germany (w)	5.9	4.8	3.7	4.3	5.6	6.7	—	8.1	-0.7	-0.3	-0.1	-0.1	1.1	2.1	—	2.3
Germany (u)	—	—	13.4	15.3	16.1	15.7	8.2	8.6	—	-13.7	-2.9	-5.3	-5.0	-3.5	0.5	1.8
Spain	42.5	39.3	37.2	39.7	46.6	49.6	48.1	48.3	-14.9	-13.7	-11.9	-11.8	-7.5	-8.2	-11.6	-11.7
France	23.0	23.1	22.6	24.9	27.6	30.5	30.7	30.3	-6.7	-6.3	-5.6	-6.2	-4.0	-3.4	-7.0	-5.2
Greece	34.1	32.6	33.5	34.1	36.1	36.8	37.9	41.4	-17.1	-17.4	-16.7	-16.9	-17.2	-17.0	-18.4	-19.8
Ireland	19.6	18.2	21.1	20.8	22.8	20.6	17.1	16.9	4.1	2.7	3.7	3.6	4.1	4.6	3.5	2.3
Italy	38.5	35.3	33.4	32.2	34.4	35.4	37.6	39.1	-12.7	-11.9	-9.7	-8.9	-8.1	-6.7	-8.5	-9.1
Luxembourg	(3.8)	(4.3)	(2.6)	(3.2)	(4.2)	(7.3)	(10.0)	(11.1)	-0.8	-1.5	0.1	1.0	0.2	1.2	-0.9	-1.1
Netherlands	13.8	12.0	12.0	8.5	9.5	9.0	12.8	11.7	-1.4	-1.8	-1.7	-0.8	1.7	4.5	-1.3	-0.4
Austria	—	4.2	8.1	7.0	7.6	7.0	6.7	7.1	—	-1.2	-3.7	-2.4	-2.4	-2.5	-2.2	-2.1
Portugal	15.9	13.4	11.8	10.7	14.7	16.9	17.2	19.9	-7.7	-5.5	-5.5	-2.0	-4.7	-4.4	-2.1	-5.5
Finland	—	13.5	17.2	20.9	40.7	41.5	39.9	39.0	—	1.1	4.4	8.3	2.2	1.4	-3.2	-1.6
Sweden	—	6.7	7.1	11.1	19.0	19.8	18.4	20.4	—	0.1	1.4	4.9	7.0	5.5	2.4	1.3
UK	9.3	9.3	11.5	11.6	13.5	12.8	12.5	11.3	1.9	2.0	4.5	7.4	7.4	6.4	5.4	6.6
E12 (w)	20.1	18.7	18.7	19.0	21.6	22.7	—	23.6	-5.0	-4.4	-3.1	-2.1	-0.8	-0.6	—	-2.3
E12 (u)	—	—	30.3	18.9	21.3	22.4	22.9	23.2	—	—	-8.5	-2.3	-1.0	-2.4	-2.7	-2.3
E15 (u)	—	—	17.9	19.1	22.0	23.0	23.2	23.3	—	—	-2.6	-1.9	-1.1	-1.6	-3.0	-2.7

Source: European Labour Force Survey (1989–1996); data for Sweden, Austria, Finland and E15 are from CEC (1996b, 1997c).

Notes
(u) data include the New German Länder.
(w) data exclude the New German Länder.
— indicates no data available.

dramatic than that for employment (see Tables 1.4 and 1.5). In 11 countries female unemployment rates exceeded male rates throughout the period, with the gap only narrowing noticeably in 6 countries. In Ireland, male and female unemployment rates remained roughly similar over the same period while the UK, Finland and Sweden all started off the period with relatively equal unemployment rates by gender, but by 1994 male unemployment rates were at least 3 percentage points higher than female unemployment rates in each country. Thus much of the narrowing at the E15 level is attributable to the emergence of higher male unemployment rates in these three countries.

The trends within E15 as a whole and within the majority of the EU member states do provide some grounds for the increased concern expressed over men's employment prospects in the mid 1990s: overall men fared relatively badly in both employment and unemployment terms. These trends have given rise to increasing public concern over employment opportunities for unemployed men, and young men in particular. During the 1990s recession young male unemployment rates rose faster than those for young females, although on average female youth unemployment rates were still higher (Table 1.6). The focus on youth unemployment as the target for employment policy has been fuelled by a concern about what will happen to young men, in particular, who are excluded from the labour market; concern not only over their opportunities and life chances but also over the implications for levels of violence and crime in the community. While the previous method of allocating the scarce resource – employment – through the exclusion of women has broken down, it has yet to be replaced with a new and socially acceptable system of distributing available work and rationing access to employment. A golden age of full employment when young people experienced no difficulty in finding work is frequently invoked, but without acknowledgement of the low levels of female employment at that time. Young people are the outsiders on the labour market and for this reason they, together with many older women who are still outside or only partially integrated into wage work, tend to bear the burden of unemployment and job shortage. This burden has increasingly taken the form of casual and part-time work as well as periods of unemployment (see Box 1.11). There is thus some evidence of greater equality between men and women in their involvement in precarious employment, a consequence of the deteriorating opportunities for young people to move into relatively secure employment. Placing the burden of adjustment on young people would not necessarily be regarded as an insuperable problem if there were good prospects that after a period of part-time or casual employment they would be able to make the transition into permanent and secure full-time work. However, the destabilisation of the employment system is such that flexible work appears to act more as a trap for the most disadvantaged young people than as a bridge for easing the transition from education to work (see Box 1.11). These deteriorating prospects for men in general, and for young people in particular, have meant that demonstration of unequal

---

Box 1.11 The increasing casualisation of the youth labour market

In **Italy** in 1992 two-thirds of new entrants into manual work in manufacturing, most of whom were young men, were on temporary contacts, while
in non-manual work in manufacturing, a gender-mixed occupation, two
thirds were still on permanent full-time contracts. The casualisation of the
youth labour market thus tends to be seen as a male problem, but if data
on the service sector were available this view might have to be revised
(National reports, Italy: Bettio and Villa 1996:8).

Young people join women in **Spain** as the main group of latecomers
to the labour market who thereby share the burden of unemployment
and casualisation in a period of severe job shortage. The gender gap in the
shares on a temporary contract has been narrowing as a consequence of
the concentration of temporary contracts on the young where men and
women are relatively equally represented (National reports, Spain: Moltó
1996:24).

In **Finland** there has been a rapid increase in the share of temporary
contracts among new hires – from 38 per cent in 1989 to 60 per cent in
1993. Women predominate among temporary job holders (National reports,
Finland: Keinänen 1996:27).

In the **UK** increased equality between young people has been brought
about through a levelling down of the prospects for young men. More young
men have become involved in part-time work, a trend which has been
fuelled by the reduction in financial support for students and the withdrawal
of access to benefits, thereby forcing increased reliance on family and
household support. The possibilities for young people to make an early transition to adult independence have been reduced (National reports, UK:
Rubery 1996:27).

---

opportunity for women in absolute terms is no longer necessarily sufficient
to win the argument that policy should be directed at improving the
position of women in the labour market. The 1990s have witnessed the
re-emergence of significant labour market problems for men and have
refocused attention on the problem of the distribution of work, both between
the sexes and between the generations. It is undoubtedly significant that at
the 1997 Luxembourg Jobs Summit, the main quantitative targets agreed
by the member states related to the provision of training and work place-
ments for the long-term unemployed and the young unemployed, with targets
for the fourth pillar, equal opportunities, left unspecified (see Chapter 9).

However, against this diagnosis of relatively poor performance for men
must be set the following factors. First, women's measured unemployment
remained higher than men's in most EU countries and for the EU as a whole
(see Chapter 4); second, women's measured unemployment is more likely
to understate the true rate of female unemployment more than is the case
for men; third, women's employment rates fell by less but from lower levels;
and fourth, women's employment rates were in some cases boosted by the
growth of part-time jobs. In some countries, the extension of leave arrange-

ments for parents also exaggerated the share of women in employment (see Box 1.7). Most seriously of all, the downturn in women's employment has come against a background of fairly consistent rises in women's employment over the past two decades and perhaps indicates the beginning of a period in which structural change is likely to work against the interests of women in the labour market.

Summary: swimming against the tide

During the first half of the 1990s the gap between male and female employment rates continued to narrow, reinforcing the trends during the 1970s and 1980s towards more equal participation in wage work by men and women. Unemployment continued to be higher for women than for men but again, the gender difference was reduced. Meanwhile, equal opportunities policy has been given a higher profile at the European level, the EU has committed itself to mainstreaming gender into general labour market and social policy and the European member states have agreed to common employment guidelines which involve commitments to both the promotion of women's employment and equal opportunities.

However, this upbeat summary of recent trends in women's employment position hides some worrying developments. First, the narrowing of the employment and unemployment gaps has, particularly in some member states, resulted mainly from a reduction in male employment rates. Second, much of the demand for female labour has been boosted by the opportunity to employ women in more flexible and often low-paid jobs. Third, the next stage of economic restructuring appears set to be relatively less favourable to women's traditional employment areas. Particularly vulnerable areas are the public sector and clerical employment in sectors such as banking. Fourth, while equal opportunities policy has been placed on the policy agenda of the European Union, there is as yet little evidence of significant commitment to such a policy objective at the member-state level, where policy initiatives are still designed and implemented. Thus the main thrusts of economic policy have been on the one hand that of meeting the Maastricht convergence criteria and, on the other, that of reducing the problem of employment shortage, with the problem of the unemployed male clearly in mind. It is yet to be determined whether the recent incorporation of equal opportunities as a fourth pillar of European employment policy will be sufficient to begin to shift the agenda to one of jobs for both men and women. Women's employment prospects over the next decade will still be influenced primarily by the general trends in the world economy, and the overall policy approach to the macroeconomic and labour market environment. As such, without further progress towards mainstreaming, any policy initiatives to reduce gender inequality may simply be swimming against the tide of economic policy, which could indeed still threaten the gains that women have made over the past two decades.

2   Organisational and employment change

State policy and the macroeconomic context provide the framework for the evolution of women's employment position. Progress towards or retreat from gender equality in employment ultimately depends upon employment decisions and practices at the level of the organisation. Unfortunately there is little, if any, harmonised information on employment practices by type of employer. Even the distinction between public and private sector employment is not identified in the European Labour Force Survey. Available information by member states is also extremely patchy and arguably often unrepresentative. Much emphasis has been placed on efforts within organisations to improve women's position through positive action programmes (see de Jong and Bock 1995; Rubery *et al.* 1996) but an even more important first step may be to gather more information on the range of different practices by organisation and to consider the implications of recent developments in human resource strategies for gender equality. The identification of new trends in employment practices must be a critical objective of mainstreaming; unless changes are focused on in their embryonic stage, policy is likely to be too little and too late. Nevertheless, it is important not to generalise from limited developments in a small number of organisations or member states, and not to assume that employment practices and policies are all developing at a similar pace and in a similar direction.

Clear differences still remain between member states in the culture and structure of organisational practices. In some member states employer practices are tightly constrained by either legal regulations or national-level collective regulations, or both, such that changes introduced into these regulations can be considered the prime determinants of change in the employment system. Where the system of regulation is relatively loose, the pace of change depends more on the independent initiatives of organisations. More research is usually carried out in these countries at the organisational level compared to those where the regulatory system is expected to deliver greater uniformity across organisations.[1] Yet this assumption of uniformity may remain relatively untested.

Current trends and developments in organisations and employment practices

Five areas can be identified which have been the site of key developments in employment practices with particular implications for gender equality:

- employment security and employment restructuring;
- flexibility in contracts and working-time arrangements;
- decentralisation of wage bargaining and individualisation of the employment relationship;
- changes in structure of jobs and organisations;
- change and continuity in the system of gender segregation and gender inequality.

Employment security and employment restructuring

The 1990s have exacerbated the trends evident in the 1970s and 1980s towards less stable employment relationships. The security of employment in the boom that followed the Second World War in many European countries was bolstered not only by stable product markets but also by legal or collective bargaining protection over dismissals. Where these controls have in the past been strong, the 1980s and 1990s have seen a weakening of these regulations (see Box 2.1; Rodgers and Rodgers 1989). This weakening of regulation coincided with increasing instability in product markets and changes in organisational structures which led employers to make rapid changes in employment levels, often through compulsory redundancy. A further dimension to employment instability was added in the late 1980s and 1990s with the extension of flexibility to public sectors, through policies such as privatisation, competitive tendering, weakening of public service employment rights and the extensive use of temporary contracts.

Box 2.1 Changes to regulations relating to dismissal

The 1994 reform of the labour market regulation system in **Spain** included changes to the regulation of dismissals. The end result of the reforms is likely to have been reduced firing costs for large firms, but enhanced rights for temporary workers will have increased costs for small firms (National reports, Spain: Moltó 1996:16, 25).

Luxembourg, alone among the EU member states, strengthened regulation against collective dismissal in 1993 in an effort to protect employment during the recession (National reports, Luxembourg: Plasman 1996:9).

In **Portugal** legislation in 1989 made the renewal of fixed-term contracts more difficult but the termination of permanent contracts easier. Thus the statistical trend towards lower shares of temporary workers in Portugal in part reflects this change in regulations (González and Castro 1996:4).

The collective impact of these developments was to weaken severely expectations of a job for life, even within what had previously been the most stable employment environments such as the public sector. In countries such as Spain there has been a long-term expectation of stable employment contracts, particularly during the Franco period:

> the Spanish employers no longer establish indefinite relationships with their workforce ... temporary jobs become permanent and long term relationships are becoming more temporary ... The last decade of the twentieth century is witnessing one of the most important sociological changes affecting most Spanish families: the end of stable employment.
> (National reports, Spain: Moltó 1996:29)

In East Germany not only had the previous government provided stable employment conditions, but in addition there had effectively been a labour shortage; thus adjustment to the new conditions of employment insecurity and unemployment marked a major transformation in social and economic life.

As the stable and continuous employment opportunities have traditionally been dominated by men, this reduction in the power of the insiders relative to the outsiders could be seen as having shifted the balance of advantage away from men and towards women. There are, however, some problems with this analysis. First, the changes mainly decreased male privileges in the labour market, without in any way directly enhancing women's position. The reduction in stability within core sectors has gone hand in hand with increased insecurity in the periphery, re-establishing the gender difference in job security but at a lower level.

Second, men were still more able than women to persuade both governments and employers to compensate for the loss of employment or to provide assistance with reintegration into work (see Box 2.2). Thus large-scale redundancies in manufacturing and heavy industry tend to attract more public attention and public funds to assist with the retraining and redeployment process than when restructuring occurs in the service sectors or female-dominated manufacturing sectors.

Third, the increasing attack on the security of employment in the public sector is likely to have a disproportionate impact on women, who have found in the public sector the main refuge from the unstable secondary employment segments of the private services sector.

Fourth, the trend towards the subcontracting out of key activities and the selling off or disposal of activities outside a company's core business has significant implications for women, as this facilitates the breakup of activities into areas which may be male- and female-dominated. Under current equal pay laws, segregation by organisation facilitates gender pay differentiation, as comparisons must be made within the same organisation. Thus subcontracting and fragmentation decrease the scope for pay and conditions to be governed by the principle of equal pay for work of equal value (Jones 1993).

Box 2.2 Reintegrating the redundant: a male-dominated policy?

Most of the unemployed in **Italy** are excluded from unemployment benefits. This inequality in treatment increased as the level of redundancy payments was repeatedly revised upwards and the period of coverage of
payments extended. Short-time working schemes also expanded in
large firms as an alternative to redundancy. Women tended to be under-
represented among those eligible for redundancy payments, although the
extension of the schemes in the 1990s to some service sectors should have
helped more women (National reports, Italy: Bettio and Villa 1996:4).

In **France** the greater scope employers enjoyed to determine redundancies since 1986 was tempered by increased requirements to help with the
reintegration of redundant workers. After 1987 there were retraining agreements for redundant workers, but since 1993 firms initiating large-scale
redundancies have been obliged to draw up social plans. In contrast to
other active labour market policies, women's involvement in these retraining and restructuring programmes was relatively low. This was because the
large firms involved in these schemes tended to be in male-dominated
sectors or in sectors with strong trade unions, where women were under-
represented (National reports, France: Silvera *et al.* 1996:21–22).

In the former **East Germany** it was the female-dominated and mixed
labour force manufacturing sectors such as textiles, electronics, food
processing, optics and precision engineering which were exposed most
rapidly to market forces after unification, leading to almost immediate
mass lay-offs and redundancies. In the core male-dominated heavy industries such as steel, shipbuilding, cars and mechanical engineering the
restructuring process was slowed down by state and trade union intervention. Even though some of the mixed labour force industries such as optics
and precision mechanics had the best prospects in the world market, most
of the subsidies were directed towards the heavy industries. In some areas
the demise of female-dominated sectors such as textiles led to women
accounting for 80 per cent of all the registered unemployed. Women's
position was made worse by their concentration in administrative roles,
which were deemed to be overstaffed, and in welfare support services
which were drastically reduced. Also, where women were employed in typically male jobs, it was found that they had a higher risk of dismissal than
their male counterparts (National reports, Germany: Maier *et al.* 1996:24).

Flexibility in contracts and working-time arrangements

The 1990s have witnessed further development of employer policy towards
more flexible employment contracts and new forms of working-time
arrangements (Bosch *et al.* 1994; Rubery *et al.* 1995; OECD 1995a). The
growth of flexible employment contracts has continued despite the weakening of the protection accorded to workers on standard or permanent contracts
and despite in some cases the enhancement of rights for those on temporary

Box 2.3 Flexibility policies at the company or sectoral level

After 1994 working-time in **Spain** was subject to collective bargaining instead of legal regulation, and working-time could be calculated on an annual basis and distributed irregularly, subject only to a 12-hour weekday rest period and a 36-hour rest period at weekends. This more flexible regulatory structure has also been implicated in the increased use of part-time contracts by employers. This move seems to be dominated by demand-side considerations, as less than 10 per cent of female part-timers in Spain worked these hours because of family responsibilities (National reports, Spain: Moltó 1996:14, 28).

In **Finland** employers expressed preferences for more flexible working arrangements in the early 1990s, especially more variable distribution of hours, but also more part-time, weekend and shift work. Some innovatory working-time arrangements were found at the local level but most adjustment still came through lay-offs and dismissal, not through part-time work or work sharing (National reports, Finland: Keinänen 1996:37).

A 1996 act in the **Netherlands** allowed more variable distribution of working hours, including longer working days. At the sectoral level there was significant interest in new working-time arrangements, including shorter working weeks and four-day working weeks, with banking, retail and chemicals leading the way. These moves were accompanied by reductions in payment for unsocial hours for full-timers. Flexibility strategies no longer solely affected part-time, temporary and zero-hours staff but also permanent staff. Unions decided to negotiate on new flexible working systems on the grounds that it was better if these systems were controlled by collective agreements (National reports, Netherlands: Plantenga *et al.* 1996:11–13).

In **Italy** changes to working hours in the early 1990s within the public sector were related to the discretion granted to city mayors to set new shop and public service opening hours. This resulted in some diversification of hours but around a relatively slow pace of change. These changes may be considered positive from the perspective of women as consumers but negative from the position of women as employees, particularly in the public sector. The previous system of six-hour days, six days per week was considered to be advantageous for women, not least because it followed the school system (National reports, Italy: Bettio and Villa 1996:5–6)

Irish employers called for more flexibility in the 1990s. In some sectors, for example retailing, increased casualisation of employment was accompanied by increased Sunday working coupled with reductions in premia paid for both Sunday and overtime working. The Labour Court upheld the right of employers to extend Sunday working and to reduce premia for new recruits, although it opposed the development of zero-hour contracts. Within the manufacturing sector, multinational companies were particularly implicated in the development of part-time employment, with a 30 per cent increase in part-time and contract work in this sector in 1995 alone (National reports, Ireland: Barry 1996:11).

Denmark has short working hours for full-timers but a high degree of flexibility relating to the organisation of working hours, resulting in a high level of unsocial hours and weekend working (National reports, Denmark: Boje 1996:19; Rubery *et al.* 1995:203).

In the first half of the decade employers in **Belgium** were active in pressing for a range of measures to increase flexibility but maintained opposition to general reductions in working-time. They were successful in obtaining a permanent right to grant up to four temporary contracts in succession, together with simplification of the regulations governing a typical workers and working-time, and opportunities to determine working-time on an annualised basis (National reports, Belgium: Meulders and Hecq 1996:23–28).

In the **UK** employers increasingly required employees, both full- and part-time, to adopt new working-time arrangements to meet the needs of organisations involving flexible, unsocial and long hours of work. Full-timers were increasingly subject to the withdrawal of overtime and unsocial hours premia but part-timers still provide the highest degree of flexibility with the least amount of compensation (National reports, UK: Rubery 1996:39). Moves towards higher levels of unsocial hours working were fuelled by the relaxation of restrictions on shop and pub opening hours over recent years.

In **France** company strategies were directed towards a search for multiple forms of flexibility, with priority given to numerical and external forms of flexibility. Within this overall strategy there was a gender divide with collective methods of work redistribution applied to male employees and individualised methods of working-time reduction reserved for women (National reports, France: Silvera *et al.* 1996:29–30).

Since 1994 employers in **Germany** have had greater scope to determine working-time at the local level, to vary its distribution within negotiated working-time levels averaged over a six-month period and to introduce Sunday or Saturday working if they could establish that otherwise they would lose international competitiveness. This last clause was opposed by trade unions who expected an increase in Sunday working. Both employers' organisations and trade unions joined together to oppose deregulation of shop opening hours, although some relaxation of these restrictions was eventually allowed so that shops could open in the evenings and on Saturday afternoons, but not on Sundays (National reports, Germany: Maier *et al.* 1996:36–43).

and atypical contracts. To some extent the continuing popularity of temporary contracts with employers relates to uncertainty over the actual change in legislation for those on permanent contracts and the potential negative impact on industrial relations, company image and the like of making permanent workers redundant. Employers have focused the burden of insecurity onto new hires and young people in particular. These policies have impacted on women in all societies but perhaps particularly in those where women have a low share of current employment or discontinuous careers. In these cases movement towards integration in the labour market has necessarily involved women being disproportionately represented among new hires.

New forms of working-time arrangements have been associated with changes to operating and opening hours, to changes in employers' wage cost strategies and to issues of work sharing (see Box 2.3). However, there has been no uniform pattern of change, and working-time arrangements at the organisation level have remained strongly conditioned by societal institutions, values and practices (see Chapter 7). Moves towards the extension of operating and opening hours have been associated with deregulation of the product and service markets, particularly retailing, and with the move towards decentralisation of collective bargaining, which often allows for new and innovative forms of working arrangements to be negotiated at local level. Countries which traditionally have had very rigid and predictable working-time patterns have been finding organisations experimenting with novel systems of work scheduling, involving flexibility over the year, the week and the day (Bettio *et al.* 1998a). These novel schemes were also being extended to the public sector in some countries.

The extension of operating and opening hours may be met either through increased use of atypical contracts or through rearrangement of the working schedules of full-time employees (through overtime or more flexible scheduling, including annualisation of working hours). Organisations have not only extended coverage to match customer demand or to introduce just-in-time production systems but have also sought to reduce the costs associated with such developments (Bosch 1995; OECD 1995a). Atypical workers have provided an important source of labour for cover at low costs: for example, part-timers might not be entitled to unsocial hours premia or to overtime premia until they have worked full-time hours. Full-timers have either retained their entitlements to premia or have seen them incorporated into higher basic pay agreements associated with new flexibility or annualised hours contracts. However, there was evidence in some countries that organisations might also now be seeking to reduce such payments to full-time core workers. Under these conditions current practices which primarily affect women and young people have implications for the future terms and conditions of men's employment as well.

Men and women offer different types of flexibility to employers; men are assumed to be available for long hours and unsocial hours but up until now have been able to negotiate significant wage supplements for extra or unsocial hours or indeed for short-hours working; women have been assumed to be available for short hours without compensation, to be willing to provide additional flexibility at basic wage rates, and to accept movement between economic activity and inactivity (Rubery *et al.* 1998b). Up until now men may perhaps be considered as having been more engaged in changes in working-time arrangements organised or negotiated at a collective instead of an individualised level (National reports, France: Silvera *et al.* 1996:89). Thus male workers have been more involved in negotiated reductions in working weeks, new collectively negotiated annualised hours contracts, short-time working schemes for spreading the burden of recession, and such like. In contrast, women have been more subject to the individualisation of working-time, including the creation of part-time jobs, individualised work schedules and the use of flexible contracts. Where part-time jobs have been created through collective schemes aimed explicitly at work sharing – as under the French system of providing subsidies for annualised part-time contracts – there does appear to be evidence of greater involvement of men, perhaps as these work-sharing schemes may be considered hybrids, incorporating both collective and individualised elements, involving some forms of compensation and protection of full-time employment rights (National reports, France: Silvera *et al.* 1996:94).

Decentralisation of wage bargaining and individualisation of the employment relationship

The trend towards decentralisation of wage bargaining increases the scope both for variations between organisations and, within more weakly organised establishments, for greater managerial discretion (Traxler 1996; Katz 1993; Marsden 1992). Both tendencies may have negative implications for women. Women may be located in the less strongly organised sectors, and even when employed within the same firm, may be less likely to receive supplements and bonuses (Rubery and Fagan 1994, 1995a). Thus these developments herald a trend towards an intensified two-tier bargaining structure, with those in the weaker sectors still dependent on centralised but limited regulation, leaving more scope for managerial discretion (see Chapter 6). Where decentralisation deprived the sectoral or national framework of its role in maintaining the real value of minimum wages, the impact on women is likely to have been particularly negative. In the more extreme cases, for example the UK, decentralisation resulted in the collapse of national and sectoral-level agreements, leaving many workers, and particularly women, outside the regulatory net.

The extent of the trend towards decentralisation is very different between member states; for example Sweden experienced a significant change in its highly centralised system with much greater scope for wage determination at the local level but Finland, which faced an even more severe economic crisis, largely retained its centralised system. Other countries differed in the timing of the decentralisation, with the move away from indexation and centralised wage bargaining occurring in Denmark in the early 1980s, compared to the much later collapse of centralised bargaining in Sweden and the movement away from indexation in Italy in the 1980s and 1990s. In Spain the trend was away from legal regulation to greater emphasis on collective regulation, which increased the scope for variations between organisations because of differences in the capacities for collective negoti-ation. However, there has, of yet, been no retreat from the principle of the universal application of collective agreements.

Alongside decentralisation there has been a parallel trend towards increased individualisation of the employment relationship and, in particular, towards greater emphasis on performance criteria for pay determination over collec-tively agreed norms and values (see Chapter 6). This change put in question the use of seniority payment systems in many member states. Seniority payments can be argued to have been instrumental in maintaining gender pay differentials, as women tend both to have less seniority than men and to be concentrated in part-time or temporary jobs where there are reduced rights to seniority payments. However, the change to individual merit and performance is not necessarily benefiting women, for two reasons (Rubery 1995a): first, there is much greater scope for managerial discretion and second, the extra payments tend to be much greater for those at the top of the hierarchy. Finally, it appears somewhat paradoxical that it was precisely at the point at which women were drawing equal with men in seniority terms that the system of extra rewards was called into question (Rubery *et al.* 1997b).

Changes in structure of jobs and organisations

Changes have taken place not only in the terms and conditions of employ-ment but also in the nature and organisation of work. Four trends in particular can be identified: towards flatter hierarchies; towards greater functional flexi-bility; towards polarisation between upgraded skills on the one hand and downgraded skills on the other; and towards higher initial qualifications and more continuous or further training over the life cycle.

The move towards flatter hierarchies can be argued to be having contra-dictory effects for women (see Box 2.4). On the one hand, men have been further up the occupational ladder than women so that the removal of steps in the ladder – the displacement of middle management – should in the first instance primarily affect men. Yet the impact of the change is to increase the gulf between management and others, removing possible intermediate promotion opportunities for both men and women, and increasing the barriers that women have to breach to break the glass ceiling. In addition, the taking out of layers of middle management has often coincided with devolution of responsibility to staff below managerial level, many of whom are women, and who may have received no compensation for the extra responsibilities (Coyle 1995). This devolution has been accompanied by increased central-

---

Box 2.4 Towards flatter hierarchies, functional flexibility and greater gender inequality?

A study in the **UK** of the implications of changes in organisational structures (Coyle 1995) found problems for gender relations. Devolved power to line managers created problems for the implementation of equal opportunity policies even when there was commitment at head office; reductions in the numbers of middle managers coincided with increasing levels of responsibility for the mainly female administrative employees without necessarily providing compensating rewards; competition had increased between men and women for fewer middle management jobs and a widening gap had emerged between senior and other levels of management, creating 'a wide chasm' for women to cross; and increasing work intensity, coupled with devolved responsibility, had reduced possibilities for employees to match working-time to domestic needs (National reports, UK: Rubery 1996:45).

Under the 1994 reform in **Spain** there was a weakening of the traditional job classification system, paving the way for greater functional flexibility within organisations and greater scope to adapt job structures. The movement away from traditional job classifications also allowed for the elimination of the practice of describing jobs by the gender of the person employed (National reports, Spain: Moltó 1996:14, 1993). There have been significant differences between sectors and types of firms in Spain in their work organisation strategies. Large enterprises have done much to develop flexible, polyvalent production systems, but small firms have competed on the basis of low labour costs. Women have tended to remain concentrated in this secondary sector (National reports, Spain: Moltó 1996:24).

Some changes have been taking place in women's employment in **Austria** related to new methods of working and new systems of human resource management. These included, in particular, the increasing integration of secretarial work with administrative and executive work; the decentralisation of responsibility accompanied by increased centralised control via the use of new technologies; the flattening of hierarchical structures; the development of teamwork; the increase in flexible working and the increasing emphasis on techniques to motivate workers and to instil company loyalty (National reports, Austria: Pastner 1996:12–14).

---

ised control and surveillance, which might result in a deterioration of women's employment situation.

Trends towards greater functional flexibility can also be regarded as having ambiguous consequences for gender equality. First the move away from traditional job classifications in principle opens up possibilities of changes to the pattern of occupational segregation, and undermines men's labour market power where it is based on such traditional demarcations. However, as suggested above, the net result could be a reallocation of more skilled work towards women, but without extra compensation. Alternatively, the development of functional flexibility could also call into question the specific demand for female labour in areas such as clerical work, as the growth of new technology allows for clerical functions to be recombined with other tasks. How these new developments will impact on the gender division of labour is by no means predetermined. One of the important equal opportunities issues over the next decade will be how to steer a clear course between making certain that women are not excluded from the new systems of work organisation while equally making certain that the employment of female labour is not used as means of downgrading the pay and status of skilled functions. Similar concerns can be voiced about telework, which in principle offers the possibility of a more flexible and possibly more family-friendly organisation of working life, but which also raises the spectre of an increase in the number of women working at home in isolation and on inferior terms and conditions of employment (Huws 1995).

Changes in job content come about not only through changes in work organisation but also through restructuring of sectors and the introduction of new management systems in both public and private sectors. Some of the more notable changes taking place in work organisation have resulted from the growth, for example, in industrial concentration in retailing which has led to the increased use of deskilled part-time flexible labour to replace the skilled and family labour employed in the independent retail sector. Trends in the nature of jobs are unlikely to be in one direction, and the overall trend may be towards an increased polarisation between high-skilled, high-value-added jobs and low-skilled service sector employment. These trends towards polarisation have also been affecting the male labour market, but women have remained dominant in the low-paid service areas.

New management systems have been introduced into the public sectors based on private sector management principles, with potential significance not only for job security and work intensity but also for skill levels and the professional ethos within many traditionally female-dominated areas of the public sector (National reports, UK: Rubery 1996:24). These trends have developed to a greater extent in the UK than elsewhere but other countries have been actively considering changing methods of management of the public sector. For example, Finland introduced changes allowing much more flexibility in the management of public service provision by local authorities.

Access to employment has become increasingly dependent upon initial qualifications, such that entry into many job areas has been restricted to graduates, while previously access might have been obtained through internal labour market systems. In some respects the trends have been favouring women, as over recent years they have markedly improved their acquisition of qualifications, thus placing them in a stronger position to compete in the external labour market. They still face disadvantage within internal labour markets by virtue both of more interrupted careers and of discrimination in internal promotion systems. Yet competition through qualifications only benefits some women, and may confine the rest of the female work-force to even poorer employment opportunities as credentialism removes opportunities for the less educated to move up the job hierarchy.

The increased requirement for continuing access to training and retraining also presents women with some problems. Training opportunities have tended to be reserved for those in work and thus by definition fewer women have been eligible for these opportunities. Training also has tended to be given to those higher up the hierarchy, thus further disadvantaging women (Tuijman and Schömann 1996).

However, the available data on access to training of men and women is mixed; in some countries women appear to have fared relatively well,

---

Box 2.5 Access to training: some mixed feelings

In **Finland** women are underrepresented in labour market training and overrepresented in personnel training and adult education. Training for women had been maintained during the recession while the incidence of male training had fallen. However, training periods for men tended to be longer than for women (National reports, Finland: Keinänen 1996:35).

Women in **Portugal** faced difficulties obtaining access to vocational training as courses were often held after work, with employers reluctant to give time off during working hours. Women had less spare time and less access to transportation (National reports, Portugal: Lopes and Perista 1996:21).

In **Sweden** in 1995 45 per cent of women had a training period compared to 39 per cent of men. White-collar workers and those with higher education were the most likely to receive training; similar patterns applied to both men and women (National reports, Sweden: Gonäs and Spånt 1996:20).

Many of the problems that **Austrian** women faced in gaining access to promotion were related to discrimination against women in further vocational training at the company level. Only a fifth of women attended training at their workplace in 1989 compared to a quarter of men and they were often excluded from career advancement courses (National reports, Austria: Pastner 1996:19).

Women in **France** have been almost as likely as men to take part in training courses. However, men have dominated continuing training courses, and training in industrial techniques, while more female training has been related to teaching, IT and medico-social areas. In 1993 under 7 per cent of employees were promoted at the end of a training course, but in this respect men and women had the same likelihood of promotion (National reports, France: Silvera *et al.* 1996:24).

By 1994 women in **Denmark** accounted for the majority of course partic-ipants, both in the case of those undertaking vocational training of less than three years and of those in long further education courses lasting between three and five years (National reports, Denmark: Boje 1996:Tables 4 and 5).

although it is difficult to obtain data on not only frequency of training but also length of training and its impact on careers (see Box 2.5).

Change and continuity in the system of gender segregation and gender inequality

At the organisation level, the number of initiatives to reduce gender inequality and gender segregation appear to have been modest and relatively infrequent. Moreover, evidence has come to light that the practice of classifying jobs by gender at the point of recruitment is still alive and well, at least in some countries (see Box 2.6). Where initiatives have been taken to reduce segregation, these have often had to compete against opposite countervailing trends towards greater emphasis on performance and the individual and less reliance on fair structures and systems to determine recruitment, promotion or rewards.

Box 2.6 The persistence of gender discrimination

Indirect evidence of continuing discrimination by employers in **Finland** came from complaints to the Ombudsman over dismissal, in which women who were pregnant or returning after parental leave frequently sought the advice of the Ombudsman. Complaints about discrimination in recruitment were also frequent (National reports, Finland: Keinänen 1996:35).

Research in the early 1990s in the **Netherlands** revealed that when employers were asked which characteristics were important in selection decisions, gender was considered relatively unimportant when the question was posed in the abstract, but when related to specific vacancies gender, along with age and health, took on much greater importance. Moreover, women were more likely to obtain employment in sectors where women were already reasonably well represented in the workforce (National reports, Netherlands: Plantenga *et al.* 1996:9).

In **Austria**, although the law required public advertisements to be gender neutral, a study found that the employment services agency, when making direct contact with employers, still asked whether they had a preference for the sex of the applicant for a particular vacancy. In 1994, almost 38 per cent of all job vacancies were intended exclusively for men and only 29 per cent for women. Gender was regarded as irrelevant in only a third of vacancies (National reports, Austria: Pastner 1996:15–18).

In **France** a study found a strong link between career success and an expressed willingness to be mobile. It was also still assumed that men were mobile and women were not, even though in practice most promoted men had not been mobile, some men were beginning to express difficulties associated with mobility, and some women were actively keen to be mobile, especially when this offered the chances of promotion (National reports, France: Silvera *et al.* 1996:23–24).

There is limited information available on positive action plans (Rubery *et al.* 1996; Box 2.7). In some countries these have been required by or facilitated by the state, but the effectiveness of these measures at the organisational level has depended upon the political and social climate. Thus most organisations have complied with the requirement for equality audits in Sweden, while in Italy the act has had little or no effect.

In the Netherlands there has been considerable activity within collective agreements in drawing up equal opportunity policies, but the number of companies implementing a company-specific plan has been found to be limited. Where implemented, such plans have been found to have positive effects. The UK has had perhaps the largest voluntary programme to promote women into higher-level jobs – Opportunity 2000 – which by 1994 included 275 organisations, up from 61 in 1991. However, as the scheme was entirely voluntary, and most organisations decided not to set targets or goals, the end results of such policies remain in doubt. Nevertheless, early evaluations indicated some positive effects (Hammond 1994) and the scheme at least helped to keep equal opportunity on organisations' agendas, even if still towards the bottom of the list of priorities. One of the problems in launching further equal opportunity policies at the organisation level has in fact been the change of business climate to a more performance-orientated environment. Such changes have also been reported to be affecting the attitudes of women. For example, in Austria women felt that they should not be given special privileges, and that they should not be regarded as victims (National reports, Austria: Pastner 1996:23). Increasing emphasis on individualised employment relationships might also be harming the effectiveness of job evaluation schemes as a mechanism for promoting equal value (see Box 2.8) even though their use may be spreading. As performance and merit awards increase in importance, the relationship between job grade and earnings is reduced. In Scandinavia, job evaluation could be considered to have a more positive role to play in enhancing gender pay equity, as its use is being promoted specifically with this objective in mind.

Gender prejudice in the selection and recruitment process was still reported in a number of countries where new research had become available, revealing the persistence of this problem despite gender equality laws. In Austria and the Netherlands personnel officers revealed a high degree of gender preference, particularly when discussing specific vacancies (see Box 2.6). Male jobs appeared more likely to be seen as only open to men, while female jobs were more likely to be open to both sexes. In France there was still a high attachment to geographical mobility clauses and a strong belief that women could not comply with this requirement, despite evidence to the contrary. There was also indirect evidence of the continuation of discrimination in dismissals. The tendency to dismiss women in East Germany more rapidly than men has already been noted, but evidence from Finland shows more women make complaints to the ombudsman about dismissal issues.

Box 2.7 Positive action policies

By the mid-1990s around half of the collective agreements in the **Netherlands** included some form of agreement to strengthen the position of women, but only around 5 per cent had adopted a fully developed structural approach to affirmative action; at the company level only 4 per cent had adopted an affirmative action approach. Yet where such programmes were adopted research had found them to be effective in both raising the share of women in the workforce and increasing the share of women in higher level jobs (National reports, Netherlands: Plantenga *et al.* 1996:10–11).

The 1991 act officially sanctioning and providing incentives for positive action in **Italy** was largely ignored by enterprises (National reports, Italy: Bettio and Villa 1996:1). Employers expressed opposition to the requirement to provide information on the position of women in enterprises when the law was passed and expressed their intention to boycott it. No sanctions were imposed on employers not complying with the legislation (de Jong and Bock 1995).

A growing number of private enterprises in **Sweden** were establishing positive action programmes, in accordance with the National Equality Plan of 1988–93, which had as one of its goals an increase in the number of women in management (National reports, Sweden: Gonäs and Spånt 1996:18).

Equal opportunity policies faced little chance of being implemented in **Austria** in the private sector. One reason, among others, was the clash between the equality principle and the growing ideology of the performance principle. Women were not seen as needing special treatment, so most equal opportunity policies at the company level focused on the reconciliation of work and family and few measures were taken to help women to break into management (National reports, Austria: Pastner 1996:23). In the public sector, a federal Law of Equal Opportunity passed in 1993 required not only the implementation of equal opportunity but also positive action. Recruitment and promotion of women were to be given priority if the share of women fell below 40 per cent at each grade level.

In **Belgium** positive action has been compulsory in all public sector organisations for some time. Equal opportunities officers have had to be appointed, reports published on the situation of women and plans for positive action developed. Since 1992 positive action plans have had

Summary: towards a more or a less segmented labour market

Many of the policy thrusts and developments in employment practices over the first half of the 1990s could be argued to have threatened the traditional privileges of labour market insiders. The destabilisation of employment both within the private and the public sectors, the increasing use of flexible to be included in the restructuring plans of private organisations. Nineteen sectors included positive action plans in collective agreements in 1991–1992 and 40 companies participated in a government-sponsored project on positive action from 1989 to 1993 (de Jong and Bock 1995:189, 192).

The **UK** has opposed any notion of positive or affirmative action involving either legal compulsion or quotas, but there has been a significant voluntary initiative, known as Opportunity 2000, with 275 signed-up members in 1994 compared to 61 in 1991. These organisations pledged themselves to try to improve the position of women but chose to do so through methods such as monitoring and offering flexible working arrangements and by and large decided not to set targets. Opportunity 2000 has been working within the framework of the business case for equal opportunity, instead of the social and ethical considerations that dominated equal opportunity policies in earlier periods (National reports, UK: Rubery 1996:40).

In principle, **France** went further and took action earlier than other countries, since 1983 requiring organisations to prepare an annual report on the position of women and to discuss it with the works council. In practice the law had little effect; by the early 1990s only about 30 companies had drafted a positive action plan under the Roudy Act and 'the obligation to submit an annual report on the position of women within the organisation also seems to have faded quietly away' (de Jong and Bock 1995:190).

The **German** positive action plan for federal government employees brought in after the 1994 law included increased rights to work part-time, protection against discrimination for part-timers and the appointment of women representatives to monitor positive action plans. The plan did not go as far as many *Länder* schemes in pressing for positive action to break the glass ceiling. The Kalanke case against the Bremen positive action policy was successful as under this scheme women were automatically given priority if they had the same qualifications as men, but most of the *Länder* schemes allowed for individual circumstances to be taken into account in the application of positive action programmes, thereby probably escaping the ruling, as in the Kalanke case, that the positive action plans were illegal under European law if individual circumstances were not considered (National reports, Germany: Maier *et al.* 1996:45–46). However, European law was subsequently amended to allow more scope for positive action.

contracts and flexible working-time arrangements, the individualisation of employment contracts, the move from seniority to more merit-related pay and the development of more functionally flexible job structures are all consistent with the dismantling of traditional internal labour market systems based around the continuous full-time male worker. On that basis recent trends might be expected to have reduced segmentation in the labour market and with it the extent of gender segregation and difference.

Box 2.8 Pay equality policies

Spain introduced the principle of equal pay for work of equal value in 1994, opening the way for a critique of existing job-evaluation criteria. Modification of the professional classification within the old Labour Ordinances which had maintained a gender-specific set of job classifications also provided scope for improvements for women, but these remained conditional on increasing bargaining power in female employment areas (National reports, Spain: Moltó 1996:27).

In **Finland** the collective agreements of 1991 and 1995 allowed for an equality supplement, worth 0.4 per cent of the wage bill in 1991. Additionally, in the 1990s there was increasing interest in the use of job evaluation as a tool for narrowing the gender pay gap with the central labour market organisations setting up a joint working group to investigate methods of job evaluation, particularly in female-dominated jobs (National reports, Finland: Keinänen 1996:29).

The continuation of occupation-based collective bargaining systems in **Greece** presented a barrier to the use of job evaluation in the application of the principle of equal pay for work of equal value. The planned privatisation of large parts of the public sector was also likely to increase the gender pay gap as the highly regulated system in the public sector had probably helped gender pay equality (National reports, Greece: Cavouriaris and Symeonidou 1996:7).

In **Sweden** each employer has had to provide an annual report on wage differentials between men and women in the organisation and an annual plan detailing actions to be taken to reduce differentials. The details of the plan are required to be determined in consultation with unions. All local authorities have had plans approved. Most employers have observed this requirement and presented both the survey and the plan (National reports, Sweden: Gonäs and Spånt 1996:15–16).

In the **UK** job evaluation schemes have become more widely used, but they have had less impact in determining actual earnings, which increasingly depend upon not only the job grade but also upon individualised merit or performance assessment (National reports, UK: Rubery 1996:41).

However, the reality is somewhat different. While employment security has been reduced for the more privileged workers, the risk of either unemployment or temporary or insecure employment tends to have risen even more for the outsiders. Similarly, while new working-time arrangements have begun to impinge on core workers, the burden of flexibility has still been borne by part-timers and others on atypical contracts. The breakdown of traditional job functions has been displacing areas of traditional female work such as clerical work as much as it has opened up new opportunities to break into traditionally male-dominated areas. Thus the new developments, while undermining traditional sources of insider power, also create opportunities for new and possibly more intense forms of both segmentation

and segregation, based around more individualised employment relationships that are difficult to monitor for gender equity.

Nor is the breakdown of insider power proceeding at an even pace; it is
those on the edge of internal labour markets, the male manual workers and
the women in lower-level clerical and administrative or service jobs, who
tend to be the first to suffer from the dismantling of traditional forms
of employment protection and regulation, or from the privatisation or
contracting out of public sector services. The restructuring process has been
taking place within a gendered labour market, and gender has been and
remains a key factor in the strategies deployed by employers at the
organisation level. Gender divisions are central to the restructuring of
working-time arrangements, pay structures and the division of labour
(Rubery *et al.* 1998b). However, the role of gender has also become more
complex, with more women employed in higher level jobs and more men
trapped in insecure jobs or unemployment. Thus divisions within male and
female populations need to be considered alongside the processes of gender
differentiation and segregation.

3 Changes in women's labour supply and household composition

Chapters 1 and 2 examined developments in macroeconomic conditions, government policy and organisational change within firms. These features of the economy structure the quantity and type of jobs available, and the conditions under which men and women supply their labour. The focus in this chapter is at the micro-level; namely upon women as social actors within this institutional context. The analysis reveals some important elements of convergence in women's labour supply patterns across countries, including a universal closing of the gender gap in activity rates and average education levels. At the same time there are signs of persistent divergence, for example in patterns of full-time and part-time employment for mothers in different societies. A second, related theme is divergence between women with high qualifications and relatively good labour market opportunities, and the experience of women with less educational and occupational capital.

Women's labour supply behaviour, and the lifestyle to which they aspire, is changing with every generation. The education system has expanded in most countries, and women have grabbed the increased opportunities to enhance their human capital with the 'educational lever' (Crompton and Sanderson 1990). In most countries women's average qualification levels now match or even exceed those of men, although gender differences by subject area persist. Education, complemented by equal treatment legislation and policies in the labour market, and the more general influence of feminist ideas, raises employment aspirations, opportunities and earning power. The increased opportunity for economic and social independence influences women's fertility patterns. Women are delaying the age at which they start their families, they are having fewer children, and a growing minority are remaining childless, at least in some countries. As well as reducing their fertility rates, women are also more likely to remain in the labour market while raising young children than they were in previous generations (Kempeneers and LeLievre 1991; Rubery et al. 1995). This increased continuity in women's labour market behaviour coincides with greater discontinuity and diversification in household organisation. Marriages are becoming less stable, first marriages are occurring later in people's lives and divorce, cohabitation and lone parenthood are becoming more common (PA Cambridge Economic Consultants 1991). Rising male unemployment and the squeeze on disposable income for low- and middle-income households in many countries are increasing the financial pressures for women to enter waged work. These changes in labour market behaviour and household organisation make the traditional sexual division of labour between male breadwinners and women as primary caregivers and secondary paid workers increasingly outdated. This is widely recognised, at least in principle, because there was a marked shift in people's values across Europe during the 1980s. A growing proportion of people favour equal roles for women and men, and the preferred household arrangement for both sexes is more often one in which they both have a paid job rather than the traditional breadwinner arrangement in which the women stays at home (CEC 1988).

The analysis in the next section reveals the persistent increase in women's activity rates which result from these behavioural and attitudinal changes, but at the same time indicates continual national differences which mean that a simple convergence across Europe cannot be confidently predicted. This theme is developed first with an analysis of women's increasing average educational attainment, and the divergent labour market experiences within countries between highly educated and less educated women. The section following turns to examine trends in family formation, household composition and activity rates for mothers with young children. Mothers' full-time and part-time employment rates are examined then, and differences between countries, as well as between women with different educational levels, are identified. The concluding section suggests that the fall in fertility rates and other changes in women's family and economic roles may help to push the importance of reconciling work and family life and updating the 'gender contract' further up the political agenda, but that the outcome may still be increased pressure on women to choose between either a career or children.

Trends in women's labour market activity

The gender gap in activity rates is closing in each country, for women's participation rates have risen consistently over time, while men's have remained stable or declined (Meulders *et al.* 1993; Rubery *et al.* 1995). However, 1990 marked a turning point in both Sweden and Finland, where activity rates started to fall for women, while male activity continued to decline. This turning point was the result of the recession, which also fuelled the extension of education for young people, and the extension of parental leave in the case of Finland (see Box 3.1).

Labour market activity is becoming concentrated in a narrower age range for both sexes. This is due to later entry as young people spend more years in education, combined with a trend towards earlier retirement. The majority

---

Box 3.1 The 1990 turning point in Sweden and Finland: female activity rates start to fall

In **Finland** activity rates for women started to fall in 1990, although the decline was less than that for men. In 1990 72.5 per cent of women and 78.9 per cent of men aged 15–64 were economically active but by 1994 the rates were 69.6 per cent and 75.3 per cent respectively. The decline was concentrated on young people, but rates fell for all women under 40 years and all men under 55 years. The main reason was that young people were spending longer in education. Another important factor was the introduction of extended parental leave in 1986, which was recorded as inactivity, unlike the basic parental leave entitlement of 11 months. The introduction of this extended leave coincided with a decline in activity rates for women aged 24–39 years. Activity started to rise again in 1995 with the economic upturn (National reports, Finland Ilmakunnas 1995:37, 60, 63).

Similarly, activity rates also started to fall in **Sweden** in 1990, also concentrated on the younger age groups (16–24 years). The main cause was the recession and the associated cuts in public expenditure. Between 1989 and 1994 activity rates for the 25–54-year-old population fell from 95 to 90 per cent for men and from 90 to 86 per cent for women. Activity rates for the immigrant population were disproportionately hit (National reports, Sweden: Gonäs and Spånt 1996:22–25).

---

of men participate continuously in the labour market over the working life (a plateau curve). A similar, but still lower, pattern of labour market continuity characterises women's participation in the Nordic countries and France (Figure 3.1), as well as in the former East Germany.

The high and continuous activity curve for the working life in the Scandinavian countries was showing signs of shifting from the plateau curve of the 1980s to one with a right-hand peak during the 1990s. The highest female activity rates were now to be found among those aged in their later thirties and early forties. This was partly to do with a marked fall in activity rates for young people associated with the extension of education. The conjunction of high unemployment rates and the extension of parental leave schemes in Denmark and Finland in the 1990s may also be operating to encourage some women with poor employment prospects to withdraw from the labour market when they have young children.

European member states without a plateau curve for women's activity have previously been classified into those with a 'woman returner' pattern of interrupted activity (the m-shaped curve), and those with curtailed participation associated with more lengthy or permanent labour market exits due to marriage and childbearing (the left-hand peak curve). While this distinction was still relevant at the end of the 1980s (Meulders *et al.* 1993), by the mid-1990s it had become increasingly outdated. Higher and more continuous activity patterns have been emerging as younger generations of women move through their working lives making shorter and fewer labour market interruptions than their predecessors (see Box 3.2). By the mid-1990s, therefore, the m-shaped curve had almost disappeared in the UK and Germany (even before unification) and had become flatter in the Netherlands. This evolution mimics the earlier disappearance of the m-shaped curve for women in France and Denmark (Rubery *et al.* 1995:Figure 1.1; National reports, France: Silvera *et al.* 1996:36). Among the other countries there was a clear movement from a left-hand peak in female activity curves at the end of the 1980s towards a higher and more continuous activity pattern indicated by a plateau curve.

Box 3.2 Generational increase in women's labour market continuity.

In the **Netherlands** only a quarter of women continued in employment after the birth of their first child in the early 1980s, but this had risen to nearly half (48 per cent) ten years later. Women who delayed having their first child until they were 30, and highly educated women, were more likely to remain in employment (National reports, Netherlands: Plantenga *et al.* 1996:17–18).

Longitudinal analysis reveals a generational increase in employment continuity for women in the former **West Germany**. The share of all women who remained continuously employed until the age of 45 rose slightly for mothers, from 14 per cent for those mothers born prior to 1929 to 20 per cent for the cohort born between 1930 and 1939. However, the majority of women had discontinuous work histories, and the propensity for mothers to enter and re-enter the labour market increased, with the result that the interruption for childraising fell to an average of 6 years (National reports, Germany: Maier *et al.* 1996:24).

In **France** female activity rates rose between 1983 and 1994 and activity rates for mothers with one child approximated those for women without children in most age groups. The increase in activity was less significant for women with two or more children. Between 3 per cent and 6 per cent of women aged 20–49 left the labour market between 1989 and 1991, indicating that discontinuity is still a feature of women's employment. However, these exit rates remained stable over the ten-year period, while entry rates have risen steadily since 1982, indicating that the long-term trend is a 'reduction in the duration of career breaks' (National reports, France: Silvera *et al.* 1996:35).

By 1982 one-third of women in **Austria** were continually employed from the end of their training until retirement. The proportion with uninterrupted careers continued to rise, but coexisted with at least two other common patterns for women: namely a pattern of several short career breaks or of one extended interruption. This diversity reflects differences in women's education levels and the number of children they have, as well as other personal attributes (National reports, Austria: Pastner 1996:22–23).

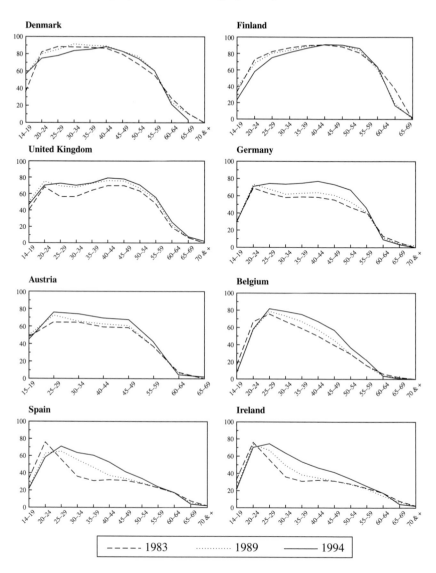

Figure 3.1 The evolution of female age-related activity curves, 1983–1994

Source: European Labour Force Survey (1983–1994).

Notes
Data for Germany in 1994 include the New *Länder* in 1994.
Data for Finland are for 1990 instead of 1989.

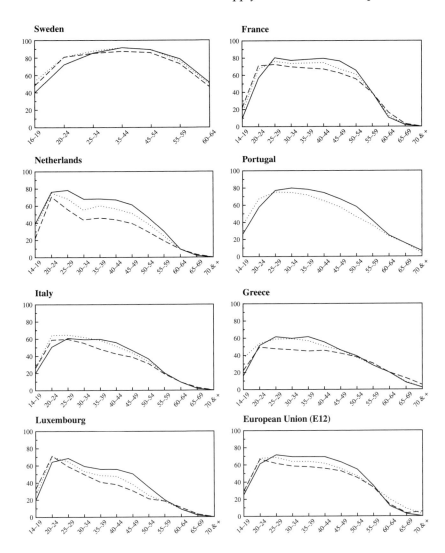

Despite this long-term trend towards increased labour market continuity for women, marked differences in the pattern and level of activity can be detected. The heights of the emerging plateau curves vary across countries, and are generally lower than the more established continuity curves found in France and the Nordic countries. The lower level of these aggregate curves in some countries is likely to conceal divergence within the female population. In countries such as the UK where the m-shaped curve was disappearing from aggregate statistics, more detailed cohort analysis has suggested that the 'woman returner' pattern still dominated individual employment profiles, albeit with shorter average gaps and greater differentiation between different groups of women (see for example, Brannen *et al.* 1994). In contrast, high unemployment and relatively strong employment protection for labour market 'insiders' in the Southern European member states have result in a particularly stark distinction between those women who have maintained continuous employment careers, and others who either opted out due to their inability to gain 'insider' status (Bettio and Villa 1993; Kempeneers and Lelievre 1991) or become trapped in a cycle of entry and exits between inactivity and temporary employment (National reports, Spain: Moltó 1996:37). In these countries increased aggregate female activity may have reflected a greater propensity for women to continuously 'opt in' rather than an increase in the rate of re-entry (National reports, Italy: Bettio and Villa 1996:36).

As we shall see below, a major source of divergence among women within different national labour markets is educational attainment. Highly educated women are more able and willing to maintain a pattern of high and continuous activity owing to their access to higher-level, better-paid and more secure employment; and the associated greater promotion prospects and financial returns of working (Rubery *et al.* 1995). Another source of difference is that between migrant workers. In Luxembourg there was a much higher activity rate among migrant women than in the resident population (National reports, Austria: Plasman 1996:16). High rates of migration among the Irish also influence the interpretation of the activity rates for the resident population: among young people there is a high propensity to emigrate to escape unemployment, particularly for young women (National reports, Ireland: Barry 1996:18). From this perspective the recorded activity rates for young Irish women are deflated because they exclude the large numbers who have migrated to the UK or North America for work. In the UK there is a strong differentiation in women's activity rates according to ethnic status. Some ethnic minority women have a much lower participation rate than the white female population, for example the Pakistani and Bangladeshi community. Afro-Caribbean women have the highest activity rates, but this consists of a higher exposure to unemployment and a lower employment rate than white women. These differences in activity rates are a product of historical differences in the causes and patterns of migration for earlier generations of ethnic minorities, combined with cultural differences in norms concerning appropriate economic and social roles for women (Dale and Holdsworth 1998).

In sum, the higher activity rates of women over the life cycle indicate that motherhood disrupts women's activity rates less now than in the past. Differences persist among women as a result of two sets of forces that are influencing women's activity rates over their working lives. At the broad national level, differences in social institutions and norms affect female, particularly maternal, activity patterns. Favourable employment conditions and employment policies which facilitate the reconciliation of employment with childraising are clearly important factors which influence labour market aspirations and their fulfilment (Fagan and Rubery 1996a; Rubery *et al.* 1998a). At the same time there is a convergence across countries in the norms and labour market resources of certain groups of women, particularly those who are highly educated, who are following higher and more continuous patterns of participation. To improve our understanding of these processes we need to look at trends in women's educational and family characteristics.

Trends in women's qualification levels and their impact on labour market behaviour

Qualifications enhance an individual's job prospects, earnings potential and employment aspirations, as well as access to many of the intrinsically more rewarding parts of the labour market. Women with qualifications have higher activity rates and employment rates than less qualified women (Eurostat 1994a:Table 30). They also have higher wage rates and are found in a wider range of occupations and industrial sectors, for example in Ireland (National reports, Ireland: Barry 1996:62 and Tables 26 and 27). Highly qualified women may have a stronger commitment to following a career than women with fewer qualifications (Hakim 1991, 1996). Households containing highly educated women also show the most sign of change in the traditional domestic division of labour, through a modest increase in men's involvement in childcare and housework plus purchase of childcare and other domestic services in (Brannen and Moss 1991; Dale and Egerton 1995; Corti *et al.* 1995). Thus, labour market continuity is easier for highly educated women to achieve, because they have more employment opportunities, are more able to afford to pay for childcare, and educated women (and men) are generally less supportive of the traditional social norms and roles embodied in the 'male breadwinner' presumption of family life.

The expansion of the education system in most countries during recent decades means that average qualification levels have risen with each generation (Rubery *et al.* 1995:Appendix Table 1.5). This generational increase in educational experience has been particularly strong for women, facilitated by equal treatment legislation and policies; a necessary influx to counter the much lower educational opportunities experienced by older generations

Table 3.1 Index of gender differences in education by age group, 1992

	Age 25–34	Age 55–64
Belgium	–0.9	7.0
Denmark	–0.2	10.3
France	0.9	6.5
Germany	3.4	18.4
Ireland	–2.8	–1.0
Italy	0.0	5.1
Netherlands	2.1	11.7
Portugal	–1.8	2.6
Spain	–1.2	4.5
UK	2.8	10.7
Austria	5.8	15.4
Finland	–1.6	2.2
Sweden	–1.6	1.3

Source: OECD (1995b:Table CO2:28).

Notes
1991 figure used for Portugal.
Data not available for Greece and Luxembourg.
A positive value indicates a higher level of education among men and a negative value a higher level of education among women.
For details of construction of index see OECD (1995b:349).

of women. Gender differences in the level of educational attainment have fallen as a result; indeed the average educational level of women is now higher than that for men among the younger generation in many countries (see Table 3.1). Overall women are generally performing better than men in the education system, particularly at school level, for example in the UK, France, Ireland, Portugal and Austria (National reports, UK: Rubery 1996:71; France: Silvera *et al.* 1996:32; Ireland: Barry 1996:18; Portugal: Lopes and Perista 1996:39; Austria: Pastner 1996:35). More younger women now hold graduate-level qualifications in many countries (Rubery *et al.* 1995: Appendix Table 1.5; National reports, France: Silvera *et al.* 1996:32–33; Austria: Pastner 1996; Finland: Keinänen 1996:38).

While the gender gap in educational levels has been closed, and there are growing indications that women are overtaking men in qualification levels, segregation by subject area persists, maintaining patterns of labour market segregation (see Chapter 5). Table 3.2 shows that at graduate level women have been particularly under-represented in engineering and, to a lesser extent, in the natural sciences, matched by a disproportionate concentration in arts and social sciences. This segregation by subject area feeds into employment, with women using the 'qualification lever' (Crompton and Sanderson 1990) to gain entry to the professions, but clustering in the caring and public sector professions, while areas such as engineering remain male dominated (Rubery and Fagan 1993 and Chapter 5 below). Segregation at graduate level partly reflects earlier specialisation in school, with girls having a lower participation in mathematics and science, which limits their options at graduate level (National reports, France: Silvera *et al.* 1996:32; Netherlands: Plantenga *et al.* 1996:17). Nevertheless, women have been increasing their involvement in science and engineering subjects in many countries (Box 3.3).

Box 3.3 Women's increasing participation in non-traditional education and training

In the **UK**, women increased their share of university places in physical science from 27 per cent in 1989 to 35 per cent by 1993, and their share of places in engineering and technical subjects also rose from 9 per cent to 26 per cent over this period (National reports, UK: Rubery 1996:72).

In **Ireland**, by 1993 women held 51 per cent of places in university and higher education institutes (National reports, Ireland: Barry 1996:60).

By the 1990s women made up half of all university students In **Italy**, and were relatively well integrated, holding between 45 per cent and 55 per cent of places in most subject areas. Engineering remained male dominated, but women increased their share to 23 per cent over a ten-year period, while 80 per cent of literature students were women (National reports, Italy: Bettio and Villa 1996:11).

In **Portugal** the female share of engineering places rose from 24 per cent in 1986–1987 to 30 per cent by 1990–1991, but over this period women also increased their share of already feminised subject areas such as education and medicine (National reports, Portugal: Lopes and Perista 1996:32).

In **Austria** only 4.5 per cent of students in technical sciences were women in 1961: by 1991 this had climbed to 15 per cent (National reports, Austria: Pastner 1996:35).

In the former **West Germany** women's share of new entrants in non-traditional university subjects such as engineering rose from 12 per cent to 16 per cent between 1989 and 1993, and in medicine women achieved 50 per cent of new entrant places in 1993, up from 46 per cent in 1989. In the former **East Germany** women increased their share of all university entrants following unification, up from 39 per cent in 1990 to 49 per cent in 1993, and increased their share in all subject areas. Women's share of new engineering students increased from 19 per cent to 21 per cent and of medical new entrants from 44 per cent to 55 per cent (National reports, Germany: Maier *et al.* 1996:Table 2.1.9).

Vocational training courses have remained more highly segregated than those in formal education (see Box 3.4). This pattern of segregation in vocational training courses has also been reflected in training projects co-financed by the European structural funds. Evaluation of European-financed schemes has shown that to promote desegregation of vocational training it

Table 3.2 Concentration by subject for women who graduated in 1992

(a) Countries ranked by female concentration in human sciences

	Engineering	Natural science	Medicine	Law and business	Human sciences
Finland	7.3	9.4	11.9	11.4	60.0
Ireland	3.8	16.9	6.3	15.4	57.8
Greece	6.5	13.3	14.1	12.2	53.9
Denmark	6.4	4.9	22.3	13.0	53.4
Spain	3.0	8.1	15.3	22.7	50.9
Netherlands	4.3	5.1	22.6	15.7	52.4
UK	9.2	14.4	7.7	21.5	47.2
Sweden	6.7	7.9	22.4	22.4	40.7
Germany (w)	7.2	14.9	13.3	24.7	39.8
Italy	4.8	11.7	23.1	24.2	35.0
Belgium	10.2	10.7	16.5	30.3	32.4

(b) Gender difference in concentration: female concentration minus male concentration

	Engineering	Natural science	Medicine	Law and business	Human sciences
Finland	−32.0	−12.1	4.6	0.8	38.5
Ireland	−16.3	−4.4	0.9	−2.7	22.7
Greece	−16.3	−7.8	8.1	−0.5	16.5
Denmark	−22.8	−7.5	18.1	−15.6	27.8
Spain	−15.7	−5.4	4.5	−5.9	22.5
Netherlands	−22.0	−8.7	13.0	−8.9	26.7
UK	−11.2	−5.0	1.6	−0.6	15.1
Sweden	−21.8	−9.0	11.7	−2.2	20.0
Germany (w)	−23.9	−4.3	2.6	0.0	25.6
Italy	−13.2	−1.0	−3.9	−5.9	24.5
Belgium	−23.9	−2.4	6.4	1.6	18.4

Source: OECD (1995b:222–223).

is necessary to monitor the gender profile of entry and completion rates, and to provide backup measures, including childcare, plus targeted information and courses (Rees 1995a, 1995b).

Rising educational levels do not solve the issue of labour market discrimination. Women are overqualified relative to men in any given job in many countries, even in Denmark (Rubery and Fagan 1993; National reports, Denmark: Boje 1996:32 and Chapter 5 below). This 'gendered job queue' (Reskin and Roos 1990) is likely to be reflected in unemployment. For example, in Spain female graduates have much lower employment rates than male graduates, even when they have studied the same subject. The concentration of female students on humanities courses has made them even more vulnerable to unemployment than men (National reports, Spain: Moltó

Box 3.4 High and persistent segregation of vocational training courses

In **Portugal** in 1994 women were over-represented in courses in the decorative arts and librarianship, and virtually absent from electronics (National reports, Portugal: Lopes and Perista 1996:31).

In **France** in 1993 young women only held one-third of all apprenticeships (National reports, France: Silvera *et al*. 1996:23).

In **Denmark**, the vocational training system remained segregated, although the degree of segregation diminished in the 1980s (National reports, Denmark: Boje 1996:60–61).

In **Ireland**, government training schemes remained highly segregated, with women more likely to be found on short-term general courses rather than specific skills training and apprenticeships (National reports, Ireland: Barry 1996:22).

In **Finland**, gender segregation was much higher in vocational education than in universities, with only 3 per cent of students entering vocational training institutes being in mixed fields (41–60 per cent of places held by men) in 1992, compared to 40 per cent of university entrants (National reports, Finland: Keinänen 1996:38).

In **Austria**, only one-third of apprenticeships were held by young women in 1992, although this was a marked increase on previous years. Young women remained concentrated into a narrow range of service-based training, despite positive action initiatives, while young men had a more diverse training profile (National reports, Austria: Pastner 1996:29).

In the former **West Germany** the dual-apprenticeship system became somewhat less segregated in the 1980s as men entered service occupations and women expanded their shares of traditional male apprenticeships in manufacturing. The recession in the 1990s put this process into reverse as women lost ground in their share of manufacturing and technical apprenticeships, although not in every trade. In the former **East Germany** women were increasingly excluded from manufacturing apprenticeships, while men found a new interest in entering service apprenticeships, resulting in a desegregation of feminised areas but a resegregation of male areas and an overall fall in the female share of apprenticeships, from around half to 38 per cent by 1994 (National reports, Germany: Maier *et al*. 1996:Table 2.1.7).

1996:Table 1.3.3.). This lower return to education for women has been exacerbated by downward occupational mobility after labour market breaks for childraising in countries with 'returner' profiles, such as the UK and Germany. Furthermore, the goal posts are moving. As labour markets restructure and formal qualifications become more rapidly outdated, the issue of access to workplace training and lifelong learning takes on more importance in at least some national labour markets (National reports, Finland: Keinänen 1996:39; Denmark: Boje 1996). Segregated employment constrains women's access to workplace-based training schemes. Thus, in Germany, a further penalty of downward mobility into low-skilled jobs is exclusion from workplace-based training schemes (National reports, Germany: Maier *et al.* 1996:24). Access to workplace training is also lower for women in France, but when women do get this training their rate of post-training promotion seems to be the same as that for men (National reports, France: Silvera *et al.* 1996:24).

A final point to note is that average qualification levels vary across countries owing to national differences in educational systems. For example, in the 20–39 age group in 1991 there were more graduates in Denmark, Belgium, Netherlands, Greece and Ireland (18 per cent) than elsewhere, falling to less than 10 per cent of the population in this age group in Italy, Luxembourg and Portugal (Rubery *et al.* 1995: Appendix Table 1.5). The majority of women do not, therefore, have the relative protection that graduate-level qualifications provide. Women with basic qualifications tend to be highly segregated into female-dominated, low-paid areas; for example in 1992 in Ireland 51 per cent of unqualified female school leavers worked in personal services, compared to only 39 per cent of similarly unqualified males. This leaves them vulnerable to structural and cyclical unemployment in these areas (National reports, Ireland: Barry 1996:58). In Portugal some girls in the 1990s were still being denied full educational opportunities, for they were more likely to quit compulsory education prematurely in order to contribute to household income (National reports, Portugal: Lopes and Perista 1996:30).

The divergence in experience between women according to qualifications is indicated in Figure 3.2, which examines women in the 20–39 age group in 1994. In each country activity rates increased with educational attainment for women with and without dependent children. The only exception was for women without dependent children in France, where there was little variation by qualification level. Much of the national variation in activity rates discussed in the previous section can be attributed to divergent behaviour among women who only have the basic, compulsory level of schooling. To consider women without dependent children first, participation in the formal labour market was particularly low for those women with basic educational attainment in Greece, Spain, Italy and Finland (see Figure 3.2a). In part this may be because some of these women were economically inactive as they were still completing their education. In addition, in the Southern European member states some economic activity by this group of women might be hidden in the informal economy. In contrast, there was evidence of a strong convergence across countries for graduate women, who exhibited high activity rates of around 90 per cent or more. This positive effect of qualifications on women's activity rates meant that it was among the graduate population that the smallest gender gap in activity rates is found.

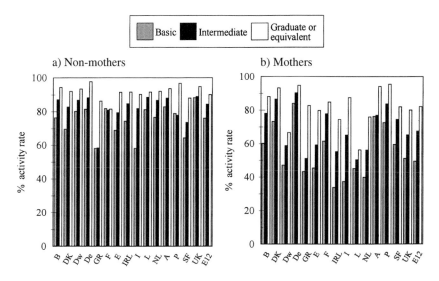

Figure 3.2 Impact of educational attainment on the activity rates of non-mothers and mothers aged 20–39, 1994

Source: European Labour Force Survey (1993, 1994, 1996).

Notes
Data for Austria and Finland are for 1996; those for Denmark are for 1993.
Data relate to women who are the household head, either individually or as part of a couple.
Mothers have at least one child under 15.
See data box (p. 8) for details of educational groups.

Qualifications also boost activity rates for mothers (see Figure 3.2b). As for women without children, the widest national differences in activity rates were found among mothers with the lowest education level. The activity rates for this group of mothers ranged from just over 30 per cent in Ireland to over 70 per cent in Denmark, East Germany, Finland, Austria and Portugal in 1994. Harmonised data are unavailable for Sweden, but the pattern in this country was similar to the other two Scandinavian member states: high activity rates for all women but with qualifications still exerting an additional pull on activity (National reports, Sweden: Gonäs and Spånt 1996:21). Graduate-level qualifications produced a particularly strong increase in mothers' activity rates in Italy, Greece, Spain, Ireland and the Netherlands. The cross-national divergence in activity rates for mothers narrowed for those with graduate-level qualifications, but the divergence was much greater than that for women without childraising responsibilities. Evidently, higher education only partly offsets the influence of country-specific activity patterns for mothers.

Trends in family formation, household structure and women's activity rates

Since the late 1970s young people have been delaying the age at which they get married, countering the trend towards earlier marriages observed for many countries in the 1960s (Eurostat 1994b:Table F-5). This reflects changing attitudes towards marriage, as well as structural changes such as longer periods of study and the increasing difficulties which young people face in gaining employment and setting up independent households (National reports, Belgium: Meulders and Hecq 1996:36) By 1993, the average woman in the EU got married for the first time at 26 years, ranging from 24.5 years for Portuguese women to over 28 years for women in Sweden and Denmark (Table 3.3). In France, for example, in the mid-1980s more than half of women were married by the age of 24 (56.5 per cent), falling to just over a quarter (26.5 per cent) ten years later (National reports, France: Silvera *et al.* 1996:40). In Austria, the percentage of women who were remaining single tripled in one generation (National reports, Austria: Pastner 1996:43). Later marriages have been contributing to the long-term fall in the marriage rate which continued in the 1990s in most countries. Greece and Luxembourg were the only countries where the marriage rates increased between 1990 and 1993, which in Luxembourg may have reflected the 1990 fiscal reform which removed financial disincentives to marriage (National reports, Luxembourg: Plasman 1996:21).

Marriage remains a common institution, and most women still usually get married before they reach 30 years (CEC 1992). However, marriages have become less stable: there has been a general rise in the divorce rate since the 1960s, and a growing proportion of marriages involve at least one previously married person. Cohabitation has also become more popular, accounting for example for about 12 per cent of all couples in France in 1990 and 16 per cent of all families in Finland (National reports, France: Silvera *et al.* 1996:41; Finland: Keinänen 1996:45). While these trends in marital behaviour are evident in all countries there is little evidence of convergence towards new family patterns and arrangements. Rates of divorce and remarriage remain low in the Southern European countries and Ireland, and in Ireland it is only in the early 1990s that divorce was legalised after a narrow majority vote. At the other extreme, the Nordic member states and the UK have high divorce and remarriage rates.

Later marriages and more remarriages have been accompanied by significant changes in fertility. Women are starting their families later in their lives; the average age at first birth rose from 24.6 years for women in the EU (E12) in 1977 to 26.2 years in 1989 (CEC 1992). They have also been having fewer children. In 1960 the fertility rate exceeded 2 in every member state and was close to or greater than 3 in Ireland, Spain, the Netherlands and Portugal (see Table 3.4). By 1993, the fertility rate had declined to less than 2 across Europe, with the exception of Sweden, although in Sweden

Table 3.3 Marital trends in the European Union, 1960–1993

Country	Women's mean age at first marriage			Crude marriage rate (/1,000 pop.)			Crude divorce rate (/1,000 pop.)			Female remarriage rate as % of all marriages		
	1960	1989	1993	1960	1989	1993	1960	1989	1993	1960	1989	1993
Belgium	22.8	23.6	24.9	7.2	6.4	5.4	0.5	2.0	2.1	9.0	17.3	19.2
Denmark	22.8	26.9	28.5	7.8	6.0	6.1	1.5	3.0	2.5	13.4	26.3	26.8
Germany(u)	23.4	24.6	26.1	9.5	6.7	5.5	1.0	2.2	1.9	10.9	22.3	22.9
Greece	25.2	24.4	25.3	7.0	6.1	6.0	0.3	0.6	0.7	3.5	8.1	8.1
Spain[a b]	26.1	25.0	25.9	7.7	5.7	5.0	—	0.6	0.7	1.3	3.0	4.0
France	23.0	25.3	26.4	7.0	5.0	4.4	0.7	1.9	1.9	9.5	16.0	16.4
Ireland[a b]	27.6	25.8	26.6	5.5	5.2	4.4	—	—	—	1.3	0.7	0.6
Italy[a c]	24.8	25.4	26.0	7.7	5.7	5.1	—	0.5	0.4	1.1	3.4	3.8
Luxembourg	—	25.1	25.7	7.1	5.8	6.0	0.5	2.3	1.9	5.7	18.4	19.4
Netherlands	24.2	25.5	26.7	7.8	6.1	5.8	0.5	1.9	2.0	6.4	15.5	17.5
Austria	24.0	24.6	25.6	8.3	5.6	5.6	1.1	2.0	2.0	12.7	19.9	20.2
Portugal	24.8	23.8	24.5	7.8	7.4	6.9	0.1	1.0	1.2	2.3	5.4	5.6
Finland	23.8	25.8	26.6	7.4	4.9	4.9	0.8	2.9	2.5	8.7	15.8	18.0
Sweden[d]	23.9	30.4	28.1	6.7	12.8	3.9	1.2	2.2	2.5	11.3	19.0	20.2
UK[a c]	—	24.8	25.6	7.5	6.8	5.9	0.5	2.9	3.1	9.3	25.6	26.9
E15[b]	24.1	25.2	26.1	7.9	6.2	5.3	0.5	1.7	1.7	7.4	15.8	15.6

Source: Eurostat (1995:Tables F3, F15, F19, F7).

Notes
— indicates no data available.
a Women's mean age at first marriage: 1992 figures used for 1993 for Spain, Ireland, Italy and UK.
b Remarriages as a percentage of total marriages: 1991 figures used for 1993 for Ireland and E15.
c Remarriage as a percentage of total marriages: 1992 figures used for 1993 for Spain, Italy and the UK.
d Data for Sweden calculated as total marriages of women living in the country. In Sweden there was a rapid rise in the number of marriages in 1989 after a change in the law on pensions payable to widows (Eurostat 19945:x).

Table 3.4 Trends in childbearing in the European Union, 1960–1993

Country	Women's mean age at child birth			Share of live births outside marriage			Crude fertility rate (/1000 pop.)		
	1960	1989	1993	1960	1989	1993	1960	1989	1993
Belgium[a]	28.0	27.8	28.1	2.1	11.3	12.6	2.6	1.6	1.6
Denmark	26.9	28.3	28.9	7.8	46.1	46.8	2.5	1.6	1.8
Germany[b]	27.5	27.6	28.1	7.6	15.5	14.8	2.4	1.4	1.3
Greece	—	27.0	27.8	1.2	2.1	2.8	2.3	1.4	1.3
Spain[a]	—	28.7	29.3	2.3	9.4	10.5	2.9	1.4	1.3
France[a]	27.6	28.2	28.7	6.1	28.2	33.2	2.7	1.8	1.7
Ireland	—	30.2	30.3	1.6	12.8	19.5	3.8	2.1	1.9
Italy	29.2	28.9	29.4	2.4	6.1	7.3	2.4	1.3	1.2
Luxembourg	—	28.2	28.6	3.2	11.8	12.9	2.3	1.5	1.7
Netherlands	29.8	29.2	29.8	1.4	10.7	13.1	3.1	1.6	1.6
Austria	27.6	27.0	27.4	13.0	22.6	26.3	2.7	1.4	1.5
Portugal	—	27.2	27.7	9.5	14.5	17.0	3.2	1.6	1.5
Finland	28.3	28.8	29.0	4.0	22.9	30.3	2.7	1.7	1.8
Sweden	27.5	28.6	29.0	11.3	51.8	50.4	2.2	2.0	2.0
UK	—	27.6	27.9	5.2	26.6	31.8	2.7	1.8	1.8
E15	—	28.1	28.6	5.1	18.9	21.7	—	1.6	1.5

Source: Eurostat (1995:Tables E4, E9).

Notes
— indicates no data available.
a Share of live births outside marriage: 1991 figure used for 1993 for Belgium; 1992 figures used for 1993 for Spain and France.
b Data for all years refer to combined West and East Germany.

it subsequently fell to 1.7 by 1995 (National reports, Sweden: Gonäs and Spånt 1996:30). Most national average fertility rates have fallen substantially below the 2.1 threshold which is required for general population replacement (CEC 1995a:64). If these lower fertility rates persist, the population size will fall over the long term. Higher fertility rates have tended to be found in the Nordic countries and the UK, that is in those countries with high rates of marital instability, while below average or average fertility rates have been found in the Southern European countries. Ireland this time did not fit the Southern European pattern and instead had a high fertility rate, in fact the highest in all the EU when completed fertility rates are considered (see Table 3.5).

Table 3.5 shows that each generation of women of childbearing age had smaller families between 1970 and 1990.[1] This generational decline in fertility continued over the 1990s in many countries, but in the Nordic countries, France, Belgium and Luxembourg there were signs of a stabilisation or even increase in fertility rates (see Table 3.4; National reports, Luxembourg: Plasman 1996:19–20; France: Silvera *et al.* 1996:40). In the particular case of East Germany, fertility had fallen by a massive 70 per

Table 3.5 Generational decline in fertility rates for selected cohorts

	Completed fertility for women aged 35				
	1970	*1980*	*1990*	*1992*	*1995*
Belgium	2.27	1.94	1.82	1.83	1.83
Denmark	2.38	2.06	1.83	1.84	1.84
Germany[a]	2.16	1.79	1.67	1.65	1.63
Greece	2.02	2.00	2.03	1.92	1.92
Spain	2.67	2.43	1.90	1.85	1.69
France	2.58	2.22	2.13	2.12	2.06
Ireland	3.44	3.27	2.68	2.54	2.39
Italy	2.29	2.07	1.77	1.70	1.59
Luxembourg	2.00	1.82	1.68	1.68	1.69
Netherlands	2.50	1.99	1.87	1.86	1.83
Austria	2.45	1.93	1.77	1.72	1.68
Portugal	2.85	2.31	1.97	1.93	1.86
Finland	2.30	1.87	1.88	1.91	1.91
Sweden	2.14	1.96	2.04	2.05	2.07
UK	2.41	2.17	2.02	1.99	1.93
E15	—	—	1.89	1.85	1.78

Source: Eurostat (1995:Table E10).

Notes
— indicates no data available.
90 per cent of women have children before age 35 (Eurostat 1995:65).
a   data for all years refer to combined West and East Germany.

cent since unification. This might indicate a postponement rather than decline in childbirth, in response to the deterioration in labour market conditions and a convergence with West German mothers in the average age at first birth (National reports, Germany: Maier *et al.* 1996:25). The net result of having fewer children and having them later in life was that the average age of women giving birth – and hence entitled to maternity leave – rose to 28.6 years across the European Union (Table 3.4). Furthermore, the proportion of women in the labour market who remain childless has increased, for example in the Netherlands 20 per cent of the cohort born in 1985 have been predicted to remain childless, in contrast to 15 per cent of the cohort born in 1950 (National reports, Netherlands: Plantenga *et al.* 1996:20). In the UK the proportion of women who expect to remain childless also rose (National reports, UK: Rubery 1996:50).

   A weakening of the link between marriage and fertility is the other significant trend, so that by the end of the 1980s more than one in ten children were born to unmarried parents in every country except for Italy, Spain and Greece. At the other end of the spectrum the share of children born outside marriage rose to one in three or more in the Scandinavian countries, France and the UK. These differences suggest wide variations in the acceptability of having children outside marriage across the member

Table 3.6 One-parent families as a share of all families with children,[a] 1994

| | 1994 | Activity rates for single adults with 1 or more children | |
		Male	Female
Belgium	8.6	87.0	71.2
Denmark[b]	15.0	96.9	78.1
Germany (u)	9.3	87.8	74.7
Greece	2.8	(93.4)	71.4
Spain	2.1	89.9	79.4
France	8.4	91.9	84.0
Ireland	5.8	—	40.4
Italy	3.7	93.2	73.3
Luxembourg	5.8	—	69.0
Austria[c]	8.3	(98.8)	88.1
Netherlands	6.6	84.1	50.1
Finland[c]	12.1	95.0	71.7
Portugal	4.0	(98.5)	74.3
UK	16.4	70.0	44.4

Source: Eurostat (1996a, 1996b).

Notes
— indicates no data available.
a Share of private households with children under 15.
b Data for Denmark are for 1993.
c Data for Austria and Finland are for 1995. No data available for Sweden.

states, differences in social norms which may then impact upon the observed fertility rates.

Many of the children born outside marriage are to cohabiting parents; for example 75 per cent of all births outside marriage in the UK in 1993 were registered by both parents (National reports, UK: Rubery 1996:52). Nevertheless, a growing incidence of single motherhood, combined with increased divorce means that in some countries lone-parent households are an increasingly common living arrangement for families with children (see Table 3.6). In most countries divorce, rather than widowhood, is now the main reason for lone parenthood, even in countries such as Spain with relatively low, although rising, divorce rates (National reports, Spain: Moltó 1996:31).

Alongside the changing patterns of fertility and household formation, and the overall increase in activity rates of women over the lifecourse, the labour market involvement of women with young children has also been changing in most countries.[2] The effect of motherhood on activity rates is illustrated for women aged 20–39 in Figure 3.3. In most countries mothers had much lower activity rates than women of a similar age without dependent children. The exceptions were the countries with high plateau activity curves for women (see Figure 3.1): namely Denmark, East Germany, Finland, Sweden (although Sweden is not shown in Figure 3.3 because harmonised

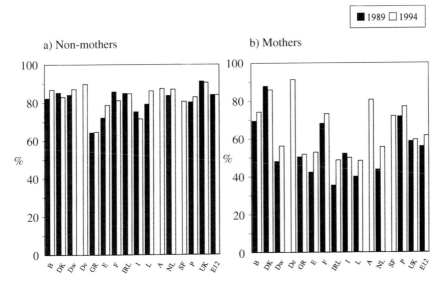

Figure 3.3 Activity rates of mothers and non-mothers aged 20–39, 1989 and
1994

Source: European Labour Force Survey (1993, 1994, 1996).

Notes
Data for Austria and Finland are for 1996; those for Denmark are for 1989 and1993.
Data relate to women who are the household head, either individually or as part of a couple.
Mothers have at least one child under 15.
See data box (p. 8) for details of educational groups.

data are unavailable) and France. In Denmark, East Germany and probably
Sweden (see Box 3.5), mothers had higher activity rates than women without
dependent children, reflecting the latter's younger average age and greater
involvement in the education system. More detailed national French and
Finnish data also showed that being a mother in itself did not reduce women's
labour market activity. In France, it was mothers who had the highest activity
rates when comparisons were drawn within the categories of single, married
and cohabiting women (National reports, France: Silvera *et al.* 1996:36). In
Finland mothers with pre-school children had even higher activity rates than
women without children (National reports, Finland: Keinänen 1996:63),
although activity rates for mothers with young children fell in the early
1990s (see Box 3.5).

Over 80 per cent of women aged 20–39 years without children were
economically active in most of the member states in 1994. Lower rates
were recorded in Italy, Spain and Greece, but in the case of Spain there
had been a rapid increase in activity rates. The decline for Italy between
1989 and 1994 was due to a statistical adjustment to the recording of unemployment (National reports, Italy: Bettio and Villa 1996:11). Mothers'

Box 3.5 Maternal activity rates in Finland and Sweden

In **Finland** activity rates for mothers are high by international standards, although in the early 1990s they fell, associated with the poor economic conditions, the introduction of extended parental leave and a homecare allowance in 1986. In 1993 73 per cent of mothers with a child under 7 and 56 per cent of mothers with a child under 3 were active, compared to 78 per cent and 67 per cent in 1989 (National reports, Finland: Keinänen 1996:42). Parents on basic parental leave (11 months) are counted as active, while those on extended leave are defined as inactive.

In **Sweden** activity rates are high for both sexes of working age, exceeding 85 per cent for women and 90 per cent for men in the 25–54-year age group in 1994 (National reports, Sweden: Gonäs and Spånt:Tables 1.9 and 1.10). Among parents with a child under 7 years old, 81 per cent of mothers and 93 per cent of fathers were active (European Childcare Network 1996: Appendix Table 1). These figures include parents on parental leave.

---

activity rates rose markedly during the first half of the 1990s in most countries where this group of women had much lower activity rates than other women, reflecting the longer term trend for women to retain their labour market involvement with the onset of motherhood. The exceptions were Greece and Italy. By 1994 maternal activity rates for this cohort of women exceeded 70 per cent in Denmark, East Germany, Austria, France, Finland, Portugal (and Sweden). Maternal activity rates for this age group crossed the 50 per cent threshold in Spain and the Netherlands by 1994, so that only Ireland and Luxembourg remained below this level by the mid-1990s.

Activity rates for lone mothers were high in most countries, although lower than those for the minority of lone parents who were men (see Table 3.6 above). This group of mothers displayed more similar activity rates across countries than the overall pattern for all mothers, probably reflecting the common financial pressures of marital breakdown or widowhood. The UK, Ireland and the Netherlands stood out for their relatively low activity rates for lone mothers. One important reason is likely to be that limited childcare facilities in these countries, combined with the organisation of the welfare benefit system, meant that there were limited financial gains from employment for lone mothers. For example, many lone mothers were caught in a 'poverty trap' in the UK due to a combination of low average female wages, childcare costs and the high effective taxes on earnings in the social security system. Benefit reforms and credits for childcare costs under the new Labour government's 'Welfare to Work' programme have been designed to reduce this trap. However, the lower average qualifications of lone mothers, and their geographical concentration in areas of high unemployment also reduces their access to employment (National reports, UK: Rubery 1996).

The trends of lower fertility rates and rising female activity rates are inter-related, but the causal relationship runs in both directions. Having children can influence women's labour supply, but these childbearing decisions are influenced by women's labour market experiences and prospects (PA Cambridge Economic Consultants 1991). If motherhood incurs high labour market penalties in terms of reduced earnings, the pressures of combining care responsibilities with job commitments and so forth, then women may opt to have fewer children. Across Europe there are signs of a divergence among women in their employment and fertility behaviour. To start with, there is evidence that the trend towards smaller and later families is most pronounced among highly educated women, who have the greater labour market prospects and expectations. For example, in the UK graduates were the least likely to have formed partnerships or to have had children by the age of 33 (Dale and Egerton 1995). Education also deferred the age at which women started their families in Finland and Austria (National reports, Finland: Keinänen 1996:44; Austria: Pastner 1996:44). By starting families later in their lives women are able to acquire more years of labour market experience prior to taking on childraising commitments. Evidence from the Netherlands suggests that this work history experience has a subsequent effect on mothers' activity rates: within each category of educational attainment it was women who started their families later in their lives who had the highest activity rates (National reports, Netherlands: Plantenga *et al.* 1996:19–20). More generally, there is a division between women's activity rates according to family size, for the minority of women who have three or more children these days also tend to have much lower activity rates in comparison to women with smaller families (see Figure 3.4).

These fertility patterns offer some support for Hakim's (1991, 1996) thesis that some women are more committed to having an employment career and make plans on this basis, in comparison to other women who prioritise a domestic career of marriage and children. It is probable that 'career-oriented' women are more likely to try to manage their fertility to minimise the labour market costs by delaying the start of their family until their employment career is established, and by having fewer or no children. However, the relationship between work orientations and planned behaviour on one hand, and actual behaviour on the other hand, is complex. Hakim's (1991, 1996) thesis largely attributes differences in women's labour market behaviour to differences in their work orientations and the labour market plans they made early in their working lives. Others have questioned this causal inference, arguing that the influence of women's work orientations on their working lives requires an explanation of the origins of these different work orientations, and more attention to the way that orientations and plans develop and adapt over the lifetime in relation to labour market opportunities and experiences (see Devine 1994; Fagan and Rubery 1996b; Ginn *et al.* 1996; Crompton and Harris 1998a; 1998b and Hakim 1998 for a response).

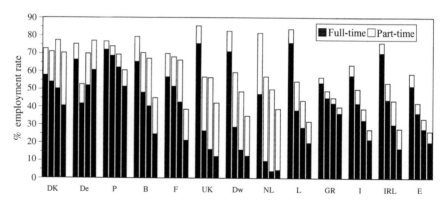

Figure 3.4 Full- and part-time employment rates of non-mothers and mothers aged 20–39 by number of children, 1994

Source: European Labour Force Survey (1994).

Notes
Data for Denmark are for 1993.
Countries ranked by employment rates of all mothers with a child under 15 years.
Data relate to women who are the household head, either individually or as part of a couple.
Number of children: 1st bar = no child; 2nd bar = one child; 3rd bar = two children; 4th bar = three or more children.

For example, in circumstances where it is difficult to combine employment with childraising – such as when childcare is expensive or when jobs involve long or variable hours of work – then women who are trying to establish a career, or simply to retain a foothold in the labour market, may adapt their earlier plans and delay starting a family or have fewer or no children. Another example is that women who do become mothers often experience slower career progression or even loss of occupational status as a result, in part because they are often penalised for adjusting their working hours to accommodate their childcare responsibilities. Even if their labour market behaviour remains unchanged, though, they may suffer discrimination if their managers believe that motherhood makes women less committed employees. Thus, the difficulties of combining employment with raising children, and the more general experience of sex discrimination at the workplace are likely to reduce levels of work commitment for some women in an adaptive process (Dex 1988). These women may invest more heavily in their home life as a source of self-fulfilment, perhaps resulting in them having more children than originally planned and in reduced labour market involvement. In particular, women with low formal qualifications face the greatest difficulties of reconciling motherhood with employment. The combination of low wages, job instability and high childcare costs thwarts any plans to remain in the labour market after maternity leave (for example McRae 1991a), and constrains their ability to re-enter employment after a labour market exit or period of unemployment.

Motherhood, education and women's employment rates

While activity rates are a widely used indicator of labour market involvement, it is increasingly recognised that it is employment and hours worked rather than the activity rate which are the key indicators for comparing women's labour market behaviour (Hakim 1993a; Jonung and Persson 1993). One reason is that women's unemployment is often hidden among those defined as inactive (see Chapter 4). Women with domestic partners or children may be discouraged from declaring themselves to be actively seeking work by high unemployment rates, and in many countries the organisation of the unemployment benefit system also encourages women in these domestic circumstances to define themselves as inactive rather than unemployed (Rubery *et al.* 1998a). Even women who do not consider themselves to be looking for work are likely to be more willing to take jobs in periods of strong labour demand. That the unemployment rate undercounts the hidden female labour supply is revealed by the significant inflow of women from the inactive, non-student population into employment over the 1980s, with the result that the employment rate rose as jobs were created, but the unemployment rate remained static (Rubery *et al.* 1998a). The second reason for the difficulty of measuring women's unemployment specifically, is the limitation of this indicator as a measure of labour market performance. This was recognised in European employment policy by the early 1990s, when a shift in focus occurred towards using the employment rate rather than the unemployment rate as an indicator of labour market performance (CEC 1994). A third reason is that the volume of hours worked varies among the employed, and for women the key difference is the marked variation in the rate of part-time work across countries, as well as by occupation and sector. In this section, therefore, we focus on the employment rate to analyse variations in the labour market involvement of women according to maternal responsibilities and education, focusing on the generation of women currently in the peak years for becoming a mother and having young children to raise (20–39 years).[3]

Fully comparable data on maternal employment rates are not yet available for all 15 member states. The European Childcare Network collected the most harmonised data available, which refer to mothers with children aged 10 years or under for 13 member states; the data for Austria refers to children aged under 15 and for Sweden they only include mothers with children under the age of 7. The result is an overstatement of the labour market involvement of mothers in Austria and an understatement in the data for Sweden. The available data also does not identify women on parental leave, who are recorded as employed in some countries, such as Sweden where women make extensive use of parental leave, but are counted as inactive in others, such as women on child homecare leave after the exhaustion of parental leave in Finland.

Despite these limitations, these data reveal that employment rates for this group of mothers were highest in the three Scandinavian member states,

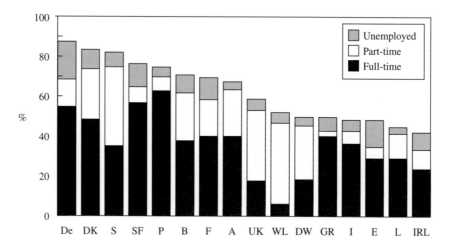

Figure 3.5 Economic activity of mothers with a child aged 10 or under, 1993

Source: European Childcare Network (1996).

Notes
Unemployment rate for Austria is the average for all women.
Austrian mothers defined as women with children under 15.
Swedish mothers defined as women with children under 7.

Portugal, Austria and the former East Germany (see Figure 3.5). The data also reveal that the national variations in employment rates for mothers is composed of differences in levels of full-time and part-time employment. The highest proportion of mothers engaged in full-time employment was found in Portugal, Finland and the former East Germany. Although part-time employment was still untypical for mothers in Finland, their involvement in part-time employment had increased during the recession of the 1990s (National reports, Finland: Keinänen 1996:64). In comparison, the high employment rates for mothers in Denmark, Sweden and Austria rested upon a much higher level of part-time employment. The comparison of full-time employment rates reveals that this form of employment was particularly rare for mothers in the UK, the Netherlands and West Germany.

Swedish labour force survey data shows that part-time employment was traditionally most common in the 25–34 year age band, partially substituting for full-time employment at this stage in women's lives. However, this began to change over the 1990s. At the turn of the decade, there was a pattern of age-related peaks in the level of full-time employment for younger and older women, mirroring the m-shaped curve for women's activity seen in many other countries (National reports, Sweden: Gonäs and Spånt 1996:68–69). This m-shaped curve for full-time employment had disappeared by 1995 owing to the spread of part-time employment into the younger age groups as a result of the shortage of full-time jobs in the recession. A different change was occurring in Denmark, where the percentage of employed women who worked part-time in the core years of family formation had fallen over time, from 32 per cent of the 25–44 year age group in 1981 to only 14 per cent in 1994 (National reports, Denmark: Boje 1996:Table 8), suggesting a move towards a model of full-time employment as the norm for a growing proportion of younger generations of mothers. In contrast, the high rates of part-time employment for mothers in the Netherlands, the UK and West Germany (at 41 per cent, 35 per cent and 28 per cent respectively) seem to be a substitute for full-time work, given the very low rates of full-time employment for mothers.

Another issue of importance is the number of hours worked. In the UK, the Netherlands and West Germany, part-time work was the most common form of employment for mothers, and most of these jobs involved short or marginal hours, in contrast to the longer hours for mothers employed part-time in Sweden, Denmark, Belgium and France (Rubery *et al.* 1995:Table 1.20; National reports, Sweden: Gonäs and Spånt 1996:28). Short part-time hours were also common for women in Austria: they were more likely than men to work less than 24 hours, and accounted for 60 per cent of all marginal part-timers working less than 12 hours (National reports, Austria: Pastner 1996:18, 42). The number of hours involved in full-time work for mothers also varied across countries, reflecting both working-time regulations in the public and private sectors, and the relative importance of the agricultural sector, which typically involves long hours of work (Rubery *et al.* 1997a).

The extent and form of employment for mothers is clearly organised quite differently across the member states. The variation in full-time employment rates for mothers across countries indicates that differences in overall employment rates for mothers cannot simply be attributed to differences in the opportunities for part-time work. Furthermore, preferences for part-time work cannot be inferred from these data on circumstances, because involvement in part-time work may be more to do with labour market policies to promote flexibility or work sharing (see Chapter 7 below).

Figure 3.5 also shows the level of recorded unemployment for mothers in 1993, which accounted for 10 per cent or more of all mothers in the former East Germany, Denmark, Finland, France and Spain. East German mothers had the highest rates of economic activity, but only the fourth-highest employment rates. The highest rates of hidden unemployment among mothers could be expected to be found in the Southern European countries given the particularly high levels of unemployment there. Despite high unemployment, the employment rate for mothers rose over the period 1985–1993 in all the old member states except Denmark (European Childcare Network 1996:Figure 1a). The decline in employment for mothers in Denmark over this period reflected the disproportionate concentration of unemployment on women with small children, particularly lone mothers (National reports, Denmark: Boje 1996:47–48). Maternal employment rates also fell in Finland, but proportionally less than the job loss for other women (National reports,

Finland: Keinänen 1996:64). In contrast, employment rates for fathers fell in 7 of the 12 old member states, indicating that the ability of fathers to support their children, let alone pursue a traditional 'breadwinner role', was being undermined by the poor economic climate.

The influence of the age and number of children on women's employment rates

In some countries, the number of children that women have is the key factor influencing activity rates, while in others it is the age of the youngest child that is more important (Delacourt and Zighera 1988; Meulders *et al.* 1993; Joshi and Hinde 1993). This is illustrated in Figures 3.4 and 3.6, using data for the 12 member states in 1994.

The arrival of the first child has little impact on women's overall employment rate in Denmark and Portugal. Although in Denmark there is a slight shift into part-time employment (see Figure 3.4). Belgium and France also maintain relatively high employment rates for mothers after the arrival of the first child, partly, as in Denmark, through a move into part-time employment for some mothers. Women maintain high employment rates with the arrival of the first child in Sweden, Finland and Austria as well (harmonised data unavailable). In Sweden this is maintained, through women working reduced hours while their children are young (National reports, Sweden: Gonäs and Spånt 1996:42), and a similar strategy is pursued by women in Austria where such jobs are available (National reports, Austria: Pastner 1996:41).

In these countries where women maintained a high employment rate after the birth of the first child it was only with the arrival of the third child that maternal employment rates fell sharply (see National reports, Finland: Keinänen 1996:63; Sweden: Löfström 1995:7, for Finland and Sweden). More detailed French data which combined both the number of children and their ages indicated that the third child was much more of a constraint than the age of the youngest first or even second child (National reports, France: Silvera *et al.* 1996:35). This might reflect a weaker labour market attachment, combined with the strong institutional incentive for French mothers with large families to leave the labour market. The 'childraiser's allowance' has traditionally been paid for the third child, although it is now extended to the second child, but the family tax system and early retirement options in the public sector also favour mothers of large families.

The former East Germany is the only country where employment rates dipped sharply for women with one child before recovering for mothers with two or three children. This was likely to be related to the high unemployment rates during the 1990s resulting from the unification process, which may have had a particularly negative impact on employment opportunities for new mothers.

In the remaining member states the first child precipitated a sharp fall in employment, followed by a steady decline in employment as family size increased. The impact of increasing family size is partly due to a reduction in work experience and hence labour market returns, and once work experience is taken into account the effect of family size is reduced (National reports, Ireland: Barry 1996:65). The arrival of the first child may trigger the beginning of a 'filter process' among mothers, for a UK study found that women who remained in the labour market after the birth of their first child had a high rate of return following maternity leave, compared to the average rate for first-time mothers, due to a combination of work commitment and conducive workplace factors (McRae 1991b). The arrival of the first child produced a further effect in the UK, West Germany and the Netherlands, where women who combined employment with motherhood did so through switching to part-time work, a pattern which might be emerging in Ireland as well.

Figure 3.6 shows that women with young children tended to have the lowest employment rates, but the effect of the age of the youngest child was slight in Denmark and Portugal, where over 70 per cent of women with a child under the age of 2 were in employment. Mothers in Sweden also had a high level of employment, although this was partly because periods of parental leave are recorded as employment. Mothers in Finland still have high employment rates despite falls in the 1990s due to the combination of the economic recession and the impact of women making use of the new extended element of the parental leave scheme, which resulted in them being counted as economically inactive (see Box 3.5). High

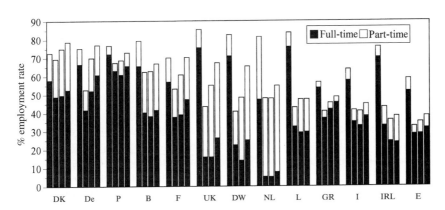

Figure 3.6 Full- and part-time employment rates of non-mothers and mothers aged 20–39 by age of youngest child, 1994

Source: European Labour Force Survey (1994).

Notes
Data for Denmark are for 1993.
Countries ranked by employment rates of all mothers with a child under 15 years.
Data relate to women who are the household head, either individually or as part of a couple.
Age of youngest child: 1st bar = no child; 2nd bar = less than 2 years; 3rd bar = 3–6 years; 4th bar = 7–14 years.

employment rates for mothers were also maintained when children were young in Belgium, France and East Germany, although in East Germany and France there was a pronounced dip in employment when children were very young.

Among countries with lower employment rates for mothers there was little variation with the age of the youngest child in Italy, Spain, Greece or Ireland. It was in the UK and West Germany, and to a lesser extent in the Netherlands, that the age of the youngest child was critical. Full-time employment rates for mothers were very low in these countries; even when the youngest child is of school age the full-time employment rate remained below that for mothers with a child under 2 years in the other member states. Mothers' employment increases steadily as the youngest child grows up, mostly through a re-entry to part-time employment. In the UK the fastest increase in activity occurred for women with children under 5 years old, from an activity rate of 27 per cent in 1973 to 46 per cent in 1989 and reaching 54 per cent in 1993, but rates of part-time work for employed mothers only fell slightly, from 72 per cent in 1973 to 70 per cent in 1993 (National reports, UK: Rubery 1996:Table 1.3.11).

This overall comparison for mothers aggregates the experience of different groups of women. The picture for lone mothers is likely to differ from that for mothers with partners in many countries. We have already mentioned the unusual case of the UK, where lone mothers have lower activity rates than other mothers (see above, Table 3.6). In Luxembourg, the higher overall employment rate for lone mothers masked a higher part-time employment rate for women with pre-school children. This may be due to the ability of some lone mothers to claim the guaranteed minimum income (RMG) without having to accept a job (National reports, Luxembourg: Plasman 1996:22). The occupational position of mothers is also an important determinant. In the UK, mothers of new babies in professional jobs had much higher full-time employment rates than mothers in manual jobs, and the full-time employment increased more rapidly with the child's age (Glover and Arber 1995). There were also marked differences in employment patterns in the UK according to ethnic origin, whereby part-time employment was mainly a model of motherhood for white women (Dale and Holdsworth 1998). Other attributes, such as migrant status or regional location, may be important in several other member states. A major influence is education, which we discuss next.

The influence of education on maternal full-time and part-time employment rates

In every country, graduate-level qualifications increased women's likelihood of being in the labour market, and more specifically of being in employment. Conversely, women who only had basic qualifications were more likely to be inactive or unemployed (Eurostat 1994a:Table 30).

Education and training might be expected to influence the extent to which mothers engage in full-time employment, for human capital theorists such as Becker (1985) assume that this investment reflects pre-existing preferences and aspirations towards a high level of labour market involvement. This thesis is echoed by Hakim (1991, 1996) who argues that a strong career orientation leads women to engage in full-time employment. A demand-side perspective might also predict that women with educational resources are more able to maintain full-time employment because they are less vulnerable to job loss. On the other hand, highly educated women may be concentrated in parts of the labour market, particularly professional jobs within the public sector, where they are more able to negotiate reduced hours of work and extended parental leave.

Figure 3.7 shows that mothers with high education levels did have higher full-time employment rates than those with lower educational qualifications. However, the higher employment rates for highly educated mothers were due to a greater involvement in both part-time and full-time employment. Involvement in full-time work did increase more sharply than part-time employment with qualification level, except in the Netherlands and West Germany. Nevertheless, the share of graduate mothers who were employed full-time varies between countries. So while graduate mothers had a full-time employment rate in excess of 60 per cent in the former East Germany, Finland and the four Southern European member states, the share fell to

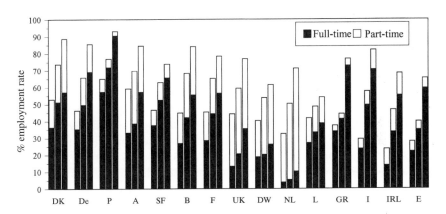

Figure 3.7 Full- and part-time employment rates of mothers aged 20–39 by educational attainment, 1994

Source: European Labour Force Survey (1993, 1994, 1996).

Notes
Data for Denmark are for 1993.
Data for Austria and Finland are for 1996.
Countries ranked by employment rates of all mothers with a child under 15 years.
Data relate to women who are the household head, either individually or as part of a couple.
Educational attainment: 1st bar = low, ISCED (0–3); 2nd bar = medium, ISCED (3–5); 3rd bar = high, ISCED (6–7).

33 per cent in the UK, 25 per cent in West Germany and to as low as 9 per cent in the Netherlands.

Conclusions

Women have continued to increase their share of employment despite economic recessions and the collapse of employment opportunities for the young and for many prime age men. These trends suggest that women, far from acting as a labour reserve, are instead forming a permanent part of the labour force and will resist any pressure for their integration into employment to be reversed. Women's increased determination to participate within the wage labour market is indicated by their reduced fertility rates and their increasing acquisition of educational qualifications.

Much of this change in women's labour supply behaviour is reinforced by changes taking place in the organisation of family life. Not only are women more likely to work when they have children, they are also having fewer children and at an older age. Women are entering into marriages later and more are remaining single or childless. Moreover, in some countries marriage is by no means a prerequisite for having children and a growing proportion of children are born to single women and to cohabiting couples. These changes in family formation are being initiated by both women and men and reflect change in social values as well as changes in women's labour market position. The importance of social values in conditioning behaviour is indicated by national differences in the pace and form of these changes. In some countries, particularly the Nordic countries, the traditional life-cycle model of commitment to lifelong marriage followed by having children is giving way to more complex family and life-cycle patterns. In others, notably the Southern European member states and Ireland, there is more pressure on women to opt into the traditional pattern of marriage and children or else to remain childless. However, the common theme is more diversity in household structures and living arrangements. This is undermining the validity of the stable 'male breadwinner' model of family life which still underpins family and labour market policy in most countries, with the exception of the 'weak breadwinner' Scandinavian countries (Lewis 1992; Rubery *et al.* 1998a).

Fertility rates have fallen in many countries. The traditional family form of marriage preceding childbirth and marital stability is strongest in the Southern European member states, yet it is here that fertility rates fell rapidly and have shown no immediate signs of recovery. The control of fertility can be regarded as an important means of resistance by women to their traditional family roles, and in these countries, as well as in other parts of the EU such as West Germany, the fall in fertility might indicate that a growing proportion of women were 'opting-out' of motherhood by having fewer or no children in response to the difficulties of juggling labour market activity with private care responsibilities (National reports, Italy: Bettio and

Villa 1993; Germany: Maier *et al.* 1994:5–13). Similar pressures could account for the recent fall in fertility rates in Sweden, which coincided with rising unemployment, and where the fertility decline was most marked in regions with the highest unemployment (National reports, Sweden: Gonäs and Spånt 1996:30). Studies show that the Swedish parental leave system has had an important effect on the timing of births, for women delayed leave until their career was established in order to enhance their leave entitlements (OECD 1995c), so in the current recession young women might be postponing childbirth.

It is striking that the Nordic states are characterised by both the weakest adherence to the traditional norm of married life – fewer and later marriages combined with high rates of divorce, remarriage and births outside marriage – and some of the highest fertility rates in the European Union. State family and labour market policies in these countries are largely organised to facilitate the reconciliation of individual women's and men's employment and parental responsibilities, rather than supporting a particular marital living arrangement (Fagan and Rubery 1996a; Rubery *et al.* 1998a). The result is high and continuous labour market involvement for the majority of mothers over the early years of childraising. The United Kingdom provides an alternative example of a country with high fertility combined with unstable marital patterns and a high rate of cohabitation. However, in contrast to the Nordic countries, women in Britain receive little state support to move outside their traditional roles. This suggests that there is no deterministic relationship between state policies and family patterns and that, as in the United States, traditional family relations may be breaking down, even when the result may be many women trapped in poverty as single parents facing a low-wage labour market and limited state support for the family.

The increased involvement of women in the labour market, declines in fertility rates and increased diversity and movement between different household types over the lifecourse in contemporary societies is stimulating debate about which policies are required to respond to these economic and demographic trends. One line of debate is the pro-natalist concern to raise fertility rates that is increasingly voiced in some countries which have experienced rapid falls in fertility. A commonly proposed solution consists of efforts to prop up the traditional 'male breadwinner' model of childraising, for example by extending childraising allowances or tax subsidies to encourage married women to quit the labour market to raise children. However, comparisons of national fertility trends suggest that a natalist policy has more chance of success if it focuses upon the Nordic examples of reforming the gender contract implicit in labour market and family policies in ways which help both mothers and fathers to combine employment with their childcare responsibilities. The debate in Italy in the mid-1990s about the need to redress the fall in fertility rates is one example of where this wider policy agenda has not yet emerged. Yet equal opportunities policies and the transfer of some services from household provision to the market or public domain is likely to be as important as family policies in redressing fertility rates in Italy (National reports, Italy: Bettio and Villa 1996:1, 12). Without this wider modernisation of the gender contract in Italy, and indeed most other member states, the risk is that a growing proportion of women will opt for having few or no children in order to be able to compete in the labour market.

The final demographic issue to note is that the relative size of the elderly population is growing across Europe, due to a combination of the long-term trends of fertility decline and rising life expectancy. This demographic shift has contributed to the increase in the dependency ratio[4] over recent years, which population forecasts indicate will remain high over the next 30 years (Eurostat 1994b). The 'ageing' of the population has particular implications for women. First, there is a growing need to provide care for elderly frail people. In many countries this responsibility is likely to fall on families, and in practice on women, as welfare services are curtailed or held constant due to public expenditure constraints, thus adding to the domestic workload that women must manage with paid employment. For example, although the incidence of extended families living together declined in Spain over the 1980s, 28 per cent of men and 32 per cent of women over the age of 60 live with their child or other relative (National reports, Spain: Moltó 1996:31). A large amount of family care is provided even in countries such as the UK where it is usual for elderly relatives to live on their own or in residential care homes (Finch 1989). These elder-care responsibilities raise additional policy issues about how to reconcile employment with private care responsibilities. If caring for elderly relatives makes it difficult for women to remain in employment, then this will impact on the quality of family relationships as well as on the income of the carers. Second, women's greater longevity, combined with their lower earnings-related pension entitlements, makes them more vulnerable than men to poverty in old age in most member states (Ginn and Arber 1994, 1998). It is, therefore, essential to improve women's labour market position and hence their prospects for gaining an adequate income during their working lives and into retirement.

Part II

Indicators of women's employment in the 1990s

Introduction

Part II examines the four main dimensions to gender inequality in waged work. Chapter 4 begins by comparing women's and men's employment rates. This indicator measures the proportion of the working-age population who have a job, and is also desegregated into the full-time and part-time employment rate. The employment rate has two main advantages over the more widely used economic activity rate, which records the proportion of people in paid work or looking for employment. First, in societies where women's ascribed work is primarily as wives and mothers and the female activity rate is relatively low, the boundary between 'unemployment' and 'inactivity' is rather blurred. The result is that a large amount of women's unemployment is hidden. This was vividly demonstrated in the European Union throughout the 1980s, when the majority of net job growth was filled by women entering the labour market from 'inactivity', rather than by those from recorded unemployment. Second, given the persistently high unemployment rates in many economies, there is a growing acceptance that it is the employment rate rather than the activity rate which is the better indicator of the health of the economy. Chapter 4 goes on to consider how the different types of labour market organisation mean that the nature of the unemployment problem varies considerably between countries. The chapter also examines the nature of the welfare system and the rate of progress within European labour markets towards institutions that reflect the social economic changes outlined in Part I.

Occupational segregation, pay and working-time are analysed in Chapters 5, 6 and 7. These are well-established indicators of women's economic position, but there are still conceptual and measurement debates, such as that around the issue of how to measure segregation. In addition, there are often limitations in the available data, particularly when drawing international comparisons. These issues connected with the adequacy of the different indicators are addressed in the course of the analyses.

While each of the four dimensions contributes to gender inequality in waged and unwaged work, the impact is not necessarily cumulative. A high level of gender inequality on one dimension can be offset by a low level of gender inequality on another. Furthermore, there is no general relationship between women's employment rates and gender equality in the terms and conditions of employment: where gender differences in the employment rate have narrowed, this feminisation of employment does not inevitably lead to declines in segregation, wage inequality or working-time differences. For example, in the Scandinavian countries there are high female employment rates and high levels of occupational segregation, but women's segregation is associated with relatively low rates of gender pay inequality because of the compressed wage structure in these economies. The emergence of a high rate of part-time work in the Netherlands has helped to reduce gender inequality in employment rates and has not led to a significant increase in gender pay inequality (measured by hourly earnings), but has done little to alter gender differences among the employed workforce in the number of hours worked. In the UK, the relatively high employment rate for women is based on high levels of gender segregation and pay inequalities combined with particularly poor terms and conditions for the large proportion of women who are in part-time jobs.

Gender differences in employment are found in all of the member states, but the extent and form of inequality varies, so that important differences in the 'gender order' (Connell 1987) are found between societies. Many of these national differences in the relation between gender and employment outcomes can be traced to systems of labour market regulation which shape, for example, the wage structure and the pattern of working-time. Differences in welfare state regimes and family systems also influence gender relations in waged work. Member states can be arrayed on a spectrum from 'strong' to 'weak' male breadwinner states (Lewis 1992), with many occupying contradictory positions because of inconsistency between different policy areas, so that the male breadwinner system of family organisation may be encouraged in some parts of life while discouraged in others.

Gender differentiation in waged and unwaged work – even in those countries where the extent is more muted – means that gender plays a key role in the process of economic restructuring and labour market reorganisation. The growth of service sector employment, the expansion of non-standard contractual and working-time arrangements, the tendency for net job growth to be filled by recruits from the inactive rather than unemployed pools of the population, are all linked to the gendered pattern of labour market organisation and development.

Political and economic pressure in most EU countries over the 1980s and 1990s led to various moves to deregulate the labour market (see Chapters 1 and 2 above). If this increases the scope for women's different family and social position to influence the terms and conditions on which they are employed the result may be to stall or reverse what progress has been made in reducing gender inequalities. Public sector restructuring is another general trend which may threaten women's employment position. Large welfare states have tended to facilitate the 'weak' male breadwinner system in which high female employment rates are supported on one hand by a high demand for women's labour in the public sector, and on the other by high levels of provision of public services, backed up by rights to parental leave or reduced working hours. This is clearly illustrated by the case of Sweden.

However, attempts to reintroduce a strong male breadwinner system of household organisation seem doomed to failure. Even in countries where state policy is still premised on this form of family life, this is increasingly adrift from how women and men are actually organising their lives. As we saw in Chapter 3, women continue to increase their participation in paid work and lifestyles and household formation patterns are becoming increasingly complex.

Thus, any roll-back of welfare state provision and labour market regulations is set to increase gender differentiation, but the outcome is unlikely to be the recreation of a stable male breadwinner gender order in the household and the labour market. Governments and employers appear unwilling to address the consequences of cutbacks in welfare provision or in policies to facilitate work and family life. Reductions in welfare provision on one hand, and increased pressure to work long or variable hours on the other, all exacerbate the problems of reconciling work and family life. There is little evidence of any systematic rethink of either welfare state or labour market policies in the light of changes in women's employment patterns and in family formation. The result is likely to be further fragmentation of the social and economic system, particularly along the division between those households with and without employment, and greater inconsistency between the wider needs of society and how labour markets are organised, in which children may be the losers.

4 Wage work, care work and welfare

This chapter explores changes and continuity in women's role in wage work, care work and welfare. The first section explores women's contribution to trends in the employment rate in Europe. It demonstrates that the rising employment rate for women has partly compensated for the decline in men's employment rate and hence reduced the overall decline in the European employment rate. Much of the increased employment rate for women has occurred due to the decline in inactivity rates of women in the core working years, thereby reducing the gender divergence in labour market behaviour. However, current measures of labour market activity are also shown to be inadequate for capturing the full range of gender differences in labour market integration; employment rates may overstate women's integration into wage work, while unemployment rates understate the proportion of women excluded from the labour market.

Notwithstanding the limitations of standard measures of unemployment, in 12 of the 15 member states the unemployment rate is higher for women than for men. This greater vulnerability of women to unemployment in most labour markets does, however, emerge within labour market conditions which vary nationally and hence require different types of policy intervention. This is demonstrated in the second section, which explores the nature of unemployment within European labour markets and the position of women within patterns of both adult and youth unemployment.

Differences in men's and women's integration into wage work coexist with differences in the gender division of domestic labour within the household. This gender division is reinforced by state policies concerning the organisation of social welfare, which are still largely premised on a 'male breadwinner' model of family life. Yet in recent years the 'specialisation' of women in domestic work has been declining as more and more women are integrated into the wage labour market, although often at the cost of undertaking the 'double shift' of adding waged labour to their already time-consuming responsibilities of care work and domestic labour. In some countries the state has played an active role in integrating women into waged work through the extension of public sector employment and services and through the adoption of a 'dual-earner' model of household organisation as an organising principle of the social welfare system. Other European countries have been slower to modernise their welfare system to meet the changing role of women in the labour market, retaining a strong 'male breadwinner' presumption in state policies and failing to provide the child-care support necessary to facilitate a high labour market participation rate for women without jeopardising either the birth rate or the well-being of children and their mothers. While state policies in many countries have made some moves away from the 'strong' breadwinner principle, few have made the transition past a 'modified' to a 'weak' breadwinner state (Lewis 1992). These 'modified' regimes have dismantled the breadwinner presumption to some degree and in some policy areas, but this may coexist with the preservation or reinforcement of the breadwinner presumption in others (see Box 4.1).

Box 4.1 Strong, modified and weak male breadwinner states

A **strong male breadwinner** state is designed around the presumption of a male breadwinner and a dependent wife. Taxation systems tend to be household based, so that the total tax take is usually lower on married couples than on two single adults, but the effective marginal tax faced by the second earner is greater than for a single person. Welfare benefits involve high levels of derived rights for the spouse, and access to benefits may be dependent upon aggregate household income. Family policy encourages childcare in the family through extended but unpaid parental leave or through childraising allowances.

A **weak male breadwinner** state is based on the assumption that all fit adults of working age are likely to be in work or looking for work. Taxation and benefit systems are based around the individual, although welfare benefits may still involve household means-testing once individual entitlements are exhausted. The presumption of economic activity is supported by paid leave systems, by opportunities to reduce hours and by childcare provision.

A **modified male breadwinner** system may involve contradictory elements from the strong and the weak male breadwinner systems, combining, for example, household taxation with childcare provision (for example France) or individual taxation with means-tested benefits and little or no childcare provision (for example the UK). (Adapted from Lewis (1992).)

The third section explores the rather slow progress of change within the welfare and family system, which has tended to lag behind changes in women's behaviour in the waged economy. Care work is still regarded as primarily the responsibility of women in welfare policies, while changes in policies in response to constraints on public expenditure have tended to narrow rather than extend access to social protection for women working on atypical contracts or with non-continuous work histories. Finally, there is little evidence to show any significant change in the household division of labour; the main way in which women escape from the double shift of wage and domestic work is through the substitution of public and private services for their domestic labour rather than any significant redistribution of care and domestic work between the sexes. The implications of the analysis in this chapter are summarised in the closing section.

Gender and the employment rate

The share of the population in employment came to be regarded as a better indicator of labour market performance than measured unemployment rates in the 1990s (CEC 1994; Freeman 1995). However, even on this indicator Europe has tended to fare relatively less well than its main competitors, the US and Japan. Moreover, with the exception of the second half of the 1980s, the trend of the European employment rate has been largely downward since the mid-1970s (CEC 1994). Closer inspection reveals that trends in the overall employment rate over the 1980s were based on very different patterns by gender, and also very different employment rates between European countries, primarily related to different shares of women in employment (Rubery *et al.* 1998a). This section explores the role of gender and age in the divisions between employment and non-employment; the organisation of labour markets and the impact on the pattern of unemployment.

Changes in employment and non-employment

During the 1980s the trend in the European employment rate was upward (rising by over two percentage points from 59.4 per cent in 1983 to 61.6 per cent in 1989 at the E10 level), fuelled by the continued expansion of female employment. In the 1990s the trend was downward again; between 1989 and 1994 the overall employment rate fell by 1 percentage point at the E10 level, by just over a percentage point at the E12 level and by over 2 percentage points at the E14 level.[1] The increase in the 1980s was the result of the expansion of female employment as male employment rates fell in many countries and even the overall employment rate declined in a number of countries, including Greece, France, Ireland and Italy (Rubery *et al.* 1998a:21–22). Similarly, in the early 1990s significant differences emerged between member states and between women and men. In eight member states – Denmark, Germany, Spain, Italy, Portugal, Finland, Sweden and the UK – the overall employment rate fell by between 2 and 3 percentage points while only in the Netherlands, Ireland and Belgium were there rises of more than a percentage point (4.7, 2.3 and 1.9 points respectively). In the former West Germany the employment rate rose by a percentage point while in the former East Germany there was a 10 percentage point fall between 1991 and 1994 following unification. Overall, between 1991 and 1994 the male employment rate fell by 4 percentage points (E12) and by

5 at the E14 level, while the female employment rate continued to rise, with a 2 percentage point increase at the E12 level, or a 1 percentage point increase if 14 countries are taken into account.

Female employment rates were more robust than male employment rates in the first part of the 1990s, although the increases were generally more modest than during the 1980s. Six countries recorded increases in the female employment rate of 2 or more percentage points and three smaller rises of less than a percentage point (see Table 4.1). Five, however, recorded falls, relatively small in size in Greece and Italy but of more than 2 percentage points in Sweden, Finland and Denmark. Between 1991 and 1994 the female employment rate in the former East Germany in fact fell by more than the male rate (11.5 compared to 9.5 percentage points), reflecting the devastating impact of reunification and adjustment to a market economy on East German women. Elsewhere, men fared not only worse than women but also worse than during the 1980s, with employment rates falling in every member state except the Netherlands where only a small rise was recorded (1 percentage point).

Table 4.1 Employment rates in the European Union

	1989			1994		
	Total	Male	Female	Total	Male	Female
Belgium	53.8	67.9	39.7	55.7	66.5	44.8
Denmark	75.3	80.9	69.5	72.4	77.6	67.1
Germany (e)	73.0	78.6	67.7	62.7	69.1	56.2
Germany (w)	64.1	77.8	50.3	65.1	75.3	54.7
Germany	67.9	78.4	57.2	64.7	74.1	55.0
Spain	48.0	67.0	29.5	45.0	60.1	30.2
France	60.8	71.4	50.6	58.9	66.6	51.3
Greece	55.2	74.1	37.6	54.1	72.2	37.1
Ireland	50.3	66.4	33.9	52.6	65.3	39.8
Italy	53.3	71.3	35.8	50.9	66.5	35.6
Luxembourg	59.3	77.0	41.3	60.2	74.9	44.9
Netherlands	59.1	73.5	44.4	63.8	74.5	52.7
Austria[a]	—	—	—	56.8	67.7	47.0
Portugal	65.1	78.9	52.4	62.9	72.5	54.1
Sweden	82.9	85.1	80.7	72.2	73.5	70.9
Finland	73.2	75.9	70.5	59.1	60.3	58.0
UK	70.6	80.2	60.9	67.7	74.1	61.1
E12	60.1	74.1	46.3	58.9	69.8	48.0
E14	62.5	75.3	49.8	60.3	70.6	50.0

Sources: (E12) European Labour Force Survey (1989, 1994, 1995); Finnish Labour Force Survey (1989–1994); Swedish Labour Force Survey (1989–1995).

Notes
— indicates no data available.
a Data for Austria are for 1995.

Table 4.2 decomposes the changes in EU employment rate between 1989 and 1994 and identifies the negative impact of falling male employment rates in 13 out of 14 member states, compared to the positive contribution to the employment rate from changes in female employment in all but 6 countries (data exclude Austria). Falls in female employment only reduced the overall employment rate by 1 percentage point on average in those countries where women did bear a more equal share of the economic downturn, that is the Nordic countries and the former East Germany between 1991 and 1994. In Sweden, Finland and Denmark the negative contributions from men and women were similar, although still slightly higher for men, while the reverse is true for the former East Germany.

Changes in overall employment rates may reflect changes in the age structure of the population, towards or away from high-activity age groups, or alternatively may reflect changes in employment rates within age groups. Using a shift share analysis, we find that changes in the age structure of the population exerted a positive force in most countries and for both sexes as the weight of the population shifted towards those age groups that tended to have higher employment rates (Table 4.2). Falling male employment rates within age groups in fact had the greatest negative impact on overall employment rates, and without the beneficial changes to the population structure the overall decline would have been greater in many countries. Every member state recorded falls in male age-specific employment rates. This pattern is similar to that found in the 1980s for men (Rubery *et al.* 1998a:29) but what was different about the period from 1989 to 1994 was that nine member states also recorded falling age-specific employment rates for women, offset or partially offset by shifts in the structure of the working-age population in seven of the countries. Without the positive population effect there would in fact have also been a negative female contribution to the overall employment rates in France and the UK.

The increase in women's share of employment in the 1980s was in most countries relatively evenly accounted for by changes in the industrial composition towards more female-dominated sectors, and by increasing female shares within sectors: out of a 3 percentage point increase in the female employment rate between 1983 and 1992 for nine EU countries (that is excluding Spain, Portugal and Italy as well as Sweden, Finland, Sweden) 1.34 percentage points were accounted for by the changing industrial composition of employment and 1.63 by increasing female shares within sectors (Rubery *et al.* 1998a:103). Increasing female shares within industries were somewhat more important than changing composition effects in the majority of countries, and also more important in the period from 1987 to 1992 compared to that from 1983 to 1987. Unfortunately we are not able to identify if this pattern continued into the early 1990s because of a change in industrial classification used in the European Labour Force Survey after 1992.

Table 4.2 The percentage point contribution by gender to changing employment rates within EU member states, 1989–1994 (for the 15–64 population), decomposed by population and age-specific employment rates

	Men				Women				Employment rate		
	Population age structure effect	Change in age-specific employment rates	Interaction term	Male contribution	Population age structure effect	Change in age-specific employment rates	Interaction term	Female contribution	Change in total employment rate	1989	1994[b]
Belgium	0.67	-1.41	0.03	-0.71	0.43	2.03	0.14	2.59	1.88	53.8	55.7
Denmark	0.15	-1.81	0.04	-1.63	0.41	-1.60	0.00	-1.19	-2.82	75.3	72.4
East Germany[a]	-0.55	-3.99	-0.13	-4.67	-0.78	-5.21	0.16	-5.83	-10.50	73.0	62.5
West Germany	0.27	-1.63	0.07	-1.28	0.04	1.91	0.25	2.19	0.91	64.1	65.1
Germany[a]	0.13	-2.30	-0.02	-2.19	-0.05	-1.07	0.05	-1.07	-3.27	67.9	64.6
Spain	0.35	-3.76	0.00	-3.41	0.13	0.17	0.05	0.35	-3.06	48.0	45.0
France	0.49	-2.82	-0.01	-2.35	0.50	-0.24	0.14	0.40	-1.95	60.8	58.8
Greece	0.08	-0.98	-0.02	-0.93	-0.02	-0.21	0.01	-0.22	-1.15	55.2	54.1
Ireland	0.36	-0.92	0.02	-0.54	0.09	2.73	0.10	2.92	2.38	50.3	52.7
Italy	0.45	-2.78	-0.04	-2.37	0.36	-0.48	-0.01	-0.12	-2.49	53.3	50.8
Luxembourg	0.52	-1.62	0.08	-1.01	0.13	1.49	0.16	1.78	0.77	59.3	60.0
Netherlands	0.65	-0.15	-0.02	0.49	0.08	3.93	0.12	4.13	4.62	59.1	63.7
Portugal	0.11	-3.19	-0.01	-3.10	0.12	0.76	-0.01	0.87	-2.22	65.1	62.9
Sweden[a]	0.37	-6.47	0.22	-5.88	0.34	-5.39	0.21	-4.84	-10.72	82.9	72.2
Finland	0.03	-8.05	0.16	-7.86	0.22	-6.58	0.15	-6.21	-14.07	73.2	59.1
UK	0.43	-3.62	0.15	-3.04	0.20	-0.28	0.21	0.12	-2.92	70.6	67.6

Sources: (E12) European Labour Force Survey (1989–1994); Finnish Labour Force Survey (1989–1994); Swedish Labour Force Survey (1989–1995).

Notes
a Refers to change 1991–1994 for former East Germany, unified Germany and Sweden.
b Employment rates standardised for differential population change between men and women.

Labour market activity of the young (15–24 years)

Youth employment rates are low and declining in most countries. Gender differences in this age group are, however, relatively small and the period from 1989 to 1994 witnessed further convergence between the employment rates of young women and men. Much of the convergence was the result of the impact of economic conditions on job opportunities for the young combined with, or resulting in, a rising share of the age group staying on in full-time education.

These trends were already evident in the 1980s as youth employment rates fell for men in eight countries and for women in seven, and participation in education increased. Only the Netherlands displayed a large rise in youth employment, possibly explained by a change in the survey design that led to the inclusion of more short part-time jobs, often taken by young people (Rubery *et al.* 1998a:41–43). Between 1989 and 1994 youth employment rates fell in every European member state for both women and men, except for the Netherlands where rates rose for women and men (see Figure 4.1). At the E12 level (excluding East Germany) there was a 10 percentage point fall in the youth male employment rate but only a 7 point fall for women, leaving the female rate lower but with the gap reduced to just 6 percentage points, the lowest of all age groups. Using the combined data for E14 there was nearly a 21 percentage point fall for men and a decline of just less than 14 percentage points for women, reflecting the large falls in Sweden and Finland. In all 13 countries where youth employment rates fell, the male rate fell by more than the female rate. The former East Germany provided an exception to this trend, with female employment rates falling by 2 percentage points more than male rates between 1991 and 1994, leading to some divergence in male–female youth employment rates but from a relatively equal starting point. In Austria youth participation rates rose over the 1980s for both men and women, but between 1987 and 1992 the female activity rate for 15–19 year olds fell from 49.8 per cent to 44.1 per cent, diverging from the male rate which fell from 56.4 per cent to 54.7 per cent. However, for those aged 20–24 activity rates converged, as there was an increase for women (71.8 per cent to 75.3 per cent) while the male rate fell (81.5 per cent to 76.4 per cent) (National reports, Austria: Pastner 1995:12). By 1994 the gender gap only remained greater than 8 percentage points in the four Southern European countries (up to nearly 13 points in Greece) while in six member states the gap was less than 4 points in favour of men. In the Netherlands and Sweden the female rate actually exceeded the male rate by around a percentage point.

Differences in employment rates between countries are to some extent the result of variable rates of participation in education but also the differences in economic behaviour of students. In Denmark a fifth of all students under 25 were also in employment in 1994 and in the Netherlands and the UK the share was around 10 per cent. In the majority of other countries

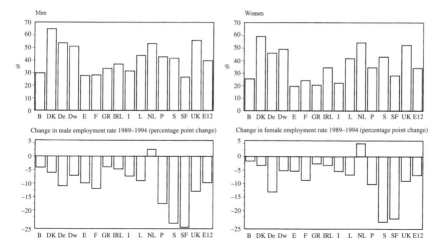

Figure 4.1 Youth employment rates and the change between 1989 and 1994

Source: European Labour Force Survey (1989–1994).

the share was around 1 per cent or less (Rubery *et al.* 1998a:43). The countries where there were high shares of young people both in education and active in the labour market were also those where there was a good supply of part-time jobs and where a relatively low proportion of the young unemployed were first-time jobseekers. The higher youth employment rates in Germany and Austria reflect the more structured training system that provides training and employment for young people and has traditionally eased the transition from education to employment, leading to lower levels of youth unemployment (Ryan and Büchtemann 1996).

Gender differences in youth unemployment rates, measured as a share of the labour force, also converged over the period from 1989 to 1994. By 1994 male youth unemployment rates exceeded female rates in seven countries, compared to only five in 1989. However, unemployment rates for young women remained higher than men's in the other eight countries, and the differential was particularly high in the Southern European countries of Spain, Greece and Italy.[2] Furthermore, the period after 1994 saw some renewed divergence in male and female unemployment rates (see Chapter 1).

Extended periods of unemployment may lead to inactivity, encouraging increased participation in education or discouraged job search. Figure 4.2 shows the extent of youth non-employment as a proportion of the population and the changes in inactivity and unemployment between 1989 and 1994. Reflecting the falling employment rates in nearly all member states, non-employment increased, mainly in the form of inactivity. Unemployment rates rose by much less and actually fell in the case of Italy, Ireland,

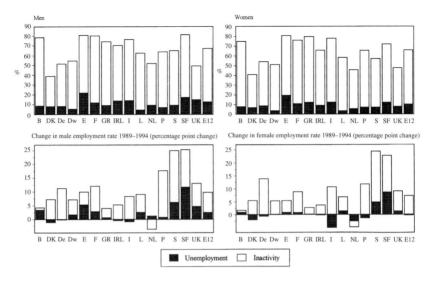

Figure 4.2 Youth non-employment rates and the change between 1989 and 1994
Source: European Labour Force Survey (1989–1994).

Denmark, and the former East Germany (1991–1994) for both men and women and for women in the case of the Netherlands and Portugal. The severe impact of the recession on the Swedish and Finnish labour markets led to a large increase in youth unemployment as well as rises in inactivity for both men and women, exceeding all other member states. Recession also caused dramatic increases in non-employment for young men in Portugal and the UK and for women in the former East Germany.

The very high unemployment rates of young persons as a share of the active population in Table 1.5 are greatly reduced in most countries when unemployment is measured as a share of the population, as in Figure 4.2. Nevertheless, unemployment rates were still high (more than 10 per cent) in 1994 in Spain, Italy, France for both men and women, in Ireland and the UK for men and in Greece for women. Previously, female unemployment rates as a share of the population remained higher than male rates despite the lower activity rates of young women. However, whereas in 1990 female unemployment rates by the population measure were higher than the male rate in 10 of the 14 countries for which we have data, by 1994 this was reduced to only 4 countries, including France and Belgium in which the shares were almost equal. This worsening of the position of young men in the labour market shows the degree of similarity between the sexes in this age group, but attention solely on the plight of young men disguises the fact that women have been equally disadvantaged in almost all countries, and even more so in some.

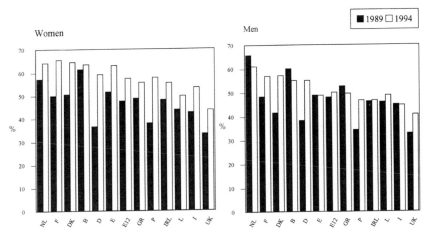

Figure 4.3 Share of young women and men aged 15–24 in full-time education, 1989 and 1994

Source: European Labour Force Survey (1989, 1994).

Notes
1994 data for Germany include the New *Länder*.
Countries ranked by share of all young people in education.
Figure for D refers to West Germany 1989, unified Germany 1994.
Figures for West Germany are 53 per cent men, 47 per cent women.

Deteriorating labour market opportunities for the young and new demands on the jobs market led to an increase in participation in education for women in all of the 12 original member states and for men in most of these countries (Figure 4.3). In 1989 young women's participation in education lagged slightly behind that of men (48.4 per cent and 48.8 per cent) but by 1994 there were slightly more women in education than men at the E12 level, 57.4 per cent compared to 57.2 per cent, emphasising the increased number of women exercising the 'qualifications lever' (Crompton and Sanderson 1990). There were particularly large increases, 10 percentage points or more, found in the share of young women and men in education in France, Denmark, the UK and Portugal and for young women in Italy and Spain. In the E12 countries, the share of young women and men in education in 1994 was roughly equal in four countries; male shares exceeded female shares by 2 percentage points or more in five countries, while in Spain, Portugal and Italy more young women than men were in education. In Austria, Finland and Sweden the participation of young persons in education has traditionally been high, reflected in the high level of educational attainment of the population in general. The poor economic conditions for the young in Sweden and Finland led to a rapid additional rise in participation in education.

While the differences between the participation of young women and men in education within countries became weaker, by 1994 strong country differences remained. The share of the 15–24-year-old population in education ranged from a high of 67 per cent in the Netherlands to less than half in the UK (45 per cent) and rankings by gender reflected a similar pattern, with the UK at the bottom, but the highest share of young women in education was found in France.

Although a high share of inactive young people were in education, there were some who can be regarded as 'fully inactive', neither seeking work nor participating in education. In 1992 nearly 7 per cent of young people in the EU (E12) were 'fully inactive'. Young women dominated this group with one in ten young women inactive and not in education, compared to only 3 per cent of men. In some countries 'full inactivity' was as high as 13 per cent and reached 17.9 per cent for young women in Ireland (Rubery *et al.* 1998a:43). High rates of youth unemployment are a cause for concern, but if the young at the start of their working lives do not even define themselves as part of the labour market there may be even greater potential for future serious social problems.

Labour market activity of core working age population (25–49 years)

The core age group of 25–49-year-olds is where some of the highest male employment rates are found, but much lower female employment rates. This age group covers the peak childrearing years for women as well as the years when men have traditionally felt most secure in the labour market. As a result, rising unemployment rates for 25–49-year-old men tend to create even more concern among policy-makers than those for the young, the old and women. The declining male employment rates during the 1980s were mainly the result of falling employment rates in the older and younger age groups while the core age experienced only small falls in most countries (Rubery *et al.* 1998a). The period from 1989 to 1994 was quite different, with core-age employment rates for men falling in all but one country, Ireland (Figure 4.4). In contrast, in the majority of countries the female employment rate for the core age groups continued to rise, reflecting the pattern observed during the 1980s. The rises were particularly strong in countries where female employment was lower than the European average, such as Ireland, Luxembourg and the Netherlands. However, unlike the 1980s, women's employment also fell in the 1990s in some countries, namely the Scandinavian countries and the former East Germany. What is characteristic about all four of these countries is that they are all based, or were at the start of the 1990s, around an employment system of high levels of employment for both men and women of working age and this more equal distribution of work between the sexes led to a more equal share of the employment decline.

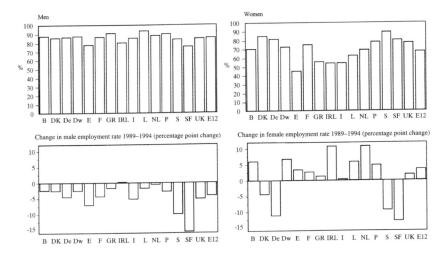

Figure 4.4 Core-age employment rates and the change between 1989 and 1994
Source: European Labour Force Survey (1989–1994).

Figure 4.4 shows how the E12 female core-age employment rate rose by 3.5 percentage points during the early 1990s while the male rate fell by just over 4 percentage points. Looking in greater detail at the individual member states, we find that, despite the economic downturn, female employment rates rose by more than 10 percentage points in Ireland and the Netherlands, and by more than 6 percentage points in Belgium, Luxembourg and the former West Germany. The contrasting fortunes of women in the former West and East Germany could not be more stark: the female core-age employment rate in the former East Germany fell by more than 11 percentage points between 1991 and 1994 compared to a fall in the male rate of half that amount, while in the former West Germany the female rate rose by more than 6 percentage points and the male rate declined by around two and a half percentage points.

The better fortune of core-age women compared to their male counterparts led to the continued convergence in employment rates for this age group over this period, particularly in the countries where there were large increases in the female employment rate, but also where more modest increases for women combined with large falls for men. Even in Finland and Sweden, where female employment rates were high at the start of the period, core-age women managed to reduce the gap with core-age men to around 3 percentage points by 1994 as a result of larger falls in the male employment rates. Only in Denmark and the former East Germany did the male–female differential in core-age employment rates increase over this period. By 1994 there were fewer than 10 percentage points between male and female core-age employment rates in the Scandinavian countries and between 10 and 20 percentage points in the other high-employment-rate countries of Portugal, the UK, France and the former East Germany. At the other extreme, the gap remained larger than 30 percentage points in Spain, Italy, Ireland and Luxembourg and greater than 40 percentage points in Greece. The range of female employment rates in the EU in 1994 was still large, at nearly 40 percentage points compared to just 18 for men but had narrowed from 52 percentage points in 1989, with the convergence between countries the result of a narrowing of the top and the bottom end of the distribution.

Education has a positive effect on both male and female employment rates, but with even greater effects on women (Table 4.3). Seven countries stand out as having particularly high returns to education, with the difference between the employment rates of basic-educated and university-educated women in 1994 exceeding 30 percentage points, rising to more than 40 percentage points in Belgium, Italy and Ireland. Rising employment among women with post-compulsory education accounted for most of the increase in female core-age employment rates in seven countries while in four – the UK, the Netherlands, former East Germany and Spain – the increases were more equal between women with post-compulsory and higher education.

Table 4.3 Employment rates by educational attainment for the 25–49 age group, 1994

	Low		Medium		High	
	Women	*Men*	*Women*	*Men*	*Women*	*Men*
Belgium	44.8	81.1	68.1	90.5	85.0	93.6
Denmark	60.7	74.3	76.3	86.2	87.2	91.2
Germany (e)	49.4	68.4	68.6	85.6	86.5	91.2
Germany (w)	52.4	78.4	67.3	86.9	77.7	93.8
Greece	42.1	91.1	48.7	90.4	78.4	91.2
Spain	31.7	75.1	49.6	79.7	66.0	83.8
France	55.6	80.3	71.4	89.4	81.4	90.2
Ireland	29.3	71.4	56.9	87.9	77.5	92.7
Italy	36.7	84.3	62.4	85.9	78.4	90.5
Luxembourg	50.1	93.0	60.8	94.3	67.0	93.3
Netherlands	42.8	73.4	62.7	90.8	79.8	91.0
Austria	70.9	91.8	70.4	81.4	88.1	93.8
Portugal	64.9	89.7	74.7	88.7	93.9	94.9
Finland	70.0	74.2	67.5	76.0	82.0	87.5
Sweden	76.9	84.2	84.3	86.2	89.7	92.3
UK	60.4	77.9	74.1	86.3	86.2	93.3

Source: European Labour Force Survey (1995).

Notes
Data for Austria, Finland and Sweden are for 1995.
Educational attainment: low is equivalent to ISCED levels 0–3; medium 3–5; high 6–7.

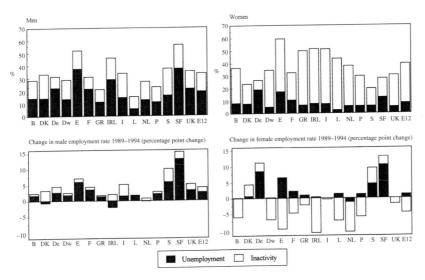

Figure 4.5 Core-age non-employment rates and the change between 1989 and 1994

Source: European Labour Force Survey (1989–1994).

Core-age non-employment

In all countries core-age women were more likely than men to be inactive and in most countries they were more likely to be unemployed, although the gender gap in unemployment rates fell during the early 1990s (Figure 4.5). Women were between five and six times more likely than men to be inactive in most member states. The exceptions were the Scandinavian countries and the former East Germany at one extreme, with lower ratios of less than two, and Luxembourg and Greece at the other, with ratios close to ten.

Measuring unemployment rates as a share of the labour force, we find that female rates exceeded male rates in the majority of countries in 1994, except for the UK, Sweden and Finland, where male rates were higher, and Ireland, where they were equal. The largest gender gaps were in Spain, Italy, Belgium and the former East Germany, with female rates exceeding male rates by between 4.8 and 12.4 percentage points. Measured as a share of the population aged 25 to 49, female core-age unemployment rates were lower and closer to the male rates, reflecting women's lower overall activity rates. However, even under this measure, women's unemployment exceeded male rates in 10 of the 14 countries, although the gap was less than 2 percentage points. The marked exception was the former East Germany where 18.9 per cent of the female core-age population were unemployed compared to 9.6 per cent of men.

In the 1980s female inactivity rates fell in all countries (Rubery *et al.* 1998a) but between 1989 and 1994 the decline in female inactivity rates only continued in 11 countries, ranging from just 0.3 of a percentage point in Italy to 11.2 points in Ireland (Figure 4.5). Rises in women's unemployment rates were found in the three countries where employment rates fell most significantly, namely Denmark, Sweden and Finland, with the latter two recording very dramatic increases. Spain was the only other country to see a large rise in unemployment, with all other countries experiencing little or no change. For men, the story was quite different: inactivity rates continued to rise over the 1990s, combined with rising unemployment rates in all countries except the Netherlands and Denmark.

Women's greater risk of unemployment declines rapidly with educational attainment, so that at higher-qualification levels there is a convergence in unemployment rates for women and men. The impact of educational attainment on reducing women's unemployment rates was particularly strong in those countries where employment rates were also boosted by educational attainment (see above and Table 4.3). For example, for women in the former East Germany the unemployment rate declined by 30 percentage points for graduate women compared to those with only basic education while the differential for men was just 15 percentage points (Table 4.4). In all countries except the UK and the former West Germany, the impact of educational attainment in reducing unemployment rates was greater for women than for men.

Labour market activity of the older-age working population (50–64 years)

Much of the restructuring that has occurred in the labour markets of the European Union in the 1980s and 1990s was at the expense of older workers, mainly male, many of whom found it too hard to re-enter employment and took advantage of the many early retirement schemes that proliferated over the period (Casey 1996). Some older workers chose to take early retirement while others were effectively forced out of the labour market as a result of too few job opportunities. For women the story was quite different in most countries. Older women tended to be of a generation in which low labour-market activity was expected, as part of a male breadwinner system of household organisation.

During the 1980s male older-age employment rates fell considerably, resulting in rising inactivity, particularly in Belgium but also in Greece, France, Ireland and the Netherlands (Rubery *et al.* 1998a:52–55). Over the same period employment rates rose for women in the majority of countries as inactivity rates fell but the expansion of employment was much lower than for women in the core-age groups. During the early 1990s male employment rates for the older-age group continued to fall in all 14 countries, although the magnitude of the fall varied from just 0.4 of a percentage point

Table 4.4 Unemployment rates as a share of the labour force by educational level, 1994

	Men			Women		
	Low	Medium	High	Low	Medium	High
Belgium	9.8	5.5	3.5	19.5	11.2	4.3
Denmark	10.7	6.8	4.4	14.2	9.9	5.2
Germany (e)	24.1	10.4	6.8	39.7	25.4	9.2
Germany (w)	14.9	5.5	3.4	11.7	6.3	5.2
Spain	19.5	14.8	11.6	33.5	29.2	21.8
France	14.2	8.1	6.4	18.7	12.8	7.1
Greece	4.7	5.6	4.5	11.6	13.5	7.3
Ireland	20.0	8.9	4.1	23.7	11.2	5.9
Italy	7.9	5.7	5.1	15.7	11.2	9.6
Luxembourg	3.4	(1.2)	(2.4)	5.3	(3.2)	(3.2)
Netherlands	12.2	4.8	4.9	13.5	7.8	5.9
Austria	7.5	4.3	4.0	8.1	5.8	4.3
Portugal	5.3	4.4	3.2	8.3	9.5	2.1
Finland	40.3	35.4	14.9	32.6	38.2	13.1
Sweden	18.1	20.3	7.0	15.4	16.6	6.3
UK	14.3	8.9	4.0	8.8	6.0	3.3

Source: European Labour Force Survey (1994, 1995).

Notes
Data for Austria, Finland and Sweden are for 1995.
Education attainment: Low is equivalent to ISCED levels 0–3, medium 3–5; and high 6–7.

to 16 percentage points in the former East Germany (see Figure 4.6). Reunification in Germany disproportionately affected women and older men in the former East Germany, whereas core-age men were relatively more protected. Employment rates for this group of men also fell by more than 5 percentage points in the UK, Sweden, Finland and Spain. The patterns for women were also similar to those during the 1980s, with employment rates rising in the majority of countries, albeit by relatively small amounts in many cases. In Sweden, Finland and the former East Germany, female older-age employment rates fell, but from higher levels than in most other countries and by much less than the decline in the male rates. In Greece, the female older-age employment rate also fell, but in this case the rate was already very low, 29.3 per cent in 1989, and the fall was actually slightly larger than that for men.

The generation effect on female older-age employment rates was clear, with employment rates much lower than for the core-age groups, even though they continued to rise in most countries during the early 1990s. Except for Sweden, female older-age employment rates were at least 20 percentage points lower than the core-age rates in all countries and in five countries – Belgium, former East Germany, France, Luxembourg and the Netherlands – the difference was more than 30 percentage points. In some countries (the UK, Italy, Belgium, Spain, Sweden, the former East Germany and the

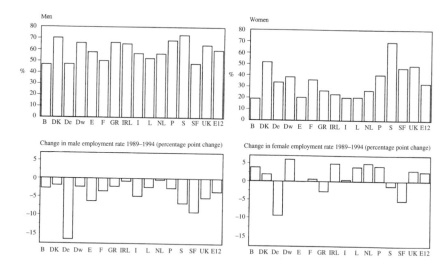

Figure 4.6 Older-age employment rates and the change between 1989 and 1994
Source: European Labour Force Survey (1989–1994).

Netherlands) there was a similar gap between male employment rates in older-age and core-age groups, reflecting the large rise in early retirement for men. In Finland, Luxembourg and Greece the percentage point fall in male employment rates between core-age and older-age groups was even greater than for women. Differences between countries in official retirement ages and in societal norms regarding early retirement explain much of the variation by country.

The contribution of older people to employment is likely to continue to fall, as rising levels of labour market involvement for older women may be insufficient to offset the increasing levels of inactivity among older-age men (Figure 4.7). This trend, combined with the increased time that the young spend in education, is leading to ever shorter working lives. The reduced time spent in the labour market represents on the one hand a decline in labour supply for a scarce amount of employment but on the other hand an increase in the already large dependent population. However, rising educational levels among the younger cohort reduce labour supply in the short term but in the medium term enhance both the quality of the labour supply and the propensity to remain in the labour market (Rubery and Smith 1997). Increasing the employment rate for older people would raise the tax base, provided employment did not fall in other age groups, as well as making use of the skills that many have accrued over their lifetimes.

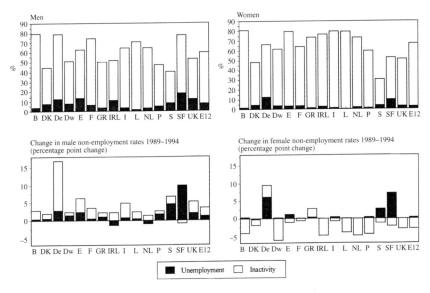

Figure 4.7 Older-age non-employment rates and the change between 1989 and 1994
Source: European Labour Force Survey (1989–1994).

Summary, and the problems of definition of economic activity status

The convergence in employment rates between women and men at an aggregate level that was noted through the 1980s continued in the early 1990s as men's employment position was weakened, particularly in the older- and younger-age groups. There was an even stronger convergence among young men and women as employment rates fell and participation in education rose for both sexes. In part, this rise in education was in response to weakening employment opportunities but it also signalled the importance of education for labour market success, suggesting that perhaps disadvantage in the future will not necessarily be mainly along gender lines. Higher education is also associated with convergence in employment rates by gender for core-age workers, with wider gender gaps at lower educational levels. Again there is some evidence of educational divisions applying to men as well as women in influencing employment chances.

Convergence in the older age ranges arises out of different processes: women moving into employment and older men taking up early retirement. Further convergence can be expected in some countries as younger cohorts of women with high participation rates move into the older age brackets (see Chapter 8).

So far we have been considering conventional definitions of economic activity status. However, as we have argued previously (Rubery *et al.* 1998a), these conventional definitions are not fully satisfactory and may require updating to recognise the increasingly fuzzy boundaries between employment, unemployment and inactivity (see Box 4.2). We have argued that it may not be appropriate, for example, to categorise individuals as belonging to only one status; students may be mainly inactive but still undertaking some paid work; those without work may wish to work, but may find it impossible to search continuously for work because of, for example, the care of children. Yet if a job were to become available, alternative childcare arrangements would be made. Some may regard themselves as primarily homemakers while still undertaking paid work, while those on parental leave are treated as in the labour market whether or not there is a high return rate to employment. The Labour Force Survey, by treating one hour of paid work as sufficient to give an individual employment status, tends to overstate the number of people in employment but its definition of unemployment, which requires people to be without work, to have been looking for work over the past four weeks and to be available for work within two weeks, is perhaps too restrictive, causing many people, particularly women, to be classified as inactive when they wish to work, thus swelling the ranks of the hidden unemployed.

This tendency is evident in Figure 4.8, in which we show the shares of inactive women and men who may perhaps be more properly regarded as part of the hidden unemployed. These include those who have been looking for work but are not immediately available for work within the ILO requirements (jobseekers), those who say they want to work but have not been looking as they believe no jobs are available (discouraged workers) and other inactives who wish to work but have not been currently looking for work. This increased the share of the working-age population who could be regarded as unemployed under a broad definition by 2.2 percentage points for men and by 4 percentage points for women for E15 in 1995. For women the share of the working-age population in 'unemployment' was increased by almost 60 per cent as a result, with ILO-measured unemployment accounting for just over 7 per cent of the working-age population in 1995. The incidence of hidden unemployment varied by country as well as by gender, with the largest rises found in the Netherlands, Ireland, Italy and the UK. This reworking of the definitions of unemployment indicates the sensitivity of labour market analysis to the definitions used – and indeed the sensitivity of gender estimates to such measures. Alternative indicators of potential labour supply other than measured unemployment rates are clearly necessary, together with richer information on the nature of individuals' activities, such as education or childcare, as well as current employment and job search activity patterns.

Unemployment and labour market organisation

The organisation of labour markets has a major effect on the incidence of unemployment, including the incidence by gender. The tendency for unemployment to be higher among women than men, except in the UK, Finland

Box 4.2 Problems with the definitions of economic activity status

Finland provides an example of a country where the downturn in economic activity led to the growth of an informal economy not captured by official statistics. The informal sector includes worker cooperatives, marginal jobs, voluntary work, homeworking, secondhand markets and exchange of services. Both men and women were involved in these activities but women were more active in initiating them (National reports, Finland: Keinänen 1996:73).

Unusually, the **Irish** national register of the unemployed, called the Live Register, records a higher and a growing number of female unemployed compared to the Labour Force Survey. Indeed, female unemployment was some 70 per cent higher in the Live Register, and grew by 23 thousand between 1987 and 1994 while remaining virtually constant under the Labour Force Survey estimates. The reason for this divergence was not clear; for some the increase on the Live Register related to more women claiming their rights to benefits, which was unwelcome from the government's point of view. Registration was also a requirement to obtain access to many training and employment schemes. Others saw the reason as lying in the underestimates of the Labour Force Survey, perhaps because of the high number of women who categorised themselves as engaged on home duties and not as unemployed despite recent job search activity (National reports, Ireland: Barry 1996:79–81).

In **Italy** the change in the national definition of unemployment to coincide more with the ILO definition in 1992 led to a reduction in measured unemployment which particularly affected the most vulnerable sectors of the labour force: first-time jobseekers, women and the unemployed in the south; women accounted for 60 per cent of the statistical contraction in unemployment (National reports, Italy: Bettio and Villa 1996:22–23).

In **Sweden** the recession increased not only open but also partial unemployment, revealed by a marked increase between 1989 and 1995 in the share of both men and women on short and long part-time working wanting to increase their working-time. The increase was particularly noted among elderly women working short part-time hours on temporary contracts among whom the share wishing to increase working-time rose from 15 per cent to 61 per cent. There was a similar increase in the 'latent unemployed', that is those classified as inactive who still regarded themselves as active: for women the increase was from 4.6 per cent to 13.3 per cent of the inactive and for men from 5.1 per cent to 15.7 per cent. If the partial and latent unemployed were added to the measured unemployment rate then unemployment as a percentage of the working-age population rose to 17.4 per cent for women and 12.6 per cent for men (National reports, Sweden: Gonäs and Spånt 1996:87–89).

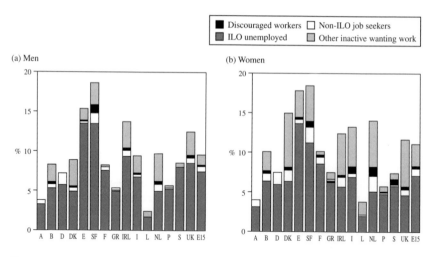

Figure 4.8 Unemployment and hidden unemployment by gender in the EU, 1995
Source: European Labour Force Survey (1995).

Note
Data for Germany, Austria and Ireland have all non-searching inactive included in the 'other
reason' category.

and Sweden, does not mean that the gender gap in unemployment arises
out of the same conditions. Unemployment in European member states varies
significantly along a number of dimensions. These differences include the
relative concentration of unemployment on the young or other age groups,
or among first-time jobseekers as opposed to those with recent employment
experience or those returning from inactivity; the level of flows into and
out of unemployment and the significance of flows in and out of inactivity
as well as between employment and unemployment; the tendency for movements out of unemployment to be into stable or into unstable employment;
the role of family networks or more formal employment systems in helping
the unemployed find work; the risk of unemployment by educational level,
or by social characteristics such as the presence of a young child; and the
availability of jobseekers for full-time or part-time work.

These characteristics of the unemployment problem are related to both
labour market and social institutions, including the family system, the system
of labour market regulation, the use of internal labour markets and the
overall macroeconomic conditions. They will also impact upon the nature
of gender differences in the unemployment problem. While comprehensive
data are not available in all cases, we can provide some indications of differences along these dimensions, both by member states and by gender (see
Table 4.5). Moreover, while youth unemployment tends to be higher than
adult unemployment in all countries, there are major differences between

countries in the size of the gap, such that those countries with strong youth training programmes, for example Germany, Austria and the Netherlands, have relatively low youth unemployment rates. This suggests that there are also differences in the nature of youth unemployment between countries (Table 4.6).

The economic activity status of the unemployed before entering unemployment provides some clues to the nature of unemployment. Differences in the relative importance of youth unemployment are reflected in the share of the unemployment who are first-jobseekers (see Table 4.6). It is in the Southern European countries that first-time jobseekers dominate the unemployed, and the majority of the young unemployed were first-time jobseekers in Greece and Italy as well as in Belgium, Netherlands and Finland in 1994. In contrast, in Sweden the share of first-time jobseekers was less than a quarter for men and just 12.6 per cent for women in 1995. Similarly, the proportion of the unemployed who had entered unemployment from domestic activity also varied markedly for women, ranging from 3 per cent in Denmark to around 40 per cent or more in Italy, Luxembourg, Greece, the UK and Ireland (see Table 4.5). These different statuses prior to entering unemployment clearly affect access to benefits and the nature of the unemployment problem, whether it involves making entry into the labour market, re-entering with possible problems of downgraded skills or re-employment following job loss. Where unemployment is concentrated among first-time jobseekers it tends to be the family which provides support and also the networks through which jobs are sought. In the Southern European countries around 60 per cent of young people found a job through the family, while in the Northern European countries the share tended to be a third or less in 1991 (Eurobarometer data quoted in National reports, Italy: Bettio and Villa 1996:Table 16). However, evidence suggests that these networks are used less effectively in the interests of daughters than of sons (National reports, Italy: Bettio and Villa 1996:34–35; Bettio and Villa 1998; Pugliese 1995).

Member states also differed in the rate of inflows into unemployment and the rate of outflows: the Scandinavian countries tended to have high rates of inflow into unemployment and high rates of outflow from unemployment; Greece had a low rate of both inflow and outflow, while the high unemployment in Spain emerges out of medium rates of inflow and low rates of outflow. While the precise ranking of countries by these measures depends on the stage of the economic cycle, there were clear differences in the extent to which unemployment was concentrated on a few or involved high inflows and outflows. There were also clear gender differences: women's inflow rates into unemployment were usually lower than or comparable to men's in 1993, but as these were measured as a share of the population, and women had lower activity rates, this in fact suggests an over-representation of women in inflow rates. Moreover, outflow rates from unemployment for women were lower than men's in six countries and

Table 4.5 Characteristics of unemployment in the European Union, 1994

	Unemployment rate		Unemployment rate of mothers with at least one child		Share of 1st-time jobseekers among unemployed		Share of unemployed seeking part-time work		Share of unemployed Women Previously in domestic work (1992)	Share of long-term unemployed among the unemployed	
	Male	Female	Under 15	Under 2	Male	Female	Male	Female		Male	Female
Belgium	7.7	12.4	13.9	14.0	23.5	20.7	..	16.4	22	53.4	62.6
Denmark	7.2	9.0	14.0c	16.4c	(3.3)	4.6	8.7	13.6	(3)	31.9	32.4
Germany (u)	7.5	10.3	9.7	8.5	4.2	3.9	3.5	26.5	14	41.2	47.2
Greece	6.0	13.7	12.1	12.6	37.2	52.3	3.3	5.7	39	41.3	57.2
Spain	20.0	31.4	33.0	31.8	14.8	25.8	1.9	7.7	21	46.3	59.4
France	11.1	14.6	17.4	20.0	9.1	11.2	3.0	20.4	17	36.8	38.1
Ireland	14.5	14.7	18.4	14.4	15.1	19.0	..	29.3	39	68.5	57.4
Italy	8.8	15.6	15.5	15.5	46.2	54.0	4.8	26.7	45	59.6	63.3
Luxembourg	3.0	4.3	5.8	3.5	..	(29.0)	..	(23.5)	(42)	(33.8)	(24.6)
Netherlands	6.5	8.1	10.8	9.0	34.1	25.6	27.6	69.9	21	50.0	48.7
Austria	3.9	4.9	5.6	..	(4.5)	9.2	..	34.2	..	24.6	30.6
Portugal	5.9	7.8	8.9	9.4	11.4	17.0	..	3.7	30	42.3	44.3
Finland	17.8	16.2	17.6	..	26.5	30.6	4.7	11.1	..	42.0	31.5
Sweden	8.8	7.4	..	..	8.8	7.7	9.9	17.5	..	23.4	15.9
UK	11.4	7.4	10.3	11.6	8.7	12.2	5.5	48.4	38	51.2	33.9
E12	10.2	13.0	..	..	15.9	21.4	4.3	22.7	..	46.8	49.6

	Rate of inflow into unemployment (1993) [a,g]			Rate of outflow from unemployment (1993) [b,g]			Ratio of unemployment rate of those with less than upper secondary education to those with third level of education (1994)	
	Total	Male	Female	Total	Male	Female	Male	Female
Belgium	0.42	0.43	0.41	8.6	9.2	8.0	2.7	4.3
Denmark	1.75	1.91	1.61	21.4	21.6	21.4	2.2	2.6
Germany (u)	0.57	0.64	0.51	9.0	9.3	8.8	3.5	2.0
Greece	0.30	0.30	0.30	4.7	5.6	4.0	1.1	1.4
Spain	0.56[e]	0.44	0.67	2.7[e]	2.9	2.4	1.7	1.5
France	0.37[e]	0.37	0.38	3.0[e]	2.9	3.0	2.1	2.4
Ireland	0.55[f]	0.60	0.52	3.8[f]	2.8	5.7	4.3	3.9
Italy	0.41	0.44	0.38	9.5	8.9	10.0	1.7	1.6
Luxembourg	..	..	..	..	..	..	1.4	..
Netherlands	0.24	0.28	0.19	6.4	6.5	6.3	2.5	2.3
Austria	..	..	..	..	..	..	(2.0) 4.6[d]	(2.2) 5.5[d]
Portugal	0.34	0.37	0.31	15.3	18.3	12.6	1.8	3.8
Finland	2.83	0.37	0.31	15.3	18.3	12.6	1.8	3.8
Sweden	1.14[e]	1.25	1.02	18.4[e]	17.7	19.5	2.8	2.9
UK	0.67	0.82	0.53	9.3	7.8	12.4	3.0	2.5
E12	..	..	..	..	..	..	2.3	2.0

Sources: European Labour Force Survey (1992, 1994); OECD (1995c:Tables R, S).

Notes

.. indicates no reliable data available.
a Source population = working population minus the unemployed.
b Source population = the unemployed.
c Data from 1993.
d Data from National reports, Austria: Pastner (1996:69).
e Data from 1994.
f Data from 1992.
g Data from OECD (1995c:Table 1.9).

Table 4.6 Characteristics of youth (15–24 years) unemployment by member state, 1994

	Unemployment rates[a]		Share of 1st-time jobseekers among the unemployed[a]		Share of long-term unemployed among the unemployed[a]		Share of unemployed searching for part-time work[a]		Monthly rate of inflows and outflows from unemployment (1993)[b]		Share of unemployed receiving benefits (1993)[a]	
	Men	Women	Men	Women	Men	Women	Men	Women	Inflows	Outflows	Men	Women
Belgium	20.5	23.4	59.1	56.1	38.9	40.5	..	6.2	3.45	29.4	78.0	81.6
Denmark	10.2	10.2	..	17.1	14.8	13.9	23.0	18.2	0.76	13.9	45.2	44.8
Germany (u)	9.4	8.4	14.3	15.8	22.4	32.7	2.2	13.7	0.95	6.1	64.7	64.1
Greece	19.8	36.9	74.9	76.9	36.1	54.1	4.7	4.6	1.06c	3.9	..	..
Spain	41.4	49.7	35.4	45.2	41.0	51.1	2.5	5.9	0.48c	4.4	14.7	12.5
France	27.2	30.5	29.5	30.2	20.6	23.2	3.3	10.3	0.89	5.5	31.0	31.0
Ireland	25.1	20.5	44.2	44.7	56.8	47.2			0.82d	9.6	71.4	57.7
Italy	28.7	35.4	69.8	72.7	59.9	62.5	5.0	15.0	..	..	3.2	3.1
Luxembourg	8.5	7.2										
Netherlands	13.6	9.0	71.4	64.6	43.4	37.0	45.0	54.0	0.41	11.4	36.1	25.5
Austria	5.7	6.2	..	32.9	(14.3)	..	..	(19.2)	..	..	60.6	46.1
Portugal	12.5	16.9	27.6	36.7	31.7	36.9	..	23.0	0.63	19.2	7.4	11.7
Finland	41.3	41.1	74.6	74.5	23.4	11.3	14.4	23.0	4.2	22.6	50.9	31.9
Sweden	20.2	17.8	23.4	12.6	16.9	(8.1)	11.0	14.9	2.26	28.2	53.9	48.4
UK	19.3	12.8	26.0	34.5	37.6	23.9	10.1	34.6	1.7c	11.4	..	..
E12	21.7	22.4	39.7	46.2	38.9	42.6	6.1	13.4	0.93	11.7	19.5	18.9

Sources: European Labour Force Survey (1994, 1995); OECD (1995c:27).

Notes

.. indicates no reliable data available.
a Data from Austria, Finland and Sweden refer to 1995.
b Data from OECD (1995c:Table 1.9).

c Data from 1994.
d Data from 1992.

roughly equal in three. The lower chance of exit from unemployment contributes to women's over-representation among the long-term unemployed in nine countries, so that women often face a doubly higher risk, of moving into unemployment and of staying there. Women in all countries tended to move more rapidly between economic activity statuses, with flows between employment, unemployment and inactivity all exceeding the relevant flows for men. This higher mobility probably reflects a less stable attachment to labour force participation, but also greater job instability; for example, in a number of countries a higher share of women tend to enter unemployment from the ending of temporary contracts. Countries vary in the actual rate of flow between employment statuses (see Rubery *et al.* 1998a:134), but what is perhaps interesting is the increasing flows of men between employment and inactivity, suggesting that there is some convergence in male and female employment patterns, with men becoming less firmly integrated into the labour force at the same time as the permanency of women's attachment is increasing.

Table 4.5 also shows the ratio of unemployment rates for those with higher education to those with just compulsory education, for both men and women. The ratios were all greater than two in 1994, implying at least a doubling of the risk of unemployment, except in Greece, Spain, Italy and Luxembourg for both women and men and in Portugal for men only. High unemployment among first-time jobseekers in the Southern European countries and higher labour force commitment among the more educated women in the South may help explain the lower ratios. In contrast, Austria has particularly high ratios, implying a much greater risk of unemployment among the less educated. The gender gap in unemployment rates tends to narrow with education (see Table 4.4), so that the gap was less than 3 percentage points for highly educated core-age workers in all countries except Spain and Italy. The greatest narrowing was found in Belgium, where it fell from nearly 10 percentage points for the lower educated to under 1 percentage point for the higher educated, and in the UK where it fell from over 5 to under 1 percentage point. However, the gender gap in Belgium was in favour of men, but in the UK in favour of women, so that it was less educated women in Belgium and less educated men in the UK whose unemployment risk was very high.

Having a child increased the risk of unemployment for women in most countries, with Germany and Greece the exceptions. This risk increased particularly in Denmark,[3] the UK and France, but there was no systematic tendency for it to be higher when the child was very young. Very different shares of unemployed women were looking for part-time work in 1994, ranging from under 10 per cent in Greece, Spain and Portugal to 48 per cent in the UK and 70 per cent in the Netherlands. These differences reflected labour market institutions, with low shares of the unemployed seeking part-time work in countries with limited part-time opportunities. However, the matching was not complete, with Germany, Belgium, Denmark, Sweden and France recording lower shares of the unemployed seeking part-time work than might be expected from the share of part-time work in the labour market.

Differences in systems of labour market organisation were particularly evident in the case of the youth labour market. Female youth unemployment rates exceeded male rates in 7 out of 15 countries, with the largest gaps in favour of men found in Ireland, the UK and the Netherlands, but the gender gap was generally lower than for all age groups. In some countries, particularly Italy and Greece but also Belgium, the Netherlands, Spain, Finland and Ireland, high youth unemployment rates resulted from a high share of first-time jobseekers (see Table 4.6). In Italy in particular, initial entry into employment is a major problem for many young people so that first-time jobseekers under 25 accounted for around a quarter of ILO unemployed women and men in 1994.

The difficulty that young people face in finding a first job in some countries, or a permanent job in the case of countries such a Spain, was highlighted not only by the high unemployment rates but also the high incidence of long-term unemployment. In Spain, Greece and Italy, more than half of unemployed young women had been out of work for more than a year and the same was true for unemployed young men in Ireland and Italy. Looking at the share of the youth unemployed who were searching for a part-time job, we find that it is the young women who were more likely to be looking for part-time work, except in Denmark. However, the proportion of ILO unemployed women looking for part-time work was lower among those aged under 25 than over 25 in all countries except Finland, but the opposite was the case for young men. In the Netherlands, Denmark and the UK there were particularly high shares of the young unemployed searching for part-time work. There were also significant differences in the proportions of young unemployed receiving benefits (see Table 4.6), although gender differences in shares were less significant than for the unemployed as a whole (see Table 4.7).

Thus the characteristics of the unemployed, both male and female, measured by age, education, relationship to past employment experience, the period spent in unemployment and desire for future employment, all varied between member states, calling for specific approaches to employment policy which take into account gender- and country-specific differences.

The welfare state and family system

State policies influence the integration of women into the labour market through their shaping of both the household or family system on the one hand and the labour market system on the other. While full economic independence for women and full equality at the family and household level has yet to be achieved in any member state, by the mid-1990s countries had made very different rates of progress towards equality. Member states ranged across a spectrum from strong male breadwinner states, to modified male bread winner states to weak male breadwinner states (Lewis 1992; see Box 4.1). A strong breadwinner state – for example Ireland or Germany – tends to define wives as dependent upon their spouse and either discourages or provides little incentive for women's employment when they are married or have children. A weak breadwinner state – found in most Scandinavian countries – is organised on the presumption that all fit adults of working age are employed or looking for work, that taxation and entitlement to benefits should be mainly based on the individual and not the household, and that parental employment needs to be facilitated through childcare subsidies or leave for care responsibilities. Somewhere between these two extremes fall the modi- fied breadwinner states which do provide some facilities for parental leave and/or some incentive or encouragement for women to work but whose policies may be contradictory, with some elements supporting independence for women and others reinforcing dependency. France, for example, has a family-based taxation system, associated with strong breadwinner states, but significant support for childcare. The UK, on the other hand, has indivi- dualised taxation, but a high level of means-testing in its welfare system and has provided little or no support for childcare.

The influences that state policies may have on women's employment posi- tion include direct employment effects, in the sense of a large welfare state increasing the demand for female labour (see Chapter 1); indirect employ- ment effects, through influences on the incentives for women to enter the labour market or on the types of jobs for which they make themselves avail- able; and effects on the system of social reproduction, including the fertility rate and the system of childcare, which in turn shapes the pattern of employ- ment for both women and men in the labour market. The impact of state policies on women's access to employment provides too narrow a frame- work for assessment of gender equity; also at stake is the more general issue of whether they promote gender equity in access to resources, and not only for those who have adopted the standard lifestyle of a married couple. Assessment of the equity implications should also take into account the interests of children and of the rights of both parents to engage in child- care. With these criteria in mind, we look at how the welfare state systems in the member states have promoted or hindered gender equity, and consider the recent and predicted future developments in state policies within this assessment framework. Welfare state policies are examined under four head- ings: passive and active labour market measures; social security and pension policy; taxation and benefits; and family policy. Then trends in the gender division of domestic labour and housework are reviewed.

Passive and active labour market policies

While women's employment rates rose in all member states in the 1980s and early 1990s, the share of women who were non-employed varied dramatically between member states. The share of the non-employed who define themselves as unemployed may depend on the form of state policies towards unemployed women and on social norms. In strong male bread-winner states it may be more common for women to define themselves as inactive or as housewives, compared to those member states where most adults are expected to be either working or looking for work (see Figure 4.8). In these states, access to unemployment benefits often requires contribution records showing recent and relatively continuous employment, and often for more than a minimum number of hours per week. These requirements present a barrier for women who may have interrupted careers and return to work part-time. In addition, some systems – particularly Germany, the UK and Finland – normally require unemployment benefit recipients to be available for full-time work and, if applicable, to be able to make alternative childcare arrangements at short notice. Under these conditions women who have contributed to unemployment benefits while in employment are not able to claim benefits as they have made insufficient contributions, are unavailable for full-time work or cannot meet the availability for work tests. For example, stricter eligibility conditions in Spain reduced the coverage of the unemployment benefit system by 10 percentage points between 1993 and 1994, from 67.2 per cent to 57.8 per cent of the registered unemployed. Women were disproportionately excluded as they did not meet the rising requirements for continuous employment records (National reports, Spain: Moltó 1996:76).

Table 4.7 shows the share of the ILO unemployed receiving benefits by gender and by country. The Scandinavian countries, together with Belgium and Germany, had relatively high and gender equal rates of benefit coverage in 1994, while the Southern European countries and Luxembourg had low rates for both men and women. It was in the middle-ranking countries, together to some extent with Spain, that the main gender differences emerged. In Ireland, the UK, the Netherlands and Spain the proportion of unemployed men who received benefits was at least 1.8 times the incidence for unemployed women. This applied to Greece too, but here the main problem was the low overall rate of coverage, as even with this gender advantage only 10 per cent of men received benefits.

The wide variety of eligibility conditions between member states by length of contributions required are also outlined in Table 4.7, while Figure 4.9 shows the variety in the maximum length of time for which benefit recipients received non-means-tested benefits in 1995. These two factors together determine access to non-means-tested benefits. Duration of benefits varied from an unlimited period in Belgium (in theory, but subject to restrictions, especially for those – mainly women – who were not household heads), to six months for ordinary unemployment benefits in Italy, together with the UK, which cut the maximum length from one year to six months at the end of 1996. The direction of change over the early 1990s was towards a reduction in non-means-tested benefits, except in Finland. In Finland access to

Table 4.7 Unemployment benefit systems in the EU member states

	A Share of ILO unemployed receiving unemployment benefits or assistance, 1994		B Continuity requirements for unemployment benefits	C Requirements affecting access of part-timers to unemployment benefits	D Duration of non-means-tested benefits
	Male	Female			
High share					
Finland	90.4	91.6	Low	High	Medium
Belgium	84.0	85.8	Medium	High	Long
Sweden	78.7	76.8ᵃ	Low	High	Short
Denmark	68.2	70.4	Low	Medium	Long
Germany	77.5	69.2	Low	High	Medium
Medium share					
Austria	74.6	56.5ᵇ	Medium	Lowᶜ	Short
France	53.5	43.8	Medium	Low	Medium
Ireland	82.0	42.9	High	High	Short
UK	71.0	36.8ᵈ	Medium	High	Short
Netherlands	62.2	33.9	Medium	Low	Long
Low share					
Luxembourg	26.6	30.7ᵉ	Medium	Medium	Medium
Portugal	25.5	23.5	High	—	Medium
Spain	37.4	19.2	Low	Low	Medium
Italy	8.5	7.1	Mediumᶠ	—	Short
Greece	10.2	5.2	Low	—	Short
E12	38.1	33.0	—	—	—

Sources: European Labour Force Survey (1994, 1995); Grimshaw and Rubery (1997a).

Notes
— indicates no data available.
Column B:
Low: less than 6 months in past year or equivalent;
Medium: approximately equal to 6 months in past year or equivalent;
High: greater than 6 months in past year.
Column C:
Low: minimum hours' threshold of 12 hours or less; no requirement to be available for full-time work;
Medium: minimum hours' threshold more than 12 hours but less than 17; no requirement to be available for full-time work;
High: minimum hours' threshold of 17 hours or more, or minimum earnings requirement, or requirement to be available for full-time work.
Column D:
Short: 15 months maximum or less;
Medium: more than 15 months maximum but less than 3 years maximum;
Long: more than 3 years maximum.
a 1990 data.
b Data for share in receipt of benefits in Austria is for 1995.
c In Austria, benefits are earnings related with no minimum level for part-timers.
d Data is missing from the Eurostat data for the UK and therefore derives from national LFS data for the UK, Winter 1995/96.
e Data is missing for Luxembourg and therefore figures refer to 1991 data based on the annual ILO census (National reports, Luxembourg: Plasman 1995).
f Italy details refer to 'ordinary unemployment benefits'.

180 days of the flat-rate labour-market support benefit, after the exhaustion of the 500 days' unemployment entitlement benefits linked to previous income, was excluded from means-testing. However, an employment qualification of six months' employment in the past two years was imposed for the 180 days' labour market support, with the result that in practice the proportion of unemployed women claiming this benefit decreased, as fewer were able to meet the employment requirement. Thus, in practice, whether more women appear under means-tested or insurance benefits will also depend upon the employment requirements for the insurance benefits. A similar perverse effect was found in Spain, where women were more likely to receive the means-tested unemployment assistance than unemployment benefit, as the former had less stringent employment record requirements, such that some young women coming to the end of a temporary contract qualified for assistance (National reports, Spain: Moltó 1996:77).

The level of unemployment benefits varied considerably between countries, an institutional constraint on labour markets recognised in all the major analyses of employment patterns and prospects. However, what is less well recognised is that both the level of benefits and access to benefits varied markedly by gender. The OECD Jobs Study (OECD 1994a) did try to address this issue, but its efforts at introducing a gender dimension into the analysis were inadequate. First, it failed to deal with differences in coverage of benefits by gender, as revealed in Table 4.7. Second, although the OECD did consider differences in the replacement rates for women and men, in practice the only adjustment made in the estimated replacement rate related to the greater likelihood that men would receive a dependent spouse

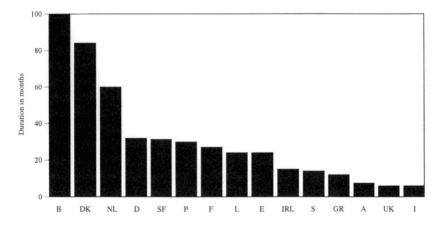

Figure 4.9 Maximum duration of non-means-tested unemployment benefits

Source: Rubery *et al.* (1998a: Table 5.4).

Note
Duration of benefits is the maximum where duration is subject to contribution record.

allowance; otherwise replacement rates were calculated on the basis of women and men receiving the same wage, that is the average male production worker's wage.

Table 4.8 estimates replacement rates based on average female wages for women and average male wages for men. Where the unemployment benefit system provided a fixed percentage replacement rate the ratio was the same, but where the system provided an element of flat-rate benefits, or minimum or maximum thresholds, the replacement rates varied, usually with the female replacement rate exceeding that for men, except in Germany where the benefits were based on net earnings, which tended to be higher for men because of the tax system (see Table 4.10). The replacement rate was often higher for women, particularly under flat-rate systems, simply because women earned lower wages. Care must be taken in interpreting this result, as often these flat-rate payments were so low that in practice the unemployed also claimed additional means-tested benefits for which only household heads tend to be eligible.

Debates about whether the level of unemployment benefits reduces incentives to work, or alternatively whether minimum wage levels are too high, are often conducted at a relatively unsophisticated level, without reference to the different entitlement to benefits among the unemployed, or indeed to differences in the level of wages on offer to groups of the unemployed (Grimshaw and Rubery 1997a). Where many people are excluded from benefits, the unemployment benefit system fails to provide a floor to wages during periods of high unemployment. Those without access to benefits may take on low-wage work, either within the formal sector in deregulated markets or in the informal sector. Where wages are allowed to fall to very low levels the effect may be to decrease the flexibility of the labour market as it becomes more difficult for the unemployed to move into work at wages that would be sufficient to provide for their subsistence (Gregg and Wadsworth 1995). Thus labour market deregulation can lead to increased labour market segmentation, in which wage levels in some job areas are so low that jobs can only be taken by those who are living in households with other employed persons such as married women and young people or by those outside the benefit system. Yet the failure to recognise this wage segmentation leads to pressure to reduce benefit levels rather than to establish a better floor to wages in the labour market.

Once benefits are means-tested, women are much less likely than men to receive benefits as they are more likely to have a spouse whose employment income places them outside the scope of the means-tested benefits. When the male unemployed move on to means-tested benefits, their spouse's income is usually less likely to be sufficient to provide an alternative to benefits and women may be under pressure to leave the labour market (McLaughlin 1995). The result is not only to deprive women of independent income but also to promote the social exclusion of whole households. Means-tested systems often impose very high marginal tax rates on additional

Table 4.8 Replacement rate for the initial period of unemployment benefits based on average gross weekly earnings of men and women working as full-time manual workers in manufacturing[a] (October 1993)

	Formula for replacement rate	Addition for dependent spouse	Threshold level	Actual replacement rates for full-time manufacturing manual workers			
				Ratio of gross benefits to gross earnings for a single person		Ratio assuming men claim for a dependent spouse	
				Men	Women	Men	Women
Belgium	55%	5%	Yes	0.44	0.55	0.48	0.55
Denmark	90%	No	Yes	0.63	0.77	0.63	0.77
Germany[b]	60% (of net earnings)	No	Yes	0.36	0.38	0.41	0.5
Greece	40%	10% of benefit	Yes	0.25	0.32	0.28	0.32
Spain	70%	No	Yes	0.66	0.70	0.66	0.70
France	(40.4% + 1645FF) or 57.4%	No	Yes	0.58	0.63	0.58	0.63
Ireland	IR£55.60 p.w.	IR£35.50	n/a	0.21	0.33	0.33	0.33
Italy	20%	No	No	0.20	0.20	0.20	0.20
Luxembourg	80%	No	Yes	0.80	0.80	0.80	0.80
Netherlands	70%	No	Yes	0.70	0.70	0.70	0.70
Austria[c]	60% of net earnings	Yes[d]	Yes	—	—	—	—
Portugal	65%	No	Yes	0.65	0.65	0.65	0.65
Finland	Ranges from 38% to 77%[e]	No	No	0.58	0.62	0.58	0.62
Sweden	75%	No	Yes	0.70	0.75	0.70	0.75
UK	UK£45.45	UK£28.05	n/a	0.15	0.25	0.25	0.25

Source: Rubery *et al.* (1998a).

Notes
a See Rubery *et al.* (1998a:Appendix) for details.
b Calculation of replacement rates for married men and women is complicated by the impact of the 'joint assessment system' (see p. 158 for details).
c We have been unable to collect figures for average gross earnings for men and women, and therefore have not reported estimates for actual replacement rates.
d A small nominal addition up to 600 Austrian shillings per month is available in the form of a family allowance which also covers long-term partners, children and other family members (National reports, Luxembourg: Pastner 1995:71).
e The range is based on an earnings-related formula.

household earnings, discouraging labour market participation of spouses. Figure 4.10 shows that the likelihood of an individual being unemployed in 1996 was increased if his or her spouse was also unemployed. This concentration of unemployment among certain households is likely to be associated with the characteristics of household members, including educational levels, but what is notable is that women were much more likely to be pulled into unemployment by the unemployment of their spouse than were men. Household means-testing has taken on greater not lesser importance in the unemployment benefit system in many countries (OECD 1996), with potentially negative consequences for women.

In the 1990s member states promoted the advantages of flexible employment contracts and flexible employment careers, but the overall direction of change was towards stricter entitlements for benefits, based on more continuous employment, and without improved access for part-timers, except for those who entered part-time work directly from unemployment. This latter group may be offered the protection of unemployment benefit, a policy that could create a gender divide amongst part-timers, as more women than men enter part-time work directly from inactivity and thus will not benefit from this enhanced protection (Rubery 1998a). The direction of change in the past was towards wider coverage of social protection, especially in Southern European countries such as Spain and Portugal, but as we have seen above, there was a reversal of this policy in Spain, with tighter restrictions on eligibility and also a failure to extend coverage to the growing atypical employment forms such as part-time work and apprenticeship contracts. More women and young people were thus likely to remain outside the social protection system (National reports, Spain: Moltó 1996:4). In the 1990s Italy failed to reform its social protection system, which covered only a small minority of the unemployed. While most of the unemployed in Italy were first-time jobseekers, the unemployment protection largely covered those made redundant from large companies. Policy objectives to widen the unemployment coverage and reduce protection for the redundant failed to materialise (National reports, Italy: Bettio and Villa 1996:34); instead more resources were devoted to those made redundant as soon as the 1990s recession began to bite. These policies systematically discriminated against both young people and women. In Denmark, where there was scope for individual choice over whether to join an unemployment insurance scheme or not, there was a reverse process. More women than men were insured in 1993, and more women were opting for full-time instead of part-time insurance, with the growth of full-time insured women exceeding the already rapid growth of full-time female employment in Denmark (National reports, Denmark: Boje 1996:Table 29). These changes underline the commitment by Danish women to economic independence.

However, Denmark stands out as one of the few countries in which the share of part-time work fell in the early 1990s. The changes in labour market organisation, away from full-time and continuous employment contracts and

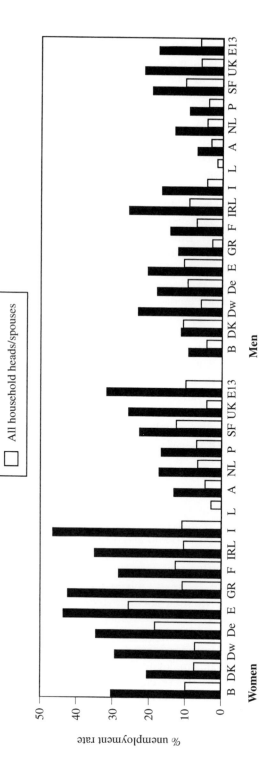

Figure 4.10 Unemployment rates for women and men with an unemployed spouse, 1996

Sources: European Labour Force Survey (1996); Eurostat (1993).

Note
Data for Denmark refer to 1990.

towards high levels of unemployment for those without recent employment experience, call into question the principles underlying the unemployment benefit system in many member states. There was no evidence that proposed reforms involved a redesign of the system in order to match developments in the labour market. For example, Austria and Germany cut benefits or increased contribution records to meet the Maastricht convergence criteria but with no significant change in the principles behind the insurance system. The burden of flexibility was increasingly being borne by labour market participants, particularly women and young people, whose employment patterns often excluded them from independent access to benefits.

In the 1990s policy-makers stressed the advantages of active over passive labour market policies for both personal and economic reasons. An emphasis on active labour market policies characterises the Nordic welfare states, which have also been associated with gender equity. However, the Nordic welfare states have combined an active labour market policy for all fit adults with extensive provision not only for childcare but also for parental leave. The effect of a switch to active labour market policies that place more pressure on those not in work to participate, but without adequate childcare or parental leave protection, may be to further reduce the importance accorded to care work. In the Netherlands the reform of the welfare system resulted in the presumption that all claiming benefit should be seeking work, except for those with responsibility for a child under 5 (National reports, Netherlands: Plantenga *et al.* 1996:50). The implications of this change were that care work was no longer to be regarded as a basis for state support once children reached the age of 5. Similarly, in the UK single mothers faced increasing pressure to seek work during the 1990s. The individualisation of care responsibilities in the name of creating a working society marginalises the interests of both children and women.

Access to active labour market policies has itself still often been restricted to those eligible for benefits. Consequently, many women were excluded because of their lower entitlement to benefits. Even those who had recently been in employment had less eligibility because of short-hours or temporary contracts and many unemployed women might be returning to the labour market after an extended break to look after children. Some countries extended eligibility rights to women returners, but often only on special schemes or on standard schemes only if places were available.

Thus despite their over-representation among the unemployed, women were often under-represented in active labour market schemes, especially where these involved direct work experience and participation in workplace-based training or job creation schemes. Concentration of policies on the registered unemployed or those claiming benefits, or indeed on the redundant from heavy industry, leads to indirect discrimination against women. The tendency to regard unemployment as mainly a problem for men was evident in many countries in the 1990s: in the distribution of resources in Germany to ease the transition in heavy industries in East Germany; in the development of short-time programmes for the redundant workers in Italy, and in the reduced representation of Finnish women in active labour market policies focused primarily on the longer-term unemployed among whom men were over-represented (National reports, Germany: Maier *et al.* 1996:24; Italy: Bettio and Villa 1996:34; Finland: Keinänen 1996:75). Mainstreaming gender into active labour market policies requires a rethink of current practices; Box 4.3 outlines some principles that could be integrated into a new gender-sensitive approach to active labour market policy. Through NOW (New Opportunity for Women) and the subsequent Employment-NOW initiatives the European Commission attempted to provide some assistance to offset this discrimination by providing some of the structural funds for programmes targeted specifically at women. The results were mixed, in part because the schemes have been concerned to provide retraining opportunities for women but without any policies to change the attitudes and practices of employers. As a consequence, in Spain the programmes designed to help women establish new businesses in which they were not dependent upon employers appeared to be the most successful (National reports, Spain: Moltó 1996:87).

Box 4.3 Towards gender-friendly active labour market policies

Mainstreaming gender equality into the design of active labour market policies involves consideration of the following issues:

- eligibility requirements, including extending access to women who want to work but who do not fulfil requirements for unemployment benefit;
- the design of policies to ensure that women are not concentrated in programmes remote from employment while men are over-represented in on-the-job, employer-led programmes;
- the coverage of programmes to ensure that male-dominated jobs or sectors are not given priority over female-dominated jobs and sectors;
- the provision of access to childcare, especially in countries where childcare is limited;
- closer integration of positive action and women-only training courses with actual job opportunities and targeted in areas of expanding employment;
- policies to ensure that the encouragement of participation by welfare recipients does not involve unreasonable pressure on single parents to work without adequate childcare facilities.

Social security and pension policy

Social security systems in many countries are still organised around the principle of a primary and thus male breadwinner. In strong male breadwinner states spouses derive most of their rights to social security benefits, including pensions and health care, through their partner. This practice creates the potential for married women to act as a cheap labour supply to the formal and the informal sector, including jobs outside the social security net. Incentives to accumulate individual rights, for example to pensions, may be weak if such benefits are means-tested on household income or if the benefits, for example attached to part-time jobs, are unlikely to provide a significant source of independent income. Evidence from many member states points to periods out of the labour market caring for a child being less favourably treated than periods of sickness or unemployment, for entitlements to pensions (see for example CEC 1993). Where it is difficult to make up for these gaps in employment history, women may not be concerned to find work within the social security net. Moreover, the unemployed, including here many women, may be more likely to take up low-paid or informal sector work where they are excluded from access to unemployment benefits. Some countries have extended social security rights to atypical workers over the 1990s, including freelance workers and homeworkers, but the effectiveness of these measures depends upon the incentives for both employers and employees to comply with the regulations. There are few grounds for believing that the extension of social security to cover homeworkers or freelance working in Greece, Spain and Portugal, for example, in the early 1990s successfully brought these sectors within the social security net. Nevertheless, this extension of coverage, including for example the extension of pension coverage to the self-employed in Italy, can be regarded as an important point of principle, that pension rights should not be limited to those in full-time wage employment.

Three types of pension systems can be identified: the basic security system in which pensions are universal, based on citizenship and not employment history; the income security system in which pensions are based on employment history and are strongly earnings related; and a residual pension system which provides only a low level of benefits and the gap between the basic pension and required income standards is made up either through private pension provision or through means-tested benefits (Ginn and Arber 1994, 1998 and see Table 4.9).

Women tend to fare best in those countries that provide a basic pension system in which access is based more on citizenship and less on employment record; they fare worst in the residual protection systems. The most popular European pension system is the income security system which tends to provide relatively high pension entitlements based on past employment records. Men are more likely to accumulate such rights but the income security system also often provides better derived rights to women than the residual systems. Such systems still discriminate against those women who are outside stable partnerships.

Figure 4.11 shows pension entitlements as a percentage of male average net earnings in manufacturing, comparing entitlements under a full contributory pension and a pension based on social assistance. The best pension

Table 4.9 Pension systems in EU member states

Pension system	Country
Residual	UK, Ireland
Income security	Germany, Belgium, France, Greece, Italy, Spain, Portugal, Luxembourg, Austria
Basic security	Denmark, Netherlands, Finland, Sweden

Sources: Rubery *et al.* (1998a); Ginn and Arber (1994).

Notes
Residual = state plays a minimal role, family and market roles emphasised.
Income security = state ensures high earning-related benefit for those with adequate employment record.
Basic security = state provides a universal benefit.

entitlements as a percentage of earnings were provided in countries following the income security model, but these pension entitlements varied with earnings and thus favoured men. Moreover, those who rely on social assistance, which may include many women outside conventional family relationships, face a much lower replacement rate. In Portugal, for example, a much higher percentage of women were found on the basic social assistance pension than men (National reports, Portugal: Lopes and Perista 1996:62). The basic security systems, illustrated here by Denmark, the Netherlands and Sweden, tended to provide a reasonable social assistance pension and there is less advantage, at least for low-paid workers, in obtaining a full contributory pension (except in Sweden). In the residual systems the replacement rate

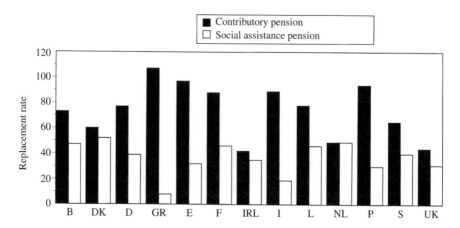

Figure 4.11 Average replacement rates for a full contributory state pension and a social assistance pension

Sources: CEC (1993); National reports, Sweden: Gonäs and Spånt (1996).

for both the state full contributory pension and for the social assistance minimum was low, indicating the need to rely on private pension systems or additional means-tested benefits for an adequate income in old age.

Women would benefit more from a move towards higher basic benefits as a citizen's right than towards pension rights based on women's own work histories. Even in the Scandinavian countries which have moved to individualised rights within a context of a universal pension entitlement, the evidence showed that women received lower pension entitlements than men on account of interrupted work histories, shorter working hours and lower pay rates. In Sweden no credits have been granted for those out of the labour market to raise children within the supplementary pension system (National reports, Sweden: Gonäs and Spånt 1996:94). A move to individualisation of rights thus needs to be combined with a rapid improvement in women's labour market position or towards a universal pension provision based on citizenship.

In the 1990s many pension systems were moving in the opposite direction, from a universal benefit provision towards reduced basic pensions, longer contribution periods for full pensions, increased reliance on private or occupational provision and a rising retirement age for women to meet requirements for equal treatment. Women are likely to be the losers because their weak position in the labour market reduces their access to private pension provision. Moves towards longer contribution periods clearly disadvantage women, but changes to the period over which pension entitlements are calculated can have perverse effects: for example, in France the extension of the period from 10 to 25 years in practice hit men harder than women because their earnings rose more steeply with age. However, the move towards calculating entitlement based on lifetime earnings, as for example in the UK state earnings-related system, clearly disadvantaged women as they were more likely to have had breaks out of the labour market (National reports, UK: Rubery and Smith 1995). The only trend towards improvement in women's pension rights came in countries such as Austria, in which credits for periods out of the labour market spent in childcare were granted for the purpose of qualifying for the basic state pension. The high level of marital instability causes severe problems for the principle of derived rights, with European member states differing in regulations as to rights of former wives and husbands. Furthermore, in a residual system divorced women can suffer if they have spent time out of the labour market caring or in low-paid part-time work. In 1998 the UK government began implementing legislation to provide for pension splitting in divorce settlements.

Tax and benefits policy

Male breadwinner systems of household organisation can only function if men are able to earn wages in the labour market sufficient to support themselves and their dependants or if households with a dependent spouse and children receive state subsidies and support. Support for male bread-winner households is often provided through the taxation system. Systems which take the household instead of the individual as the basic unit of taxa-tion tend to impose high marginal taxes on second-income earners, thereby discouraging participation by the spouse, while providing tax subsidies to households with dependent wives and children.

Eight countries had adopted the principle of individual taxation by the mid-1990s while in seven the household remained the unit of taxation (although options for individual taxation exist in a further five) (see Table 4.10). Three of the seven with household systems aggregated household income for tax purposes, two split the joint income between partners and two divided the income by a family quotient which took into account the number of adults and children. Household taxation provides a particularly strong disincentive to participation when it is based on income splitting and when, as in Germany, the marginal tax rates vary significantly by income level. In Belgium the effect was less strong, as only 30 per cent of the partner's earnings could be transferred to a non-working spouse for tax purposes, while in Germany a full 50 per cent could be transferred. On the other hand, individualised taxation systems provide strong incentives to participation on an equal basis when marginal tax rates are high, as was the case in Sweden in the early 1990s.

Just as the household systems mainly provide an option for individualised taxation, some of the individualised systems may also be regarded more as hybrids than as full individual taxation. In two of the countries there was still an allowance for a dependent spouse and one, the UK, gave an allowance for marriage, although this fell in value in the 1990s. In a further two, unused allowances could be transferred to spouses, which again raised the marginal tax rate for the spouse entering employment. The commitment to independent taxation in some countries which had adopted it remained fragile in the early 1990s; in Austria the dependent spouse allowance was increased, albeit from a low level, and a return to household taxation was debated by politicians (National reports, Austria: Pastner 1996:98).

Thus in the majority of EU countries married women faced the prospect of a higher marginal tax rate than would apply to their single counterparts, although the overall taxation rate on the married couple still tended to be lower than that for two single adults. Few countries provided these advan-tages to cohabiting couples, even though such couples were normally taken to constitute a household when means-tested benefits were calculated. The French tax system can be considered an anomaly in this respect for until 1996 the system actually provided a subsidy to cohabiting couples, as each parent could claim a full allowance for a child. The new system treated cohabiting and married couples equally. Nevertheless, the tax system in most countries reinforced the status of marriage.[4] A tax system can be said to support the economic independence of women only if the individual is

Table 4.10 Taxation systems in EU member states

	Taxation system	*Modifications*
Belgium	Income splitting	Maximum 30% of income can be transferred to spouse. Individual taxation option.
Denmark	Individualised	Allowances transferable to spouse.
Germany (u)	Income splitting	Individual taxation option.
Greece	Individualised	
Spain	Aggregation	Individual taxation option. Dependent spouse allowance.
France	Family quotient	
Ireland	Aggregation	Individual taxation option. Dependent spouse allowance
Italy	Individualised	Dependent spouse allowance
Luxembourg	Family quotient	
Netherlands	Individualised	Allowance transferable to spouse.
Austria	Individualised	Dependent spouse allowance.
Portugal	Aggregation	Individual taxation option. Higher allowance for married couple.
Finland	Individualised	
Sweden	Individualised	
UK	Individualised	Marriage allowance.

Source: Rubery *et al.* (1998a).

Notes
Aggregation = household taxation based on the aggregation of earnings of married couples.
Income splitting = aggregated earnings of married couples is divided in two.
Family quotient = aggregation includes children's income; aggregated income is divided by
   family quotient which includes allowance for children.

the basic unit of taxation, and extra tax relief relates to the care of children and not marriage or adult dependence.

However, the impact of household taxation on marginal tax rates may be low and in any case many countries switched from high direct to higher indirect taxes in the 1990s. Rising female earnings more than offset taxation policies designed to promote male breadwinner households in France (National reports, France: Silvera *et al.* 1996:133). Nevertheless many women, even those in cohabiting couples, face severe financial penalties if they enter the labour market because of the loss of means-tested benefits, even where taxation is fully individualised. Thus, for example, women in Finland faced high marginal tax rates when considering re-entering the labour market because of means-tested housing benefits and because of the loss of the child homecare allowance, even though the taxation system is individualised. In contrast in Denmark there were few means-tested benefits in the early 1990s that affected women in couples. However, even here the welfare system imposed high marginal tax rates on lone parents returning to work.

Where means-tested benefits are significant in the support of the unemployed, the result is likely to be social exclusion of whole households. Where governments responded to these problems by providing means-tested benefits for those entering low-paid work, the result has been very high marginal tax rates for the spouses of those receiving in-work benefits. The Family Credit system in the UK imposed very high marginal tax rates on spouses entering the labour market. The unemployment benefit system only allowed couples to retain UK£10 per week, while half any remaining earnings were forfeited to the state and half saved to be reclaimed when the couple moved off benefits and into work.[5] In Ireland the spouse could retain IR£60 before losing benefits when on unemployment benefit and IR£45 when on unemployment assistance. Thus, while means-testing of some sort may be unavoidable, countries differed in the extent to which they allowed the spouse or cohabitee to have some level of independent income before taxing at rates of 100 per cent or more.

The direction of change in benefits was, if anything, towards more means-testing, as governments attempted to increase their targeting of resources to the most needy and to reduce automatic entitlements to benefits. As we have seen above, these changes work to the disadvantage of women. Moreover, in attempting to ease the transition from benefits to employment, new means-tested benefits were introduced (and more measures may be brought in in the future) which increase the constraint on economic activity by the partners of recipients. The disincentive effects of means-tested benefit systems on women's participation tend to be much greater than household-based taxation systems, if only because the former impose very high marginal tax rates. Priority thus needs to be given to designing benefit systems which provide the spouses of benefit recipients with incentives to maintain their employment or to re-enter employment, in the interests both of gender equality and of combating whole-household social exclusion (OECD 1996, 1997b).

Family policy

While taxation policy shapes the incentive to work, childcare and leave policies may be essential to facilitate continuous employment careers for women (see Table 4.11). Family policy may be directed, however, not at facilitating employment but at raising the fertility rate or at improving the education and care of children. Thus the impact on women's participation rates can be contradictory.

State policies with respect to facilitating childcare can include;

- incentives for mothers and/or fathers to take leave on a full or part-time basis;
- direct provision of pre-school childcare;
- help with childcare costs;
- arrangements of school entry dates and school hours to facilitate the participation of parents in employment;
- the provision of after-school care.

Table 4.11 Parental leave and childcare in EU member states

	Length of maternity and parental leave in months after birth of each child	Payment for parental leave	Publicly funded childcare[f] 0–3 of age group covered	School hours
Belgium	27	FR	30	Long day
Denmark	30	FR	48	Medium day
Germany (u)	36	FR[c]	2 (w), 50 (e)	Half day
Greece	9	U	3	Half day
Spain	36	U	2	Long day[g]
France	36	FR[d]	23	Long day
Ireland	3[a]	—	2	Medium day
Italy	9[a]	ER[e]	6	Half day
Luxembourg	2	—	n/a	Half day
Netherlands	15[b]	U	8	Long day[g]
Austria	24	FR	3	—
Portugal	27	U	12	Half day[h]
Finland	36	ER + FR	21	—
Sweden	36	ER	33	—
UK	7[a]	—	2	Medium day

Source: European Childcare Network (1994; 1996).

Notes
FR = flat rate.
ER = earnings-related.
U = unpaid.
a Maternity leave only.
b Includes 6 months per parent part-time leave only.
c Means tested.
d Only paid for families with two or more children.
e Low earnings-related benefit.
f Greece 0–2½, Netherlands 0–4, UK 0–5.
g Long day but with a long lunch break which may or may not be supervised.
h Half day as shortage of places has meant children attending in shifts.

There were major differences in provision between member states in the first half of the 1990s. While maternity leave was provided in all countries, in part under the impetus of an EC directive, the UK, Ireland and Luxembourg[6] had no provision for parental leave prior to the passing of the parental leave directive in the second part of the decade (see Table 4.11). The Netherlands only had the opportunity for part-time leave while three more countries – Spain, Greece and Portugal – only provided unpaid leave. Seven countries provided some paid parental leave but in four of these payment was either low or means-tested – or in the case of France only available for the second child (previously only for the third child). Only three countries, all of them Nordic countries, provided parental leave which was paid at a reasonably high level despite recent reductions in benefit levels. Even here the Danish leave was paid only at 80 per cent of unemployment benefits and was subsequently reduced to 60 per cent in 1997

(Bettio *et al.* 1998b). Sweden and Finland stand out as having parental leave systems involving high individual income replacement ratios, at 75 per cent for Sweden for all women and 66 per cent maximum for Finland, which fell to 25 per cent maximum for high-income earners. Sweden had the most flexible and best-remunerated system, and the opportunity to take full or part-time leave for a maximum of 15 months until a child reached 8, with opportunities for additional unpaid hours' reductions. The EU directive on parental leave agreed will apply to all countries, but it was left to member states to decide whether or not it will be paid.

Parental leave has complex effects on women's labour supply: it strengthens their labour force attachment in a context in which the alternative would be for them to quit work, but it may weaken attachment if it is introduced as a substitute for direct childcare. Where state policy does not back up extended leave with childcare facilities, the system may fail to provide a bridge back into employment and may mainly serve to postpone labour market quits. Such an outcome was evident, for example, in Germany. Leave arrangements in Denmark, Belgium, France and Finland were introduced in a context of a broader work-sharing policy and also in a context where childcare facilities were relatively widely available. If childcare provision were to be cut, the long term impact could be to reduce female involvement in employment and to reinforce their position as carers. The extension of eligibility for extended leave to those with two children in France and to all Finnish women, whether or not in employment, runs the risk that it may reduce the continuity of female participation rather than strengthen it. However, in France the opportunity to take part-time leave was not as popular as expected, confirming perhaps French women's commitment to full-time work (National reports, France: Silvera *et al.* 1996:39). In Finland there was an increase in the number of women in their twenties who were defined as housewives, probably as a result of the introduction of child homecare leave (for all, up until the child is 3) at a time of very poor employment prospects. However, Finnish children still had the right to a childcare place, which should aid women's re-entry to the labour market once the child homecare leave is exhausted.

Most parental leave opportunities were in practice only taken up by women, even when available to men. Only Sweden among EU countries currently required some of the parental leave to be taken by men, and here the take-up rate among fathers was around 40 per cent, even though the number of days taken only accounted for 9 per cent of all leave in 1992 (National reports, Sweden: Lofström 1995:66). The new directive on parental leave moves in the same direction by making the entitlement to parental leave an individual and non-transferable right. However, even in Sweden the parental leave did not fundamentally change the gender division of labour and the result was a high share of women in part-time employment, albeit on a voluntary basis, and a consequent retention of men as dominant household providers, even within an almost universal dual-earner family system.

The spectrum of systems of family and welfare organisations still ranged from strong to weak male breadwinner models, and not from strong male breadwinner to equality models.

Most EU countries failed to provide childcare facilities for children under 3: the Scandinavian countries, the former East Germany, France and Belgium stood out as the only countries with significant provision (see Table 4.11). Coverage above age 3 depended in part on the start of compulsory schooling, which varied significantly between member states. The organisation of schooling has a major influence on women's employment, with some countries only providing part-day schooling, or having unsupervised lunch breaks (see Table 4.11). Out-of-school care can compensate for short compulsory schooling but only Scandinavia, France and Belgium had significant out-of-school provision. The countries which appeared to be doing most to extend childcare provision were those which already provided more publicly funded childcare than most EU countries. Thus France increased resources for childcare by 9 billion francs in 1994, and Sweden established a requirement for childcare places to be available for children under 12 for all couples where both were in work, although more of the childcare costs were to be borne by parents. There is little evidence of convergence in childcare provision across member states. In the early 1990s the UK, with almost the worst provision level, attempted to introduce a controversial system of vouchers for nursery education for all children aged 4 (National reports, UK: Rubery 1996:29). This was scrapped by the incoming government in 1997 in favour of a 'national childcare strategy' based around after-school clubs and childcare tax relief for low-income households. However, the impact may be limited due to low levels of funding and limited coverage.

Most member states provided some elements of this range of family policies, but it is the combination of policies, and the specific form that they take, which determines whether they reinforce women's role as carers or promote the employment of women. The types of policies which do little to support the employment of women, or which may even reinforce the position of women as dependent spouses and carers include:

- extended periods of unpaid or low-paid parental leave combined with limited or no childcare facilities at the end of the leave period to facilitate re-entry into employment;
- short school hours or interrupted schooldays and/or long holidays, combined with limited after-school or holiday childcare arrangements;
- limited provision of publicly funded childcare for pre-school children and a late starting age for compulsory schooling.

It can by no means be assumed that the Nordic example of providing relatively high replacement rates for parents on leave can provide the model for the remaining EU states in implementing the parental leave directive. Most interest in parental leave systems over the 1990s lay in extending either the length of leave (for example in Finland, Denmark and Austria) or extending eligibility (to the second child in France or to both parents as in Sweden and Denmark, or introducing career breaks into the private sector in Belgium). This interest in expanding the amount of leave or the eligibility conditions is consistent with parental leave being used as a relatively cheap form of work sharing in a period of high unemployment. Even this type of policy was under threat with the retrenchment of the welfare state: the extended leave in Austria was cut back shortly after being introduced from two to one and a half years, with a further six months available for fathers only. As the leave was low paid, few fathers took up the option and the move was seen as a means of cutting costs. Indeed, in all countries, except to some extent the Nordic countries, extended parental leave maintains economic dependency and where leave was low paid or unpaid there was very little chance that men would take up the opportunities for leave, even when these were provided as an individual right. In Denmark it was suggested that the system was too inflexible for men to participate in; they had to take at least 13 weeks full-time leave which was regarded by many as too long, involving too large a risk to careers. Shorter or part-time leave was expected to be more popular and the directive on parental leave provided for flexible arrangements, with leave to be full-time, part-time or even based on a time-bank arrangement (Bettio *et al.* 1998a). Here family policy comes up against the reluctance of employers to recognise the care responsibilities of their employees. On the other hand, there is an equal reluctance by the state to take responsibility for children, especially when these children are outside conventional couple households (see for example Austria and the UK, where single mothers were the target of cutbacks in the 1990s). Thus family policy still tends to be oriented towards women in standard couple households.

While welfare state cutbacks, increasing organisational pressures for competitiveness and the political backlash against alternative lifestyles might be expected to lead to a withdrawal of parental and childcare support by both the state and employers, there is another factor, the widespread decline in the fertility rate, which may ensure that family policy stays on the policy agenda. Women seem to be displaying strong resistance to pressure to reverse their labour market emancipation; instead of recession and the cutbacks in welfare provision leading to a return to domestic work, women increased their education, postponed marriage and motherhood and demanded continuous employment in the labour market. Family policies designed to shore up the male breadwinner model do not appear to have worked, and governments may have to stop trying to hold back the tidal move away from the male breadwinner family and belatedly begin to remodel their welfare state systems to match the new patterns of social and labour market organisation emerging in all European societies.

The gender division of domestic labour and care work

Although women on average commit fewer hours to waged work than men (see Chapter 7 below), differences in the total working week – waged and unwaged work – are comparatively small or even reversed (Gershuny *et al.* 1994; Kiernan 1991; Juster and Stafford 1991; Spain and Bianchi 1996; Rubery *et al.* 1998a:198–201). Juster and Stafford (1991, cited in Plantenga 1997) show that the amount of time which women spend on non-waged work is relatively similar across countries, at between 27–33 hours per week in the countries studied, while men's time-contribution to non-waged work varies markedly, from a low of 3.5 hours in Japan to a high of 18 hours in Sweden. However, even in Sweden, it is women who increase their hours of unpaid labour and reduce their hours of waged work when there are young children present. The major factor helping women to retain high and continuous employment rates in Sweden is thus not a more equal gender division of unpaid labour but greater support from the state through paid leave entitlements and a public sector infrastructure for childcare and elder-care (see Table 4.11).

Some research has revealed a lagged adaptation, in that men's contribution to domestic labour has slowly increased in recent decades (Gershuny *et al.* 1994; Van der Lippe and Roelofs 1995). This trend is more pronounced in households where women are in full-time employment, among couples with high levels of education, and for those who endorse a gender role ideology of egalitarian behaviour, with all three characteristics being highly correlated (Corti *et al.* 1995; Dale and Egerton 1995; Deven *et al.* 1997; Gershuny *et al.* 1994; Vogler 1994; Rubery *et al.* 1995:105–108; Seymour 1988). The organisation of the labour market also affects the adaptation of men's behaviour. Men do more domestic work when they themselves have shorter working hours (Fagan 1997; Van der Lippe and Roelofs 1995) and in Britain they also increase their contribution when their 'breadwinner' role is weakened through unemployment or retirement, particularly if their partners remain in, or enter, full-time employment (Pahl 1984; Morris 1985; Laite and Halfpenny 1987; Gallie and Marsh 1994:Table 3.4). Similarly, men's use of parental leave entitlements is affected by the flexibility and wage compensation structure of the scheme, with the highest take-up found in Sweden, although it is still women who are the major users of the Swedish parental leave scheme (Fagan and Rubery 1996a).

The general adjustments made in the household organisation of domestic labour in response to women spending more time on waged work can be summarised as follows (Gershuny *et al.* 1994; Horrell 1994; Van der Lippe and Roelofs 1995). When their partners are employed, men increase their time-input to domestic labour through doing more shopping, cooking and routine housework, but compensate by spending less time on traditionally male tasks (gardening, car and household maintenance) so that their overall time commitment to domestic labour remains largely the same. Women devote less time to domestic work the more hours of paid work they do, although the adjustment is slight for those working short part-time hours. Overall employment increases women's workloads and the main difference is that employed women have less time for leisure, sleep and to spend with their children. Putting men's and women's behaviour together, the overall amount of time allocated to housework falls in dual-employed households, mainly through less time being spent on meal preparation, cleaning and other tidying up. Part of the explanation is probably that less time is spent at home and so less meal preparation and cleaning is required, and lower domestic standards may be accepted. Dual-employed couples may also make more use of private or public sector services to substitute for family-based childcare and domestic production. For example, in Britain dual-earner households purchase more prepared food (Horrell 1991) and certain services, notably childcare and to a lesser extent cleaning and some household maintenance work (Brannen *et al.* 1994; Gregson and Lowe 1994; Warde 1990). However, substituting purchased goods and services for self-provisioning is as much to do with the higher household income that results from the second wage as with the time squeeze when both partners are employed, for among couples with similar income levels expenditure patterns are similar regardless of whether they are dual-employed or single-earner households (Horrell 1991). Thus, consumption patterns in connection with market services and the use of domestic technology are more to do with cultural norms and purchasing power than differences between households in the amount of time available for domestic labour.

The process of lagged adaptation is slow and occurs across generations, and it trails after the increased integration of women into waged work, rather than accompanying or preceding changes in women's workloads. So far, the adjustment which men have made is small and insufficient to compensate for women's increased workloads. A number of studies reveal men's reluctance to do more of what they still see as 'women's work'; the tensions which result as women try to redistribute the domestic division of labour in their households; and how what is accepted as a fair or equitable division of labour is influenced by a number of factors, including gender ideology, the behaviour of peers, the size of the contribution women make to the household's income, and the extent to which women perceive that their partners have increased their effort (Hochschild 1990; Spain and Bianchi 1996; Seymour 1988). It is the slow and so far incomplete process of lagged adaptation that is the reason policy needs to focus on providing the initial infrastructure to support women's participation in the labour market, although in the longer term there will need to be a major change in the gender division of labour within the household if full equality in the labour market is to be achieved.

Summary

The share of the population inside and outside the labour force has been shaped to a considerable extent by the development of state policies (Esping-Andersen 1990). Large welfare states tend to encourage more people to enter the labour force and define themselves as a permanent part of it; yet they also provide more employment through the creation of public sector service jobs, and provide in some cases the possibility of combining permanent attachment to the labour force with forms of work sharing, such as leave arrangements. Both the strong and the weak male breadwinner states face problems, the former because this system is less and less relevant for the large shares of the population who do not live in traditional nuclear families, or do not stay in them over their lifecourse, and the latter because of the perceived high costs of large welfare state provision and the increasing economic and political pressure to cut back on policies which relieved women of some of the burden of care and provided them with independent access to resources. The outcome of these pressures is not yet known; what is perhaps notable is that female employment has been rising in all member states, and this suggests that any policy based on a reinforcement of the male breadwinner model is unlikely to be successful. Thus state policies influence but do not determine social organisation or the aspirations and behaviour of women.

Despite the clear inconsistency between state policies and current family patterns and modes of behaviour (OECD 1994b), there are few signs of a rethink of the male breadwinner model which still underpins many countries' welfare state systems. Instead many trends are in the opposite direction, towards more means-testing, fewer individual rights and more limited support for parents in their attempts to reconcile work and family life (Rubery *et al.* 1998a) – yet at the same time family systems are becoming more complex and fertility rates are falling. The danger is that current policies will promote the principles of employment and self-support without providing the framework of either a large welfare state or a stable family system to guarantee a secure environment for those in need of care. The fragmentation of family systems is coinciding with the cutback of collective social provision, leaving a vacuum to be filled by an individualised, market-based system of care provision in which inequalities between and within sexes and generations will be reinforced. A new gender contract is needed (OECD 1994b) to match current social patterns of organisation with changing labour market patterns and behaviour, but the construction of a new gender contract cannot be left to individual households. Instead, the state needs to play a major role in the updating of the institutional framework within which work and family life can be reconciled.

5 Occupational segregation

European labour markets, in common with most other economies, are highly sex segregated (Anker 1998; Hakim 1992; Watts and Rich 1993; Rubery and Fagan 1993). This is despite a decline in segregation in recent decades, and more generally this century, according to available data series, although some studies suggest a greater degree of change (Anker 1998; Hakim 1981) than others (Blackburn *et al.* 1993). In European economies where a relatively high proportion of jobs are filled by women, this usually coincides with high rather than low levels of sex segregation, thus providing little ground for optimism that further entry of women into the wage economy will in itself bring about the desegregation of the labour market, one of the key objectives of both the third and the fourth action programmes for equal opportunities.

Sex segregated patterns of employment arise from a combination of labour supply and demand conditions (for example Beechey 1977; Walby 1998; Crompton and Sanderson 1990; Reskin and Roos 1990; Rees 1992; Siltanen 1994; Rubery and Fagan 1995b; Rubery *et al.* 1996). On the supply-side, men and women may have different types of skills and qualifications, arising from different socialisation processes or different investments in human capital. The domestic division of labour associated with the 'male bread-winner' presumption of family life also produces gender differences in labour supply conditions, with women expected to take primary responsibility for unpaid care work and housework and men expected to be the main earners. From the demand-side, employers may discriminate against women because they perceive women to be less productive workers due to their actual or presumed domestic responsibilities (statistical discrimination), or because they simply prefer to employ men, owing to their own preferences, the preferences of their existing male workforce or perhaps those of their customers (taste discrimination). More generally, employers may take advantage of the domestic division of responsibilities, along with men's resistance to women entering 'their' jobs, to segregate the sexes into different job areas. This enables employers to restrict access to the better wages, employment security and other employment conditions to those men who have the most market power because of their skills or union organisation. Women may be crowded into a narrow range of jobs as a result, leading to excess supply and lowering wage levels (Bergmann 1974).

The dynamics of change to patterns of occupational segregation arise in a number of ways (Cockburn 1991; Crompton and Sanderson 1990; Reskin and Roos 1990; Rubery and Fagan 1995b; Rubery *et al.* 1996). Employers may start to recruit women in a number of different circumstances. There may be a shortage of male labour, either because the occupation is expanding rapidly or because the occupation has become less attractive to men, owing to it moving down the job hierarchy in terms of relative falls in pay, status or promotion compared to employment opportunities elsewhere. In both circumstances employers may face the choice of recruiting less well qualified men, or turning to equally well qualified or even better qualified women. In other circumstances employers may actively decide to start recruiting women. This may be because the content and structure of the occupation is changing to meet market or technical conditions in such a way that it becomes labelled as 'women's work'. This may be to do with a cost-cutting strategy of reducing labour costs, or the requirement for new skills which women are perceived to possess to a greater extent than men, such as interpersonal communication skills in a more customer-service oriented market. Recruitment practices may also change, owing to anti-discrimination legislation and policies and more general changes in societal norms. From the supply-side, women may start to make different career plans and investment in education, and to adopt more continuous patterns of labour market participation. As we saw in Chapter 3, there have been major changes in women's labour supply. Women's qualification levels are rising and providing a lever for their entry into some of the better-paid professional jobs, although they are still under-represented in certain areas such as engineering, and sex segregation in vocational training is still marked. Women's labour market involvement is also becoming more continuous across the lifecourse with each generation.

In this chapter we look at recent trends in the pattern of segregation across the European Union and assess changes and continuity in this aspect of the organisation of gender differences in the labour market. The first section reviews the problems involved in measuring segregation. This is followed by an analysis of the level of segregation and gender differences in the concentration of employment across the member states, then a section that takes a more disaggregated approach through looking at occupational groups and sub-groups. The chapter then looks at other job features which contribute to the pattern of segregation, particularly the effect of atypical employment contracts. Trends in the level of occupational segregation and vertical segregation over the 1980s and into the 1990s are reviewed. The implications of the analysis for policy are drawn in the final section.

Measuring sex segregation

There is considerable controversy over the appropriate measurement of occupational sex segregation. This controversy relates to three issues. The first problem area is the structure of occupational classification schemes. The schemes themselves tend to reflect patterns of gender segregation and gender inequality, such that a more detailed differentiation is drawn in the classification of occupations in which men's employment is concentrated, while women tend to be concentrated into a smaller number of job classifications. Another problem with the classification scheme is the relationship between occupations and industrial structure. Some occupational categories specify both job grade or skill and industrial sector, while others can be found across a range of sectors. International comparisons of occupational data produce further problems. Such comparisons require harmonised occupational schemes as different schemes clearly give rise to different results, but work organisation practices differ between countries. Apparently similar tasks may be divided up into different sets of tasks and job slots, or similar jobs in terms of job content or skill accorded different positions in the organisational and labour market hierarchy (Marsh 1986). Here lies one of the major conceptual problems for cross-country comparisons of occupational segregation. The interest in occupational segregation lies in the different positions of women and men in the labour market hierarchy, but similar measured levels of segregation may have very different implications for gender inequality such as wage outcomes (see Chapter 6 below). At a more basic level countries may just adopt different procedures in allocating jobs to occupational classification schemes (Elias and Birch 1995).

The second set of problems, much discussed in the literature of recent date, relates to the issue of measurement (see Blackburn *et al.* 1993; Garnsey and Tarling 1982; Hakim 1992, 1993b, 1993c; Jacobs 1993; OECD 1980; Siltanen 1990a, 1990b; Siltanen *et al.* 1993; Tzannatos 1990; Watts 1990, 1992, 1993; Anker 1998). The conventional way of measuring segregation is to use an index measure. The most commonly used measure, at least until recently, has been the index of dissimilarity (ID). This measure indicates the proportion of the workforce which would need to change jobs in order for there to be no segregation. However, there are problems in interpreting changes in this index over time as they can be produced by changes in the occupational structure of the economy, in the female share of total employment or in the female share of different occupational groups. Thus the index may change value even if the female shares of occupations remains constant. Two main competing solutions have been proposed to deal with these problems. Watts (1990, 1992, 1993) advocates the standardised or Karmel and MacLachlan index (IP). This also measures the share of the workforce which would need to change jobs, but in contrast to the ID index, keeps the structure of jobs and the female share of the workforce constant. The second solution proposed is the index of segregation (IS), calculated according to the marginal matching method (Blackburn *et al.* 1993). This does not attempt to decompose the effects of changes in occupational structure, the sex composition of the workforce or female shares of occupational groups. Instead, it directly incorporates changing female shares of the labour force, on the basis that the appropriate definition of segregation at the occupational level is itself determined by the female share of overall employment.

The debate about the relative merits of these two approaches in part relates to differences in the concept of segregation that is to be measured and the associated issue of interpreting change in levels of segregation over time. The proponents of the standardised index of dissimilarity are concerned with the disaggregation of changes over time to identify the relative impact of the changing occupational structure of the economy and changes in women's share of different occupational categories. In contrast, the proponents of the marginal matching approach are seeking a measure of change in segregation over time which is constructed to incorporate directly any changes in the occupational structure and in women's share of employment. It is therefore meaningless to attempt to disaggregate the index of segregation which results from this latter approach (see Blackburn *et al.* 1993).

The third controversy over how to measure segregation relates to the usefulness of single index measures of segregation as the appropriate tool for comparisons between countries or over time. Several different arguments can be made that index measures obscure rather than illuminate patterns of change. The first argument is that evidence of little change in an index measure may hide trends pulling in two different directions, resulting in an overall small net change in segregation, but with major changes taking place in the experience of women and men in the labour market. The previous work by the current authors on this issue found just such a pattern, with limited change in the segregation index reflecting women increasing their shares in both previously male-dominated and already female-dominated occupations, the former decreasing segregation and the latter increasing it (Rubery and Fagan 1993, 1995b). A second objection is that index measures provide no information on the extent of female-dominated, male-dominated or mixed occupations, and that a more informative approach may be to look at how many occupations and how many persons are employed in these three categories (Hakim 1993b). The third objection is that the international comparisons of indices provide no information on the similarity or otherwise of the ranking of occupations by the female share of their workforce, that is whether it is the same or different occupations which are highly female- or male-dominated. Thus index measures may exaggerate the degree of similarity between countries. Instead, it is suggested that international comparisons should pay more attention to differences in the gender and societal structure of occupations (Rubery and Fagan 1995b).

These considerations have all informed our exploration of patterns of occupational sex segregation. Earlier research used the harmonised Eurostat occupational data based on the ISCO-68 system of occupational classification to assess change over the 1980s (Rubery and Fagan 1993). A simple extension of this time series is not possible because this classification was discontinued in 1991 in favour of the revised ISCO-88. Here we focus on comparing the levels of segregation across the EU using data for 1994. These data only cover 12 member states, although for the first time there are harmonised data on Italy. We also refer to data from Austria, Sweden and Finland, but these are each based on different occupational classifications from ISCO-88 and, indeed, from each other. Thus caution is advised in drawing comparisons between these 3 member states and the 12 for whom harmonised data were available. The continued contention about which index is the most appropriate relates primarily to measuring and interpreting changes over time in the level of segregation, which we cannot fully engage in given the limited time series available in the harmonised data for the member states. Instead, our strategy is to present all three measures for our inter-country comparison. What this largely shows is that on all aggregate measures the relative rankings of countries by levels of segregation were similar. As well as examining the aggregate level of segregation across the employment structure we also examine two related dimensions. One is employment concentration, which shows that women's employment was clustered into particular occupational groups while men clustered into different parts of the occupational structure. The other is the female share of employment within each occupational group, which permits a distinction to be drawn between 'male-dominated' 'mixed-sex' and 'female-dominated' occupations.

Indices of occupational segregation and concentration

Table 5.1 compares national levels of occupational segregation patterns using the ISCO-88 classification at the 3-digit level for 1994. This is a more detailed classification system than the ISCO-68 2-digit breakdown (116 job categories compared to around 80), used in our earlier work for the period 1983–1990, shown in Table 5.2. This increase in detail in the classification system can be expected to produce a higher measure of segregation, simply because there is a more precise allocation of women and men between a larger number of categories rather than because there has been any actual change in the level of segregation over time. However, what this comparison does indicate is that the three different indices tell slightly different stories for the 11 countries with data for 1990 and 1994, which underlines the problems of interpreting changes over time according to which index measure and classification scheme is used. The index of segregation does show a fairly systematic tendency to be slightly higher in 1994 in eight countries, but with no change evident in the UK and a slightly lower value found in Denmark and Ireland (see Tables 5.1 and 5.2). The picture for the index of dissimilarity shows a similar pattern when the more detailed classification system used in 1994 is compared with the 1990 data: slightly

Table 5.1 Indices of segregation for all in employment, 1994

	Index of segregation	Index of dissimilarity	Karmel and MacLachlan index
Belgium	52	54	26
Denmark	58	58	29
Germany (u)	54	54	26
Germany (w)	54	55	27
Germany (e)	62	62	31
Greece	37	43	20
Spain	49	51	23
France	55	55	27
Ireland	51	54	25
Italy	42	47	21
Luxembourg	56	56	26
Netherlands	52	53	26
Portugal	47	49	25
UK	56	56	28

Sources: European Labour Force Survey (1994); Elias (1995).

Notes
Data are unavailable for Sweden, Finland, and Austria.
Based on ISCO-88 (COM) 3 digit classification.

Table 5.2 Indices of segregation for all in employment

	Index of segregation			Index of dissimilarity			Karmel and MacLachlan index		
	1983	1987	1990	1983	1987	1990	1983	1987	1990
Belgium	49	49	48	55	56	47	25	26	22
Denmark	—	—	59	—	—	59	—	—	29
Germany	—	52	51	—	55	54	—	26	26
Greece	50	50	35	53	53	43	23	24	20
Spain	—	46	48	—	51	53	—	21	23
France	53	53	53	54	54	54	26	26	26
Ireland	52	52	53	57	56	56	24	24	25
Luxembourg	61	56	54	63	61	59	28	27	26
Netherlands	—	50	51	—	54	57	—	25	27
Portugal	—	43	43	—	47	46	—	23	22
UK	59	57	56	62	59	57	30	29	28

Sources: Rubery and Fagan (1993).

Notes
— indicates data are unavailable for this year.
No harmonised data are available for Sweden, Finland or Austria.

higher levels of segregation are recorded in seven countries, but this now includes the UK and Ireland, alongside a decline in Denmark and no change in unified Germany and in Greece. The Karmel and MacLachlan index presents a more stable picture of no change in seven countries, but with a higher score in Belgium, France and Portugal and a lower score in the Netherlands.

Despite the problems of comparing indices across different occupational classification schemes, and the problems that result according to which index measure is used, a comparison of the ranking of countries using the different measures and different classification schemes does suggest that these international comparisons are tapping systematic differences in the degree of segregation between countries (Table 5.3). If we look first at the index of segregation in both 1990 and 1994, the countries retain largely similar positions in the ranking by degree of segregation. Only 2 countries out of 11 move more than one rank (Belgium up two ranks and Ireland down four). With the index of dissimilarity, 3 out of 11 change more than one rank (France and Belgium move up and the Netherlands moves down). Comparisons of the Karmel and MacLachlan index between 1990 and 1994 also find the Netherlands relatively less segregated in 1994 and Belgium and Spain more segregated. Although each index reveals some variations in the pattern of change, the countries at the top and bottom of the segregation league remain relatively constant, with most movements in ranks occurring in the middle range where the actual size of variations in the index measures are in any case small.[1]

This relatively high degree of similarity in the rankings, particularly in the case of the segregation index, allows us to be fairly confident that the results can identify countries with relatively high and low levels of segregation in ways which are not contingent upon the choice of occupational classification scheme. It also provides us with support for our earlier conclusions that the results from the Eurostat data were relatively robust, despite justifiable doubts over the ISCO-68 classification system (Rubery and Fagan 1993).

The 1994 indices of segregation for 7 out of the 12 countries were found to be within a 6-point range, from 58 in Denmark to 52 in Belgium and the Netherlands (with a value of 0 indicating no segregation and a value of 100 indicating complete segregation) (see Table 5.1). Levels of segregation were lower in Ireland and the Southern European member states, with Italy and Greece recording much the lowest values at 42 and 37 respectively. In part, as we explore below, these low segregation scores resulted from the high incidence of agricultural employment in some Southern member states, for segregation by contractual form rather than job title tended to be more salient in this part of the economy. However, even when the self-employed were removed the segregation indices for employees in Italy, Greece and Ireland remained notably below the other countries. At the other end of the spectrum, high levels of segregation were found in Denmark, the UK, France

Table 5.3 Countries ranked in descending order from highest to lowest levels of segregation using selected indicators and datasets

1990 ISCO-68 2-digit data			1994 ISCO-88 (COM) 3-digit data		
Index of segregation	*Index of dissimilarity*	*Karmel and MacLachlan index*	*Index of segregation*	*Index of dissimilarity*	*Karmel and MacLachlan index*
(1) DK	(=1) DK	(1) DK	(1) DK	(1) DK	(1) DK
(2) UK	(=1) L	(2) UK	(=2) UK	(=2) UK	(2) UK
(3) L	(=3) UK	(3) NL	(=2) L	(=2) L	(3) F
(4) F	(=3) NL	(=4) L	(4) F	(4) F	(=4) L
(4) IRL	(5) IRL	(=4) D	(5) D	(=5) IRL	(=4) D
(=6) D	(=6) F	(=4) F	(=6) B	(=5) D	(=4) NL
(=6) NL	(=6) D	(7) IRL	(=6) NL	(=5) B	(=4) B
(=8) B	(8) E	(8) E	(8) IRL	(8) NL	(=8) IRL
(=8) E	(9) B	(9) B	(9) E	(9) E	(=8) P
(10) P	(10) P	(10) P	(10) P	(10) P	(10) E
(11) GR	(11) GR	(11) GR	(11) I	(11) I	(11) I
			(12) GR	(12) GR	(12) GR

Sources: European Labour Force Survey (1994); Rubery and Fagan (1993).

Notes

1990 data not available for Italy.

1990 and 1994 data not available for Austria, Finland or Sweden

1994 data for Germany relates to unified Germany.

and Luxembourg. The index of dissimilarity displayed a similar ranking using the 1994 data, except for Ireland which moved further up to share a rank position with Germany and Belgium (see Table 5.3). Using the standardised Karmel and MacLachlan index we also found relatively little change in rank ordering.

Austria, Finland and Sweden also had high levels of segregation according to national data sources (see below, Table 5.15). For example, in Finland the index of dissimilarity and the index of segregation had a value of 58 in 1995, for an 85 occupational classification, which matched Denmark as the highest ranked country using the ISCO-88 classification of 116 occupational categories. Sweden joined Finland and Denmark with similar scores on both indices, even though this was based on a more highly aggregated occupational classification of 52 categories which, as we discussed above, tended to depress the level of segregation recorded. In Austria the dissimilarity index for 175 occupations in 1991 had a value of 56.6, ranking it higher than all the 12 member states in 1994 except for Denmark, but this was in part due to the use of a more detailed occupational classification. So, although direct comparisons cannot be made, it is clear that these three member states, and particularly Sweden and Finland, appeared to have levels of segregation at the top end of the European spectrum. Disaggregated data for unified Germany also revealed that the former East Germany had a higher level of segregation than any European member state at over 62, while West Germany had a value around 54 (Table 5.1).

Many of the economies with high levels of occupational sex segregation were also characterised by women holding a high proportion of all jobs, notably the former East Germany and the Scandinavian countries, together with the UK and France. However, this pattern was not universal: Luxembourg had a high level of segregation but a lower female presence in employment and Portugal had the opposite, a high female share of all employment but a low level of segregation. Highly sex-segregated economies tended to be associated with high proportions of women employed in services, particularly public sector services. In Portugal, the high rate of female employment had occurred in the context where the service sector was still relatively small and the agricultural sector, although declining, still accounted for a relatively large proportion of economic activity. In economies where a large proportion of employment is concentrated in agriculture, lower levels of segregation tend to be recorded, in part because of the use of a rather aggregated occupational classification scheme in this area of work, which results in men and women working in apparently mixed occupations. The scheme may not be detailed enough to identify the gender division of labour within this area of employment; as we shall see further (pp. 191ff.), the main lines of segregation may in any case not be defined by job category but by employment contract, with, for example women found among unpaid family workers and men as self-employed.

While segregation refers to the degree to which women and men work in different occupational areas, the concept of concentration offers another perspective on this phenomenon. Figure 5.1 compares the proportion of the male and female workforces who were employed in 'male-dominated', 'female-dominated' and 'mixed' occupations. Much higher shares of men worked in occupations dominated by their own sex compared to women. Two-fifths or more of men worked in occupations where the workforce was less than 20 per cent female in all EU countries. In contrast, the concentration of women into occupations where the male share of the workforce was less than 20 per cent varied from under 10 per cent in Greece and Italy to just under half of employed women in Denmark and East Germany and over 50 per cent in Sweden and Finland (but using different occupational classification schemes). In addition to the Southern European countries, Belgium and the Netherlands had a relatively low share of employed women working in very female-dominated jobs. What is perhaps most surprising was the very low shares of women employed in relatively mixed occupations (where women hold 40–59 per cent of the jobs), particularly in France, Ireland, the UK, former East Germany, Austria, Finland and Sweden, where the share was 16 per cent or less in all cases. Similar low shares of men were employed in mixed occupations. The unusualness of mixed-sex occupations is emphasised by the analysis in Table 5.4, which also demonstrates the much higher number of job categories which were male dominated in each country, ranging from 42 to 78 of the 113 ISCO-88 categories, compared to the number of female-dominated occupations which range from 13 in Spain to 32 in former East Germany. This confirms the male bias in occupational classification schemes, for larger proportions of women are concentrated into a limited number of broad occupational categories while more detailed delineation is drawn between the different jobs which men typically do. The number of occupations categorised as 'mixed-sex' was also very low, ranging from 3 in Ireland[2] to 23 in Portugal and 25 in the former East Germany. Most countries had between 11 and 19 occupations out of 116 occupational groups in this category (note each country has some missing occupations[3]).

Although the ISCO-88 classification was introduced as an attempt to overcome some of the problems of previous ISCO-68 classification schemes for creating a harmonised database, examination of the distribution of men and women by major occupational group suggests that problems still remain. For example, there were considerable differences between countries in the share of the workforce classified to corporate managers, professional or associate professional jobs. In part these variations were likely to be reflective both of differences in the occupational structure between, for example, Southern and Northern European countries, and of national customs and practices, such as the tendency to class higher-grade workers as professionals or cadres in France and not as managers. Some indication of the seriousness of these problems can be understood from the fact

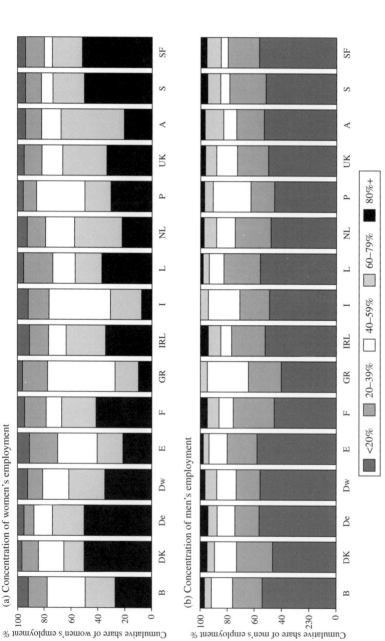

Figure 5.1 The concentration of women's and men's employment into segregated occupations

Sources: European Labour Force Survey (1994); national data for Austria, Finland and Sweden.

Notes
No data exist for a considerable number of occupations in Ireland.
Based on ISCO-88 (COM) 3-digit data except for Austria, Sweden and Finland, for which national data are used.

Table 5.4 The distribution of women and men's employment between female-dominated, mixed-sex and male-dominated occupations, 1994

	Female-dominated (workforce 60%+ female)			Mixed-sex (workforce 40–59% female)			Male-dominated (workforce < 40% female)			Missing occupations	Total no. of occupations
	No.occs	Fi/Fn	Mi/Mn	No.occs	Fi/Fn	Mi/Mn	No.occs	Fi/Fn	Mi/Mn		
Belgium	23	50	8	10	28	15	73	22	76	7	113
Denmark	28	65	11	19	19	17	59	16	73	7	113
Germany (e)	32	74	13	25	14	14	49	12	74	7	113
Germany (w)	22	62	13	17	20	14	67	19	74	7	113
Spain	13	40	7	17	30	14	78	30	80	5	113
France	20	67	14	13	12	11	63	21	76	17	113
Greece	17	27	5	17	51	30	73	22	65	6	113
Ireland	10	64	16	3	13	7	42	23	77	58	113
Italy	16	31	6	14	46	24	76	23	70	7	113
Luxembourg	19	57	7	11	18	12	74	25	81	9	113
Netherlands	20	58	12	15	22	14	70	21	74	8	113
Portugal	22	50	10	23	37	28	61	14	67	7	113
UK	21	67	12	16	16	15	64	18	73	12	113
Austria	12	68	18	6	15	10	39	18	73	0	57
Sweden	16	74	15	4	9	7	32	17	78	0	52
Finland	28	75	16	12	5	5	44	20	79	1	85

Sources: European Labour Force Survey (1994); national sources for Austria, Sweden and Finland

Notes
In the case of Ireland, data are not available for a significant number of occupations (58).
Fi/Fn = Females in occupation 'i' as a proportion of all females in employment.
Mi/Mn = Males in occupation 'i' as a proportion of all males in employment.
Based on ISCO-88 (COM) 3-digit classification for twelve member states in 1994.

that something like three-quarters of all female corporate managers in the EU were found in the UK, suggesting perhaps more a tendency to class people as managers and not professionals (Elias 1995). Other differences occur in the classification of jobs as professional or associate professional, skilled service or elementary, craft or operative. In order to minimise these problems, and also to identify major differences between broad job categories, we grouped together ISCO-88 1-digit categories 1, 2 and 3 for managerial, professional and associate professional jobs; groups 5 and 9, which are service workers and elementary occupations; and groups 6, 7, and 8, which are skilled agricultural, craft and productions related jobs. Only the clerical category (group 4) and armed forces (group 0) remained ungrouped.

Figure 5.2 shows that this classification highlighted the major differences in the gender concentration by broad occupational type in the European Union for the 12 member states (E12), while the data for the individual member states are shown in Table 5.5. In the E12 as a whole around one-third of employed persons were in higher-level jobs (managerial, professional and related), 14 per cent in clerical jobs, 23 per cent in service and elementary jobs and 30 per cent in agriculture, craft and production. This distribution diverged sharply when examined by gender: the only similarity between the sexes was the percentage concentrated into higher-level jobs. Over one-fifth of employed women were concentrated in clerical jobs, a degree of concentration which was some 60 per cent higher than the concentration of all employment in this category. In contrast, only 8 per cent of men were clerical workers, some 40 per cent lower than the overall concentration level (see Table 5.5). Women were also disproportionately concentrated in service and elementary jobs, while men dominated in the agricultural, craft and production jobs. The differences between full-timers and part-timers shown in the figure are discussed on pp. 201ff.

A similar pattern of gender differences in occupational concentrations was found within the individual member states (see Table 5.5a). Portugal, Greece and to a lesser extent Italy tended to have higher female shares in agriculture, craft and production jobs but in all cases women remained under-represented (Table 5.5c). Women's disproportionate concentration in clerical and service and elementary work was also found in every country, ranging from 32 per cent to 89 per cent above parity in the case of clerical and from 21 per cent to 68 per cent in the case of service and elementary jobs. The tendency for men and women to be relatively evenly concentrated in higher-level jobs was also borne out by the individual country analysis. The concentration of women in this occupational grouping relative to the concentration for all employed persons ranged from 9 per cent below to 27 per cent above in 13 economies (the former East Germany taken separately and accounting for the 27 per cent over-concentration). Women were in fact under-represented in this broad category of higher-level occupations in six cases and over-represented in seven.

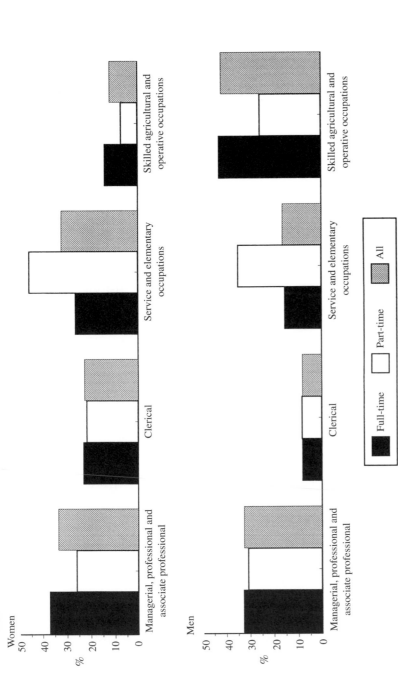

Figure 5.2 Concentration of employment in broad occupation groups by gender and working-time, EU12

Source: European Labour Force Survey (1994).

Note
Based on ISCO-88 (COM) data.

Table 5.5 Concentration of employment by broad occupational groups and by gender

(a) % distribution of all employment by broad occupational groups

	B	DK	D	D	E	F	GR	IRL	I	L	NL	P	UK	E12
Males														
1+2+3	35	37	28	35	23	34	26	26	22	32	49	26	41	33
4	12	6	3	9	8	6	8	7	11	13	7	8	8	8
5+9	13	18	16	14	22	13	15	23	22	14	13	18	15	16
6+7+8	38	38	52	41	47	45	50	42	44	42	30	46	36	42
Total	100	100	100	100	100	100	100	100	100	100	100	100	100	100
Females														
1+2+3	40	33	45	36	28	31	27	30	28	30	43	27	35	34
4	24	20	17	22	17	25	16	27	21	26	20	14	27	22
5+9	27	38	30	32	40	32	24	31	32	38	31	31	32	32
6+7+8	10	9	9	9	15	12	33	10	19	6	6	27	6	12
Total	100	100	100	100	100	100	100	100	100	100	100	100	100	100
All														
1+2+3	37	35	35	36	25	32	26	27	24	31	47	27	38	33
4	17	12	9	14	11	14	10	14	15	17	12	11	17	14
5+9	19	27	22	21	28	21	18	26	26	23	20	24	22	23
6+7+8	26	25	33	28	36	31	44	30	35	29	20	37	22	30
Total	100	100	100	100	100	100	100	100	100	100	100	100	100	100

(b) Over-/under-concentration of male employment relative to total employment within broad occupational groups[a]

Males	B	DK	D	D	E	F	GR	IRL	I	L	NL	P	UK	E12
1+2+3	95	105	79	99	93	105	99	94	92	102	105	101	107	99
4	72	47	37	61	71	41	73	47	77	72	60	74	48	58
5+9	71	67	74	63	78	59	81	88	37	60	63	75	66	71
6+7+8	142	153	158	148	130	148	113	139	125	146	148	121	159	142

(c) Over-/under-concentration of female employment relative to total employment within broad occupational groups[b]

Females	B	DK	D	D	E	F	GR	IRL	I	L	NL	P	UK	E12
1+2+3	107	94	127	102	113	94	101	111	116	96	93	99	91	102
4	142	163	179	155	157	174	149	189	143	148	159	132	164	160
5+9	143	139	133	152	143	151	134	121	124	168	154	131	142	141
6+7+8	36	37	28	32	41	40	75	34	54	22	30	73	28	40

Source: European Labour Force Survey 1994.

Notes
1+2+3 = managerial, professional and associate professional.
4 = clerical.
5+9 = service and elementary occupations.
6+7+8 = skilled agriculture, craft and operative occupations.
a Share of male employment divided by share of total employment × 100.
b Share of female employment divided by share of total employment × 100.
A score of less than 100 = under-concentration; more than 100 = over-concentration.

Differences between member states in the pattern of segregation and occupational structure

So far we have been looking at indices of segregation and rates of employment concentration, with little reference to national differences in the pattern of segregation. To explore the similarities and differences between countries we used the broad occupational categories at ISCO-88 1-digit level. We compared the gender composition of these categories and the employment concentration for both sexes by occupation for the 12 member states for which we have data. Then we used the more detailed occupational classification (2- and 3-digit levels) to identify the occupations which were the most male dominated and most female dominated.

Figure 5.3 shows the gender composition of the main occupational groups. The aggregate picture for the E12 was that the most female-dominated occupational group was clerical work, followed by service workers, elementary occupations, technicians, and professionals. Relative to their share of all employment in the E12, women were under-represented within skilled agricultural occupations, legislators and managers, plant and machine operatives, craft and related occupations and the armed forces. The actual female shares of the different occupational groups ranged from 66 per cent of clerks to 11 per cent of craft and related jobs and under 5 per cent of the armed forces. This ranking tended to hold across member states, but variations are still evident, particularly in the female share of different occupational categories.

To take the most feminised area, clerical work, first, we find that women's share of these jobs ranges from between 50 and 55 per cent in four countries to over 70 per cent in five countries. The pace and level of feminisation of clerical work varied strongly between countries but all countries have now an absolute female majority in these job areas, including the Southern European and Benelux countries, where at the beginning of the 1980s the majority of clerical workers were men (Rubery and Fagan 1993, 1995b). Thus women were over-represented relative to their share of the labour force in clerical work in all countries (see Table 5.6b).

Service work presents a very similar picture: in all cases women made up a higher share of the service workforce than their overall share of employment, but there was an even wider range of rates of feminisation, from 45 per cent and 48 per cent in the case of Italy and Greece to over 70 per cent in four countries (or five if we count the former East and the former West Germany separately) (see Table 5.6a). The category of elementary occupations was a more evenly divided job area in most countries, with nine countries recording female shares of between 40 and 57 per cent, while in Ireland only 24 per cent of these workers were female. Luxembourg had the most feminised elementary occupations, with women holding 64 per cent of these jobs. Again, women were over-represented among elementary workers relative to their share of all employment in all countries except Ireland and the former East Germany.

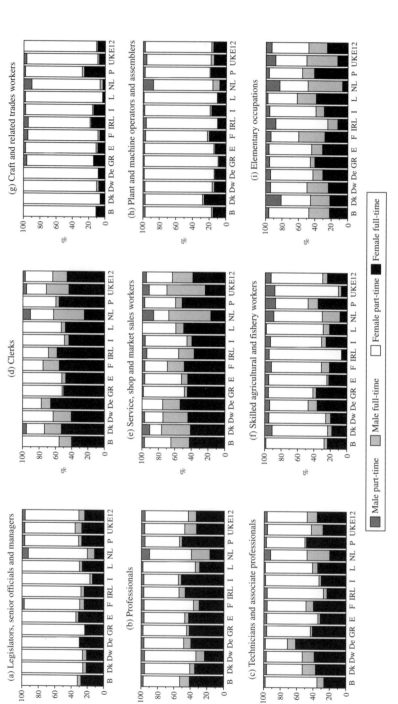

Figure 5.3 The female and male full- and part-time share of major occupational groups, 1994

Source: European Labour Force Survey (1994).

Note

Based on ISCO-88 (COM) 1-digit data.

Table 5.6 Occupational sex segregation by occupational group

(a) Female share of employment in each occupational group

	B	DK	D	D	E	F	GR	IRL	I	L	NL	P	UK	E12
Armed forces (0)	:	:	(1.7)	:	:	4.9	(8.9)	(18.2)	—	:	:	(7.7)	(5.0)	4.6
Legislators, officials and managers (1)	30.3	23.4	23.9	29.8	32.6	27.8	22.7	25.5	14.7	28.3	20.2	29.2	33.7	28.9
Professionals (2)	53.0	39.9	32.2	47.7	46.1	35.4	43.6	53.9	54.2	33.9	38.6	53.2	46.6	42.4
Technicians and associate professionals (3)	35.4	53.5	53.6	71.5	34.1	49.3	43.4	27.0	33.0	41.5	48.8	50.6	42.9	48.0
Clerks (4)	56.6	74.5	64.2	79.6	53.4	77.3	52.5	70.2	50.3	54.6	64.6	58.9	73.8	65.8
Service workers, shop and market sales workers (5)	65.3	76.7	75.4	75.1	51.8	70.0	48.0	55.5	45.6	59.2	68.9	59.7	71.2	64.4
Skilled agricultural and fishery workers (6)	27.5	23.6	25.9	48.2	24.4	31.5	42.1	6.0	31.6	29.6	30.4	48.8	10.7	31.2
Craft and related trades workers (7)	11.2	6.2	10.2	8.3	9.9	8.7	15.1	18.9	16.1	(3.4)	6.8	29.2	9.5	11.6
Plant and machine operators and assemblers (8)	16.3	28.0	16.1	13.3	13.8	22.3	9.0	10.4	19.0	(9.4)	15.7	19.9	17.7	17.8
Elementary occupations (9)	48.4	46.8	50.9	43.2	45.3	61.4	46.4	24.2	40.1	63.8	49.9	57.0	51.8	49.4
Total (0–9)	39.9	45.7	41.4	44.5	34.0	44.3	35.3	37.2	35.1	36.9	40.5	44.5	44.9	41.0

(b) Over-/under-representation of women relative to the female share of total employment[a]

	B	DK	D	D	E	F	GR	IRL	I	L	NL	P	UK	E12
Armed forces (0)	:	:	(4)	:	:	11	(25)	(49)	—	:	:	(17)	(11)	11
Legislators, officials and managers (1)	76	51	58	67	96	63	64	68	42	77	50	66	75	70
Professionals (2)	133	87	78	107	136	80	123	145	154	92	95	120	104	103
Technicians and associate professionals (3)	89	117	130	161	100	111	123	73	94	113	120	114	96	117
Clerks (4)	142	163	155	179	157	174	149	189	143	148	159	132	164	160
Service workers, shop and market sales workers (5)	164	168	182	169	153	158	136	149	130	160	170	134	159	157
Skilled agricultural and fishery workers (6)	69	52	63	108	72	71	119	16	90	80	75	110	24	76
Craft and related trades workers (7)	28	14	25	19	29	20	43	51	46	9	17	66	21	28
Plant and machine operators and assemblers (8)	41	61	39	30	41	50	26	28	54	25	39	45	39	43
Elementary occupations (9)	121	102	123	97	133	139	131	65	114	173	123	128	115	120

Source: European Labour Force Survey (1994).

Notes

[a] Female share of employment within the occupation divided by female share of all employment x 100.

Based on ISCO-88 (COM) 1-digit classification.

Women's share of professional jobs ranged from 32 per cent in the former West Germany to slightly over half in Belgium, Ireland, Italy and Portugal (53–54 per cent). It was notable that some countries with a low female share of professional jobs had relatively higher female shares of associate professionals or technicians. This suggested there might be some differences between countries in the allocation of jobs across these two categories, as discussed above (see also Box 5.1 for information on the classification of teachers across these two categories). Thus the low female presence in professional jobs in West Germany (32 per cent) existed alongside women holding 54 per cent of associate professional jobs, which was the third-highest rank position across the countries. The Netherlands, Denmark and France also had relatively low female shares of professional jobs but higher relative and absolute female shares of associate professional jobs. The highest rates of over-representation of women in professional jobs tended to be found in the Southern European countries, together with Ireland. This suggested that in these countries there was a starker polarisation between women, according to whether they were in high-level jobs, in low-level work or out of the labour force entirely. There was a certain similarity in women's share of managerial jobs across EU countries, ranging between 20 per cent and 30 per cent in 9 of the 12 countries. Spain had the highest female share of managerial jobs, close to the expected share given the female share of all employment in this country, but in all cases women were under-represented in managerial jobs.

The remaining job categories in which women were under-represented were skilled agricultural workers, craft and related jobs and plant and machine operatives. In every case women were under-represented relative to their share of all employment, with the exception of skilled agricultural workers in the former East Germany, Portugal and Greece. Women's share of craft and related jobs was particularly low relative to their share of all employment, with slightly higher levels generally found among plant and machine operatives (see Table 5.6b).

Another method of comparing the pattern of segregation across countries was to consider the composition of the most feminised and the least feminised occupations, defined here as those occupations which fell in the top or the bottom quartile of occupations ranked by the degree of feminisation. At the 2-digit level the top quartile showing the most feminised categories consisted of 6 occupational sub-groups, and we see from Table 5.7 that the same 6 occupations occured in the top quartile in at least 10 cases (out of a maximum of 13; East and West Germany are treated as separate countries for this analysis). These occupational sub-groups which were among the most feminised in almost all countries included two categories of clerical workers, health and teaching associate professionals, and two categories of sales workers. Two other categories appeared in the top quartile in the majority of countries: personal and protective service workers (group 8) and teaching professionals (group 7). Among male-dominated occupations there

Table 5.7 The most female-dominated and male-dominated occupational sub-groups[a] (ISCO 88 (COM), 2-digit data)

(a) The most female-dominated occupational sub-groups

Occupation (ISCO-88 (COM), 2-digit)	Number of countries
2 *Professionals*	
22 Life science and health professionals	4
23 Teaching professionals	7
3 *Technicians and associate professionals*	
32 Life science and health associate professionals	12
33 Teaching associate professionals	10
34 Other associate professionals (former East Germany)	1
4 *Clerks*	
41 Office clerks	11
42 Customer services clerks	10
5 *Service workers and shop and market sales workers*	
51 Personal and protective services workers	8
52 Models, salespersons and demonstrators	12
7 *Craft and related trades workers*	
74 Other craft and related trades workers (Portugal)	1
9 *Elementary occupations*	
91 Sales and services elementary occupations	11
92 Agricultural, fishery and related labourers	4

(b) The most male-dominated occupational sub-groups

Occupation (ISCO-88 (COM), 2-digit)	Number of countries
0 *Armed forces*	
01 Armed forces	11
1 *Legislators, senior officials and managers*	
11 Legislators and senior government officials (Greece)	1
12 Corporate managers	8
2 *Professionals*	
21 Physical, mathematical and engineering science professionals	12
3 *Technicians and associate professionals*	
31 Physical and engineering science associate professionals	2
33 Teaching associate professionals (Ireland)	1
6 *Skilled agricultural and fishery workers*	
61 Skilled agricultural and fishery workers	2
7 *Craft and related trades workers*	
71 Extraction and building trades workers	13
72 Metal, machinery and related trades workers	11
8 *Plant and machine operators and assemblers*	
81 Stationary-plant and related operators	11
82 Machine operators and assemblers	2
83 Drivers and mobile plant operators	13
9 *Elementary occupations*	
92 Agricultural, fishery and related labourers (Luxembourg)	1
93 Mining, construction, manufacturing and transport labourers	3

Source: European Labour Force Survey (1994).
Notes
[a]Occupational subgroups which occur among the seven most female- or most male-dominated occupations within each country.
Based on ISCO-88 (COM) 2-digit classification.

were again 6 sub-groups which occured repeatedly, this time in a minimum of 11 cases. These included construction and metal trades craft workers, drivers and operators of stationary plant, the armed forces and physical, mathematical and engineering professionals. The only other occupation to occur in a significant number of country lists of the least feminised occupations was corporate managers (8 countries).

Considerable consistency was found even at the 3-digit level in the ranking of occupations by female share (Table 5.8a). At this level of disaggregation the upper and lower quartile consisted of 29 occupational categories (except where there were a number of missing occupations in the data set). No less than 20 occupations fell in the top quartile of the most feminised occupations for 10 or more countries and a total of 36 occupations appeared in the lists of at least four countries. In most cases this analysis served to identify the sub-groups within the larger 2-digit categories which occurred among the most feminised 2-digit groups. Only 4 of the occupations at the 3-digit level which appeared in this list did not fall into the most feminised 2-digit groups: sub-groups 243, 244, 826 and 829. A similar pattern was found in the lists of the most female-dominated occupations for Austria, Finland and Sweden, based on country-specific occupational classifications. In all 3 countries the feminised occupations were found primarily in health and education, welfare and related professions, clerical work and retail, catering and domestic service work (see Table 5.8b).

Consistency in patterns of segregation also characterised the list of the 29 most male-dominated occupations; 22 occupations occured in the lists of at least 10 countries, and 34 occured in the lists of at least 4 countries. No fewer than 21 of these consistently male-dominated jobs were found in the craft and related or production and machine operative occupational groups, and a further 3 in the managerial category. The male-dominated elementary occupations were the traditional male-dominated jobs of refuse collector and labourers in mining and construction and transport. The most male-dominated occupations in Austria, Finland and Sweden, based on national data (see Table 5.8b), revealed a remarkably similar picture, with almost all the most male-dominated occupations occurring in construction, transport or heavy industry.

Although there were clear and strong similarities between countries in which occupations appeared in the female-dominated and the male-dominated sections of the employment system, there were also marked differences, both in the female shares of the occupational categories, as we had already seen, and in the precise ranking of occupations. Thus the pattern of segregation has a country-specific dimension which became clearer once occupations were examined at a more detailed level. This was evident in our previous research, in which we selected six occupational areas for more detailed analysis (Rubery and Fagan 1993, 1995b). In these occupational case studies we found national differences in the female share of the occupations and in the degree of change in recent years, which were not simply

Table 5.8 Occupations which occur among the most female- and male-dominated occupations in the new member states

(a) Austria[a]

Most female-dominated (occupation 2-digit)		Most male-dominated (occupation 2-digit)	
02	Medical professions	37	Protective service workers
03	Teaching professions	43	Train guards
05	Religions and social groups	44	Drivers
11	Office and bank clerks	45	Transport workers
13	Numerical clerks	47	Crane and building-machine operatives
14	Other office and administrative clerks	48	Machinists and wood operatives
22	Sales assistants	61	Miners
32	Waiting staff, cooks	71	Bricklayers
33	Housekeeping	72	Carpenters
34	Cleaning occupations	74	Other construction trades
35	Personal care workers	75	Civil engineering construction jobs
36	Health ancillary workers	76	Construction labourers
81	Textile workers	86	Fitters, mechanics, etc
82	Fur and leather workers	88	Plumbers and pipe layers

(b) Sweden[a]

Most female-dominated (occupation 2-digit)		Most male-dominated (occupation 2-digit)	
153	Children's nurses	79	Other building and construction workers
36	Pre-primary education teachers	50	Mining, quarrying workers
23, 24	Accounting, clerical and related workers	XI	Military occupations
152, 154, 155, 159	Managers in social welfare, home helpers, social workers, nec[b]	42–44	Wildlife, fishing, forestry workers
932	Cleaners	86	Stationary-engine operatives
		87	Material handling and related workers
10, 14	Health, nursing, veterinary workers	761–763	Electrical and electrical machinery workers
12	Dental workers	78	Painting and floor-laying workers
11, 13, 16, 192, 199	Pharmaceutical workers, environmental, health protection, nec[b]	64	Motor vehicle drivers and delivery work
91	Lodging and catering service workers	931	Building caretakers
		00	Technical workers
70–72	Textile, tailoring, shoe and leather workers	73	Metal-processing workers
92, 94–96, 99	Private household work, hygiene, laundry, training	75	Metal machine work and building metalworkers
151, 191	Social welfare workers	60–63, 65–66	Ship, aircraft, railway work and other transport workers
333	Shop assistants		
01, 02	Chemical, biological workers		

Table 5.8 (cont.)

(c) Finland[b]

Most female-dominated (occupation 2-digit)		Most male-dominated (occupation 2-digit)	
8	Library, archive, museum, and information service workers	00	Architectural and engineering workers
10	Medical and nursing workers	43	Fishing workers
11	Therapeutical workers	44	Forestry and logging workers
12	Dental workers	50	Ship's officers
13	Pharmaceutical workers	51	Deck and engine room crew
15	Social workers	52	Air transport workers
16	Child day care workers	53	Locomotive and railcar drivers
17	Psychological workers	54	Road transport workers
22	Personnel and employment affairs workers	55	Traffic supervision and service workers
23	Financial planning and accounting workers	60	Mining and quarrying
24	Secretarial and clerical workers, etc.	61	Oil drilling and peak harvesting workers
26	Banking and insurance workers	62	Building construction workers
27	Travel service workers	63	Land and waterway construction workers.
39	Other commercial workers		
56	Postal and telecommunications workers	64	Construction and industrial equipment operation workers
71	Sewing workers	73	Steel, metallurgical, forging and foundry workers
91	Accommodation establishments; commercial and institutional domestic workers	75	Engineering and structural metal workers
92	Waiter service work	78	Painting workers
93	Private household work	87	Fixed engine and motor power operation workers in energy and water supply
94	Building caretaking and cleaning work		
96	Laundry, dry cleaning and pressing work	89	Manual workers nec[b]
		90	Public safety and protection workers
		98	Military personnel

Sources: Finnish Labour Force Survey (Finland); National reports, Sweden: Gonäs and Spånt (1996); National reports, Austria: Pastner (1996).

Notes
a In the top or bottom quartile (14 occupations) of occupations ranked by female share.
b nec = not elsewhere classified.
c In the top or bottom quartile (21 occupations) of occupations ranked by female share.

a product of national differences in women's share of employment. These differences in patterns of segregation at the occupational level related to variation between countries on a number of societal features. These included national differences in the industrial structure and the way that employment was organised within industrial sectors; differences in training systems and their relationship to recruitment channels and career paths; variation in labour market conditions and in trends in the relative pay and status of certain occupations associated with different systems of pay determination; and historically rooted normative differences concerning what type of employment was considered suitable for women and whether it was acceptable for them to work when they had young children. Box 5.1 and Table 5.9 consider evidence on the situation in the 1990s, updating our earlier comparison of the female share of employment in these six occupational case studies. Further country differences emerge in the next section, when we examine the contribution which atypical employment makes to patterns of segregation.

Other dimensions to segregation: atypical employment, sector and workplace

Gender differences in the distribution of employment relate not only to occupations but also to employment forms, such that gender segregation by employment contract or by working-time category can be regarded as providing another layer to segregation. Gender differences in the incidence of different contractual arrangements are addressed in Chapter 7. Here we analyse the interactions between these different employment forms and patterns of segregation and then briefly consider the influence of sector and workplace.

Segregation for non-employees and employees

The role of self-employment in contributing to the degree of segregation within employment can be shown by comparing index measures calculated for all in employment and then recalculated for employees and non-employees separately. Table 5.10 permits this comparison for the 12 old member states in 1994, using the 3 alternative indices of segregation explained above. When we compare the index of segregation score we see that the lowest degree of segregation was found among people who were non-employees (self-employed or family workers). This is because these workers tended to be found in a limited range of occupations, including in particular agriculture. In contrast, the degree of segregation among employees was much higher. Indeed, we found that in every country except Ireland the degree of segregation among employees was greater than that among all persons in employment, and in many cases the difference was quite marked. The explanation for Ireland, as we found in our previous research (Rubery and Fagan 1993) was that there was still a relatively high proportion of the workforce engaged as self-employed agricultural workers. However, in contrast to the other European countries where agriculture has remained important, in Ireland this was an extremely male-dominated activity. Thus removing the self-employed decreased measured segregation in Ireland. Segregation among employees was markedly higher than that for all persons in employment (4 points or more) in all the Southern European

Box 5.1 Sex segregation in six occupational case study areas: an update on previous research

In previous research on occupational segregation (Rubery and Fagan 1993; 1995b) six occupational areas were looked at in detail, using both national and European-wide data sources for the period 1983–1990, chosen to include higher-level, intermediate and lower-level jobs, as well as traditionally female, traditionally male and more mixed occupations. This latter group includes occupational groups in which segregation levels varied significantly by member state. The areas studied were teaching, computer professionals, and clerical workers in public administration and in finance, driving and catering. The ISCO-88 data give us an opportunity to update our previous analyses of segregation in these areas to the situation in 1994, and also to verify that the patterns we found using the ISCO-68 data are maintained under the new coding scheme.

The two occupations which were found in the earlier report to be very male-dominated in all countries, namely **computer professionals** and **drivers**, continued to employ very few women. Table 5.9 shows that women's share of driving occupations remained below 8 per cent in all 12 countries for which we had data. **Denmark** and the **Netherlands** stood out as having the largest female share of these jobs at over 7 per cent. Both of these countries were identified in the previous study as experiencing an increasing entry of women into some driving areas such as bus transport during the 1980s. Women were not quite so rare among computer professionals, accounting for over 17 per cent of these occupations at the E12 level. Where variations between member states were found, these again fitted with the earlier findings, with women having made more entry into this professional area in **Denmark** and the **Southern European countries** together with **France**. This suggested that the Southern countries might be more open to desegregation of professional-level jobs than some Northern European countries, but only in **Portugal** was the occupation truly mixed, with a female share of over 50 per cent.

Teaching is a feminised profession across the EU, but there are important variations between countries, and between grades within occupational areas. Women accounted for 61 per cent of **teaching professionals** and for 75 per cent of **teaching associate professionals** at the E12 level in 1994. However, within the teaching professionals category there is considerable vertical segregation, with women accounting for 79 per cent of primary and pre-primary educational professionals, 57 per cent of secondary teachers but only 37 per cent of college, university and higher education professionals. Within teaching associate professionals no less than 94 per cent of pre-primary teaching associate professionals were women. This common pattern of vertical segregation in teaching across the member states coexists with national differences. In **Denmark** and the **Netherlands** three-fifths of secondary school teachers were men, compared to only one in four in **Portugal** and just over one-third in **Italy** (36 per cent male). These country differences again mirrored earlier results. Comparing the pattern of segregation in teaching across countries is complicated by differences in occupational classification; for example **France** did not have any primary or pre-primary teaching professionals, with all employees in this category found among teaching associate professionals, while the **UK**, for example, had the opposite pattern, presumably reflecting the different status attached to primary school teacher qualifications in the two countries. The UK also had a high proportion of college and higher-level jobs held by women, but the large overall numbers employed in the UK in this category suggested perhaps a different definition of college lecturer than in other countries, where only higher education lecturers may be included.

Clerical work was an occupational area which tended to be male dominated in the **Southern European** and **Benelux countries** and highly feminised in the other Northern European countries during the 1980s. By 1994 women held more than 50 per cent of these jobs in all countries but there was still a similar ranking of countries, with all the Southern and the Benelux countries, except now for the **Netherlands**, having female shares of clerical employment below 60 per cent. Insight into these differences can be gleaned from analysis of segregation within the clerical area, both by job type and by sector. When we looked at clerical work by sector, in order to update our analysis of **clerical work in public administration and finance** we found that women held relatively similar or higher shares of clerical jobs in the public sector compared to the overall figure for all clerical work, except in **Italy**, **Ireland** and **Luxembourg**, where the shares were below the average share for all clerical workers. In finance there are more marked differences by country. The **Southern European countries**, together with **Germany**, **France** and **Belgium**, had lower female shares than for clerical workers as a whole. This reflected the relatively late entry of women into banking in the Southern countries and the stronger internal labour markets and higher skill levels in banking in countries such as France and Germany than exist, for example, in the **UK** (Rubery 1995b).

Table 5.9 also provides some information on horizontal segregation within clerical work. Some clerical job areas, namely material-recording and transport clerks and library- and mail-related clerks, were systematically male-dominated across countries (except for the UK and Germany). Numerical clerks had a more varied female presence, falling as low as 31 per cent in **Spain** and as high as 90 per cent in **Denmark** in 1994. **Italy** and **Portugal** also recorded low female shares among cashiers, tellers and related clerks. While secretarial and keyboard operatives are almost exclusively feminised in eight countries, with male shares below 18 per cent, in **Italy** and **Spain** over two-fifths of these jobs were taken by men. Client-information clerks were also an almost exclusively feminised area except in Italy and, to a lesser extent, Greece, where the female shares dropped to 40 per cent and 57 per cent respectively.

While there was strong evidence that clerical work was moving towards becoming a highly feminised job area in all countries, the sixth occupational area, that of **catering workers** – here defined to include also domestic workers – retained a stronger diversity between countries. Thus in **three Southern European countries** together with **France** women constituted less than 45 per cent of catering workers, while at the opposite end of the spectrum women held more than 70 per cent of these jobs in **Germany**, **UK** and **Denmark**. **Portugal** had a relatively high female share of catering workers but this may include a lot of domestic workers and a more detailed analysis again might reveal the maintenance of the Southern tradition of actual catering work being a male-dominated occupation.

Table 5.9 Segregation in specific occupations, 1994

Occupations	Share of females in employment												
	B	DK	D	E	F	GR	IRL	I	L	NL	P	UK	E12
Selected occupations within professional job areas													
(a) Computer professionals	18	31	15	23	20	(21)	*	(20)	(9)	14	(52)	15	17
(b) Teaching professionals	64	53	55	59	57	60	62	74	53	50	70	62	61
College, university and higher education	34	(25)	(28)	31	41	35	*	33	*	(22)	(48)	42	37
Secondary education	59	41	55	50	59	57	*	64	(48)	40	74	55	57
Primary and pre-primary	80	60	76	66	*	62	*	91	(61)	68	*	85	79
Teaching associate professionals	70	80	79	43	71	(69)	*	68	(62)	(19)	84	78	75
Pre-primary	95	(91)	93	*	*	*	(5)	*	*	*	(100)	(99)	94
Selected occupations within clerical area													
All clerical	57	75	66	53	77	53	70	50	55	65	59	74	66
(c) Clerical in finance sector	49	76	60	33	72	45	73	42	61	69	34	78	61
(d) Clerical in public administration	61	88	71	61	80	55	68	46	45	65	67	74	66
Horizontal segregation within clerical area													
Secretaries and keyboard-operating clerks	83	(95)	97	59	95	73	(95)	57	(86)	93	74	93	80
Numerical clerks	47	(90)	60	31	83	59	*	57	48	64	57	75	67
Material recording and transport clerks	29	41	(34)	25	19	12	(34)	20	(13)	26	25	20	26
Library, mail and related clerks	21	34	(59)	27	46	18	(6)	42	(39)	47	41	53	48
Other office clerks	55	87	67	63	72	52	63	45	35	73	63	78	68
Cashiers, tellers, etc.	77	74	58	56	77	55	75	40	(72)	78	31	79	67
Client information clerks	(81)	(89)	82	65	89	57	*	44	(81)	83	78	94	80
Selected occupations within manual area													
(e) Housekeeping and restaurant services workers	60	75	73	43	44	41	65	43	50	59	60	71	58
(f) Drivers	(2)	7	4	2	4	1	(3)	2	(3)	8	(1)	4	4

Sources: European Labour Force Survey (1994); Elias (1995).

Notes
Bracketed figures denote data based on female and male sample sizes with statistical reliability that should be interpreted with caution.
Asterisks denote sample sizes (male and female combined) which are too small to be statistically reliable.

Table 5.10 Indices of segregation for employees, non-employees and all in employment, 1994

	Index of segregation			Index of dissimilarity			Karmel and MacLachlan index		
	Employees	Non-employees	All in employment	Employees	Non-employees	All in employment	Employees	Non-employees	All in employment
Belgium	54	34	52	58	36	54	28	16	26
Denmark	59	48	58	59	48	58	30	21	29
Germany (u)	55	37	54	56	37	54	27	16	26
Spain	53	34	49	57	41	51	26	17	23
France	59	32	55	59	32	55	29	15	27
Greece	48	25	37	53	34	43	25	15	20
Ireland	49	33	50	54	51	54	26	14	25
Italy	46	28	41	52	39	47	24	16	21
Luxembourg	59	28	55	60	29	56	28	14	26
Netherlands	53	47	52	55	47	53	27	22	26
Portugal	53	34	47	55	38	50	27	19	25
UK	56	50	56	56	57	56	28	22	28

Sources: European Labour Force Survey (1994); Elias (1995).

Note
Based on ISCO-88 (COM) 3-digit classification.

countries, with France and Luxembourg also recording increases of 3 points or more. In the Southern countries these large increases occurred from the lowest levels of segregation for all employed persons in the member states. Again, the explanation is that a large proportion of the workforce in these countries were non-employees concentrated in a limited number of broadly defined categories of activity, particularly agriculture. Where agriculture was less important in the overall employment structure, the difference in segregation pattern between employees and non-employees was often less or, for example in the case of the UK, non-existent.

Some differences can be found between the three index measures, but again the differences were more in the size of the change in the index when the self-employed were removed than a change in the direction of the trend. Thus the rise in measured segregation in Spain and Luxembourg was particularly strong when considering the index of segregation and the index of dissimilarity, but weaker, although still positive, under the standardised index of dissimilarity.

We were also able to examine the different occupational concentrations of employees, employers, the self-employed and unpaid family workers across the ISCO-88 1-digit occupational groups. If we look first at employers, it should be noted that women constituted a much lower share of this category of employed persons than of other professional status groups (21 per cent). Nevertheless, the occupational profiles of employers of both sexes were dominated by managerial and professional occupations, which accounted for over two-fifths of both male and female employers at the E12 level compared to under one-fifth of employees (Table 5.11). The other major concentrations of employers were found in service work for women and craft and related work for men. The self-employed without employees were also more concentrated in managerial work relative to employees, but had a lower concentration in the professional categories, for both men and women. Nearly one-quarter of self-employed men and one-fifth of self-employed women were in agriculture. Overall, they accounted for 57 per cent of all men and 42 per cent of all women employed in agriculture in the EU (Figure 5.4). The distribution of the self-employed was also influenced by the gender division of labour found for employees, so that the share of male self-employed found in craft and related work was similar to the share of employees, at around a quarter, while the female share for both categories fell to around 5 per cent. Around a fifth of the female self-employed were found among service workers, again similar to the female employee share, while service work only accounted for around 7 per cent of male self-employed and employees. Overall, unpaid family workers had the most skewed distribution of all categories, with 50–60 per cent of both male and female family workers found among service workers and skilled agricultural workers.

Comparisons across countries revealed both some underlying differences in patterns of employment organisation, and also some of the problems of occupational classification referred to above (see Figure 5.4). For example, if we look at the managerial category, we found that in four countries

(Greece, Spain, France and Portugal) very few were employees – below 10 per cent in each case for women and below 25 per cent in the case of men – while in another four countries the employee share was above 60 per cent for both sexes (Denmark, Italy, Ireland and the UK). Three of the first four are Southern European countries and three of the second were Northern European countries, suggesting that in part these differences might be explained by the higher level of self-employment found in Southern countries. France was the fourth country with a very low share of managers who were employees and Italy the fourth with a very high employee share. The low share in the case of France was also found in the previous ISCO-68 classification and probably related more to the traditional classification of high-level workers as cadres, or professionals, not as managers, while in Italy the job classification of manager was commonly used for employees.

The distribution of employment by professional status within agriculture and service work also revealed differences both by country and by gender. Most agricultural workers were non-employees in most countries: the proportion of female agricultural workers who were employees fell below 20 per cent in 8 out of 12 cases but exceeded 40 per cent in 3, while among male agricultural workers the proportion was generally higher, but still below below 25 per cent in 6 countries and 40 per cent or above in 4 countries (see Figure 5.4). Gender differences emerged in the relative importance of family workers and the self-employed among agricultural workers. Family workers accounted for 37 per cent of all women employed as skilled agricultural workers at the E12 level and for greater than this share in six countries, while for men the E12 share was only 6 per cent, reaching a maximum of 15 per cent in Greece. Conversely, self-employment accounted for 57 per cent of male skilled agricultural workers and 42 per cent of women in this occupational category at the E12 level (see also Table 5.11).

Among service workers, Italy and Greece stood out for having a very low proportion of employees in this occupational group, particularly for women. Unpaid family workers provided the most important source of alternative labour in Greece, while in Italy all three forms of non-employees provided relatively equal contributions, together accounting for over 50 per cent of the women employed as service workers. Family workers were also concentrated in elementary occupations in three cases – Portugal, Ireland and Germany – where this occupational group accounted for nearly half of all family workers. In the UK where the category of unpaid family workers was included in the Labour Force Survey after 1992, nearly half were found as clerical workers, suggesting that in Britain many women who keep the books for family businesses are effectively unpaid family workers.

Table 5.11 Concentration and segregation of employment by professional status and gender, 1994: E12

(a) Occupational concentration

	Men				
	Employers	Self-employed	Employees	Family workers	All employed
0	*	*	1	0	1
1	29	13	6	4	9
2	14	9	12	1	12
3	8	9	13	4	12
4	2	1	10	6	8
5	10	7	8	25	8
6	6	24	2	25	5
7	26	25	25	17	25
8	3	7	14	4	12
9	2	4	10	15	8
Total	100	100	100	100	100

(b) Composition of occupational group

	Men				
	Employers	Self-employed	Employees	Family workers	All men
0	*	*	100	0	100
1	25	17	57	1	100
2	9	9	82	*	100
3	5	9	85	*	100
4	2	1	96	1	100
5	9	11	76	4	100
6	10	57	27	6	100
7	8	12	80	1	100
8	2	7	91	*	100
9	2	5	91	2	100
Total	7	12	80	1	100

Source: European Labour Force Survey (1994).
Notes
* indicates less than 0.5 per cent.
Data includes unified Germany.
0 = armed forces.
1 = legislators, senior officials and managers.
2 = professionals.
3 = technicians and associate professionals.
4 = clerks.
5 = service, shop and market sales workers.
6 = skilled agricultural and fishery workers.
7 = craft and related workers.
8 = plant and machine operators and assemblers.
9 = elementary occupations.

Table 5.11 Concentration and segregation of employment by professional status and gender, 1994: E12

Women

Employers	Self employed		workers	employed
*	*	*	0	*
32	20	3	4	5
14	12	13	1	13
8	11	17	4	16
6	4	25	11	22
25	20	20	32	20
5	20	1	28	3
6	6	5	5	5
1	2	4	1	4
3	6	12	15	12
100	100	100	100	100

Women

Employers	Self-employed	Employees	Family workers	All women
1	1	98	0	100
18	26	53	3	100
3	6	91	*	100
1	5	93	1	100
1	1	96	2	100
3	7	84	6	100
5	42	16	37	100
4	8	84	4	100
2	3	95	1	100
1	3	91	5	100
3	7	86	4	100

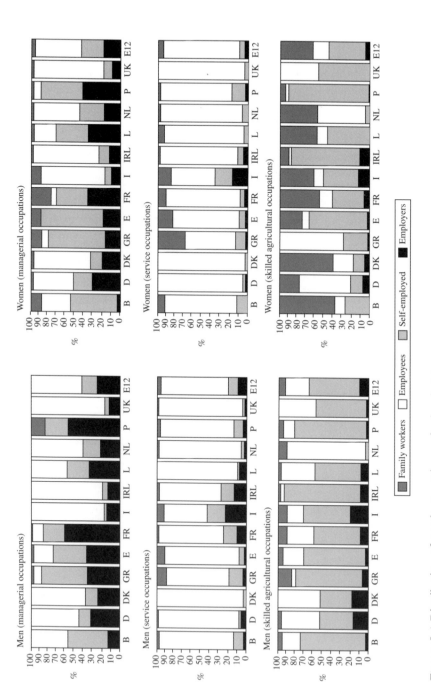

Figure 5.4 Distribution of employment by professional status

Source: European Labour Force Survey (1994).

Note
Based on ISCO-88 (COM) 1-digit data.

Segregation and part-time employment

Sex segregation within part-time employment was less than that found for all in employment, largely as a result of male part-timers being more likely than male full-timers to work in feminised sectors. However, removing part-timers from the data set and calculating the level of segregation for full-timers also reduced the measured level of segregation (see Table 5.12). This reflected the tendency for part-timers to be more concentrated in a narrow range of feminised occupations. Table 5.13 shows that a much higher share of women part-timers was found in female-dominated occupations than was the case for women full-timers in all countries except Italy. Excluding the Southern European countries at least 63 per cent of part-timers worked in female-dominated occupations in all countries. The difference in part-time concentrations relative to full-time concentrations was more than 10 percentage points in all countries except three of the Southern European countries. Spain, which experienced a rapid rise in part-time work during the early 1990s, was the only Southern country to show a much higher degree of segregation for part-timers: 58 per cent worked in jobs in which more than 60 per cent of the occupational workforce was female, compared to 37 per cent of women in full-time jobs. Only Belgium, Denmark and Luxembourg showed a similar or higher disparity between the concentrations of full- and part-timers. In Austria 70 per cent of all new part-time jobs at the end of the 1980s were created in miscellaneous office jobs, sales jobs and healthcare-related occupations, suggesting that in this country too part-time jobs tended to be concentrated in feminised jobs, and often at the lower end of the skill hierarchy (National reports, Austria: Pastner 1996:47).

While part-time work seems to contribute to higher levels of sex segregation in most countries, its actual impact was obviously greatest in countries with a high incidence of part-time work. This was evident from the segregation indices: the largest changes tended to be found in those countries with the largest part-time workforce, namely the Netherlands, the UK and the former West Germany, together with Belgium and Ireland in the case of the index of segregation (see Table 5.12). The impact of removing part-timers on the measured level of segregation in both the Netherlands and Belgium was to push these countries down, close to or even among the levels found in the Southern European countries (especially for the index of segregation), for these countries tended to have segregation levels for full-timers similar to those for all in employment. Part-time work, however, cannot be used to explain the level of occupational segregation observed. For example, Finland, in common with other Scandinavian countries, had a relatively high level of segregation but a low level of part-time work (National reports, Finland: Keinänen 1996:15).

Figure 5.3 not only showed the sex composition of different occupational categories but also the division between full-time and part-time employment for both women and men. There were four occupational groups – armed

Table 5.12 Indices of segregation for full-time, part-time and all in employment, 1994

	Index of segregation			Index of dissimilarity			Karmel and MacLachlan index		
	Part-time	Full-time	All in employment	Part-time	Full-time	All in employment	Part-time	Full-time	All in employment
Belgium	44	47	52	53	51	54	11	23	26
Denmark	47	56	58	48	56	58	18	27	29
Germany (w)	37	49	54	48	52	55	9	22	27
Germany (e)	48	61	62	57	62	62	14	30	31
Spain	46	47	49	53	51	51	20	22	23
France	42	54	55	52	54	55	15	25	27
Greece	39	37	37	41	43	43	20	19	20
Ireland	47	45	51	47	53	54	19	23	25
Italy	44	41	42	46	47	47	19	21	21
Luxembourg	62	53	56	72	55	56	14	24	26
Netherlands	31	45	52	32	50	53	12	17	26
Portugal	40	47	47	50	50	49	22	24	24
UK	40	50	56	42	52	56	12	23	28

Source: European Labour Force Survey (1994).
Note
Based on ISCO-88 (COM) 3-digit classification.

Table 5.13 The concentration of women full-timers and women part-timers in female-dominated occupations, 1994

	Share of employed women who work part-time	Share of employed women found in jobs which are female-dominated (more than 60% of the occupational workforce is female)		
		All women	All women full-timers	All women part-timers
Netherlands	65.6	58.2	48.4	63.3
UK	44.4	66.6	56.6	79.2
Germany (w)	36.5	61.3	56.5	69.8
Denmark	34.4	65.0	56.2	81.8
Belgium	28.3	49.9	44.0	64.5
France	27.8	67.1	64.4	74.2
Ireland	21.7	64.3	63.5	67.0
Germany (e)	20.0	73.1	71.7	81.5
Luxembourg	19.5	57.0	53.2	72.2
Spain	15.2	40.0	36.8	57.6
Italy	12.4	31.1	31.1	31.0
Portugal	12.1	49.7	48.9	55.5
Greece	8.0	26.5	26.3	28.9
E12	25.7	60.9	57.3	68.9

Source: European Labour Force Survey (1994).

Notes
Based on ISCO-88 (COM) 3-digit classification.
Countries ranked by share of employed women who work part-time.

forces (not shown), managers, craft and related and plant and machine operatives – with universally low levels of female and male part-time work, constituting below 7 per cent of the total workforce in every case, and even below 10 per cent of the female labour force in every case. Professionals, technicians and associate professionals and skilled agricultural workers also tended to have low levels of part-time employment, below 15 per cent of employment summing male and female part-timers, and between 7 per cent and 12 per cent of all in employment taking female part-time work alone. In individual countries, female part-time shares in these three occupational groups only rose above 10 per cent in a maximum of five cases (three in the case of agricultural workers) and over 20 per cent in one (the Netherlands). Part-time work made a much more significant contribution to the workforce in the three remaining occupational groups at the E12 level: clerical work (21 per cent including male part-time work, 19 per cent female only); service workers (29 per cent including male part-time work, 26 per cent female only); and elementary occupations (30 per cent including male part-time work, 29 per cent female only).

The role of part-time work in contributing to the feminisation of an occupation is complex. Some countries with relatively high rates of female full-time work within an occupational group also had significant female

part-time employment shares, with both full- and part-time working contributing to a high overall feminisation of the occupation (see for example
clerical work in France and Denmark). Equally, part-time work was not
always a means to increase the rate of feminisation, as it might also act in
some cases as a substitute for full-time work. This applied particularly in
the Netherlands which had a very high rate of part-time work in many occupations, but relatively low or average rates of feminisation.

If we look more specifically at the shares of part-time relative to full-
time work within occupations, we find that in the majority of occupations
and the majority of countries part-time work usually accounted for only
one-quarter or less of total female employment. There was one major exception to this pattern and that is the Netherlands, where in every case except
managerial jobs and the armed forces, the female part-time contribution was
greater than 50 per cent of the total female contribution to the occupation.
The difference with the other countries was clear when we see that with
the exception of two occupations – service work and elementary occupations – the part-time contribution only exceeded one-third of the total female
contribution in four cases (three in the UK and one in the former West
Germany), and in no case exceeded 40 per cent of the female contribution.
Within service and elementary occupations, however, the part-time contribution was significant in a number of countries. In the Netherlands and the
UK female part-timers constituted by far the majority of the workforce in
both occupations. In elementary occupations part-time work also exceeded
full-time work for women in the cases of Belgium, Denmark, France, Ireland
and West Germany. In service occupations female part-time work was nearly
equal to full-time work in Denmark and accounted for over a third of female
employment in the former West Germany, Ireland and Belgium.

Another way of considering the impact of part-time work on segregation
is to compare the actual concentrations of part-time and full-time workers by
gender within occupations to the expected employment shares, assuming
all groups are evenly represented with all occupations given their share in
overall employment. That is if women part-timers constituted 10 per cent of
employment, we would expect them to form 10 per cent of each occupational
group. On this basis we find first that within higher-level jobs both male
and female full-timers were relatively evenly represented, with even a
slightly higher share of female full-timers in this category than in that for
all in employment (see Figure 5.2 and Tables 5.14a and c). Female part-
timers were, however, markedly under-represented in these higher-level jobs
(23 per cent below expected share), as well as in agriculture, craft and operative jobs (40 per cent below expected share) (Table 5.14d). Their concentration in service and elementary work was considerably higher than that of
all women in employment. Female part-timers thus followed the overall
female employment distribution but to an exaggerated degree, with higher
rates of under- and over-representation and, in addition, marked under-
representation in higher-level jobs. Moreover, while female full-timers still

Table 5.14 Concentration of full-time and part-time employment by gender for broad occupational groups, 1994

(a) Concentration of male full-timers relative to all men in employment[a]

	B	DK	D	D	E	F	GR	IRL	I	L	NL	P	UK	E12
1+2+3	100	106	99	100	99	100	101	102	100	99	103	101	103	100
4	101	96	99	100	100	99	102	101	101	101	95	104	98	100
5+9	97	72	96	95	99	95	99	93	99	100	77	100	84	94
6+7+8	101	108	102	102	101	101	99	102	100	100	106	99	104	102

(b) Concentration of male part-timers relative to all men in employment[a]

	B	DK	D	D	E	F	GR	IRL	I	L	NL	P	UK	E12
1+2+3	95	47	121	112	138	94	67	59	(91)	139	86	87	63	95
4	74	137	140	103	88	115	(37)	(85)	(78)	46	126	(28)	126	102
5+9	229	353	232	237	142	198	125	227	(140)	133	225	101	312	215
6+7+8	72	27	45	46	64	80	122	64	(88)	71	67	123	49	61

(c) Concentration of female full-timers relative to all women in employment[a]

	B	DK	D	D	E	F	GR	IRL	I	L	NL	P	UK	E12
1+2+3	108	115	105	111	107	112	102	109	105	106	121	108	128	110
4	102	109	105	99	108	101	105	108	101	109	112	110	109	102
5+9	78	75	89	83	90	84	98	79	93	88	60	92	55	81
6+7+8	123	130	104	120	105	110	97	115	102	106	113	96	131	118

(d) Concentration of female part-timers relative to all women in employment[a]

	B	DK	D	D	E	F	GR	IRL	I	L	NL	P	UK	E12
1+2+3	81	72	79	82	60	70	75	68	61	76	90	42	65	77
4	95	82	81	101	58	98	45	71	95	62	94	28	88	96
5+9	155	148	148	129	156	141	119	176	148	149	121	156	157	142
6+7+8	42	43	84	65	72	74	133	(45)	84	(76)	93	130	61	60

Source: European Labour Force Survey (1994).

Notes
Based on ISCO-88 (COM) 3-digit classification.
1+2+3 = managerial, professional and associate professional.
4 = clerical.
5+9 = service and elementary occupations.
6+7+8 = skilled agriculture, craft and operative occupations.
a Relative concentrations calculated by dividing the share of men/women full-/part-timers within an occupational group by the share of all men/women in employment within that occupational group. A value of 100 represents the expected concentration.

had a concentration pattern markedly different from that of male full-timers, there was one significant difference compared to the concentration for all females and that was a much lower over-representation in service and elementary jobs. Like women part-timers men in part-time jobs had a concentration pattern which differed from that of full-timers (see Table 5.14b).

Male part-timers thus shared the tendency with female part-timers to be very over-represented in service and elementary jobs.

These patterns of concentration relative to total employment were largely replicated at the member state level. This can also be seen from Table 5.14, in which the concentrations of female full- and part-timers are compared to those for all females, and those for male full- and part-timers to all males. Female part-timers were systematically under-represented in higher-level jobs compared to all females, by 23 per cent at the E12 level and by margins of between 58 and 10 per cent at the member state level, and they were systematically over-represented in service and elementary jobs, by 42 per cent at E12 level, varying from 19 to 76 per cent at the member state level. Female part-timers tended to be relatively evenly represented along with full-timers in clerical work at the E12 level but there was variation by member state; seven countries recorded a slight degree of under-representation, with a deficit of up to 20 per cent and four recorded significant under-representation, at 29 per cent to 72 per cent. Female part-timers were under-represented in agriculture, craft and operative jobs at the E12 level by some 40 per cent, but there was considerable variation here by member state, with Greece and Portugal recording over-represented shares of around 30 per cent. When we compare the distributions of male part-timers to those for all men in employment we find very strong differences for two groups. In service and elementary jobs the concentration of male part-timers was 115 per cent greater than for all men in employment, while in agriculture, craft and operative jobs they were 39 per cent under-represented. Again, these patterns were replicated at the member state level, except for Greece and Portugal where male part-timers were more evenly distributed according to all male employment distributions between those two categories.

Segregation and temporary employment

Of all the forms of atypical employment, temporary work seems to have least effect in adding to segregation. By and large the pattern of temporary employment for both men and women followed that of permanent employment, with gender differences being more important than differences in employment contract for predicting allocation to occupations. These findings relate to the ISCO-68 data for 1990, and here it was found that it was only in service occupations that temporary employment had made any significant contribution to the female share of employment. Furthermore, this applied mainly in the four Southern European member states (Rubery *et al.* 1994).

Occupational segregation by sector and organisation

Much analysis of occupational segregation makes little or no reference to segregation by sector or organisation. However, occupational segregation can be regarded as having both a sectoral and an occupational dimension;

thus women tend to be concentrated in services and some specific manu-facturing sectors (Meulders *et al.* 1993), while within sectors and within organisations they tend to be concentrated in the lower skill grades (National reports, France: Silvera *et al.* 1996:44).

The overall level of segregation is itself likely to be highly dependent upon the industrial structure of employment. Those countries with a large public sector may be more likely to have an overall higher level of segre-gation when public sector services are associated with highly feminised jobs. This relationship is not determinant, as for example the feminisation rate of some public services such as teaching varies between countries, but for some countries, including here particularly the Scandinavian countries, high segregation has been associated with a large public sector. Manufacturing occupations have tended to be highly differentiated within occupational clas-sification systems, which in turn tends to lead to a high degree of measured horizontal segregation within this sector compared to the broader service and non-manual occupations.

Information at the organisational level suggests that the pattern of occu-pational segregation is much more complex than that indicated by aggregate labour market statistics – and also much more pervasive. Thus a recent study in the UK found that for each occupational group between 44 and 74 per cent of establishments employed either exclusively one sex or the other, suggesting a very high degree of complete segregation by occupa-tion at the organisational level. Perhaps even more surprising was the fact that for each of the occupational groups except for one – clerical workers – some establishments employed exclusively men and others employed exclusively women. Only in clerical work were there virtually no estab-lishments, just 2 per cent, employing only men (Millward and Woodland 1994). Thus the gender shares for an occupation at the aggregate labour market level were built up out of a mix of establishments which employed exclusively women or exclusively men, together with others in which the occupations were more mixed. We do not know if such variation is likely to be found at the organisational level in other EU countries, but research needs to be carried out at this level in order for the processes of occupa-tional segregation to be better understood.

Trends in occupational segregation

Having reviewed the pattern of segregation across the member states, what trends can be identified? As a consequence of the change in the ISCO-88 occu-pational classification system in 1992, it was not possible to assess trends in occupational segregation using harmonised data from the 1980s into the 1990s. Instead we could only seek to update the trends revealed by the Eurostat ISCO-68 data for the 1980s by reference to national data sources, which were both uneven in their availability and based on very different occupational clas-sification systems, which could give rise to very different results.

The trends during the 1980s were towards little net change. The indices of segregation for the countries for the most part either remained constant or fell slightly, although segregation in Spain, the Netherlands and Ireland even rose slightly (see Table 5.2). Only in Greece did the segregation index fall significantly, but closer examination revealed this to be connected almost entirely to a change in the classification of jobs within agriculture. Little difference was revealed in the trends when we used alternative index measures or examined national data sources. Table 5.2 shows not only the index of dissimilarity but also the Karmel and MacLachlan index, which standardises the index of dissimilarity for changes in occupational structure and female employment share. There were some differences between the index of dissimilarity and its standardised index, but again the picture was generally one of little decline in the level of segregation. The UK, Belgium, Greece and Luxembourg recorded smaller falls in their levels of segregation over the 1980s, and Ireland recorded a small increase when the Karmel and MacLachlan index was used instead of the index of dissimilarity.

There was also little evidence of change in the measured level of segregation over the 1980s for those member states for which we do not have harmonised Eurostat data. New information available for Italy on occupational segregation patterns from both the 1981 and the 1991 censuses suggest a decline across the decade at both the 3- and the 2-digit level (National reports, Italy: Bettio and Villa 1996:14 and Table 5.15). The comparison across the 3-digit level is suspect owing to the change in the occupational classification system between 1981 and 1991, but there are much greater similarities in the classification system at the 2-digit level. National data from Denmark revealed a decline in occupational segregation between 1980 and 1987, but from a high level (62 to 58, see Table 5.15). This evidence of a decline in the 1980s might have been the result of the weakening of the traditional strong division of the Danish labour market along educational lines, which reduced mobility between occupations, and was reinforced by union control of entry into occupations through control of enrolment into vocational qualifications (National reports, Denmark: Boje 1996:27–28).

Austria, Finland and Sweden, as we noted above, were still not included in the Eurostat data, but national data sources showed that the two Scandinavian countries had a similar high level of segregation to that found in Denmark (see Table 5.15 and Box 5.2). Sweden had a very high level of measured segregation which had been falling gradually since the 1960s, including through the 1980s. For Finland we only had data from 1988, but this also reveals a high level of segregation without evidence of a decline in this period, although there had been a small decrease in segregation since 1985 associated with industrial restructuring (see Box 5.2) For Austria we could compare the level of segregation in 1981 and 1991. Again, the measured level of segregation was high and the dissimilarity index showed a slight increase over the decade.[4]

Table 5.15 Trends in segregation indices in the 1980s–1990s using national data sources for selected countries

	Index of dissimilarity		Index of segregation
	2-digit	3-digit	2-digit
Germany (w)			
1989/90			52
1991/94			51
Germany (e)			
1991			61
Denmark			
1986/87			58
Ireland			
1987			53
1992			51
Netherlands			
1987	57		
1994	54		
Finland			
1988	59		59
1990	58		59
1995	58		58
Sweden[a]			
1980	(58)61	68	
1983	61		
1985[b]	(57.7)61	67	
1988	61		
1989	61		61
1990	(56)61	65	61
1991	61		60
1992	59		59
1993	59		59
1994	59		58
1995	59		58
UK			
1991	49		49
1995	48		48
Italy			
1981	43	52	
1991	37	46	
Austria			
1981	56		
1991	57		

Source: National Reports of the EC Network of Experts (see bibliography).

Notes
a Figures outside brackets are AKU 2-digit, figures inside are FOB (see National reports, Sweden: Gonäs and Spånt (1996)).
b Change in the Swedish employment classification (NYK) in 1985 (see National reports, Sweden: Gonäs and Spånt (1996)).

Box 5.2 Segregation remained a persistent feature of the labour markets in Austria, Finland and Sweden during the 1980s

In **Austria** despite very large percentage increases in some mixed or male-dominated occupations, such as executive officers in administration and the economy (up 214 per cent for women and only 97 per cent for men) or legal and social science professionals (up 77 per cent for women and 23 per cent for men), most of the new jobs for women over the decade 1981–1991 were concentrated in female-dominated jobs (75 per cent in jobs where over half of the labour force were women). Only 5 per cent of new jobs were in mixed occupations (defined as women holding 30–50 per cent of the jobs); 20 per cent were in male-dominated occupations (defined as women holding less than 30 per cent of the jobs). Overall, therefore, there was little change in the pattern of concentration of male and female employment in segregated jobs. The proportion of employed women located in female-dominated jobs, defined as where the workforce consisted of 60 per cent or more women, actually increased from 64 per cent in 1981 to 68 per cent in 1991, although the proportion concentrated in jobs with female shares of 80 per cent or more declined from 32 per cent to 20 per cent. For men the changes were even smaller and the share working in very male-dominated jobs (where the occupational workforce was 90 per cent or more male) actually rose slightly, from 41 to 42 per cent over the decade (National reports, Austria: Pastner 1996:44).

In **Sweden** patterns of female employment change were examined for two conflicting periods, 1987–1990 and 1990–1993, the first a boom period and the second a deep recession. The results found that women's employment was less cyclically sensitive than men's. The main factor determining change in women's employment was the pattern of female segregation; there was no tendency for women's share of employment within occupational groups to increase or to decrease in response to changing labour market conditions (National reports, Sweden: Gonäs and Spånt 1996:45).

In **Finland**, studies of segregation patterns in the 1970s and 1980s found the horizontal segregation of the female labour force – that is the share of women found in female-dominated jobs – increased between 1975 and 1985, while the share of men found in male-dominated jobs decreased. By 1985 the traditionally higher share of men concentrated in male-dominated jobs than of women in female-dominated jobs had disappeared. Between 1985 and 1990 there was a decrease in occupational segregation, largely as a result of industrial changes which reduced the importance of the male-dominated forestry, construction and transport industries (National reports, Finland: Keinänen 1996:42–43).

These trends towards little change in the 1980s reflected forces pulling in opposite directions: towards a desegregation of some male-dominated higher-level jobs, but towards an increased feminisation of already feminised job areas, and little change in the sex composition of male-dominated lower-level jobs (Rubery and Fagan 1993, 1995b). Thus desegregation coexisted with increasing feminisation of some job areas.

Segregation indices based on national data sources available for Germany, Ireland, the Netherlands, Finland, Sweden and the UK suggested a continuation of the above pattern during the 1990s; overall towards a slight decline in measured segregation (see Table 5.15). It should, however, be noted that the index of dissimilarity was recalculated for the Netherlands according to the standardised Karmel and MacLachlan index, and on this basis segregation had apparently remained constant in this country (National reports, Netherlands: Plantenga *et al.* 1996:26).

Within these continuing patterns of little overall change in the indices of segregation we still found trends towards both desegregation and resegregation. Female employment continued to rise in most member states in the 1990s, concentrated in certain occupational areas and with a particular impact on segregation patterns. The actual pattern of employment restructuring did vary between member states, but there was in most cases a continued expansion in the proportion of professional and higher-level jobs in the job structure overall. Within this expansion women further increased their representation within this occupational group (see Box 5.3). Low-skilled work also continued to decline in many countries, although female shares of these jobs also tended to rise. More variable was the pattern of change in clerical employment, with some countries recording noted downturns in the rate of growth or even actual declines in clerical employment compared to increases in the 1980s, while in others clerical work continued to provide a major source of female employment growth. The falls in clerical employment may signal the beginning of a process of economic restructuring in which the traditional source of middle-level jobs for women is under threat from technical change and organisational restructuring (see Chapter 8).

The end result of this process of restructuring may be increased polarisation within the female labour force at both a European and a national level. The trend towards a higher share of women entering professional and higher-level jobs was evident in all countries and was relatively independent of the overall rate of integration of women into the wage economy. This entry into higher-level jobs is associated with the women concerned pursuing more continuous and full-time careers. There was evidence of convergence across Europe in both the labour market behaviour and occupational position of the more educated and advantaged parts of the female labour force, while major differences between member states still persisted in both the labour market behaviour and the occupational position of the less educated groups of women (see Chapter 3).

While there was little change in female shares of male-dominated manual jobs, women's employment did grow, albeit from initial low starting positions, in some technical intermediate and higher-level occupations (see Box 5.4). Thus some of the effects from more diversified educational choices among young women appeared to be feeding through into the occupational

Box 5.3 Where were the new jobs for women in the 1990s: towards a segregated or desegregated labour market?

In the **UK** employment decline over the 1990s was concentrated in skilled manual jobs for men and clerical jobs for women. This coincided with relative and absolute growth in women's employment in professional and higher-level jobs. These trends suggest the continuation of the trend to desegregation at the upper end of the labour market, coupled with a decline in segregated middle-level jobs for both men and women. However, the end result might be an increasingly polarised labour force as jobs for women were increasingly concentrated in relatively low-skilled service work (with personal service workers recording the second highest job growth for women after corporate managers and administrators) at the one end and professional work at the other end. Both men and women thus perhaps face the problem of disappearing middle-level jobs (National reports, UK: Rubery 1996:81).

In **Spain** there was a rapid growth of the number of professional jobs in the 1980s, but from a low level. The coincidence of this employment growth with the entry of many well-qualified women onto the labour market allowed women in Spain to achieve a very high share of professional jobs, relative to their overall share of the labour force. This pattern continued in the 1990s, with professional jobs expanding by 25 per cent between 1990 and 1994 while overall employment fell by 7 per cent, but Spanish women increased their share of professional jobs from 42 to 47 per cent. (National reports, Spain: Moltó 1996:43).

In **Germany**, despite trends towards more mixed or moderately segregated occupations in the 1980s, the period 1989–1994 saw very little change in the share of women or men employed in segregated occupations (National reports, Germany: Maier *et al.* 1996:Table 2.1.4). In fact, the rates of change in employment in most of the major skill areas over the period 1989–1993 were remarkably similar for women in five out of seven groups, ranging from 27 to 31 per cent. The main exceptions were unskilled and semi-skilled workers (manual and non-manual combined) where there was no expansion, and head of department posts, which increased by over 62 per cent for women, but only by 22 per cent overall. Male employment also changed at a similar pace in six out of seven job areas, with the unskilled area, where a decline of 8 per cent was recorded, again the exception. However, male rates of expansion were between 10 and 15 per cent, so that the result was a relatively even rise in female shares in all job areas.

In **Ireland** in the 1990–1994 period there were above average increases in female employment in administrative, executive and managerial jobs, electrical and electronic production workers, service workers, other products production workers and commercial workers, while there was a fall of over 40 per cent in textile, clothing and leather production workers (National reports, Ireland: Barry 1996:Table 9).

In **Finland** the largest falls in employment during the deep recession of 1990–1995 occurred in clerical work, resulting in a fall of 7 per cent in total female employment, that is nearly half the total fall in women's employment of 16 per cent, and a drop in the share of the female labour force in employment from 29 to 26 per cent. Only two occupational groups experienced rises in employment: professionals and other white collar workers; and the share of women in professional jobs rose from 12 to 15 per cent and in other white-collar jobs from 17 to 21 per cent. These patterns indicate the increasing uncertainty associated with job prospects for both middle- and lower-level jobs for women, while the growth of higher-level jobs seemed more robust, even in the depths of recession. A similar pattern emerged when we looked at male employment in Finland, for although professional jobs accounted for 0.2 per cent of the total 16 per cent decline in employment, declines in production-worker employment were responsible for over half of all the fall in employment, that is for an 8.3 per cent fall in total employment (National reports, Finland: Keinänen 1996:48).

In the **Netherlands** the pattern of employment change appeared somewhat different from that in, for example, the **UK** or **Finland**, for instead of clerical work being a cause of employment decline, the category 'clerical workers not elsewhere classified' accounted for the largest growth in female employment in the first half of the 1990s. The high-growth jobs in the Netherlands were already female-dominated jobs, with medical- and dental-related workers accounting for the second-highest growth rate in female employment, followed by cashiers and related workers (National reports, Netherlands: Plantenga *et al.* 1996:24).

In **Sweden** cutbacks in the welfare state in the early 1990s primarily affected the lower-grade care jobs such as assistant nurses, childminders and administrative staff. These were also the highly gender-segregated jobs, and six out of the ten most common female jobs were expected to suffer cutbacks over the period 1996–1997 – in particular assistant nurses, shop assistants and childminders. For men, only four out of the ten most common male jobs were expected to suffer from cutbacks, and one major occupation, engineering, was projected to increase. Thus prospects for men's employment in the public sector over the 1990s might be more promising than for women, reversing the past tendency for segregation to have protected women's employment in Sweden (National reports, Sweden: Gonäs and Spånt 1996:12–13).

In **Italy** segregation appeared to be increasing rather than decreasing in the majority of occupations. Comparing female shares of the age groups 25–34 and 35–44 should indicate the direction of change, particularly as employment in Italy has tended to be relatively stable, so that once a young person is well established in an occupational area they are likely to remain in these jobs. This comparison showed that in the first half of the 1990s there were more jobs in which segregation had increased for the younger cohorts than jobs in which segregation had fallen. This applied both to male-dominated and female-dominated jobs. Thus clerical, nursing and some service jobs appeared to be becoming even more female-dominated while women's presence was declining in some male-dominated jobs such as driving. The desegregating jobs tended to be professional and public sector administrative jobs, indicating the impact of both increasing numbers of young women acquiring qualifications and the diversification of their educational choices on subsequent careers (National reports, Italy: Bettio and Villa 1996:15).

In **France** women's employment over the period 1989–1994 grew fastest within the 'cadres' and higher intellectual professions category. Its share of total female employment rose from just under 7 per cent in 1989 to 9.3 per cent in 1994, a faster increase than over the 1980s when the share rose from 5 to 7 per cent between 1982 and 1989. Over half of this increase was accounted for by academic and scientific professions which included lycée teachers, with cadres in administrative and sales positions also making a significant contribution. Overall the female share rose within this job grade by over 3 percentage points to 32 per cent: again, the largest increase in the feminisation rate. In the more feminised intermediate white-collar and lower white-collar occupations the feminisation rate still rose, and significantly within intermediate sales and administrative occupations in the private sector. Among lower white-collar workers there was some evidence of a plateauing of the feminisation rate, with the female share actually falling in the lower white-collar distributive trade jobs (National reports, France: Silvera *et al.* 1996:45).

In **Portugal** the female distribution across occupational categories remained very stable over the 1990s, with little change in the proportions of the female workforce within ISCO 1-digit categories between 1992 and 1995. Socio-economic group data also suggested that while women increased their employment shares within almost all groups the changes were relatively even across socio-economic groups. Thus while women did increase their shares of directors and management directors, from 16 to 20 per cent between 1989 and 1993, they also increased their shares of production foremen, highly skilled staff, skilled staff, semi-skilled and unskilled staff, all by 2.5 to 5.7 percentage points. The only group where women did not make a significant gain during this period was middle management, where the female share rose only by 0.7 of a percentage point to 24.1 per cent by 1993 (National reports, Portugal: Lopes and Perista 1996:18).

In **Denmark** there was a major upgrading of the skill level of the occupational structure between the late 1980s and early 1990s. For men this upgrading was reflected in a positive growth of all non-manual jobs at higher, intermediate and lower levels, and a decline in all manual jobs at skilled and unskilled levels. For women the change in structure was more skewed by skill level within non-manual and manual jobs, such that high-level non-manual employment grew by 38 per cent between 1987 and 1993, middle-level non-manual by 11 per cent and skilled manual by 15 per cent, with low-level non-manual and unskilled manual all experiencing declines (National reports, Denmark: Boje 1996:23).

structure. However, while younger, more highly educated women might be entering a wider range of courses and careers, there was little evidence of an overall trend towards desegregation.

Much of the change in women's employment pattern across occupations continued to be determined by patterns of industrial or sectoral change, but the

---

Box 5.4 Women are still bumping up against the glass ceiling, particularly in the private sector

In **Finland** women held only 21 per cent of private sector managerial posts in 1990. Moreover, within this group, women tended to be over-represented among personnel managers and administrative and financial managers while being under-represented among general managers (16 per cent) and recording their lowest share among technical managers. Women managers tended to be found primarily in either very small firms or in larger organisations, but in Finland there were relatively few large organisations, possibly restricting women's entry into management (National reports, Finland: Keinänen 1996:48–49)

In **Italy** the higher-level jobs which were found to dominate among the desegregating occupations in the first half of the 1990s did not include private sector management (National reports, Italy: Bettio and Villa 1996:16).

In the **former West Germany** the strongest job growth for women between 1989 and 1993 occurred among lower-level managers, at 62 per cent, such that women's share rose from 13 to 17 per cent, but the proportion of women among higher management only rose from 14 to 15 per cent (National reports, Germany: Maier *et al.* 1996:Table 2.1.5a). At unification vertical segregation was less strong in the East, with women accounting for 45 per cent of professional experts compared to 20 per cent in the West, and for 28 per cent of directors compared to 15 per cent in the West. Women remained better represented in higher-level jobs in the East than the West, but the female share had fallen in all these job grades, for example from 45 to 40 per cent in the case of professional experts and from 28 to 26 per cent in the case of directors by 1994 (National reports, Germany: Maier *et al.* 1996:Table 2.1.5b).

---

difference was that in the 1990s the future prospects for at least some female-dominated sectors were not as propitious as was the case in the past. There are differences in the potential for female employment growth in traditional female areas such as clerical work and services between member states, relating both to the shares of these jobs in the overall job structure and also to the current female presence within these occupational categories. Thus in some Northern European countries the female shares in these categories appeared to be reaching saturation point, while in some Southern countries and even some of the Benelux countries, the female shares in clerical and service work were still well below those found in the Scandinavian and other Northern European member states (see Box 5.1). There is of course no inevitable tendency towards convergence, so female shares may remain diverse, but in those countries where female shares were already very high, future employment change would be much more dependent upon overall changes in numbers of jobs, while in those with low female shares they still had potential for further female substitution for male labour without new job growth.

Box 5.5 Women may be facing more competition from men as male unemployment rises

In the **former East Germany** segregation prior to unification was higher than in West Germany, largely because of the concentration of East German women in services (although their share of employment in manufacturing and agriculture also exceeded that for West German women). Since unification women have been excluded from manufacturing and technical jobs more than men and have also faced much greater competition from men for entry into the service sector jobs which they had previously spurned. For example, working as a bank clerk used to be an exclusively female job, but since unification it has become one of the most attractive jobs in East Germany, attracting many male applicants. Desegregation in East Germany has thus been the result of men entering female or mixed occupations and women being increasingly excluded from the employment system (National reports, Germany: Maier *et al.* 1996:56).

In **France**, women's share of lower-skilled non-manual jobs has plateaued or even fallen, partly because the female shares could be considered to have reached saturation point. On the other hand, more men have been accepting typically female jobs, particularly in distribution and services to individuals but also in public service, such as primary teaching, perhaps because of reduced employment opportunities in traditional male areas (National reports, France: Silvera *et al.* 1996:45).

However, while in the past most of the desegregation had been in one direction, with women substituting for male labour, there was much more likelihood in the future of desegregation occurring in both directions. The loss of male jobs in manufacturing and production areas resulted in a loss of traditional job opportunities, particularly for less skilled men, and in these circumstances women can expect to face more competition in their traditional enclaves of service and clerical work. Such competition occurred in the former East Germany where women lost out in the scramble for jobs after unification (see Box 5.5). While the former East Germany represents an extreme case of dislocation, it provides a useful reminder of the potential impact on women's overall job prospects of increased competition between the sexes for work. Thus desegregation does not always work in the interests of women.

Trends in vertical segregation

During the 1990s there was evidence that the trend identified during the 1980s towards a higher share of women employed in higher level and professional jobs had continued (see Boxes 5.3 and 5.4). This reflected both the increasing share of these types of jobs within the overall employment structure and the rising share of women within these job categories. Yet while these trends suggested a decrease in vertical segregation at an aggregate

---

Box 5.6 Vertical segregation is found in both public and private sectors but is greater in private organisations

Women in **Sweden** accounted for only 9 per cent of higher-level positions in the private sector but for 29 per cent in the public sector in 1994. However, even within the public sector vertical segregation has been slow to change. Thus women only increased their share of posts as heads of finance among financial administrative staff from 15 to 18 per cent between 1991 and 1994, despite accounting for over two-thirds of employees in this area. In personnel within the public sector women accounted for four-fifths of employees, but only around 32 per cent of chief personnel officers, a situation which hardly improved in the early 1990s (National reports, Sweden: Gonäs and Spånt 1996:43).

Vertical segregation in teaching was found to be still strong and persistent in both **Ireland** and the **Netherlands**. In Ireland, women accounted for 76 per cent of primary school teachers and 55 per cent of secondary school teachers, but for only 48 per cent of principals in both types of school. However, the more equal representation among secondary schools was in part explained by the 38 per cent share of female secondary school heads, many of them nuns, who were in religious and often single-sex schools, (National reports, Ireland: Barry 1996:35). In the Netherlands women were found to be seriously under-represented among head teachers, accounting for only 13 per cent of primary head teachers while constituting 74 per cent of the teaching staff. This situation reflected in part the impact of the merger of infant and junior schools in the mid-1980s, when most of the new headships were allocated to men. Some measures had been taken to try to reduce the discrimination, but so far with little effect (National reports, Netherlands: Plantenga *et al.* 1996: 27–28).

Within the public service women's representation within the highest grades continued to rise in the early 1990s, albeit at a slow rate in both the **UK** and **Ireland**. In Ireland, the share of women at Assistant Secretary level (second-to-top grade) rose from 3 to 5 per cent between 1989 and 1992, and at Principal level (third-highest grade) from 8 to 12 per cent, but women's representation in the lowest grades increased even faster (National reports, Ireland: Barry 1996:35–36). Within the UK civil service grading structure, women significantly increased their representation in the highest grades between 1988 and 1994 – often by around 100 per cent – but from such a low level that women's share was still 10 per cent or below in the first four grades (National reports, UK: Rubery 1996:Table 2.1.10).

---

level, more detailed examination of the evidence suggests not only that progress has been slow and patchy, but also that the pattern of male and female distribution within the higher level and professional job sectors was resulting in new forms of gender segregation, particularly between the private and public sectors, but also within sectors (Crompton and Sanderson 1990; Reskin and Roos 1990; Rubery and Fagan 1993).

Women have increased their share of lower- and middle-level management jobs at a much faster rate than their share of high-level managerial posts. Part of the explanation lies in the age structure of women within management; few have reached the age or experience level to be promoted to the most senior grades. Yet this is the optimistic interpretation; the pessimistic interpretation is that the glass ceiling has yet to be cracked even if there are more women now pressing up against it (see Box 5.4).

Women's acquisition of higher and professional qualifications, coupled with the diversification of their educational and training choices, is resulting in women obtaining a higher share of vacancies in a range of professions and managerial-level jobs. The significance of education as the passport to better employment prospects for women has been seen perhaps particularly dramatically in the South, for example Spain and Italy, where educational qualifications enabled women to achieve similar shares of professional jobs to those held by women in the North, despite lower overall rates of female integration. Yet it is also the case that entry for women had been facilitated in those higher-level jobs in which most attention was paid to educational attainment, for example the professions or the public sector, where entry has tended to be regulated in many countries by examination. Where there was more scope for managerial discretion, for example in entry to private sector managerial jobs, progress had been much less dramatic (Box 5.6).

The exclusion of women from private sector management is not solely to do with modes of entry but also with slower progress in changing gender stereotypes; women tend to be more acceptable as professional experts or as specific functional managers, such as personnel specialists, than as general, technical or line managers. Thus the problem lies in the gendering of managerial jobs, and not solely in the number of female applicants or the process of selection and recruitment. As a result of this gendering, women may fare better in certain types of organisations than in others. As women have tended to be more acceptable in the lower ranks of management, and in specialist rather than general management roles, the current process of delayering organisations (see Chapter 2), that is taking out layers of middle management and increasing the significance of line management over specialised management, may increase the problems of women trying to cross the divide between managerial and non-managerial areas, as there are both fewer rungs to the ladder and a reduction in the number of routes into management.

Women have not only been entering public sector higher-level jobs at a faster rate than private sector jobs, they have also made more rapid progress up the occupational hierarchy within the public sector. Some may suggest that these improvements in women's relative position within the public sector have been associated with the downgrading of both the status of public sector employment and its associated job security. Nevertheless, women have succeeded in increasing their representation in decision-making roles in public sector professions, even if women continued to be under-represented relative to their overall share of the profession in, for example, head teacher appoint-

---

Box 5.7 Desegregation may be the beginning of a process of reseg-regation

In the **UK** the share of women among the membership of various profes-sional bodies increased dramatically over the period 1986–1992. These changes illustrate the twin processes of desegregation and resegregation. Thus while women made significant entries into some male-dominated professions, with their share of, for example, the Institute of Chemical Engineers doubling from 5 to 10 per cent, and their share of the Law Society rising from 14 per cent to nearly a quarter, other professions were clearly in the process of resegregation, with women's share of the Institute of Personnel Management rising from 42 to 60 per cent, and of health service management from 39 to 50 per cent (National reports, UK: Rubery 1996:97).

---

ments, senior nursing staff and senior administrators (see Boxes 5.1 and 5.6). Indeed, within any job area, including those where women appeared to have made most progress, there seemed to be evidence of persistent vertical segre-gation,with women always under-represented in higher-level jobs compared to their representation for the workforce as a whole.

As we argued above, processes of desegregation may not necessarily result in integration by gender but may equally well result in resegregation or the redefinition of occupations or occupational areas, previously male domi-nated, as female-dominated sectors (Box 5.7). This likelihood is evident within some professions into which women have continued to make entry, despite having already achieved a high share of employment in the 1980s. These areas, many of which are located in the public sector, but also in other jobs associated with feminine skills of communication, such as personnel management, may in the future become new ghettos of women's work. The entry of women into professional areas may lead to an increase in the number of women commanding relatively high salaries, but will not necessarily lead to the long-term erosion of job segregation. Vertical segre-gation has in the past been explained in part with reference to women's lower qualifications or experience. However, evidence suggests that women have tended to be underemployed relative to their qualifications, and also to have required more years of service or experience to achieve the same promotion as men (Box 5.8). Thus whatever the validity of the argument that women have lacked appropriate educational or work experience qualifi-cations these do not seem sufficient to account for the pervasive pattern of vertical segregation.

In this context there is clearly scope for effective equal opportunities poli-cies. Research which has attempted to evaluate the impact of equal treatment legislation and positive action programmes is somewhat limited, but overall these studies do show that strong legislation combined with comprehensive positive action programmes within companies improve women's employ-ment opportunities, their distribution across a wider range of functions and

---

Box 5.8 Women tend to require higher qualifications or longer work experience to reach the same grade

By the early 1990s, only 50 per cent of women who had completed apprenticeship training in **Austria** were employed in jobs at that level, compared to 68 per cent of men who had completed apprenticeships. Among those with vocational school qualifications only 9 per cent of women reached better or highly qualified executive positions, compared to 36 per cent of men. Even among those with higher education there were major gender disparities, with 59 per cent of men employed in better or highly qualified executive positions compared to 38 per cent of women (National reports, Austria: Pastner 1996:49)

In **Denmark** there had been a massive upgrading of both the skill level of the occupational structure and the qualifications of the labour force, particularly for women. However, several studies showed that women needed to be more qualified than men to get a job at the same occupational level. More men without vocational qualifications still got jobs at the top of the occupational hierarchy, and more men with vocational qualifications filled positions at the top of the hierarchy than women with similar qualifications. This gender gap between educational level and job position remained unchanged in the 1980s despite a strong upgrading of the female labour force (National reports, Denmark: Boje 1996).

In **Italy** a case study of an Italian bank found that the average age at which men were promoted into senior positions was 47, compared to over 50 for women. Moreover, women also required longer work experience within the bank before they were promoted (National reports, Italy: Bettio and Villa 1993).

---

their chances of promotion, although progress into the higher managerial levels is slower than in more junior positions (see Rubery *et al.* 1996 for a review and Box 5.9). However, there is also evidence that such policies may be most successful where women already constitute a relatively high share of the workforce, and there are thus fewer barriers to women being accepted in higher-level or managerial posts. Another approach to the problem of vertical segregation is to reconsider the hierarchy of occupations from an equal-value perspective. Women's unfavourable position within the job hierarchy is in part a reflection of the low value accorded to women's jobs, and also of the failure to create job ladders and career structures within female-dominated areas (Acker 1989; Phillips and Taylor 1980). Thus positive action may involve not solely adopting measures to enable women to move up into higher jobs slots previously held by men, but also reconsidering the existing job hierarchy, identifying new job grades within female jobs areas which recognise the skills and experience required in these areas, and creating links between female-dominated jobs areas and the mainstream promotion lines. Such tactics are of particular importance in the context of the ways in which structures and cultures in organisations

---

Box 5.9 Equal opportunity policies can help reduce vertical segregation but they need to be carefully targeted

A survey of some of the largest organisations in **Belgium** revealed that women only accounted for 14.5 per cent of positions at first executive level and 12.7 per cent at middle management level. In those organisations which espoused an equal opportunity policy women tended to be found in all areas of management, but in companies which were sceptical of women's role they tended to be confined to human resources and accounting (National reports, Belgium: Meulders and Hecq 1996:43; *Trends-Tendances* June 1995).

The need for policy action to reduce vertical segregation is evident from the **Swedish** findings that there was a dramatic reduction in career opportunities in occupations where women hold the majority of posts. Promotion opportunities were also lower for both men and women in female-dominated workplaces (National reports, Sweden: Gonäs and Spånt 1996:42; Le Grand 1993).

In **France** women were most likely to have gained access to skilled jobs in the service sector. This suggests that attempts to diversify women's employment should focus as a matter of priority on those industries in which women already have a presence (National reports, France: Silvera *et al.* 1996:45).

---

are moving towards flatter hierarchies and more functional flexibility. In principle the dismantling of the traditional gender order based around the bureaucratic hierarchy presents a golden opportunity for the implementation of equal-value principles; in practice women may be asked to take on many of the responsibilities taken by managerial staff in the past but without enhanced pay or status (see Chapter 2).

Summary and policy conclusions

The pattern of occupational segregation has over recent years tended to provide some protection for women's employment, both because women have been concentrated in areas with significant job growth and because these sectors have been less prone to cyclical variation. At the same time, occupational segregation is central to the persistence of gender inequality within the labour market, facilitating the maintenance of a gendered labour market in which female-dominated and male-dominated jobs are organised according to different principles, including pay, working-time and integration into career ladders and organisational structures.

This dual role of occupational segregation, in promoting the demand for female employment but at the same time maintaining and reinforcing difference, presents a major dilemma for policy towards equality. A central element of both the third and the fourth EU action programmes for equal opportunities for women and men is the desegregation of the labour market, but this policy holds many dangers as well as benefits for women. There is potential for increased competition from men in many traditional areas of women's employment. Such a development must be the eventual outcome of actions to desegregate the labour market, as much as women moving into male job areas, but if desegregation comes before equality in other areas of labour market practice, the outcome could be to the disadvantage of women. This is partly because the job prospects in many male-dominated areas have tended over recent years to be relatively poor, thus reducing the likelihood of desegregation through women's entry into male traditional areas. Declining job opportunities have been a particular feature of male manual jobs, underlining the tendency for horizontal segregation in manual and lower-skilled jobs to be maintained. Where women have made entry into traditional male jobs, it has been in the higher-level managerial and professional job sectors, where the effort of breaking into male job areas is more worthwhile and where employment opportunities have been relatively good, particularly in countries such as Spain.

While women still have a long way to go to achieve equality in the higher-level job areas, there are at least here some grounds for optimism. Women are achieving higher qualifications and diversifying their studies to include many subjects which were previously the preserve of men – and education continues to be the main lever by which women make entry into these higher-level jobs. Education alone is clearly not sufficient to overcome discrimination, though, as women still require higher educational qualifications to make entry and also higher qualifications or longer work experience to achieve promotion.

However, not all women will acquire higher education and it is amongst the less skilled that perhaps the greatest degree of inequality is found. Yet it is also here that desegregation does not provide an obvious answer to gender inequality, both because the job prospects in male-dominated areas continue to be poor and because many of the problems relate to the poor terms and conditions of employment and the poor promotion prospects in women's jobs, and not to the type of employment itself. More attention needs to be paid to the value attached to women's work and to reducing vertical segregation, both by expanding promotion opportunities through the creation of new job ladders in female-dominated areas and by the improvement of women's prospects within existing structures. Greater integration of, for example, clerical jobs into the administrative job structures of organisations may be essential if women are not to be the losers from the next stage of technological and organisational restructuring. Similarly, women workers in the care sector may benefit more from policies to improve training, pay and promotion prospects within the sector (OECD 1997b), than from the more traditional desegregation policies of training to compete with men in, for example, the construction trades. In sum, tackling the different employment conditions and rewards which women experience because of segregation may be as important as dismantling segregation. A key element is clearly wages, the subject of the next chapter.

6 Wage determination and sex segregation in employment

Trends in the gender pay gap

The gender pay gap provides the starting point for comparing the level of gender pay equality across countries. As the gender pay gap is only a comparison of average male and female earnings, it is clearly a very crude measure of gender pay equality. Simple comparisons of the gender pay gap cannot provide information on whether the major problems for women's employment lie in the pattern of occupational segregation, the structure of pay differentials between occupations and industries or in high levels of inequality within job areas or organisations. Nor can it tell us whether there is a gender pay gap for workers with similar levels of educational qualifications or similar levels of work experience. Nevertheless, the gender pay gap still provides a summary measure of progress towards gender equality in labour market outcomes. Moreover, given both the trend in all countries towards a higher share of women employed in higher-paid professional jobs, and a lower share of men in skilled jobs in manufacturing, a reasonable expectation is that, all other things being equal, the gender pay gap should narrow. Consequently, the recording of no change in the gender pay ratio may in fact disguise a worsening of gender pay inequality within jobs of a similar skill level.

In analysing the gender pay gap across Europe, the only available harmonised data was provided by Eurostat on the basis of its *Earnings in Industry and Services* publication. As previously outlined (Rubery and Fagan 1994:154), these data are inadequate for assessing the comparative position of women in the European labour market (see Box 6.1). In particular they do not provide aggregate data for the whole economy, and instead relate to manufacturing and construction, sectors in which women are under-represented. For example, three-quarters of female non-manual workers are found in the service sector. Furthermore, in 1998 there were still no Eurostat data available for Austria, Finland and Sweden or indeed for Italy. Nevertheless, Eurostat data did enable us to analyse recent trends in the relative position of women in those sectors and countries for which information was available.

Box 6.1 Statistics on earnings: some problems for the measurement of gender pay equity

The problems with current available harmonised data for the comparison of levels of gender pay equity and the identification of trends over time include:

- the emphasis on earnings in manufacturing and other industrial sectors where relatively few women are employed;
- the lack of labour-market-wide statistics and instead the provision of separate data only on manual and non-manual workers;
- the lack of harmonised information on pay in the public sector;
- the inclusion of part-timers in some countries' datasets and their exclusion in others, but the absence in all cases of separate information on part-timers' pay.

Many of these problems will be resolved through the new Structure of Earnings Survey which began in 1997, but one serious drawback remains: member states will be allowed not to collect information on pay in some major service sectors covering most of the public sector.

Women have continued to earn considerably less than men across the European Union whatever measure is used, although the extent of the overall pay gap varied markedly between countries. If we look first at average hourly manual pay in manufacturing in 1993 (see Figure 6.1a), the highest ratios were found in Sweden and Denmark at 89.5 per cent and 84.5 per cent respectively, and the lowest in the UK, where the ratio fell as low as 68 per cent. In spite of this diversity, trends within the first half of the 1990s were fairly uniform across most countries. Between 1989 and 1993, the majority of the countries witnessed a slight narrowing of this particular pay gap. The only countries where this improvement exceeded 1 percentage point were the Netherlands, where a narrowing of 2.5 percentage points continued a longer-term trend, and Luxembourg, where the gap was among the widest in the Community at the beginning of the period. On the negative side, there was no improvement at all in Denmark or Belgium, and a slight deterioration in Greece.

The gender pay gap for non-manual workers in industry (see Figure 6.1b) tends to be considerably greater than that for manual workers, in part because these salaries are given on a monthly basis, instead of hourly earnings as for manual workers. Full-time male employees are more likely than their female counterparts to work longer weekly hours and to receive overtime payments. Additionally, the non-manual group includes the highly paid male-dominated managerial professions. As Figure 6.1b shows, however, the non-manual pay gap closed more rapidly than the manual pay gap in most of the countries for which data were available; between 1989 and 1993 the

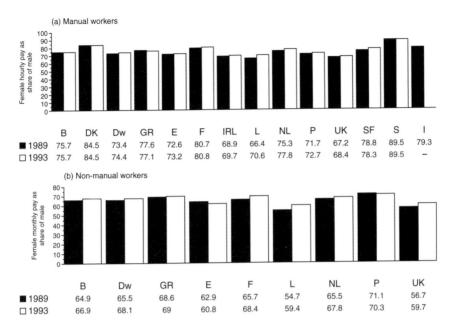

Figure 6.1 Gender pay ratios for manual and non-manual workers in industry, 1989–1993

Sources: ILO (1995); Eurostat (1994c).

Notes
Latest data for Spain, Sweden and Finland are for 1992.
Italian data are from national sources for 1989.
Data for Sweden and Finland are from ILO for 1992.

ratio improved by between 1 and 3 percentage points, except in Greece, where there was only a slight improvement, and Portugal, where the gap actually widened slightly. Once again, Luxembourg recorded a more rapid improvement but from a poor base position.

Harmonised data on pay in service sectors of the economy was limited, precluding a meaningful comparison of pay across the entire service sector. However, we were able to examine the gender pay gap in two service industries for which some data were available, namely retail, which is often associated with low pay, and insurance, which is expected to be comparatively well paid. Figures 6.2a and 6.2b show the development of gender pay ratios in the retail and insurance sectors between 1989 and 1993 (the last year for which harmonised data from Eurostat were available for most countries). It is notable that the gender pay ratios for both sectors were narrower than the figures for all non-manual workers in industry in all cases where data were available, with the exception of the UK insurance sector. Additionally, it should be noted that the gender pay gap of a certain sector

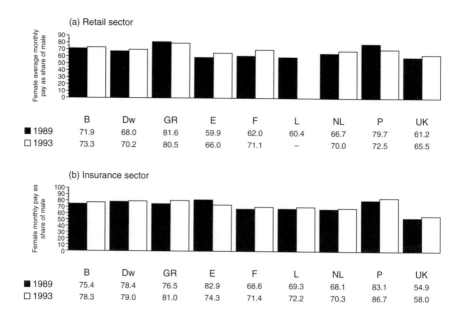

(a) Retail sector

Female average monthly pay as share of male

	B	Dw	GR	E	F	L	NL	P	UK
■ 1989	71.9	68.0	81.6	59.9	62.0	60.4	66.7	79.7	61.2
□ 1993	73.3	70.2	80.5	66.0	71.1	–	70.0	72.5	65.5

(b) Insurance sector

Female monthly pay as share of male

	B	Dw	GR	E	F	L	NL	P	UK
■ 1989	75.4	78.4	76.5	82.9	68.6	69.3	68.1	83.1	54.9
□ 1993	78.3	79.0	81.0	74.3	71.4	72.2	70.3	86.7	58.0

Figure 6.2 Gender pay ratios for non-manual workers in the retail and insurance
sectors, 1989–1993

Source: Eurostat (1994c).

Notes
Latest data for Spain are for 1992.
Greek data are for 1988 and 1992 for insurance.
No data in retail after 1990 for Italy.

can vary widely between countries: in 1993, the ratios in retail ranged from
65.5 per cent (UK) to 80.5 per cent (Greece), and in insurance the figures
ranged from 58 per cent (UK) to 86.7 per cent (Portugal). The UK was the
only country for which data were available where the gender pay gap is
wider in insurance than in retail. Clearly, however, these figures alone can
only lead us to conclusions related to the particular sector; the global position of women in the labour market can be considered determined by a
number of factors, including the degree of both horizontal and vertical segregation, and pay differentials between and within sectors.

Over the four-year period from 1989 to 1993 there was a narrowing of
the gender pay gap in both sectors in the majority of countries for which
there were data. Exceptions were found in some of the Southern European
countries: in Greece and Portugal, the gender pay gap increased in retail
(dramatically in the case of Portugal) but declined in insurance, while in
the case of Spain, a 6.1 percentage point improvement in the retail sector
was accompanied by an 8.6 percentage point deterioration in the insurance
sector.

While Eurostat is the only source of harmonised data, this information can be supplemented by data from many of the individual countries. Although such data are not comparable between countries, they are nevertheless useful in analysing trends over time and for providing information on what was happening to pay across the whole of the labour market. National data provided a particularly important source of information for those countries without Eurostat data.

In Italy national data revealed major changes in women's earnings at the beginning of the 1990s. Annualised earnings data were only available up to 1991, but even over the short period between 1989 and 1991 the gender pay ratio was found to have declined from 76.3 per cent to 72.5 per cent. Additional data from the Banca d'Italia showed a decrease of 5.3 percentage points in the gender ratio of income from wage employment between 1989 and 1993, from 79.7 per cent to 74.4 per cent (see National reports, Italy: Bettio and Villa 1996:56). The patchy nature of these data does not prevent us from reaching the conclusion that gender pay inequality has increased sharply in Italy over recent years, albeit from a relatively high level of equality which had been achieved by the mid-1980s. In 1985, the last year for which we have Eurostat Italian data, Italy had the second-smallest gender pay gap in the E10 after Denmark.

The entry of Austria, Finland and Sweden, along with the former East Germany, into the European Union should have had the effect of markedly raising the degree of gender pay equality. Sweden and Finland, together with the former East Germany, had in comparative terms achieved a relatively high level of equality by the end of the 1980s. This impact on the overall degree of gender wage equality has, however, been modified by the downward pressure on women's wages in both the Scandinavian states and the former East Germany. In the latter case after unification there was a very sharp decline in the gender pay ratio, from 85 to 76 per cent for manual workers and from 79 to 75 per cent among non-manual workers in manufacturing industry between 1991 and 1994. Trends in Sweden and Finland showed a higher level of stability, but there were hints of negative trends. Thus, although the gender pay ratio of Swedish wage earners in industry appeared to remain static at the comparatively high value of 90 per cent and that of salaried employees in industry actually increased from 75 to 77 per cent (National reports, Sweden: Gonäs and Spånt 1996:57), data on income for full-time year-round employees in Sweden suggested there had been a decline in women's relative pay. While in 1980 men earned 24 per cent more than women on this basis, by 1991 this premium had increased to 30 per cent (National reports, Sweden: Lofström 1995:59). Sectoral wage differentials may thus not provide a clear indication of trends in annual income. In Finland monthly wage and salary statistics which exclude overtime earnings showed a continuing improvement in women's relative pay position, from 80 per cent of men's average pay to 82 per cent over the period from 1988 to 1993, but annual earnings data from tax returns indicated a deterioration, with a decline from 76.8 per cent to 74.7 per cent over the period 1992 to 1994. Where equality had already reached a relatively high level by the end of the 1980s, the experience across member states does not provide us with any optimism that the gender gap would continue to close progressively over time. Not only had the movement towards equality apparently plateaued but it had also appeared to move into reverse in those countries where women had begun seriously to challenge men's share of total wage income.

Austria showed a trend towards improvement in the gender pay ratio for both blue-collar and white-collar workers, but from a very low level. The ratio in terms of the median of gross monthly incomes narrowed from 64 per cent to 65 per cent for blue-collar, and 60 per cent to 61 per cent for white-collar workers. Austria was peculiar both in the large size of the gender pay gap, and the fact that this gap was hardly any narrower for blue-collar than for white-collar workers, although this might in part be explained by the fact that, unlike in other countries, all data collected here refer to monthly earnings.

For some countries for which we had Eurostat data we could also look at trends in overall earnings statistics from national data to see if the trends identified for industry held up once the services sector was included in the analysis. Relatively few countries had data covering the whole economy. The main exceptions were the Netherlands and the UK (and Austria, see above). Data covering the whole of the labour market tended to show a somewhat smaller gender pay gap than that found for non-manual workers in industry, in part because most women in professional level jobs were employed in the services sector. Data for hourly earnings of employees in permanent employment in the Netherlands showed an increase in the gender pay ratio, narrowing 2 percentage points to 74 per cent for full-time employees but by only 1 percentage point, again to 74 per cent if part-timers and flexitime workers were included (National reports, Netherlands: Plantenga *et al.* 1996). Data from the UK New Earnings Survey showed an increase in the gender hourly pay ratio among full-time workers, from 76.4 per cent to 80.2 per cent between 1989 and 1995. This was a much higher ratio than that found for non-manual workers in industry and demonstrated the need to include service sectors, public and private, in order to understand the size and structure of the gender earnings gap. The UK had the lowest overall ratio in the Eurostat data, but there were not a sufficient number of countries with comprehensive labour market data to be able to see if there was a systematic relationship between differentials within the industrial sector and differentials across the whole of the labour market. The UK New Earnings Survey ratio also overstated the degree of gender equality, as it excluded part-timers: an estimate based on Labour Force Survey data put the full-time ratio at 78.9 per cent and the overall ratio, including part-timers, at 74.1 per cent (National reports, UK: Rubery 1996:113). National data from Portugal indicated a slight widening of the gender pay gap, both overall and when controlling for level of education (National reports, Portugal: Lopes and Perista 1996:52).

Many countries, including, for example, Germany, tend to exclude public sector workers and the associated sectors of public administration, education and health from their wage statistics. This severely restricts the usefulness of earnings data for considering gender pay equity, a problem which will be perpetuated by the new Structure of Earnings Survey for Eurostat which allows countries to exclude public sector services if they so wish. Spain had data covering industrial and service workers, excluding the public sector areas and also agriculture. On this basis we could see that there was a slight rise in the gender pay ratio in Spain, from 72.3 per cent to 73.4 per cent in terms of daily pay, and from 70 per cent to 71.5 per cent in terms of monthly pay between 1990 and 1994 (National reports, Spain: Moltó 1996:55). Even the Scandinavian countries did not have regular earnings data covering the whole economy and instead could only provide data on gender pay gaps within private and public sectors, calculated separately. These showed wider earnings differentials in private than public sectors, but the decreasing relative pay levels in the public sector over recent years would have widened gender pay differentials at the aggregate labour market level (National reports, Denmark: Boje 1996:38), although precise estimates of the size of this effect did not seem to be available.

Finally, it should be noted that the actual earnings gap between men and women is affected by overtime pay and bonus payments as well as by the nominal pay rate. The inclusion of such payments in the calculations would lead to a wider gap between the sexes. This was illustrated most clearly by data from Finland (see pp. 227–8) where the annualised earnings figures including overtime showed a widening pay gap, whereas wage and salary statistics, which excluded this source of earnings, showed an increasing gender pay ratio from a better starting position (National reports, Finland: Keinänen 1996:52). Information from Denmark showed that female state employees received only 58 per cent of the overtime payments received by their male counterparts, and 53 per cent of bonus payments. This had had the overall effect of reducing the gender pay ratio for these employees from 90 to 88 per cent (National reports, Denmark: Boje 1996:38). In Portugal in 1993, the coefficient of total earnings to basic wages was 1.189 for men but only 1.118 for women, with the obvious implication that the gender earnings gap was considerably greater than the gender gap in basic pay (National reports, Portugal: Lopes and Perista 1996:49). These differences were not only due to overtime but also to differences in access to bonuses and other extra payments. For example, in Austria the clothing industry, which had a high share of women workers, only paid 2.5 weeks' Christmas bonus instead of the normal thirteenth month payment found in most other industries.

The effect of atypical workers on the gender pay gap

The Eurostat figures used above are not consistent between countries in their treatment of part-time workers. Many countries, such as the UK, exclude part-time pay from these figures; as the vast majority of the part-time workforce is female, and part-timers in the UK are on lower rates of hourly pay than their full-time counterparts, the exclusion of part-time employees from the UK figures leads to an under-representation of the gender pay gap in the official figures. As noted above, the British Labour Force Survey gave a gender pay ratio of 74.1 per cent when comparing all female with all male workers, as against 78.9 per cent when only full-time workers were considered (National reports, UK: Rubery 1996:113).

Trends in a comprehensive measure of the gender pay gap are likely to be less favourable than those reflected in national statistics, if developments in, for example, part-time pay have been less favourable than those for the 'typical' workers included in the statistics, or if the lower paid atypical workforce has increased in size. Thus, the increase in marginal employment in the 1990s in Germany, for example, is likely to have contributed to a growing gender pay gap (National reports, Germany: Maier and Rapp 1995:16). In Austria, one country which does include part-time workers in the statistics, it has been calculated that one-third of the gender pay gap was due to the inferior labour market position of part-timers (National reports, Austria: Pastner 1996). The exclusion of part-timers and other forms of atypical worker from statistics is thus likely to lead to an underestimate of the gender pay gap. The exclusion of part-timers from pay data can also lead to hidden trends developing. For example, in France, where part-time pay is included in earnings data, recent years have shown a reduction in the gender pay gap for full-timers, but an increase in this gap for part-timers (National reports, France: Silvera *et al.* 1996:63).

The effect of part-time workers on the gender pay gap differed between countries. First, the part-time share of total female employment varied widely; for example, in 1994, the proportions ranged from 8 per cent in Greece to 65.6 per cent in the Netherlands (Eurostat 1994c). Additionally, the treatment of this group varied considerably. In the UK, the average female part-time wage declined from 73.4 per cent to 70 per cent of the female full-time median between 1989 and 1995, and represented just 57.5 per cent of the full-time male median value (National reports, UK: Rubery 1996:110), whereas in the Netherlands, part-time female hourly earnings were equivalent to those of full-timers in 1989, and by 1994 exceeded them by 1 per cent (National reports, Netherlands: Plantenga *et al.* 1996:31). The higher average hourly pay levels for part-timers could be explained in part by the tendency for earnings to increase with age: women with full-time jobs in the Netherlands tended to be young and unmarried, while part-time work was more significant for older age groups, and hourly pay tends to rise with age. Additionally the 'aggregation effect' also influenced the statistics. When the data were divided by sector, it appeared that part-timers did earn less than full-timers in most sectors (National reports, Netherlands: Plantenga *et al.* 1996:32). However, the vastly superior position of Dutch part-time workers when compared with their British counterparts was still mainly to be explained by the strong legislative protection afforded in the Netherlands, which was further strengthened in 1996 when a legal prohibition of discrimination on the grounds of hours worked was introduced (National reports, Netherlands: Plantenga *et al.* 1996:32). This situation contrasted with the removal of protection for low-paid workers in the UK including, in particular, the abolition in 1993 of wages councils which set minimum wages in part-time intensive industries, including retail and catering (for an Anglo-Dutch comparison, see Fagan *et al.* 1995).

More detailed information on earnings by hours of work in the Netherlands revealed that for those women who worked at least 40 per cent of a full-time job there was no reduction in pay, but those on short hours jobs earned 3 per cent less. However, male part-timers suffered discrimination whether they were in long or short hours jobs, with the reduction relative to male full-timers being 6 per cent and 13 per cent respectively. Part-time work is such a dominant employment form in the Netherlands that it may be regarded more as a standard than as an atypical employment form. This perspective is reflected in the wage statistics, in which three types of employees were identified: full-time, part-time and those on flexi-hours. Females on flexi-hours or variable hours workers received only 52.2 per cent of male full-time earnings or 70 per cent of female part-time earnings.

While from the Netherlands' example it is clear that improvements in the basic rights of atypical workers should be an urgent priority in many member states, it should not be forgotten that the part-time status in itself tends to be disadvantageous, even where the legal framework of protection for this group is satisfactory. Thus, although in the Netherlands only flexitime employees were found to be worse paid than their full-time counterparts, part-time employment still affected negatively the prospect of promotion. Therefore the creation of a large number of atypical jobs, more or less dominated by women, is likely to be inimical to the aim of reducing the vertical segregation of the labour market.

In countries where part-time employment was less widespread, other forms of 'atypical' work might be more important in generating low earnings. This was most evidently the case in Spain, where the extensive use of temporary contracts resulted in a large number of women receiving very low annual earnings: 21.7 per cent of female workers earned less than half the statutory minimum wage calculated on a full-time annual basis, and in total 35.1 per cent earned less than the minimum calculated on this basis, as well as 23.1 per cent of men (National reports, Spain: Moltó 1996:58). Thus, while Spanish women do not frequently work part-time on a weekly basis, in practice they are effectively part-time workers when their employment is averaged over the working year. Similarly, it is the irregular form of much of women's employment in Spain that leads the monthly gender pay gap to be much wider than the daily figure.

Given the increase in the proportion of the female workforce employed in 'atypical' jobs (see Chapter 7), pay and conditions for such workers should be a priority for gender pay policy, even if this requires more emphasis on general systems of wage protection than on measures specifically oriented to gender pay equity. A further priority is to develop earnings data sources which include atypical as well as full-time workers, both so that the aggregate picture of women's pay position can be considered and so that the differences between atypical and other workers can be monitored (see Box 6.1). Such a policy would still be likely to leave many areas of women's employment out of account, including unpaid family workers, homeworkers and other workers in the informal sector. The size of the informal sector varied widely across countries but many low-paid women in the Southern European countries were working in this sector, and thus were still likely to fall outside the official statistics. These differences between countries in the shares of the economy covered by wage statistics clearly place limitations on the use of formal wage statistics as a basis for comparing progress towards gender equality.

Systems of wage protection

Figure 6.3 categorises the systems of minimum wage protection found in the 15 member states by reference to two dimensions: the extent of coverage of the collective bargaining system and the existence or otherwise of a legal minimum wage. This categorisation of countries according to the strength of the protection provided by collective bargaining pays particular attention to the system of wage protection in services sectors, where women tend to be concentrated. The extent of collective bargaining coverage includes both direct coverage among employing organisations that are party to a collective agreement and indirect coverage, either through extension agreements or by laws which make collective agreements binding on all firms in a sector. The classification follows very much that proposed in earlier research (Rubery and Fagan 1994; 1995a), except that this time Austria, Finland and Sweden have been included. All of these additional member states had strong and relatively comprehensive systems of collective bargaining but no legal minimum wage. This strong collective bargaining protection was reinforced by the legal extension of collective agreements in Finland and Austria and by high levels of organisation in Sweden. This put these three countries in the top left-hand box of Figure 6.3, together with Italy, Germany and Denmark. With the addition of these three member states, two quadrants where most member states are concentrated can be identified: six countries with strong collective bargaining but no legal minimum wage in the top left hand quadrant of the figure, and five countries with weak collective bargaining but a legal minimum wage – that is Greece, France,

	No or partial minimum wage protection	Minimum wage protection
Strong collective bargaining	Germany Austria Denmark Finland Sweden Italy	Belgium The Netherlands
Weak collective bargaining	Ireland United Kingdom	France Luxembourg Greece Spain Portugal

Figure 6.3 Systems of wage protection in the European Union

Luxembourg, Portugal and Spain – in the bottom right corner. The remaining four countries are divided between the two other quadrants: Belgium and the Netherlands combine strong collective bargaining protection with legal minimum wages, while the UK and Ireland combine only weak protection of minimum wages through collective bargaining with limited minimum wage protection in the case of Ireland, and virtually no minimum wage protection in the case of the UK (although the new Labour government was committed to introducing a minimum wage in 1999).

There have been no changes in the classification of European countries by type of wage protection system during the 1990s, although the UK will change position to the bottom right quadrant after 1999. However, this continuity in classification masks a considerable degree of change within the systems, in particular change in the extent to which adequate protection has been provided for minimum wages. To examine the adequacy of systems of minimum wage setting, it is necessary to examine both the coverage provided by the system (that is, whether the minima apply to everyone in the workforce), and the evolution of the value of the minimum.

In the area of statutory minimum wages, during the early 1990s there was a widening of the scope of coverage of minimum wages only in the

Netherlands, where since 1993 the minimum wage has covered employees whose working hours were less than one-third of the full-time norm (National reports, Netherlands: Plantenga *et al.* 1996:35). Elsewhere, there have been few positive developments and the systems in some countries have appeared increasingly inadequate because of to the low value of the minimum wage (for example in Spain – see Table 6.1).

If we compare the effectiveness of statutory minimum wages with collective bargaining as a means of protecting low-paid workers we find, of course, that statutory minimum wages have the advantage of wider coverage. Moreover, evidence from countries which have historically used centralised agreements suggested that the trend has been moving away from the generalisation of sectoral minima and that the implementation of collective agreements in small firms or those outside the employers' association or without union members has been becoming increasingly difficult to enforce. In some countries such as Italy it became more difficult to provide wage protection through a regular upgrading of minimum wages after the abolition of the wage indexation system in the early 1990s. Thus it is difficult in the medium term to envisage the development of collective bargaining as an effective substitute for minimum wages in countries where the existing protection provided by collective bargaining has been weak. While some criticise statutory minimum wages for removing social responsibility from the social partners (National reports, France: Silvera *et al.* 1996:72), the experience in European countries which have not had a minimum wage system, such as the UK, indicates that employers cannot be relied upon to behave with social responsibility towards their employees. The extension of collective protection is perhaps a goal to be pursued in conjunction with a legal minimum wage, and not as a replacement for legal regulation. The experience in the UK following the abolition of the wages councils system (see below) is indicative of the general lack of employer social responsibility towards workers who are unprotected by statutory mechanisms or by systems of collective bargaining.

Changes in the levels of minimum wages

The effectiveness of minimum wages in reducing poverty and promoting pay equity can be judged both by trends in the real level and by trends in its value relative to a measure of average wages. Table 6.1 shows the development of the real level of minimum wages in countries for which data were available between 1989 and 1994.

Between 1989 and 1994, some governments chose to set statutory minimum wages at levels which failed to keep pace with the rate of inflation; thus, minimum wage earners in Greece, the Netherlands and Spain were worse off in real terms than in 1989, although, in part as a consequence, for example in Spain, far fewer workers were paid at the minimum rate in 1994 than five years earlier. The countries where the statutory

Table 6.1 Changes in the real and relative level of minimum wages, 1989–1994

	1994 minimum as % of 1989 minimum (real terms)	*Minimum wages as share of average male blue-collar wages*	
		1989	*1994*
Countries with statutory minimum wages			
Belgium[a]	103.4	53.6	54.4
France	102.6	61.6	61.0
Greece	93.6	55.8	49.3
Luxembourg[a]	114.0	55.7	54.5
Netherlands[b]	94.7	52.7	48.5
Portugal[a,b]	103.8	55.5	48.4
Spain[b]	98.5	44.2	41.4
Countries with selective statutory minima			
Ireland[c]	106–107.4	—	—
UK[d]	(107.9)	(41.3)	(43.2)
Countries with systems based on collective agreement			
Austria[e]	121.6	39.1	44.5
Denmark	—	—	—
Finland[f]	98.3	—	—
Germany[g]	97.9	56.4	56.4
Italy[h]	91.7	70.9	68.0
Sweden[f,i]	100.0	45.2	42.4

Sources: National reports and additional material provided by the national experts.

Notes

In calculating changes in the real value of the minimum, inflation is calculated using retail prices as the deflator (CEC 1995d).

— indicates no data available.

a Relative figures for Belgium, Luxembourg and Portugal have been calculated using hourly average wages and monthly minima.

b Latest figures for Portugal relate to 1993; Spanish '1989' figures are for 1990. For the Netherlands and Portugal the average wage for all male employees is used.

c The Irish figures refer to waiters/waitresses and clerical workers respectively, under the Hotel and Catering Joint Labour Committee.

d The UK figures relate to the 1989 and 1993 wages council minima in the hairdressing industry. There were no minimum wages in the UK after 1993 except in agriculture.

e The Austrian figure refers to blue-collar workers in the tailoring trade.

f The Finnish and Swedish minima refer to the lowest pay grade in central government agreements.

g The German minimum figure relates to manual unskilled female workers in the clothing industry. German '1989' figures are for 1991.

h The Italian minimum figure relates to the minimum for the lowest skill level in the engineering industry.

i The Swedish male average figure relates to blue-collar and lower white-collar workers; the '1994' figure is for 1993.

minimum wage increased in real terms were those in which there was an indexing mechanism for upgrading the value of the minimum wage (with the exception of Portugal). The Irish Joint Labour Committees, while only partial in terms of coverage of minimum wage protection, also produced real increases in wage protection for those covered. In the UK minimum wage levels in the Wages Councils just about kept pace with inflation before being abolished in 1993.

To give some indication of how effective protection of real wages was for those at the bottom of the labour market in countries where minimum wage protection was provided through collective bargaining, Table 6.1 also looks at the real value of the lowest available sectoral minimum over this period. The experience of the Scandinavian countries and Austria showed that it was possible to keep relatively stable minimum wages through a collectively agreed system. This did, however, require the support of the national government, and consensus on avoiding very low pay. The other difficulty with sectoral minima is that of enforceability, which may increasingly be a problem as forms of employment become more differentiated. Although detailed data were not available, the real value of the minimum wage protection provided by Italian collective agreements after the ending of the wage indexation system in 1991–1993 is likely to have decreased.

The decline of minimum wages was more dramatic compared to average blue-collar wages. For Ireland we could only compare the rate of change and not actual relative levels of pay. The Irish sectoral minimum wage thus increased by 18.9 per cent in nominal terms between 1990 and 1994, which, although resulting in a real increase in minimum wages (see above), was still insufficient to prevent a decline in the relative value of the minimum wage as average hourly earnings increased by 25.7 per cent over the same period. In the remaining countries for which we had data we compared changes in the minimum wage as a percentage of average wages. The figures reflect a wide divergence of minimum wage levels when compared to average levels. Countries with an indexation system for uprating minimum wages, namely France, Belgium and Luxembourg, maintained stable or even rising relative minimum wage levels, but in all other countries for which we had data, except for Austria and Germany, the relative level of the minimum wage declined. The decrease in relative value was dramatic in some cases, particularly in Portugal. The result of this declining level of wage protection is likely to have been increased inequality, particularly if the level of the minimum had an indirect effect on wage negotiations for those on low pay who were just above the minimum. The improvement in the lowest sectoral minimum in Austria went against this trend, but the increase in protection has been achieved from a very low starting position. In Germany the relative levels of minima seem to have been preserved, with real levels of both minimum and average wages falling in a time of recession.

Minimum wage systems in many countries thus did not prevent the low paid from becoming worse off, both in relative and often in real terms.

Pressure on the value of minimum wage levels was associated with the problems of unemployment; governments used restraint on minimum wage increases as a means to reduce inflationary pressures and to stimulate job creation. However, the impact on job creation is uncertain and the effect on gender equity and social justice of such policies need to be taken directly into account. One country, the United Kingdom, took the ultimate step during this period of abolishing wage protection for the low paid, with the sole exception of agricultural workers. While the British Wages Council system was only partial, and set low minimum rates, there was evidence that many employers took advantage of the opportunity to employ new workers at yet lower wage levels. By May 1995, a significant percentage of new jobs in the industries previously covered by the Wages Councils (for example, 22.2 per cent of full-time retail jobs, and 25 per cent of full-time hairdressing jobs) were paying less than the minimum rates of 1993 (Low Pay Network 1995; National reports, UK: Rubery 1996:104). The rate of underpayment increased considerably if we assumed Wages Council rates would have been updated by at least the rate of inflation. On this basis, 36.7 per cent of new full-time, and 49.6 per cent of new part-time jobs in hotels and catering, retail, clothing manufacture and hairdressing were paying less than the extrapolated Wages Council minima in 1995. This example strongly supports the argument that social responsibility is not an attribute that employers naturally possess, and that low wages will only be prevented through mechanisms supported by the law.

Collective agreements as systems of minimum wage setting

In evaluating collective agreements as a means of minimum wage setting, it is clear that their sufficiency has depended to a large extent on the strength of the system of collective bargaining in the country concerned. In the UK and Ireland, for example, the system of collective bargaining failed to provide adequate protection against low pay, although the Irish system was not as entirely voluntaristic as the British, in the sense that there were national guidelines for pay increases. In both countries there has been a system of legally enforceable minima in a limited number of sectors which were particularly vulnerable to low pay. In Ireland, this was extended to the retail sector, while in the UK, even this unsatisfactory form of protection was removed in 1993 (see above). In France, meanwhile, a weak collective bargaining system has been irrelevant to a large number of unorganised workers for whom the sectoral minima were lower than the statutory national minimum wage, although the government had some success in raising sectoral minima to at least the minimum wage since it adopted this as a policy goal in 1990 (National reports, France: Silvera *et al.* 1996:72).

Even in countries which have historically had stronger, nationwide collectively agreed minima, there have been trends in recent years which have indicated that the system no longer provided adequate protection against low wages. The effective operation of collectively agreed minima is to some extent dependent on there being a consensus among the social partners on the need for some form of solidaristic wage policy, as has been the case in Finland, Denmark and Sweden. In Sweden the system, until recently, was based on the premise that an individual's level of pay should depend on the skills required to perform the job, rather than the economic position of the employer. Where this consensus on the need for equality does not exist, there seems to have been a decline in the effectiveness of collective bargaining systems for protecting against low pay. In Austria, for example, there have been a fairly large number of lawsuits in small firms on the issue of minimum wage payments, suggesting difficulties with implementation (National reports, Austria: Pastner 1996:62). Generally, it is apparent that within countries the stronger frameworks of minimum wage setting through collective bargaining were to be found in the more organised sectors of the economy, which typically were not those in which female employment is concentrated.

There has also been an erosion of collective protection in some of the countries which have traditionally had stronger frameworks of collective agreement as the principal form of wage protection. This was most clearly the case in Germany, where the restructuring due to reunification was an important factor in endangering the consensus that wages should be 'taken out of competition' through sectoral-level agreements. An increase in the number of uncovered workers and sectors seems likely due to economic restructuring and the beginning of a trend towards small firms leaving employers' associations (National reports, Germany: Maier *et al.* 1996:67). The much patchier coverage of collective bargaining in the former East Germany has also posed a fundamental threat to the system of regulation: in 1993–1994 only 26 per cent of East German employers belonged to employers' associations and only 60 per cent paid wages according to collective agreements (National reports, Germany: Maier *et al.* 1996:42). Another example of the gradual erosion of systems based on strong collective agreements can be found in Finland, where employers, particularly smaller employers, have demanded an ending of the system whereby collective agreements are made binding on all firms, including those that have not participated in the negotiation of the agreements (National reports, Finland: Keinänen 1996:57). Additionally, many of the new jobs that were being created in Europe were 'atypical' jobs, and in some cases fell outside the scope of such agreements.

A further potential problem with sectoral minima is the degree of variation that is possible between sectors regarding the minimum rates (see Rubery and Fagan 1994:17), reflecting the fact that sectoral negotiations may tend to reflect the balance of bargaining power between the social partners rather than notions of what is a reasonable, or fair, level of pay. This has been reflected in demands for reduction in the minimum levels in some industries in Germany (although this debate has so far concentrated on male-dominated sectors relating to rates which have to be offered when recruiting young people or the long-term unemployed) (National reports, Germany: Maier *et al.* 1996:60). Austria has traditionally had very wide differences in pay levels between sectors (Rowthorn 1992), a factor which has been associated with the wide gender pay gap in Austria (National reports, Austria: Pastner 1996:57–58). In Spain the greater freedom which was granted in 1994 to collective agreements to determine pay, including seniority increases (see Chapter 2 above), has raised the likelihood of sectoral differences in pay practices widening according to collective bargaining strength (National reports, Spain: Moltó 1996:62).

It may to some extent be a reflection of problems with sectorally agreed minima, or in the British and Irish case with a lack of any general minimum, that there have increasingly been demands for national minimum wages in countries where these do not already apply. Generally, this demand has come from trade unions, such as in Austria where a minimum wage at the level demanded by trade unions would directly affect 8 per cent of male and 17 per cent of female employees (National reports, Austria: Pastner 1996:60). In the UK the case for a national minimum wage was taken up both by trade unions and by the Labour Party in opposition, although the two disagreed on the subject of the level of minimum wage that should be set, both before and after the election of the Labour government. In the case of Finland, however, the demand for a national minimum has come from the employers, who have indicated their willingness to agree to a minimum wage if the practice of the general extension of collective agreements was ended, as discussed above. This would be to the advantage of non-organised employers rather than employees. This example illustrates the fact that it is not wise to propose installing the same system in every country; it is of paramount importance to understand the advantages, as well as the disadvantages, of the current country systems first.

The practice of collective bargaining

One of the most noticeable developments in the area of wage determination has been the move towards decentralised, firm-based bargaining and the relative decline of national-level or industry-based bargaining. This trend has become increasingly noticeable as employers' organisations have searched for wage flexibility in those countries which previously had very centralised systems. While company-based bargaining has come to be seen as an economic necessity by leading employers, its impact on the position of women in the labour market is not necessarily favourable (see Box 6.2). If we take the example of Sweden, the relatively high level of female pay achieved in the 1970s and 1980s may be considered in large part due to the prevailing centralised bargaining system and a policy of wage equalisation based on a notion of social justice – i.e. the principle that pay should reflect the nature and requirements of the job, irrespective of industrial and firm characteristics. The change towards a policy based more on individual and differentiated pay in the 1990s resulted in widening inequalities, as pay became more dependent upon both the employer's perception of the value of a job, and the competitive position of the firm (National reports, Sweden: Gonäs and Spånt 1996:20).

Decentralisation tends to work to the disadvantage of less organised workers, and particularly those who work for small firms. Employer demands for more flexibility have been heard throughout Europe, although nowhere was the change more transformational than in Italy, where the institutional changes of 1992–1993 involved first a weakening, then abolition of the wage indexation system. This was replaced, in fact, by a centralised system of sectoral bargaining, but one which no longer provided protection against erosion by inflation. The centralised bargaining resulted in low percentage increases, supposedly related to but in practice below the government's target inflation rates, while any additional local pay increases were to be linked to the profits or productivity of the individual firm. It was thus no coincidence that Italy experienced a dramatic widening of gender pay differentials in the early 1990s (National reports, Italy: Bettio and Villa 1996:50–51) as the value of the industry-level minima were eroded. In Spain

---

Box 6.2 Decentralisation: a move towards a two- or three-tier system of protection?

The 1994 reform which made wages and wage structures subject to collective bargaining instead of legal regulation in **Spain** also ended the automatic payment of supplements related both to the job and to the person, including seniority payments. In future these supplements will be subject to negotiation. While seniority pay favoured the insiders in the labour market in the past, i.e. men, the new arrangements might yet widen the gender pay gap as women are disproportionately located in small firms and sectors with weak bargaining power where wage supplements might no longer be paid (National reports, Spain: Moltó 1996:27).

The ending of wage indexation in **Italy** in the early 1990s and in **Denmark** in the early 1980s put an end in both countries to the narrowing of the gender pay gap. In the 1980s both of these countries had led the way towards equal pay, but this progress was conditional upon a national system of wage solidarity. Gender pay differentials in both countries increased as public sector wages fell behind private sector wages and as pay dispersion within the private sector widened (National reports, Italy: Bettio and Villa 1996:43–45; Denmark: Boje 1996:4, 24). And in **Sweden** too, the traditional highly centralised system of collective bargaining gave way to a more decentralised system under pressure from Swedish employers, particularly multinational corporations (National reports, Sweden: Gonäs and Spånt 1996:16–17).

Employers in **Ireland** continued to favour a centralised system of wage control but coupled with an emphasis on local determination of pay structures and with no minimum wage. This deprived women in Ireland of the

the reforms of 1994 also in principle included the decentralisation of collective bargaining, and the transfer of regulation from the law to collective bargaining. Yet in a country with no culture of collective bargaining at the firm level, the reforms did not immediately bring about a new decentralised system of wage determination in which wages were expected to be more responsive to the economic circumstances of particular firms (National reports, Spain: Moltó 1996:15–16). Nevertheless, the long-term impact of the reforms may be to increase the scope for local wage determination.

Collective bargaining has always had an ambiguous role with respect to its impact on gender pay equity. On the one hand it provides protection against low pay but on the other it reinforces differentials, including traditional gender differentials. Similar problems exist with interpreting the function of bureaucratic rules relating to pay, such as seniority increases. These payments automatically discriminate against women who take career breaks for childbirth and are argued to be partially responsible for the high gender pay gap amongst managers in France (National reports, France: Silvera *et al.* 1996:69). Where seniority is the cornerstone of the system, as, for example, in Austria, 2 years' childcare leave results not only in the loss of income for those years but also in a substantial indirect loss,

---

normal advantage of a centralised system, as only pay increases and not minimum pay levels are subject to uniformity (National reports, Ireland: Barry 1996:12).

In **Portugal** there was only a relatively weak trend towards an increasing number of company level agreements in the first part of the 1990s with sectoral and occupational agreements still the most important (National reports, Portugal: Lopes and Perista 1996:20). Although decentralisation has not become significant in Portugal there still seemed to be some trend towards a widening gender pay gap.

In **France** there was a dual trend: towards wider coverage of sectoral agreements, encouraged by government policy to extend collective bargaining to previously non-covered sectors, such as retail and catering; and towards more decentralised bargaining as a result of the Auroux reforms (which required companies to set up systems of consultation at the workplace level). The coverage of company agreements increased from 8 to 20 per cent of employees from 1983 to 1990. These developments reinforced a dual system of collective bargaining, with the traditionally strongly organised areas developing their own system of collective regulation, while the more recently organised sectors reproduced the norms set down by the state (National reports, France: Silvera *et al.* 1996:18–20).

Collective bargaining has had a much reduced coverage of former **East German** compared to former **West German** employers. In 1993–1994 only 26 per cent of the former East German industrial companies belonged to employers' associations, and only 60 per cent paid wages related to collective agreements, while 35 per cent paid below collectively agreed rates (National reports, Germany: Maier *et al.* 1996:42).

amounting to up to 1 year's pay over a 25-year period, owing to the lack of seniority payments (National reports, Austria: Pastner 1996:64). In addition, in some sectors where women were concentrated, such as retail and catering, even uninterrupted careers were not rewarded with the high seniority payments found in some male sectors. However, not all women in all countries take career breaks and in this context, seniority may provide a guarantee of earnings improvement for women. Seniority pay has been associated with increased pay equity in Italy, where women who obtain work in the formal sector tend to have levels of seniority similar to those of men (Bettio 1988; Rubery *et al.* 1997b; Rubery 1998b).

While seniority pay may be regarded as often adding to gender pay inequality, the likely replacement for seniority pay – individualised bonuses and performance related pay – may increase rather than reduce discrimination (see Box 6.3 and Rubery 1995a). Seniority pay has the merit of being determined by objectively measured factors, and it is perhaps ironic that it is when women are beginning to close the seniority gap that this system is being replaced in some sectors and countries by more discretionary elements (Rubery *et al.* 1997b).

There is also little evidence that collective bargaining practice has been taking on board the issue of how to implement the principle of equal pay for work of equal value. Job evaluation has remained a relatively unpopular form of wage fixing in many countries and its implementation has often been associated not with gender pay equity, but with moves away from collectively determined wage systems to more management-determined systems, based on job evaluation and performance or individualised payments systems. Only in relatively few countries have unions taken up job evaluation as a means of furthering equal pay: the main examples have been found in the UK, the Netherlands and Scandinavian countries. It is in these countries that social partners have explored how to use job evaluation to implement the principle of equal value. However, not all job evaluation is associated with this aim. For example in the UK, surveys in the 1990s (IRS 1994) found an increase in the use of job evaluation but a reduction in its importance in determining actual earnings, as performance bonuses took on greater importance, often even relative to job grade, for determining actual earnings (National reports, UK: Rubery 1996:42). In the Netherlands policies to implement apparently gender-neutral job evaluation have in practice gone hand in hand with a trend towards more individualised systems of pay determination and appraisal (National reports, Netherlands: Plantenga *et al.* 1996:39).

Developments in the public sector

The public sector has traditionally employed a large proportion of women, and been a comparatively good employer. Wage determination in the public sector labour market is clearly more centralised and under political influence than in the private sector labour market. Consequently, any notion of equal pay is more easily implemented in the public labour market (National reports, Denmark: Boje 1996:35), although this does not guarantee gender pay equity; for example, the 'unisex' pay rules of the French civil service have still failed to eliminate the gender pay gap, because of the greater ease with which men earn family wage supplements and seniority payments (National reports, France: Silvera *et al.* 1996:66). One example of public sector equal opportunity laws that seem to have had some impact is in Germany, where federal and regional governments aimed to reduce vertical segregation in the public sector. These laws seemed to have been relatively successful over a short period of time (National reports, Germany: Maier *et al.* 1996:64). Two factors help to explain this role for the public sector in developing equal pay policies: first, the state may be expected to provide

---

Box 6.3 From seniority to individualised merit pay

In **Finland** one of the most common changes in the early 1990s was towards increased control of work performance and management by results, but in the mid-90s the share of the workforce affected remained small, with only 14 per cent of employees reporting being in receipt of bonuses related to performance (National reports, Finland: Keinänen 1996:36).

Austria has had a traditional system of significant seniority supplements for white-collar workers in manufacturing, which tended to favour men with continuous employment careers. These systems were under pressure, in part because of the high unemployment of the so-called older expensive employees. New performance-related systems were being introduced but research found women, again, to be the losers (National reports, Austria: Pastner 1996:22).

In the **UK** research found that performance-related pay systems, in addition to decreasing the transparency of the payment system, were also likely to lead to gender biases in assessment. Manual workers were the most likely to be excluded from performance bonuses, while non-manual workers, among whom women tend to be relatively highly represented, were more likely to be eligible for bonuses. Yet within non-manual work it was higher management, where men were concentrated, that received the most significant pay enhancements (National reports, UK: Rubery 1996:116).

In **France** women have tended to lose out in the receipt of seniority payments because of shorter tenure, over-representation among temporary staff and concentration in small firms and industrial sectors where seniority pay has been uncommon. Yet individualisation of pay, which has become fairly widespread in France – with 38 per cent of firms having implemented some individualisation by 1991 compared to 22 per cent in 1986, is unlikely to favour women, as it was replacing an objective and transparent system with a more discretionary system (National reports, France: Silvera *et al.* 1996:25–29).

an example to encourage private industry to follow; additionally, trade unions may be strong in this sector and able to negotiate for more innovative equal pay and equal opportunity policies. Another argument is that the public sector is increasingly reliant on female labour, especially where the relative pay of public sector jobs is declining, and in this context policies for greater equality for women may be considered good business sense.

However, the traditional pattern of employment in the public sector has changed over recent years, largely as a result of the tight monetary policies followed by all the countries of the European Union. France and Germany faced widespread disruption through strikes as a consequence of attempts to freeze public sector pay in the mid-1990s. In Italy, pay in the public sector declined by around 8 per cent in real terms between 1992 to 1994 compared to an overall decline in real wages of under 2.5 per cent (National reports, Italy: Bettio and Villa 1996:57). In Denmark, there has been a so-called 'wage twist' policy in place since the late 1970s, designed to keep wage increases in the public sector below those in the private sector (National reports, Denmark: Boje 1996:42). The overall increase in the gender wage gap in Denmark was not evident in the private and public sectors taken separately but arose mainly out of the reduction in relative pay in the public sector where women were concentrated. Nor is low pay confined to the private sector: in Spain, 26.5 per cent of women in the public sector earned less than the statutory minimum wage calculated on an annual basis, although the earnings distributions for women and men were much more similar in the public than the private sector (National reports, Spain: Moltó 1996:60).

Privatisation has been another factor influencing the pay and conditions of public service providers, whether the privatisation involves the actual transfer of public sector workers to the private sector or the use of what had previously been regarded as private sector pay practices in the public sector. One example which illustrates both these problems is the use of compulsory competitive tendering (CCT) in the United Kingdom, whereby public sector bodies were obliged to invite tenders from private enterprises for many of their services, with contracts awarded to the most competitive bidder. While many of these contracts were won by the local authority teams, pay, as well as terms and conditions of employment, has changed even when the contract remained in the public sector. This 'privatisation' of employment contracts has been shown to have had a differential impact on men and women, with women suffering even more than men from the deterioration in terms and conditions and the increase in work intensity (see Escott and Whitfield, 1995; National reports, UK: Rubery 1996).

As the public sector employs a large proportion of women, any comparative decline in public sector pay will impact disproportionately on the female position in the labour market even if, as in Denmark, the gender pay gap has continued to narrow in the public sector (National reports, Denmark: Boje 1996:35). This is particularly the case in the Scandinavian countries, where there is a large public sector into which women are strongly segregated. Hence, in many countries, if wage growth in the private sector is much greater than in the public sector (or in the case of Italy, if real wage shrinkage in the public sector is greater than in the private sector), this will increase the gender wage gap.

The risk of low pay

In all countries, women tend to be concentrated at the lower end of the pay scale, and to form a disproportionate number of those on the lowest wages. This means that the prevention of unacceptably low wages is important on grounds both of alleviating poverty, and of promoting gender pay equity. As occupational and industrial gender segregation remains a general feature of European labour markets, it is necessary to analyse how the different systems of wage regulation discussed above impact on the risk of low pay for women.

Throughout Europe, the lowest-paid jobs are dominated by women. This is due to the segregation of women into lower-paid 'atypical' employment and into those sectors of the labour market where collective bargaining is least effective, as well as to indirect discrimination in the valuing of 'women's jobs' within more organised sectors. The concentration of women among the lowest paid occurs both in highly regulated and less regulated labour markets. In Finland, women represented 94 per cent of the lowest decile of earners among non-manual employees in industry in 1990; 75 per cent of these workers remained in the lowest decile between 1990 and 1994. In Ireland, a less regulated country with a proportionally smaller female labour force, women represented 49 per cent of those covered by the Joint Labour Committee system (which by no means covers all those at risk of low pay) as against just 31 per cent of the total labour force. Two studies (CERC 1991; OECD 1996) have found that women have a much higher risk of low pay than male workers. The OECD study found women to have a higher risk than men of low pay in all 14 countries, and twice the risk or more in 10 out of the 14 (OECD 1996 and Table 6.2). Data on the share of the labour force receiving minimum wages in 1993 provide further confirmation of this pattern: in the four countries for which Eurostat obtained data – France, Luxembourg, the Netherlands and Portugal – the share of women receiving minimum wages was always twice that of men (CEC 1995a:161) (see Table 6.3). This risk of low pay among women also interacts with other character-istics: for example, in Luxembourg non-resident workers in the so-called 'frontier zone' were found to have a higher risk of receiving minimum wages than resident labour. In France the risk of low pay was found to be concen-trated on female workers in small firms; in 1994, 21.9 per cent of women in firms with fewer than 11 employees earned no more than the minimum wage, in comparison with 9.1 per cent of those in firms of 11 employees or more (National reports, France: Silvera *et al.* 1996).

In certain countries there were slight positive developments with respect to the percentage of women receiving the minimum wage. In Portugal, for

Table 6.2 Share of low-paid[a] full-time workers by gender

	Total	Males	Females	Female to male ratio
Australia[b]	13.8	11.8	17.7	1.5
Austria[c]	13.2	7.0	22.8	3.3
Belgium[c]	7.2	3.9	14.2	3.6
Canada[d]	23.7	16.1	34.3	2.1
Finland[d]	5.9	3.3	8.7	2.6
France[b]	13.3	10.6	17.4	1.6
Germany[d]	13.3	7.6	25.4	3.3
Italy[c]	12.5	9.3	18.5	2.0
Japan[d]	15.7	5.9	37.2	6.3
New Zealand[e]	16.9	14.4	20.7	1.4
Sweden[c]	5.2	3.0	8.4	2.8
Switzerland[b]	13.0	6.8	30.4	4.5
UK[b]	19.6	12.8	31.2	2.4
USA[d]	25.0	19.6	32.5	1.7

Source: OECD (1996).

Notes
a 'Low-paid' defined as less than 66 per cent of 8 median earnings.
b 1995.
c 1993.
d 1994.
e 1994/5.

Table 6.3 Minimum wage-earners by gender

	% of working women on minimum wage	% of working men on minimum wage
France	8.8	3.4
Luxembourg	26.0	9.0
Netherlands	4.7	1.5
Portugal	11.7	5.3
Spain	0.6	0.3

Source: CEC (1995a:161).

Notes
The data refer to 1993, with the exceptions of France (1992) and Spain (1994).
In the case of France, the data refer to people earning 1.05 times the minimum wage. The system in Luxembourg sets several minimum wages. The figures presented here refer to any person whose hourly pay is more than 130 per cent of the minimum wage for an unskilled worker with no dependants.
National data for Portugal (1994), show 8.3 per cent of women and 4 per cent of men receiving the minimum wage, which compares with 7.5 per cent of women and 4.1 per cent of men in 1993.

example, 8.3 per cent of women received the minimum wage in 1994 as against 9.5 per cent four years earlier. However, at the same time the proportion of male minimum wage earners declined from 4.8 per cent to 4 per cent (National reports, Portugal: Lopes and Perista 1996:55) and the value of the minimum dropped from 56 to 39 per cent of the average male blue-collar wage. In France, the tendency for industry-level pay scales to be fixed at the same level or even below that of the SMIC (the French minimum wage) declined in the 1990s, and there was a consequent fall in the proportion of workers failing to earn more than the minimum (8.2 per cent in 1994, compared with 10.9 per cent in 1990). However, the proportion of women among those paid the minimum increased between 1990 and 1991, when the policy of reinvigorating collective bargaining was put into practice, and this higher gender share among the very lowest paid continued through the first half of the 1990s, with the proportion of the female labour force earning the SMIC 2.8 times greater that of the male labour force (National reports, France: Silvera *et al.* 1996:72). A similar pattern was found in more dramatic form in Spain, where the percentage of women earning the minimum wage declined from 2.9 to 0.6 per cent, while the female share of minimum wage earners has increased from 42 to 50 per cent. It should be noted that the level of the minimum has fallen to a very low level in Spain, and measuring the number of those paid the minimum is an inadequate tool for measuring the extent of low pay. Nevertheless, the level of the minimum wage in Spain was still found to influence the pay of most of those not covered by collective bargaining – between 20 and 25 per cent of the female workforce (National reports, Spain: Moltó 1996:59) – and its influence spread outside the wage labour market, as the level of social security benefits in Spain has been determined in relation to the minimum wage.

In the Netherlands, a fall in the proportion of female minimum wage earners would have occurred had it not been for the introduction of the law extending the minimum to more part-timers (National reports, Netherlands: Plantenga *et al.* 1996:36–37)). Thus in 1992 78 thousand women and 50 thousand men were paid the minimum wage, but by 1994 this number had risen to 118 thousand women and 83 thousand men, as the part-timers who had been previously excluded from the system were included in the data. The number of full-timers paid the minimum wage had remained roughly constant for women, at around 33 thousand, but had risen for men from 35 to 43 thousand: the number of part-timers paid the minimum wage had risen from 46 to 85 thousand women and from 16 to 40 thousand men.

Pay dispersion trends

The evolution of earnings will clearly not necessarily follow a similar pattern for all female workers. An increase in the gender pay ratio may occur because of significant improvements for a relatively small number of women at the upper end of the female earnings distribution, while those at lower levels witness little or no improvement. Additionally, wide wage dispersion may have a strongly positive correlation with the gender pay gap (Blau and Kahn 1992). The gender pay ratio will depend both on how well women are paid relative to men, and what penalties or advantages derive from being found in the bottom or the top parts of the earnings distribution (Grimshaw and Rubery 1997b). Thus, the level of pay dispersion and its evolution provides an important dimension to the gender pay equity issue.

While in the 1970s the direction of trends was clearly towards declining pay dispersion, in the 1980s and 1990s a more variable pattern emerged, but with more countries moving towards widening pay dispersion. However, while there was a slight widening of pay dispersion in Austria and some widening at the top of the pay distributions in Belgium, Denmark, Finland, France, Portugal and Spain, it was only in the UK, together with the US if we take OECD countries as the reference point, that there was a very signifi-cant increase in pay dispersion over the 1980s (OECD 1993, 1996). Even this increase in inequality was understated, as the data provided to the OECD for many countries excluded part-timers, a fact which was not sufficiently noted, at least in the 1993 OECD report.

In the 1990s, however, the erosion of centralised regulatory systems resulted in wider pay dispersion across a wider group of countries. In Italy, for example, the structural reform of the institutional framework increased pay dispersion considerably, with the ratio of the top decile of annual income earners to the bottom decile increasing from 2.43 to 3.56 between 1989 and 1993 (National reports, Italy: Bettio and Villa 1996:55). Similarly, in Sweden income inequality increased, associated with the decentralisation of bargaining, and it was those on low incomes who suffered the most deterioration in relative income (National reports, Sweden: Gonäs and Spånt 1996: 27). In other countries, some rather less radical changes in the bargaining structure (see below) also led to some increased wage inequality (see National reports, Spain: Moltó 1996:57 and Denmark: Boje 1996:40). Meanwhile, in the under-regulated market of the United Kingdom, wage dispersion continued to grow rapidly; between 1989 and 1995 the female full-time lowest decile fell from 63.9 per cent to 59.3 per cent of the female median, while the lowest decile of female part-timers fell from 55.3 to 49 per cent of the female full-time median (National reports, UK: Rubery 1996:112–114). However, the trend towards widening pay dispersion is still not uniform: for example, pay dispersion was stable in France, the Netherlands and Portugal during the first half of the 1990s (OECD 1993, 1996; National reports, Portugal: Lopes and Perista 1996:51). Finland provides an example of a country where pay dispersion in the 1990s moved in the oppo-site direction, towards a narrower range of earnings, with marked rises for the lowest decile, possibly as a result of the lower paid being ejected from the labour market in the intense recession of the 1990s. This divergent experience suggests that the institutions of wage determination are more important than the general economic conditions in determining trends in pay dispersion.

It has generally been the case that wage dispersion among men is wider than that among women, as women are predominantly segregated into lower-paid employment, and higher-paid professional and managerial jobs are dominated by men. However, in recent years, many countries have witnessed a widening wage dispersion among women, as well as among the work-force as a whole. In Spain, dispersion for women has exceeded that for men, probably reflecting women's concentration in low-paid work and part-time jobs at the one end and the relatively high share of Spanish women in professional jobs at the other (National reports, Spain: Moltó 1996: 57). This increasing wage dispersion was a reflection of the general widening of wage differentials and the increasing differentiation between more highly educated women and other women, in terms of their occupations and their participation patterns.

If the focus is on the avoidance of poverty rather than social justice, it is evidently worrying that dispersion increased during a period of recession. This suggests that some low-paid workers, particularly women, were likely to have experienced losses in real earnings (see National reports, Sweden: Gonäs and Spånt 1996:27; Italy: Bettio and Villa 1996:54). This was certainly the case for part-time female workers in the UK, with losses in real earnings between 1993 and 1995 at lowest decile and median levels, perhaps reflecting the removal of wage protection (National reports, UK: Rubery 1996: 116).

Again, the official figures are likely to be inadequate in assessing the full extent of changes in wage dispersion, owing to the exclusion of part-time workers from many official figures (National reports, Germany: Maier *et al.* 1996:66). This is exacerbated by the increasing numbers of women that work part-time, which in itself will widen the true extent of pay dispersion if their pay is lower than that of full-time workers.

Another dimension to pay inequality is life-cycle inequality. Much of the gender pay gap is explained by widening pay differentials between men and women over the life cycle, with pay differentials at the outset of careers being relatively similar. In Luxembourg, for example, there was gender pay equality until the age of 25, from which point male earnings increased faster than those of women; after 35, the average female wage decreased, and the gender pay ratio for those over 45 years old was around 60 per cent (National reports, Luxembourg: Plasman 1996:38). Some, but by no means all, of this life-cycle inequality can be explained by women's discontinuous participa-tion patterns, but even in countries such as Italy where women tend to pursue continuous careers if they remain in work, most of the gender pay gap occurred among older men and women (National reports, Italy: Bettio and Villa 1996:58). One recent trend has been towards even greater equality in earnings among young men and women, reflecting both the upgrading of women's educational qualifications among younger cohorts and, more importantly, the downgrading of young men's earnings opportunities. In the UK this change has begun to have major impacts on lifestyles, leading to

delays in the formation of independent households and to increasing importance attached to women's earnings in partnerships (Irwin 1995).

Summary: the need to mainstream gender pay equity

Consideration of recent trends in pay determination makes it crystal clear
that far from moving smoothly towards greater gender pay equality, action
is still required to ensure that the restructuring of systems of pay determination do not result in a deterioration in women's pay and an erosion of
progress made over recent decades. The dangers for gender pay equity from
recent developments in the labour market are evident across a whole range
of indicators, including the declining coverage of minimum wage protection systems, the declining level of real and relative pay at the bottom of
the labour market, the shift towards decentralised bargaining and individualised pay, rising wage dispersion and the rising share of low-paid atypical
workers. These developments may be regarded as relatively independent of
any specific move to reverse gender pay equity, but instead may be part
of a wider movement towards greater inequality in which class, age and
gender inequalities are all increasing. It is the recognition of the significance of these broader trends for gender pay equity that becomes vital.
Lower pay for public sector workers was advocated in the interests of
meeting Maastricht conditions, lower minimum wages in the interests
of increasing flexibility and stimulating job creation and decentralisation of
pay determination in the interests of firms' efficiency and competitiveness,
but regardless of the validity of these arguments, the implications of these
policy developments for gender pay equity fail to be spelt out.

Policies directed towards equal pay, including for example the European
Commission's code of practice on equal value (see above, Chapter 1, Box
1.1), which emphasised issues of gender pay differentials within organisations, may in the end prove to have adopted too narrow a perspective in a
world in which many of the largest changes in differentials are taking place
between organisations and between groups of workers not usually considered together in any job evaluation exercises. These changes, or potential
changes, to wage systems are likely to outweigh any progress made in
formulating more gender equitable internal pay structures; as such the new
objective for gender pay equity may be to put back on to the agenda the
need to reduce pay dispersion at the labour market level and to maintain
the real and relative value of the floor to the labour market.

Without such a change in emphasis, labour market policies to stimulate
employment through reducing minimum wage levels may continue to go
hand in hand with policies apparently designed to reduce gender inequality
in the labour market. 'Mainstreaming' gender into wage determination policies should help to reveal the potential incompatibility of the policy of
flexibility with equality.

7 Gender and working-time

Time is a key gender issue both in the work place and in the home. Women and men have quite different patterns of time use in all countries, even those with the most egalitarian labour market organisation. The time women and men spend in the labour market varies not only on a daily or weekly basis, with women dominating part-time work, but also over the life cycle, with women more likely to take time out of the labour market to care for children. Women also take on a greater share of the domestic responsibilities in all countries. Even where women and men are both working full-time, women carry a double burden, doing more of the housework and caring duties and having less leisure time (Anxo and Flood 1995 and pp. 160–4 above). Labour Force Survey statistics in all countries show how women work fewer hours than men in paid employment but these results do not take account of the extra hours women work in unpaid domestic roles.

The different patterns of time use of men and women mean that they offer a different kind of flexibility in the labour market. Men's greater freedom from domestic responsibilities gives them a perceived flexibility to be available at short notice for overtime work and weekend work to cover for changes in demand. Men need to take less account of how wage work meshes with life and responsibilities in the home. Consequently, men are less likely to take time off for childcare and they are unlikely to take parental leave even if it is only available to them and cannot be taken by their partner (National reports, Sweden: Gonäs and Spånt 1996). The ability of men to concentrate on wage work gives them greater power in the labour market. Their higher involvement in full-time work and their uninterrupted labour market activity over the life cycle allows them to progress further up the labour market, granting them both higher wages and greater security in old age (see Chapter 6).

Women are more likely to adjust their labour market activity to family life, by taking part-time work, short-hours full-time work or, in countries where these options are not available, by quitting the labour market. This involves taking the risk that they will not be able to return when domestic responsibilities allow, as well as accepting reduced lifetime working and all the disadvantages it brings. In return for the 'convenience' of short and predictable working hours these labour market adjustments impose high penalties in the form of low pay and poor promotion prospects and limited pension entitlements (Maruani 1995).

These gender dimensions to working-time and flexibility lead to a paradox. Women are more time-constrained, but men are more likely to be compensated for extra or variable hours. Men are rewarded for their perceived flexibility through premia or days off, while women are penalised for the flexibility they offer in the form of low pay, low occupational attainment and low job security. In Austria, for example, men in some sectors have shorter full-time hours because of their strong collective representation (National reports, Austria: Pastner 1996:72). There is a further paradox, in that many men may be employed in areas where there is scope for part-time or casual work but only full-time work is offered. For example, temporary work is extensive in the construction industry in Austria but prohibited by collective agreement in the Netherlands (National reports, Netherlands: Plantenga *et al.* 1996:42–43; Austria: Pastner 1996:76). At the same time women very often work in areas such as hospitals and catering where there are demands for unsocial hours working that conflict with domestic commitments.

However, the patterns of flexibility by working-time and contract are by no means fixed, leaving significant scope for societal differences in the rate of involvement of women in flexible part-time and other non-standard contracts, in the spread of flexible work and long hours working and in the extent of the disadvantage suffered by flexible workers relative to full-time permanent workers. These societal differences emerge from the interaction of nationally specific regulations on wages and working-time, plus welfare state policies and social norms which influence involvement in waged work. For example, the extent and form of women's involvement in part-time work varies markedly between countries, as does the quality of these jobs (Blossfeld and Hakim 1997; Fagan and Rubery 1996b; O'Reilly and Fagan 1998). More generally a diverse range of national working-time regimes can be identified, in which the number of hours worked and the extent of unsocial hours working varies markedly between countries (Rubery *et al.* 1995, 1997a, 1998b).

This chapter first examines the expansion of part-time employment and changes in working-time in the European Union over the period from 1989 to 1994 before returning to the different kinds of flexibility that men and women offer. The second part of the chapter explores the growth of other forms of flexible employment and the different patterns of temporary employment.

The expansion of part-time jobs

In the early 1990s part-time employment increased for women and men in all countries with the exception of the Nordic countries and the former East

Germany for women and Italy, Finland and Luxembourg for men. This confirms the pattern found for the period from 1983 to 1992, in which part-time jobs accounted for more than half of new jobs in the European Union and for 54 per cent of male jobs and 56 per cent of female jobs. Three-quarters of these new part-time jobs were taken by women, but the same was also true for the new full-time jobs (Rubery *et al.* 1998a:34; Smith *et al.* 1998). In the first part of the 1990s most new jobs were again taken by women and the decline in full-time work was yet more evident.

Full-time employment declined for men in most countries (10 out of 14) and also for women in around a third (5 out of 14) between 1989 and 1994. Moreover, male part-time employment grew faster, with part-time work for men doubling in the former East Germany (between 1991 and 1994), increasing by at least a half in Spain, Belgium, Ireland and the former West Germany and by a third or more in Portugal and the UK. This rise in male part-time work reflected the increasing difficulties that men faced in the labour market and the general lack of full-time work. The growth rates of female part-time work were more modest but from a much larger base. However, in Ireland there was a 64 per cent rise in female part-time work and an increase in four countries of more than a third. The large rise in female part-time employment in Ireland was important in increasing labour market participation of core-age women (National reports, Ireland: Barry 1996:54–56). Where falls in female part-time employment occurred these reflected not only the economic conditions, particularly in Sweden and the former East Germany, but also women's increased aspirations for full participation in the labour market including, in the case of the former East Germany, their reluctance to adopt a West German pattern of part-time participation (National reports, Denmark: Boje 1996:43; Sweden: Gonäs and Spånt 1996:39–40; Germany: Maier *et al.* 1996:25). In three of the four countries where female part-time employment fell, male part-time employment actually expanded, by 14.6 per cent and 1.6 per cent in Sweden and Denmark and doubling in the former East Germany (107 per cent). Table 7.1 shows the contributions that the changes in full- and part-time employment made to the net change in overall employment between 1989 and 1994. In most cases the increases in male part-time employment had a limited impact on the change in employment, with the UK and the Netherlands the exceptions. By contrast, the changes in female part-time employment were more significant, particularly in the Netherlands but also in Ireland, the former West Germany, Belgium, France and Luxembourg. The falling rates of female part-time employment in Denmark and Sweden had a significant negative impact on overall female employment, while in the former East Germany the impact was relatively minor compared to that of falling rates of female full-time employment.

The absolute increase in part-time jobs and the greater falls in full-time work meant that rates of part-time employment also rose. At the E14 level part-time rates rose by 1.8 percentage points, from 14.8 per cent to 16.6 per

Table 7.1 Contribution of full- and part-time jobs to net job change, 1989–1994

	Male		Female		Total
	Full-time	*Part-time*	*Full-time*	*Part-time*	
Belgium	−0.9	0.5	2.3	2.6	4.5
Denmark	−2.3	0.1	1.7	−3.1	−3.6
Germany (e)[a]	−6.2	0.7	−8.6	−0.5	−14.5
Germany (w)	0.8	0.7	1.0	4.1	6.5
Spain	−5.7	0.6	0.2	1.3	−3.7
France	−2.3	0.6	−0.2	2.3	0.4
Greece	1.3	0.5	1.3	0.1	3.1
Ireland	0.6	1.5	4.6	3.5	10.2
Italy	−3.3	−0.3	−0.6	0.5	−3.7
Luxembourg	2.7	−0.4	2.9	2.1	7.3
Netherlands	1.9	1.2	0.7	7.7	11.5
Portugal	−5.2	0.8	0.5	1.1	−2.8
Finland	−8.5	−0.1	−7.2	−0.5	−16.3
Sweden	−6.2	0.6	−2.1	−2.5	−10.2
UK	−3.6	1.0	0.2	0.7	−1.7
E12[b]	−2.1	0.6	0.4	2.0	0.8
E14[b]	−3.8	0.5	−1.1	0.7	−3.8

Sources: European Labour Force Survey (1989–1994); national data for Finland and Sweden.
Notes
Contributions sum to percentage change in employment between 1989 and 1994, 1989 taken
    as the base (1991 for East Germany).
No data are available for Austria.
a Data for the former East Germany are for 1991–1994.
b Excluding East Germany.

cent and the female rate increased by 2 percentage points, while for the men
the rate rose by just over 1 point (see Table 7.2). Within member states part-
time rates for employed men rose in 12 of the 14, with small falls in the
part-time share in Italy and Luxembourg (see also Delsen 1998). For women,
the trend was generally upwards but there were some exceptions: in Denmark
and Sweden rates of part-time work among employed women fell by 5.7
and 1.4 percentage points, and in Greece the rate for women remained
unchanged and the lowest in the EU. The large falls in the female part-time
rate in Denmark in the early 1990s meant that by the mid-1990s it was at a
similar level to that in the 1970s (National reports, Denmark: Boje
1996:72–73). There were particularly strong increases in the rate of part-time
work for employed women in the former West Germany, Ireland and the
Netherlands, where rates all increased by more than five percentage points.
In Austria the female part-time rate of employment rose from 18.9 per cent
to 19.6 per cent between 1989 and 1994 while the male rate remained virtually unchanged at around 1 per cent (National reports, Austria: Pastner
1996:78). The growth of part-time employment in Austria would have been
more significant if marginal workers working less than 12 hours a week had
also been included (see Box 7.1).

Table 7.2 The share of employed women and men working part-time in the European Union, 1989 and 1994

	Male part-time rates		Female part-time rates	
	1989	1994	1989	1994
Belgium	1.7	2.5	25.0	28.3
Denmark	9.4	10.0	40.1	34.4
Germany (e)	—	2.9	—	19.4
Germany (w)	2.3	3.3	30.7	36.4
Spain	1.6	2.6	11.9	15.2
France	3.5	4.6	23.8	27.8
Greece	2.4	3.1	8.0	8.0
Ireland	3.1	5.1	16.5	21.7
Italy	3.1	2.8	10.9	12.4
Luxembourg	(1.9)	(1.3)	16.4	19.5
Netherlands	15.0	16.1	60.1	66.0
Austria	1.1	1.3	18.9	19.8
Portugal	3.1	4.7	10.0	12.1
Finland	4.7	5.5	10.4	11.1
Sweden	7.3	9.4	41.6	40.2
UK	5.0	7.1	43.6	44.4
E12[a]	3.8	4.8	28.0	31.3
E14[a]	4.6	5.8	29.0	31.0

Source: European Labour Force Survey (1989, 1994); National reports, Austria: Pastner (1996:78); Finland: Keinänen (1996); Sweden: Gonäs and Spånt (1996).

Notes
— indicates no data available.
a Excluding East Germany.

The growth in part-time employment was not related to the levels of part-time work at the start of the period. Some countries with high levels of part-time work, namely Denmark and Sweden, as we have seen, recorded falls for women, but at the other extreme, countries with the lowest part-time rates – for example Greece for women and Luxembourg for men – also experienced small falls in the incidence of part-time work. Other countries with high levels of part-time work, such as the UK and the Netherlands, experienced increases in part-time employment, particularly for women in the Netherlands and men in the UK. At the lower and middle end of the distribution of rates of part-time employment, Belgium, France and Ireland all saw increases for both men and women.

These differing trends between countries – regardless of their starting points – increased the inter-country range of part-time rates for both women and men, but in general part-time work became far more common for both sexes. Nevertheless, rates of part-time work for men were still only above 5 per cent in six countries in 1994 while women were more heavily involved in part-time work. Only the four Southern European countries and Finland recorded part-time rates for employed women below 19 per cent in 1994

(8–15.2 per cent) and only Greece below 10 per cent, while in four countries more than a quarter of employed women worked part-time and in a
further three – the Netherlands, Sweden and the UK – the rates were over
40 per cent. The proportion of employed women working part-time in the
former East Germany showed a more modest increase than in the former
West Germany, 2.7 compared to 5.7 percentage points, but even this increase
reflected the even larger fall in female full-time work in the East as female
part-time work declined in absolute terms.

Working hours and contractual status

Gender differences in working-time arise from a number of factors and along
several dimensions. Differences in working hours may be related first of all
to differences in employment contracts. This division extends beyond the
obvious divisions between part-time and full-time work to include divisions
in some countries between blue-collar and white-collar employees, between
public and private sector employees and between employees and the self-
employed (Bosch *et al.* 1994). The self-employed tend to have long working
hours which are determined more by the individual concerned than by the
regulatory system (see Table 7.3). The division between temporary and permanent contracts also has a working-time dimension, as the use of temporary
contracts may be an alternative to overtime or to forms of part-time work
such as annualised part-time work.[1] Different contractual conditions can act
as another layer of segregation in the labour market, reinforcing differences
in working-time. There are also gender differences in working-time between
men and women working under the same contractual conditions and these
differences, although more subtle, are important in terms of the impact they
have on women's progression in the labour market and the gender division
of work in the home.

   In all countries men work longer hours than women but the difference is
a result of the different levels of involvement of women in part-time work
on the one hand and of men in long-hours work, either as self-employed
or full-time employees, on the other. At the E12 level the gender gap in
average hours for all in employment was 8.2 hours in 1994. However,
in practice the gender gap in average hours ranged from around 4 to 5 hours
in all the Southern European countries and Luxembourg and in Austria and
Finland to more than 12 hours in the Netherlands and the UK (see Table
7.3). In Greece and Portugal the small gender gap arose out of long usual
hours for both men and women, with employed women in both these countries usually working more hours than men in Denmark and the Netherlands.
In Spain, Italy, Luxembourg, Austria and Finland men had working hours
similar to the European average but a relatively low incidence of part-time
work for women resulted in a smaller gender gap. In the Netherlands and
the UK the particularly large gender gap arose out of a high incidence of
part-time work with very short hours for women. However, in the case

Box 7.1 Women dominate marginal jobs

It is estimated that there were around a quarter of a million 'marginal work-ers' in **Austria** in 1992, classified as those working less than 12 hours a week and not included in the national employment statistics. Around one-third of these marginal workers were men, either young students or pensioners, and of the two-thirds who were women around half were house-wives. It is estimated that two-thirds of all marginal workers were unpaid family workers in the agricultural sector. The inclusion of marginal workers in the labour force would, it was estimated, increase the part-time rate from 19.6 per cent to 27 per cent or 28 per cent in 1992 (National reports, Austria: Pastner 1996:77).

Workers working less than 12 hours in **Netherlands** have been excluded from the definition of the employed labour force in the national surveys since 1992. Evidence suggests that these workers may be more likely to be on temporary and flexible contracts (National reports, Netherlands: Plantenga *et al.* 1996:48–49).

In the **UK** many short part-time jobs fall below the minimum income level for coverage by National Insurance and entitlement to non-means-tested benefits. One study of flexible workers also showed how only 59 per cent of male part-timers were entitled to paid holidays and only 29 per cent of female part-timers (Watson 1993; National reports, UK: Rubery 1996:162, 136).

In **Sweden** the threshold for social security protection was set at a very low insurance level, thereby limiting the marginalisation of short part-time workers in Sweden (National reports, Sweden: Gonäs and Spånt 1996:64). However, for access to the voluntary unemployment benefit schemes, work-ers have to work at least 17 hours.

In **Germany** part-timers working less than 15 hours a week and earning less than DM580 a month in the West and DM470 a month in the East were not covered by sickness insurance or old age pensions (values for 1995). This last group of marginal employees, dominated by women (70.4 per cent), experienced a 15 per cent expansion between 1987 and the 1994 (National reports, Germany: Maier *et al.* 1996:79). In addition those work-ing less than 18 hours were not covered by unemployment insurance although this last threshold has recently been reduced to 15.

of the UK this was combined with very long hours for men, second only to Greece, reflecting the polarised pattern of working-time in the UK, while the Netherlands has the shortest average hours for men as well as short hours for women. The difference in average usual hours shows the unequal distribution of work in all countries, but in particular in Ireland, the Netherlands and the UK. If we consider the average hours of employees only the gender gap falls to 7.4 hours at the E12 level and also falls in 8 of the 12 member states plus Austria, Finland and Sweden.

Table 7.3 Average hours by employment category and gender, 1994

	All in employment		All employees		Full-time employees		Part-time employees		Full-time employers		Full-time self-employed		Full-time family workers	
	Male	Female	Male	Female	Male	Female	Male	Female	Male	Female	Male	Female	Male	Female
Belgium	40.6	33.4	38.3	31.9	38.8	36.9	21.1	20.9	58.1	45.0	56.3	50.7	53.6	50.8
Denmark	39.0	32.8	37.1	32.1	39.8	38.0	14.2	21.2	54.5	50.8	54.4	47.2	(43.1)	47.7
Germany (u)	40.9	33.5	39.3	32.9	39.9	39.2	18.9	20.2	—	—	—	—	—	—
Germany (w)	—	—	—	—	—	—	—	—	50.5	49.5	51.4	46.2	50.7	46.9
Germany (e)	—	—	—	—	—	—	—	—	55.4	50.8	54.6	49.4	52.5	55.1
Greece	45.3	40.7	41.0	38.0	41.4	39.0	25.6	21.5	52.1	49.3	51.0	46.5	49.8	46.3
Spain	42.1	37.6	40.5	36.3	41.0	39.5	19.6	17.5	47.4	45.1	47.6	46.2	47.0	46.4
France	41.6	35.0	39.8	34.2	40.6	38.7	22.5	22.4	55.1	49.8	56.6	50.9	57.7	53.6
Ireland	45.1	34.7	40.4	33.9	41.5	37.8	20.5	18.3	57.9	50.9	60.0	50.5	60.7	49.2
Italy	41.4	36.1	39.5	34.7	39.7	36.3	30.1	23.0	46.6	44.1	45.9	42.6	44.6	42.6
Luxembourg	42.1	35.4	40.5	34.3	40.6	37.9	(26.7)	19.7	55.8	(53.6)	56.7	(46.6)	(65.0)	(48.4)
Netherlands	38.1	25.2	36.3	25.2	39.6	39.1	18.6	17.9	58.9	50.7	56.2	47.9	57.9	46.2
Austria	41.0	35.9	39.5	34.8	40.0	39.0	21.5	23.5	—	—	—	—	—	—
Portugal	44.3	39.2	42.4	37.9	42.7	39.3	26.3	20.2	53.9	50.2	51.2	48.2	53.1	52.7
Finland	40.1	36.3	38.2	35.7	39.2	37.9	21.6	22.1	—	—	—	—	—	—
Sweden	39.2	33.0	38.0	32.8	40.1	39.8	19.6	24.4	—	—	—	—	—	—
UK	44.4	30.6	43.5	30.6	45.4	40.5	16.0	17.9	57.3	54.5	49.7	46	45.5	52.2
E12	41.9	33.7	40.2	32.8	41.1	38.9	19.5	19.7	—	—	—	—	—	—

Source: European Labour Force Survey (1994, 1995).

Notes
Data for Austria, Finland and Sweden are for 1995.
— indicates no data available.

The gender gap in average working hours actually rose during the early 1990s, from 7.9 in 1989 at the EU12 level to 8.2 hours in 1994. This reflected slight falls in the gender gap in the UK and Ireland but widening gaps in other countries, particularly in Portugal and Luxembourg, where the gap rose by more than one hour. In Austria the gender gap for employees was 3.7 hours in 1993, slightly down from 3.8 in 1988 (National reports, Austria: Pastner 1996:70). Detailed analysis of the change in average hours between 1983 and 1995 showed that they fell from around 40 hours per week to 38½ at the E12 level, but the falls within countries ranged from around 2½ hours in Germany, Ireland, Belgium and Greece to just 40 minutes in the UK. Most of the reduction was due to a compositional shift, with the continued decline of agricultural employment, in which hours have traditionally been long, and the general expansion of part-time work, rather than negotiated reductions in full-time hours. However, negotiated reductions in full-time hours played more of a role in Belgium, Germany, Denmark and Luxembourg than in the other member states (CEC 1996b).

Employers and the self-employed in all countries tend to work very long hours free from regulatory protection and under pressure to meet demand. In 10 of the 12 member states for which we have data for men and 7 out of 12 for women, full-time employers worked more than 50 hours a week on average (Table 7.3). Despite the very long hours for female employers, the usual hours of the full-time male employers still exceeded women's by 5 hours or more in five countries, including Belgium where the gap was 13 hours. The self-employed without employees sometimes work even longer hours than employers, but in all cases they still work long hours and had a more significant effect on overall average hours. In nine countries full-time self-employed men worked more than 50 hours a week and in Ireland the average was 60 hours a week (see Table 7.3). Full-time self-employed women worked more than 50 hours a week in three countries and more than 45 hours in all other countries except Italy, where average hours were 'only' 42.6. Among the full-time self-employed, men worked longer hours than women in all countries, with a gender gap of 5 hours or more in seven countries, rising to more than 10 hours in two countries, Ireland and Luxembourg. Clearly, employers and the self-employed of both sexes work very long hours but it is men's greater domination of these statuses that pushes up their average hours in employment. Self-employment has been seen both as a way to combat rising unemployment and as a new form of labour market flexibility with the spread of 'contracting out' and 'pseudo freelance' contracts (Meager 1996). However, self-employment could be regarded as inefficient with respect to the distribution of work, given the very long hours often involved. In many countries these long hours may be a form of 'self-exploitation' induced by the low net income for many of the self-employed.

Women are also more likely to be family workers than men and here too we find long hours of work among full-timers (see Table 7.3). In some countries female full-time family workers actually worked longer hours than men on average; only in Ireland, Luxembourg and the Netherlands was there a significant gap in the hours of male and female full-time family workers in favour of men. However, this 'equality' in long hours had little impact on the overall distribution of work in most labour markets, as family workers accounted for a minority of jobs.

Among part-timers there was little difference between men and women's working hours, and indeed at the E12 level men work slightly shorter part-time hours (see Table 7.3). Women's hours in part-time jobs are longer than those for men in Denmark, the UK, Germany, Austria and Sweden. This is probably because many of the male part-timers are students working short hours while women of all ages are heavily involved in both long- and short-hours part-time work (Delsen 1998). In the Southern European countries, where part-time work is less common, it is the men who work the longer part-time hours.

Among full-time employees a gender gap was still found in all countries, although the actual size varied from less than one hour in Germany, the Netherlands and Sweden to around five hours in the UK in 1994 (see Table 7.3). The cause of a large gender gap for full-time employees in the UK appears to be the long hours worked by men, as the average hours worked by female full-time employees are longer than in any other EU country, including even Portugal, where standard contractual hours are the longest. In fact, in 1994 the UK had the highest share of both male and female employees working more than the 48-hour limit of the EC Working Time Directive (IDS 1996b). In Italy and Ireland, the two other countries with a large gender gap (i.e. over three hours), women's average hours were below the E12 average hours, particularly in Italy. Men's hours were above the E12 average in Ireland, but well below average in Italy, so that in this case the large gender gap arose out of short hours for women, not long hours for men. Here, however, we may in part be identifying a statistical problem, as average hours for full-timers are brought down in Italy by the high share of women who say they work full-time but who give their usual hours as less than 30 hours per week (Rubery *et al.* 1995:172). This may suggest a tendency for Italians not to identify themselves as working part-time even when employed for short hours, as it is not regarded as a regular form of employment and those in part-time jobs may be still included in the unemployment register (National reports, Italy: Bettio and Villa 1994). Moreover, in Italy average full-time hours are brought down by the relatively low contractual hours in the public sector, set at 36 hours (Rubery *et al.* 1995:142).

The segregated nature of the labour market by occupation and industry adds a further dimension to the patterns of working-time. The complex inter-relationships of employment within sectors by professional status and occupation combine with societal factors to produce the national pattern of working-time (Rubery *et al.* 1997a). Male-dominated occupations such as agriculture and managerial work, which are characterised by long hours, push up male average hours in many countries, while many professional and clerical jobs in which women are concentrated have much shorter full-time hours (Rubery *et al.* 1998b). Male-dominated sectors such as agriculture, transport and mining often have longer full-time hours but more feminised sectors such as public administration and other services have shorter full-time hours.

At the E12 level there were differences of more than two hours between the average hours of male and female full-time employees in 8 of the 12 industrial groups, but this disguised many different societal effects across countries in 1994 (see Table 7.4). In the UK and Ireland male full-time employees worked on average at least two hours more than female full-time employees in all sectors (except in mining and electricity in Ireland), contributing to the two largest gender gaps: 3.7 and 4.9 hours for full-time employees. In countries such as Belgium, Germany, the Netherlands and Sweden, where working-time is regulated more strictly, the gender gap within sectors was more limited. In these countries no sector had a gap of more than two hours and there was only one sector in the Netherlands, two in Sweden and five in Belgium and Germany where the gap even exceeded one hour. Of the two sectors in Sweden where the gender gap exceeded an hour, men's hours were longer in the case of hotels and restaurants but women's hours were longer in the case of agriculture. Across all 15 countries there were only five sectors where women usually worked longer hours – four in Sweden and one in Finland – but only in agriculture in Sweden did the gap rise above an hour.

If we look at full-time employees in hotels and restaurants across the EU, we see that male full-time employees usually worked at least one hour per week more than women except in the Netherlands and Austria, and more than two hours longer in all other countries except Belgium, Germany, Finland and Sweden. There was a similar strong sector effect in transport and communication in all countries except the Netherlands and Sweden. In other services there was a sector effect in the opposite direction, with a narrow gender gap of less than an hour in nine countries. However, here the societal effect of long hours in the UK and Ireland overrode this pattern while in Italy the particularly short hours of women in the public sector increased the gender gap. The strong collective regulation of working hours in the manufacturing sector reduced the gender gap in average hours to less than an hour in ten countries, only exceeding two hours in the UK and Ireland. Due to the sectoral segregation of employment, there was no clear relationship between the number of sectors with large gender gaps and the size of the overall national gender gap. France and Denmark had a gender gap of at least an hour in eight sectors but a national gender gap of less than two hours, while Portugal also had eight sectors with a gender gap of at least an hour but a national difference of 3.6 hours.

Average hours fell for men in the European Union in the early part of the 1990s, from 42.4 to 41.9, but rose for women from 33.7 to 34.5. At

Table 7.4 Gender gap in average hours of full-time employees by sector and country, 1994

	A, B	C	D	E	F	G	H	I	J	K	L	M–Q	Gender gap for all sectors
Belgium	..	..				+	+	+	+	+			1.9
Denmark	++	..	+			++	++	++	++	++			1.8
Germany (u)		..	+		+	+	+	+	+			+	0.7
Greece	++	..		+			++	++		+	+		2.4
Spain	++	..		+		++	++	++		+	+		1.5
France	++	+	++		+	++	++	++	++	++	++	++	1.9
Ireland	++	..		+	++	+	++	++	++	+	+	++	3.7
Italy	++	++		+	++	++	++	+	+	++	++	++	3.4
Luxembourg	..	..		..	++	++	++	+	+	++	++	++	2.7
Netherlands	+	..		..									0.5
Austria	++	..	+		+	+	+	+	+	+	+	++	1.0
Portugal	++	..			++	+	++	+	+	++	++		3.6
Finland	++	..			+	++	+	++	++	+	++	*	1.3
Sweden	+ *	..		*			+	*			*		0.3
UK	++	++	++	++	++	++	++	++	++	++	++	++	4.9

Source: European Labour Force Survey (1994:Table 73).

Notes

Male hours are consistently greater than female hours except in Sweden and Finland where marked *.

Data for Sweden, Finland and Austria are for 1995.

A, B = agriculture.
C = mining and quarrying.
D = manufacturing.
E = electricity, gas and water supply.
F = construction.
G = wholesale and retail trade, repairs.
H = hotels and restaurants.
I = transport and communications.

J = financial intermediation.
K = real estate and business activities.
L = public administration.
M–Q = other services
.. = indicates no reliable data for one or both sexes.
+ = indicates 1-hour gap.
++ = indicates 2-hour gap or more.

the same time, average hours for full-timers remained virtually unchanged. During the period from 1983 to 1995 male full-time hours actually rose in both industry and services in the UK, the Netherlands, Portugal and Ireland; and in industry only in France, Italy, Luxembourg and Spain and at the E12 level. For women, average full-time hours fell in both industry and services in nearly all countries and at the E12 level. However, average hours for female full-timers rose between 1983 and 1995 in both sectors in the UK, in industry in France and Spain and in Greece in services (CEC 1996b).

Policies and initiatives aimed at reducing overall working-time are regarded as the most gender-neutral way of sharing work between the sexes (Bettio *et al.* 1998a; Meulders 1996; Beccalli and Salvati 1995) but these lost momentum in the early 1990s (Bosch *et al.* 1994; Bosch and Lehndorff 1997). However, the mid-1990s saw a resurgence of policies to reduce working-time in a number of countries, particularly France and Italy but also Portugal. In Italy policies aimed at reducing overall working-time have tended to lead to increased days off rather than a reduction in the weekly or daily working-time, or money alternatives have been taken, reducing the work-sharing impact (National reports, Italy: Bettio and Villa 1996:47). Similarly, in Spain the gradual reduction of working-time slowed down, for men more for than women (National reports, Spain: Moltó 1996:68) but the second half of the 1990s saw the main unions in Spain demand progress towards a 35-hour week (IDS 1998a). Average hours have also been falling in Ireland since the 1960s, and even over the short period between 1988 and 1994 hours fell by over 2 hours to 41.1, although marked gender differences remain (Table 7.3 above). In the UK, the government of the early 1990s resisted pressure from Europe to place a maximum limit on usual hours, in spite of a European court ruling that long hours were bad for the health of UK employees (IDS 1996b). However, the incoming Labour government of May 1997 agreed to sign the EC Working-time Directive and therefore bring a limit on working hours into the UK for the first time.[2]

Over- and underworking

Figure 7.1 shows the gender differences in involvement in short- and long-hours working across the EU, but also the impact of societal systems and norms. While within each country more men were involved in long hours of work than women, and more women than men were in short hours of work, these differences do not hold between countries. Thus more men were involved in short-hours working in, for example, the Netherlands and Denmark than was the case for women in each of the Southern European countries plus Luxembourg and Finland. Conversely, more women were involved in long hours of work in Greece and the UK than was the case for men in Belgium, the Netherlands, Luxembourg and Germany. These data reveal the importance of regulation, both legal and voluntary, in reducing

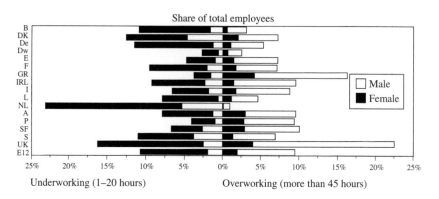

Figure 7.1 Over- and underworking of male and female employees, 1994

Source: European Labour Force Survey (1994, 1996).

Note
Data for Austria, Sweden and Finland refer to 1996.

full-time working hours in some countries, while allowing for wider dispersion of hours in others (Rubery *et al.* 1995). In all countries other than the UK, legal or voluntary regulations establish a working-time norm for full-time workers, around which the usual hours of full-timers tend to cluster (Watson 1992a, 1992b). In the UK there was no evident modal number of hours worked by full-timers and the long hours of work provide a significant source of flexibility to employers.

Short-hours working also reflects social norms and regulations; in some countries with high levels of part-time working there is a tendency for these jobs to be organised on a short-hours basis of less than 20 or even less than 10 hours, while in others with medium to high levels of part-time working – for example, Denmark, Sweden and France – most part-timers work more than 20 hours. These longer hours for part-timers are brought about in part by women's preferences for longer part-time hours in these countries (Gregory 1991; O'Reilly 1994), but also by collective agreements which have tended to favour long part-time hours over short part-time work. In France the Loi Robien of 1995 explicitly encouraged part-time contracts of 16 to 32 hours by the use of social security rebates. Part-timers working short and very short hours are more likely to be marginalised and less likely to earn a subsistence wage, reinforcing dependence on another wage earner, usually a man (see Box 7.1). Indeed, in Austria and the Netherlands those working less than 12 hours are not included in national definitions of the economically active (National reports, Austria: Pastner 1996; Netherlands: Plantenga *et al.* 1996).

Unsocial hours working

Differences in women's and men's working-time patterns not only relate to weekly working hours and contractual variation but also to the scheduling and the cover of unsocial hours. Increased operating time and opening hours demand more unsocial hours working from employees (Bosch 1995) and in most European countries in the 1990s there were moves to increase the flexibility of working hours, both by providing more scope for variable scheduling of full-time work and by expanding the opportunities for atypical employment contracts (see Box 7.2).

The expectations that some industries such as distribution and catering will have a higher incidence of weekend working, whether done by those on long or short hours, is borne out by the Labour Force Survey data. However, the shares of employees working at weekends within sectors does vary across member states as societal influences on the norms for unsocial hours working are exerted (Rubery *et al.* 1995, 1998b). In 1994 the differences were particularly apparent between those countries where a deregulated labour market allowed high rates of weekend working, compared to those where weekend work was prohibited until the mid-1990s. For example, in 1994 more than 60 per cent of employees in the UK usually or sometimes worked on Saturdays, compared to less than 25 per cent in Portugal and less than a third in Belgium and Germany. The UK and Denmark, along with Sweden and Finland (for all persons in employment), were the only countries where more than a third of employees worked on Sundays compared to less than a quarter in all other countries except Ireland.

Gender differences in unsocial hours working reflect the segregation of the labour market. Usual Saturday work was more common for women than men in 11 out of 15 countries and at the E15 level, ranging from 13.4 per cent of women in Belgium to more than a quarter in Denmark (26.7 per cent). In Italy nearly two-fifths of female employees work on Saturdays, largely owing to Saturday opening in the public sector services. Only in Portugal were men more likely than women usually to work on a Saturday, 20.9 per cent compared to 17.8 per cent. Men were more likely to work sometimes on a Saturday in all countries, reflecting opportunities for overtime, often at a premium, whereas usual Saturday work is more likely to be part of a contract and more often subject to normal rates of pay (Figure 7.2).

In 1994 Sunday work was more limited and the gender patterns less clear. Women were more likely never to work on Sundays overall. However, in Denmark, the former East Germany, the Netherlands and Sweden usual Sunday work was more common for women than men. In all other countries the shares were more equal or more men usually worked on Sundays. As with Saturdays, the share who sometimes worked on a Sunday was always greater for men (Figure 7.2). The deregulated nature of the UK labour market was clearly illustrated by the large incidence of Sunday working, with nearly half

266 Indicators of women's employment

Box 7.2 Differences and similarities in working-time preferences by gender

In **Finland** involuntary part-time work increased rapidly for both sexes between 1989 and 1993. The willingness to switch from full-time to part-time work also increased, and at a more rapid rate for men than women (National reports, Finland: Ilmakunnas 1995:19).

In **France**, 30 per cent of female full-timers in 1991–1992 were willing to work part-time with a proportionate pay cut, compared to only 18 per cent of men, but there was an upward trend for both sexes in the context of high unemployment over the 1990s. Having a child under the age of 6 increased women's preference for part-time work. An important finding was that 36 per cent of both men and women were willing to accept a 10 per cent cut in pay if they could reduce hours by 20 per cent (National reports, France: Silvera *et al.* 1996:39–40).

A large proportion of the **Swedish** labour force was dissatisfied with their working-time, particularly women and young men who wanted to increase their hours of work. Even over the peak childraising years (24–44) one-quarter of women wanted longer hours of work, compared to only 5–10 per cent of men (National reports, Sweden: Gonäs and Spånt, 1996:29 and Table 11).

In **Sweden** analysis of longitudinal studies showed how women have increasingly used short part-time work at the start of their working life but the tendency to enter part-time in mid-life has reduced, characterised by a reduced m-shape of full-time work which is in fact shifting towards a right-hand peak (National reports, Sweden: Gonäs and Spånt 1996:37–38).

In **Portugal** female employees were willing to increase their hours of work by an average of nine hours, compared to five hours for men (National reports, Portugal: Lopes and Perista 1996:37).

---

of male employees (47.8 per cent) and just less than a third of women (32.3 per cent) usually or sometimes working on a Sunday.

National data for Austria show that similar shares of men and women do 'weekend duty' with 13.1 per cent of men and 12.6 per cent of women involved, but at the end of the 1970s 50 per cent more men than women were working at weekends. For employees, 6 per cent of men and 15 per cent of women had to work on Saturday mornings, probably reflecting the concentration of women's employment in the retail and tourism sectors (National reports, Austria: Pastner 1996:75–76).

The European Labour Force Survey first collected unsocial hours data in 1992 but even over the short time to 1994 there were significant changes in some countries. In the UK, a 1993 law allowing Sunday trading in the retail sector was passed, leading to an increase in the number of women and men working on Sundays (National reports, UK: Rubery 1996:129). The increase in the share of female employees working on Sundays was particularly strong in the UK, Ireland and France and the share who never

The fall in part-time employment in **Denmark** was particularly strong in the 25–54 age group, when women were returning to full-time rather than part-time work after having children and taking advantage of public childcare facilities. At the same time, some women were forced into unemployment by the lack of adequate childcare facilities (National reports, Denmark: Boje 1996:51), but the high share of working women with young children demonstrated that the childcare problem was not as severe as elsewhere.

A survey of working-time preferences in the **Netherlands** showed that women were less satisfied with the hours they worked than men and would like to work longer hours. A higher share of women wanted to work more hours if it involved a change of hours by their partner, whereas male preferences were stronger for working for fewer hours if their partner's hours changed (National reports, Netherlands: Plantenga *et al.* 1996:48).

Only 3 per cent of **Austrian** part-timers would like to work full-time, but this reflected the poor childcare provision in Austria (National reports, Austria: Pastner 1996:80).

A survey of working-time preferences in **Spain** showed that more women would like to work fewer hours than men but the largest share of men and women would like to work between 36 and 40 hours a week (National reports, Spain: Moltó 1996:69).

Women in the former East and West **Germany** had quite different working-time patterns, even after unification. More than two-fifths (44 per cent) of women in the West worked 36–39 hours a week and a further 25 per cent worked 20 hours or less in 1994, compared to 70 per cent of East German women who worked more than 40 hours a week and only 4.7 per cent worked less than 20 hours (National reports, Germany: Maier *et al.* 1996:26).

work on Sundays fell by at least two percentage points. For men, there were similar increases in Sunday work in the UK, Luxembourg and France. The pattern of Saturday work remained more stable in most countries, but, again, in the UK and Luxembourg there was an increase in the proportion of both male and female employees who were involved in Saturday work.

Countries also differ in the use of part-time work in preference to occasional or regular work by full-timers to cover weekends (Figures 7.3 and 7.4). In Denmark, Belgium, Greece and Ireland a higher proportion of female part-timers regularly or occasionally worked on Saturdays than the share of full-timers, whereas the opposite was true in Spain, Luxembourg, Portugal, the former West Germany and the UK; elsewhere the difference was small. In the former East Germany a slightly higher share of female part-timers than full-timers regularly or occasionally worked on Saturdays (34.9 per cent compared to 33.7 per cent), in contrast to the West. In six countries – Belgium, Denmark, France, Ireland, the Netherlands and the UK – female part-timers were more likely than full-timers to work regularly on Saturdays,

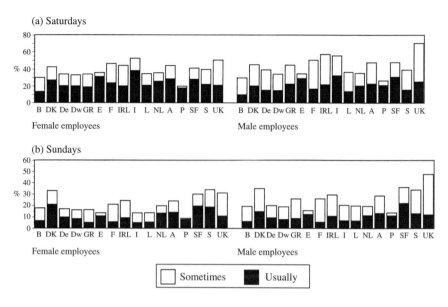

Figure 7.2 Share of female and male employees working Saturdays and Sundays by gender, 1994

Source: European Labour Force Survey (1994, 1995).

Note
Data for Austria, Finland and Sweden are for all in employment and for 1995.

suggesting that they were employed as regular cover for unsocial hours. In two of the six remaining countries, Germany and Greece, female part-timers were more likely sometimes to work on Saturdays, in these cases providing flexible cover for some weekend work. In Denmark and Belgium, again, a higher share of female part-timers than full-timers usually or occasionally worked on Sundays but in Germany, the UK, France, Spain, Luxembourg and the Netherlands proportionately more full-timers were involved in Sunday work. In Belgium, Denmark, Greece and the UK, female part-timers more often regularly worked Sundays but full-timers in nearly all countries tended to work on Sundays on an occasional basis more often than part-timers.

The pattern of weekend working of male part-timers reveals how they provide a particular sort of flexibility to employers. Only in the former East Germany were male part-timers less likely than male full-timers to work on Saturdays on a regular basis. Occasional Saturday work was more common for male full-timers than male part-timers in all countries apart from Greece and the former West Germany, illustrating the different type of flexibility provided by overtime and additional hours to meet irregular demand. The pattern of Sunday work emphasises this pattern even more, as male part-timers were more likely than full-timers to work regularly on Sundays in all countries except Greece and Luxembourg, with Italy and the

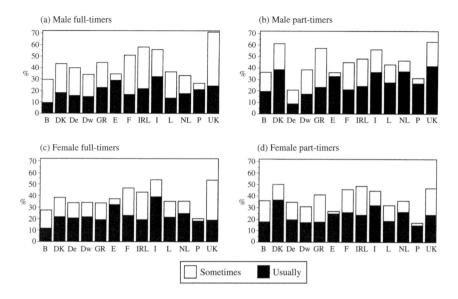

Figure 7.3 Share of full- and part-time employees working Saturdays by gender, 1994

Source: European Labour Force Survey (1994).

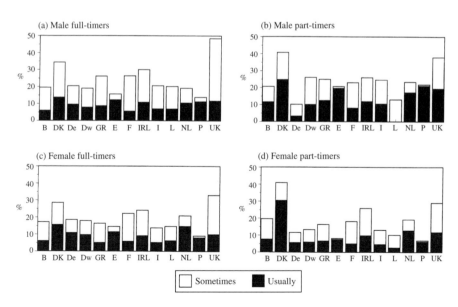

Figure 7.4 Share of full- and part-time employees working Sundays by gender, 1994

Source: European Labour Force Survey (1994).

former West Germany the only places where male full-timers were less likely to sometimes work on a Sunday.

Given that the majority of part-timers are women, the extent to which part-time work is used to cover unsocial hours working may produce a major change in the sex composition of employees working unsocial hours. However, trends in unsocial hours working by full-timers as well as part-timers depends not only on the deregulation of the labour market but also on social norms, in relation both to the acceptability of weekend working and of women working instead of participating in or orchestrating family activities. In the UK, family networks have been more fragmented than in most countries and here we see the greatest spread of unsocial hours working to all groups of the labour market. In other countries there has been a greater resistance to change and the spread of unsocial hours working (National reports, Italy: Bettio *et al.* 1996); to this extent it may remain concentrated on those who seek such work, for example, students. Indeed, in the Netherlands, Austria and Germany Sunday work was still prohibited in the early 1990s unless it was agreed to by the social partners or was necessary for the running of the business (National reports, Austria: Pastner 1996:72–73; Germany: Maier *et al.* 1996:39; Netherlands: Plantenga *et al.* 1996:45–46).

Working hours and the life cycle

Men and women not only differ in the flexibility that they offer in terms of usual hours or the scheduling of hours but also in the type of flexibility they offer over the life cycle. We have already seen in Chapter 3 how in some countries women use part-time employment as a way to reconcile the demands of work and family life, either because of poor childcare provision in countries like as the UK and Germany or because there is a legal right to reduce hours during the early years of a child's life, for example in Sweden. Here we concentrate on the use of part-time employment throughout the age groups and how it contributes to the overall level of employment within each age group.

Figure 7.5 clearly shows how the incidence of part-time work differs between women and men, old and young and between countries. In Denmark, the Netherlands, Sweden and the UK young women and men under 20 worked part-time in almost equal proportions in 1994, and in the case of Denmark and the Netherlands part-time work contributed more to the teenage employment rate than full-time work. These part-time jobs not only provide young people with some independence, often while participating in education, they also provide employers with a flexible labour supply, often keen to work unsocial hours (Marshall 1989).The proportion of young people working part-time was very small in most countries but so were the proportions of young people actually working, suggesting that opportunities for part-time work may encourage the labour supply of young in a period of rising participation in education.

In the older age groups for women a part-time wedge opened up in some countries but not in others. At the same time, part-time employment for men almost disappeared among those aged over 30, apart from in Sweden and the Netherlands. In 1994 the Southern European countries and Finland had a minimal level of part-time employment among both women and men in any of the older age groups. In Finland there was a very small contribution to age-specific employment rates from female part-time work, reflecting a tradition of full-time participation, and the share of male part-timers was roughly equal. Although women in Finland appeared not to use part-time employment to reconcile work and family life, annual average hours data by age group reveals a clear m-shape with a reduction in hours occurring over the core child-rearing years, a decrease in economic activity which is not visible in either employment or activity rates. Women in Finland tended to reduce annual rather than weekly hours (National reports, Finland: Keinänen 1996:67–68). The part-time rate for mothers increased slightly in Finland in the early 1990s and although the rate for single women and lone mothers fell, part-time rates remained highest for single women (14.6 per cent compared to 10 per cent for married or cohabiting mothers) (National reports, Finland: Keinänen 1996:64–65). In Italy, probably only 3 per cent of the entire female working population, or a third of all part-timers, chose part-time employment as a means of coping with motherhood, with the majority of mothers staying in full-time work or quitting the labour market altogether (National reports, Italy: Bettio and Villa 1996:39).

In the Netherlands and Denmark part-time employment formed more of a band than a wedge, widening with age for the Netherlands but narrowing in Denmark. The growing tendency for women in Denmark to remain in full-time employment (National reports, Denmark: Boje 1996) has pushed the Danish pattern away from this model to almost a reverse wedge. Sweden and the UK had the largest part-time wedges for women, and part-time employment was clearly important for the employment of core-age women and also for the overall level of employment in those age groups. The part-time wedge of female employment was also significant in France and the former West Germany and to a lesser extent in Ireland and Luxembourg. In spite of the sharp increase in part-time employment for women in Ireland over recent years, its impact on overall employment within older age groups is still relatively minor.

The sharp reduction in employment in the older age groups was apparent in most countries for both men and women, but there was an increased relative importance of part-time employment, particularly for men, as full-time rates are much lower and labour market opportunities in general are reduced (Paoli 1994). In the countries with higher rates of part-time work such as Sweden, the Netherlands and the UK, part-time work had taken on an increased importance for employment among older workers, particularly for men. In Portugal, Finland and France, where the rates of part-time work were much lower, there was also a role for male part-time employment for

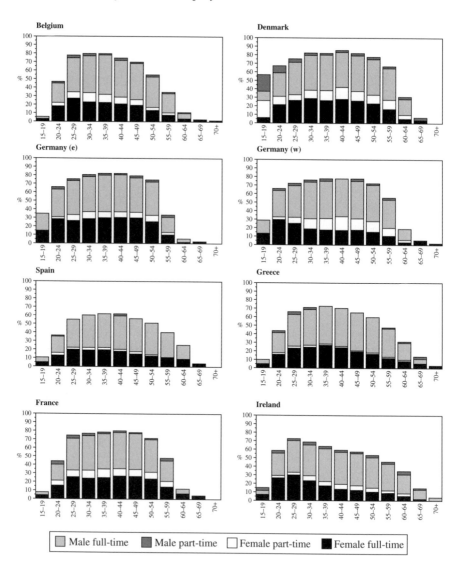

Figure 7.5 Employment rates by age and full- and part-time status for men and women in the EU, 1994.

Sources: European Labour Force Survey (1994); national data for Sweden and Finland, 1995.

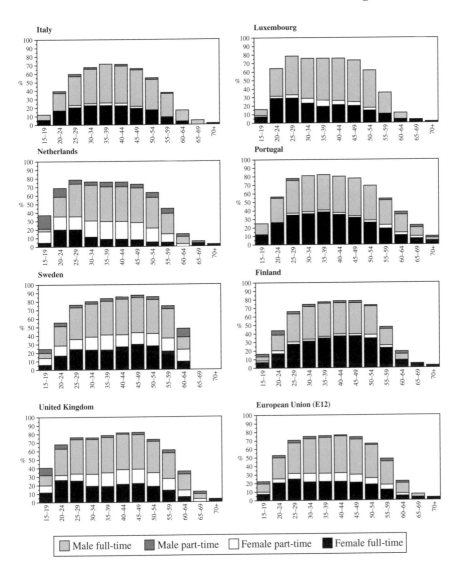

Figure 7.5 (continued)

the over 55s, evidence of part-time retirement policies aimed at increasing employment opportunities in some countries (Casey 1996).

Part-time work is particularly associated with female employment when it forms a significant part of core-age women's economic activity. This applied in many but by no means all countries. There were additional sources of part-time employment that were significant in many countries and affected men to a greater extent, in some cases, equally with women, namely part-time work among the young and the old. Here we found part-time employment that combined with study for the young and retirement for the old. These additional sources of part-time labour supply are increasing and could also be regarded as comprising disadvantaged workers; the old and the young with fewer options may be increasingly forced to take part-time jobs at the bottom of the labour market (Smith 1998).

Women's working-time patterns and preferences

Various government and employer initiatives were initiated in the late 1980s and 1990s to encourage the expansion of part-time work and working-time flexibility more generally, partly in response to rising unemployment (Rubery *et al.* 1995; Bosch *et al.* 1994; Bettio *et al.* 1998a). Part-time work is primarily carried out by women and even in the labour market for young people it often remains a feminised employment form (Rubery *et al.* 1995). Where women have increased their involvement in part-time work this is frequently assumed to reflect a choice in order to give them time to raise their children, yet closer analysis reveals that this presumption cannot be made (see Box 7.3).

Box 7.3 Not all female part-timers have care responsibilities

In **France** in 1990 46 per cent of female part-time workers did not have children, suggesting that this form of work was not voluntarily chosen for reasons of motherhood (National reports, France: Silvera *et al.* 1996:86).

In **Spain** in the mid-1990s less than 10 per cent of female part-time employees stated that they worked part-time owing to family responsibilities; more than 40 per cent of both female and male part-timers attributed their hours to the requirements of the job (National reports, Spain: Moltó 1996:29).

In 1994 only 40 per cent of women in **Ireland** worked part-time because of family responsibilities (National reports, Ireland: Barry 1996:57).

In **Finland** in 1993 the part-time rate was higher for single women than for either married or cohabiting women with or without children. Single mothers had the lowest part-time rates of just 5.5 per cent compared to 14.6 per cent for single non-mothers and 13.6 per cent for married or cohabiting mothers (National reports, Finland: Keinänen 1996:53).

The Labour Force Survey only gives information on the extent to which part-time work is voluntary or involuntary and does not provide information on the working-time preferences of those in full-time work. Between 28 and 44 per cent of all people in part-time jobs could be classified as involuntary part-timers, in 7 of the 15 member states (see Table 7.5). A higher proportion of men than women working part-time did so because they could not find full-time work, but since the majority of part-timers were women they accounted for the majority of involuntary part-time workers (see Table 7.5). It is important, therefore, to measure gender differences in working-time preferences empirically, for gender differences as well as similarities may be discovered (see Box 7.2).

Working-time preferences have to be contextualised, for employment decisions and aspirations are socially embedded and influenced by the economic context, social institutions and dominant values (Granovetter 1985; Fagan 1998). Obviously mothers will find it easier to exert a choice to remain in full-time employment while raising children where family policies, labour market conditions and dominant social attitudes support this pattern of behaviour; and preferences will be influenced by what is seen to be feasible or achievable. For example, women in the former East Germany maintained

Table 7.5 Reasons for working part-time

	Share of part-timers who could not find a full-time job			*Share of involuntary part-timers who are women*	*Female share of all part-timers*
	Total	*Women*	*Men*		
Belgium	28	27	40	83	88.1
Denmark	18	19	17	76	74.4
Germany (u)	9	9	12	84	88.1
Greece	41	32	53	46	62.5
Spain	19	19	18	75	74.9
France	39	37	49	86	82.8
Ireland	33	23	57	53	71.5
Italy	37	34	44	65	71.1
Luxembourg	(11)	(9)	..	(100)	89.6
Netherlands	6	5	10	56	73.8
Austria	7	7	10	78	83.7
Portugal	19	21	16	74	67.1
Finland	44	38	47	69	64.8
Sweden	27	27	29	80	78.9
UK	14	11	27	68	83.6
E12	18	16	26	73	81.8

Source: European Labour Force Survey (1994, 1995).

Notes
.. indicates no reliable data available.
Data for Sweden, Finland and Austria are for 1995.

a high labour market attachment despite speculation that their propensity to quit or work part-time would increase following unification. Only 13 per cent of married women with two children in the former East Germany stated that they would give up waged work if they could afford to. However, it is unclear whether this pattern of combining motherhood with employment is likely to continue, not only because of high unemployment but also because of changes in the institutional environment, with reduced support for childcare services legitimated by the rapid fall in fertility rates (National reports, Germany: Maier *et al.* 1996:25–28). Working-time preferences are more likely to be influenced by the availability of institutional support than by differences in the domestic division of labour, as in all societies women still seem to take on a higher share of domestic work (see Box 7.4 and pp. 160–4).

Finally, research has also demonstrated that it is important to distinguish whether people would prefer to work more or fewer hours, rather than

---

Box 7.4 Women are still burdened by most of the unpaid domestic work in the household

A study of time use in **Austria** showed that women with a child under 15 working full-time had a ten-and-a-half-hour day, including their unpaid work in the household, and women working part-time had only a marginally shorter day at nine and three-quarter hours. For men, their day was around nine hours irrespective of whether they worked full-time, part-time or were unemployed. On average mothers of children under 15 in Austria had one hour less leisure time then men in the same households (National reports, Austria: Pastner 1996:65–6)

Time-use studies of households in **Sweden** showed that men spent more time in the labour market than women, 41 compared to 27 hours per week, but women spent more time on unpaid housework, 33 compared to 27 hours per week (National reports, Sweden: Gonäs and Spånt 1996:43–44).

A time-use study in **Luxembourg** showed that women with a child and a husband had to spend significantly more time doing domestic activities with little help from their partner. Active women spent six hours a day on domestic tasks in addition to their labour market time. There was some evidence that men in younger couples were sharing more of the domestic tasks (National reports, Luxembourg: Plasman 1996:54–55).

In **Finland** women and men had a working day of similar length although the time spent on paid and unpaid work was quite different. Men spent an average of 243 minutes on paid work each day compared to 155 minutes for women, but 236 minutes of a women's day were spent on household work compared to 140 minutes for men (National reports, Finland: Ilmakunnas 1996:53).

In **Ireland** women accounted for the majority of those doing domestic duties, 'men simply do "not engage in home duties"' (National reports, Ireland: Barry 1996:70).

simply asking whether they want full-time or part-time work. While the majority of part-time work can be considered voluntary in, for example, the UK, Germany and the Netherlands, short part-time hours have been found to be unpopular and significant proportions of female part-timers could be considered underemployed (Fagan 1996; National reports, Netherlands: Plantenga *et al.* 1996; Germany: Maier *et al.* 1994:35–37). In France 37 per cent of part-timers stated that they wanted longer hours in 1994, an increase from 29 per cent in 1991 (National reports, France: Silvera *et al.* 1996:38). Preferred hours for full-timers also vary, and there is also a strong life-cycle component to working-time preferences (Rubery *et al.* 1995). Furthermore, it is not only the length of working-time which is important: survey evidence suggests that parents would like a more family-friendly scheduling of working hours, for example later starts for night shifts to increase the proportion of the evening spent with the family and the increased use of flexitime (Bettio *et al.* 1998a).

Temporary work and the life cycle

The expansion of temporary employment

Many countries experienced a growth in temporary contracts in the 1980s as legislation restricting their use was relaxed and employers, unsure about the economic climate, were less willing to take on permanent staff. Over the 1990s the pattern of growth was more mixed across countries (de Grip *et al.* 1997). Temporary work was less common than part-time work in most countries and the gender differences tended to be less strong, but women were still more likely to be on temporary contracts than men (see Table 7.6). Spain was the country in which temporary employment was most common, owing to a rapid expansion in the mid-1980s (Toharia 1997): just less than a third of all male employees and nearly two-fifths of women in Spain were on temporary contracts in 1994 compared to an E14 average of 11.8 per cent and 13 per cent. In ten countries, including the former East Germany, more than 10 per cent of female employees were temporary, compared to six countries for men (see Table 7.6). The share of women on temporary contracts exceeded that of men by at least 2 percentage points in all countries except Greece and the former West Germany in 1994.

Over the period from 1989 to 1994 the gender gap in temporary employment shares closed somewhat. At the E14 level the number of female temporary employees expanded by 17.3 per cent but rose by a fifth for men. Moreover, this expansion for men significantly increased the proportion of male employees on temporary contracts, as the number of male permanent employees fell by 4.8 per cent in contrast to a modest rise for women, of 4.5 per cent. In five countries male temporary employment expanded by more than a fifth, including Sweden where there was a rise of nearly 75 per cent. Female temporary employment expanded in 10 of the 14 coun-

Table 7.6 The share of female and male employees who are in temporary jobs, 1989 and 1994

	Male		Female	
	1989	*1994*	*1989*	*1994*
Belgium	3.1	3.5	8.4	7.5
Denmark	9.8	11.1	10.2	12.9
Germany (e)[a]	11.8	14.9	12.4	16.9
Germany (w)	10.2	8.7	12.3	9.5
Spain	24.5	31.4	31.2	37.9
France	7.8	9.7	9.4	12.4
Greece	18.0	10.2	15.6	10.5
Ireland	6.5	8.0	11.9	11.4
Italy	4.9	6.1	8.7	9.3
Luxembourg	2.6	2.0	5.0	4.4
Netherlands	6.8	7.9	11.5	15.0
Austria[b]	—	5.0	—	7.5
Portugal	16.9	8.5	21.2	10.5
Finland	8.7	12.3	15.5	14.7
Sweden	7.8	13.6	12.3	15.9
UK	3.7	5.5	7.4	7.5
E12[c]	9.1	9.8	11.4	11.8
E14[c]	8.8	10.8	11.7	13.0

Source: European Labour Force Survey (1989, 1994, 1995); National reports, Finland: Keinänen (1996); Sweden: Gonäs and Spånt (1996).

Notes
— indicates no data available.
a Data are for 1991, not 1989, for the former East Germany.
b Data for Austria are for 1995 not 1994.
c Excluding East Germany.

tries, in 2 countries by more than a fifth and in a further 4 by more than a third. Temporary employment fell for both men and women in Greece, the former West Germany, Portugal, Luxembourg (men only) and Finland (women only). In the former West Germany the overall falls reflected a decline in temporary full-timers and a rise in temporary part-timers, while the opposite was true for men in Luxembourg. In Portugal and Greece there were net falls in temporary employment for both men and women, particularly in Portugal where a change in the regulation of temporary employment (González and Castro 1995) saw the share of temporary employment for women fall from nearly a fifth in 1989 to less than a tenth in 1994. Although temporary employment rose in Sweden, there was an initial decline in temporary employment at the beginning of the 1990s as contracts were not renewed, particularly in the female-dominated public sector (National reports, Sweden: Gonäs and Spånt 1996:33). The decline in temporary employment for women in Finland could also have been the result of a failure to renew contracts.

Employees who are both part-time and temporary face the double dis-advantage of a limited contract and limited hours of work. In 1991 women were twice as likely as men to be in this precarious position in 11 of the 12 member states (Rubery *et al.* 1995). Further examination of the expansion of temporary employment shows that in some countries it was the part-time temporary jobs that grew fastest for both men and women. At the E12 level (data not available for Austria, Finland and Sweden) the number of female employees who were both part-time and temporary grew by more than a fifth (20.6 per cent) compared to just under a fifth for permanent part-timers (19.6 per cent), just 5.8 per cent for temporary full-timers and 2 per cent for permanent full-timers (see Table 7.7). For men the picture was more striking, with part-time temporary employees increasing by 27.7 per cent, and part-time permanent employees by 27 per cent, compared to just 1.9 per cent for full-time temporary employees and a fall of nearly 5 per cent for full-time permanent employees. The growth of this most precarious form of employment varied among member states, with net falls in six countries for both men and women but a near doubling of the number of part-time temporary male and female employees in France and a similar rise for women in the Netherlands. In the former East Germany the number of part-time temporary male employees rose by almost 600 per cent,[3] considerably outstripping the rise for women of 57 per cent. However, this was in fact the only area of employment growth for women after 1991.

The distribution of temporary employment by age group also shows a life-cycle effect on the type of flexibility that men and women offer. Temporary employment tends to be concentrated on the young in most countries, as new entrants to the labour market are often employed on temporary contracts or take temporary work owing to a shortage of permanent jobs

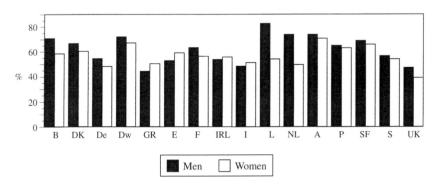

Figure 7.6 Concentration of temporary employees among those aged under 30, 1994

Sources: European Labour Force Survey (1994, 1995); national data for Sweden and Finland, 1995.

Note
Data for Austria refer to 1995

Table 7.7 Percentage change in temporary and permanent employees by gender and working-time, 1989–1994

| | Male | | | | | | Female | | | | | | All employees |
| | Permanent | | | Temporary | | | Permanent | | | Temporary | | | |
	Full-time	Part-time	Total	Full-time	Part-time	Total	Full-time	Part-time	Total	Full-time	Part-time	Total	Total
Belgium	-0.9	89.1	0.2	14.6	-2.7	10.9	10.9	35.8	17.5	10.3	-4.9	3.8	6.5
Denmark	-3.6	3.2	-3.0	8.6	22.9	11.1	2.1	-17.3	-6.1	25.9	13.8	22.6	-2.3
Germany (e)	-16.1	17.4	-15.7	0.3	594.7	10.3	-26.6	-15.0	-24.6	-0.3	56.5	8.9	-16.4
Germany (w)	1.8	82.8	2.9	-16.7	43.0	-13.7	8.2	39.1	18.0	-18.7	17.8	-11.8	6.4
Spain	-16.4	24.1	-16.2	15.1	149.3	18.2	-2.3	27.9	-0.1	26.6	67.8	34.3	-2.1
France	-5.0	-0.2	-4.8	10.0	95.5	21.7	-1.2	17.5	3.0	15.1	91.6	40.2	1.3
Greece	12.4	174.8	13.1	-45.6	-5.7	-41.6	21.6	-3.5	20.6	-27.6	-9.0	-23.4	6.8
Ireland	2.6	77.6	3.6	8.1	71.0	28.8	18.2	100.3	26.8	-2.1	42.4	20.8	13.3
Italy	-7.1	32.1	-6.8	42.2	-29.7	17.2	-3.1	54.9	0.4	40.4	-23.5	7.5	-3.2
Luxembourg	4.7	137.5	5.1	50.0	-65.5	-19.1	7.9	53.6	14.1	42.7	-19.3	0.4	7.6
Netherlands	3.0	-6.8	1.8	-15.9	79.7	21.3	4.3	30.5	19.3	-6.2	96.1	62.3	10.9
Portugal	0.1	148.2	0.9	-54.6	-35.6	-54.1	24.5	37.3	25.3	-42.0	-65.6	-45.1	-0.7
Finland[a,b]	—	—	-26.4	—	—	9.0	—	—	-16.1	—	—	-21.0	-20.3
Sweden[b]	—	—	-6.1	—	—	74.1	—	—	-0.3	—	—	34.1	1.9
UK	-10.6	54.0	-8.6	70.4	-6.6	37.0	-3.2	3.8	-0.3	53.7	-16.0	2.2	-3.8
E12 (w)[c]	-4.7	26.9	-3.9	1.9	27.7	5.3	2.0	19.6	6.9	5.8	20.6	11.1	1.1
E14 (w)[c]	—	—	-4.8	—	—	20.1	—	—	4.5	—	—	17.3	1.0

Sources: European Labour Force Survey (1989–1994); national data for Finland and Sweden.

Notes

— indicates no data available.

Net change in employment 1989–94 as a percentage of the 1989 level.

a Data for Finland are for 1989–1993.

b Data on temporary and permanent employees by full- and part-time are not available for Sweden and Finland.

c Data for E12 and E14 exclude the New German *Länder*.

Box 7.5 Many of the new jobs were flexible during and after the recession of the early 1990s, particularly for the young

In **Italy** over 70 per cent of manual workers and 27 per cent of clerical workers recruited in the metal industry in 1994 were temporary on Youth Training Contracts (YTCs), apprenticeships or temporary contracts. For women, the proportions were even higher at 79.8 per cent and 40.5 per cent respectively. Youth Training Contracts were one of the most successful policy provisions in Italy, bringing 2.5 million young people into employment between 1985 and 1994, but both women and young people in the south were less successful in gaining these jobs (National reports, Italy: Bettio and Villa 1996:33).

Data for 1994 from the national employment agency in **Spain**, 'INEM', showed that 80 per cent of contracts had a maximum duration of just six months: 80 per cent of these were part-time contracts, 89 per cent apprenticeship contracts and 74 per cent training contracts with a six-month maximum duration (National reports, Spain: Moltó 1996:71–72).

In **Finland** the share of new hires that were on fixed-term contracts rose from 28 per cent of men and 48 per cent of women in 1989 to 57 per cent of men and 64 per cent of women in 1993. Although women's relative disadvantage was reduced in the share of new hires that were temporary, the low number of new hires in 1993 means that the figures should be regarded with caution (National reports, Finland: Ilmakunnas 1995:33).

(see Box 7.5). More than half of all female temporary employees were aged under 30 in 1994 in 13 countries, with just less than a half in the Netherlands and the former East Germany, the exception being the UK where just less than two-fifths of temporary female employees were below 30. For men, the pattern was similar, with Greece, Italy and the UK the only countries where less than 50 per cent of male temporary employees were under 30 (see Figure 7.6). The concentration of female temporary employees among those under 30 was lower than that for men in most countries, reflecting the higher rates of temporary contracts among women and a more even distribution of temporary work across age groups. Women may be less able to move on to permanent contracts than men, perhaps because they are segregated into more insecure segments of the labour market. In addition, periods out of the labour market mean that older women may have to return to work on a temporary contract. Of the four countries – Ireland, Greece, Spain and Italy – in which the concentration of female temporary employees in the age groups below 30 was greater than for men, only in two, Greece and Spain, was the difference more than 3 percentage points. These two countries have particularly low rates of female employment, so the greater concentration in the young age group reflected women's greater propensity to quit the labour market at an early age.

Summary

In the early 1990s there was an expansion of flexible forms of employment as European labour markets were increasingly deregulated, albeit from very different starting points. These trends were not gender neutral. Although women and men both experienced increases in part-time and temporary employment, the male experience of flexible employment has tended to be concentrated at the beginning and end of men's working lives. Women instead face involvement in flexible employment conditions and the disadvantage that this implies throughout their working lives. This experience forms part of the penalty for taking responsibility for caring or trying to mesh work and family life.

Further moves towards deregulation could intensify gender differences in the future. Restructuring of the European labour market towards more flexible and variable working-time systems may build upon gender differences; the moves to longer service sector opening hours will result in greater use of women and part-timers to cover unsocial hours, often without additional premia. Labour market regulation tends to reduce gender differences in working hours, at least for full-timers, with the widest gender gaps appearing in the most deregulated labour markets. Dismantling labour market institutions provides renewed scope for employers to differentiate working-time conditions by gender and to impose demands for long-hours of work on full-timers, increasing the obstacles confronting women, and indeed men, who wish to have both a career and a family life. The recent move to revitalise movements towards shorter working hours for full-time workers and the developing European framework of protection for atypical workers, such as the 1997 part-time workers' directive, perhaps provide the only signs of new development to ameliorate some of the disadvantages that confront women as a consequence of the time dimension to the organisation of the labour market.

Part III

Reflections on trends and future prospects

Introduction

Trends in the 1990s have reaffirmed the increasing importance of women to European labour markets. Chapter 8 explores the likely trends in both supply and demand for female labour into the millennium. The long-term prospects for women's employment will depend to a large part on how successful European states are in achieving their long-term goal of raising the employment rate, counteracting recent trends towards declining employment rates. If employment rates are to rise, women's labour will provide the key source of additional labour supply. More complicated scenarios, however, emerge if the longer-term trend is towards lower or static employment opportunities. There seems every prospect that women will continue to increase their supply of labour to the market, fuelled by their increasing investments in education, rising uncertainty over the stability of marriage as an alternative source of income support, and their increasing unwillingness to accept a subordinate role in the home and the labour market. However, this growing labour supply may face a decreasing demand for labour in some of the key areas of female employment such as clerical work and public services. While it has been male-dominated employment areas that have faced the brunt of recent recessions, it may be the turn of female-dominated sectors in the next phases of restructuring. Under these conditions, traditional patterns of segregation may be subject to further pressure, with heightened competition between men and women to obtain entry into the labour market as the traditional systems of excluding prime-age women from the labour market finally break down.

However, it is critically important for gender equality that any increased competition between men and women for jobs in a situation of general job shortage does not become a contest based on which group is willing to accept the worst terms and conditions. Already the experience of the 1990s suggests that integration of women into the labour market can be based as much on differentiation as on equality. The possibility of a reversal of progress towards greater gender equality in treatment within the labour market has already arisen in the 1990s, thereby reducing optimism that the only direction of change is upwards, even if at a very slow pace. Moreover, even if women will not necessarily be the only ones to suffer from heightened competition within increasingly deregulated labour markets, the prospect remains that greater gender equality may only be achieved through a general deterioration in employment conditions within the labour market, involving reductions in the pay and status attached to male jobs. The objective of equal opportunities must be to remove discrimination, not to generalise poor conditions within the labour market. Moreover, gender equality is not and cannot be premised upon a purely individualised labour market in which neither men nor women, nor indeed employers, take any responsibility for the care and upbringing of children.

It is in these respects that the campaign for gender equality can make common cause with the interests of men as workers and as parents. Progress towards gender equality requires reorganisation of both paid and unpaid work and a consideration of general policy towards labour markets and social and welfare policy, and not solely policies targeted explicitly at gender equality issues. The chances of developing such an integrated and broad approach have in principle been enhanced by the dual commitments of the EU, to mainstreaming gender into all policy and to the specification of equal opportunities as one of the four pillars of European employment policy. These developments, together with the general prospects for integration through equality rather than inequality are discussed in Chapter 9. Although the prognosis is not very optimistic, it must be remembered that European member states are still in a position to shape their own futures. It is not too late for them to take policy decisions and initiatives which could reverse those trends likely to lead to widening inequalities within European labour markets. The wide divergences in labour market policies and practices which still prevail within European member states is in itself evidence of the scope for variation and for policy choice. The emergence of a new European strategy for employment, while helpful in placing employment objectives firmly on the policy agenda, should not be a reason for member states to shy away from developing their own specific initiatives and policies to reshape the labour market and welfare system to meet the emerging new patterns of social and economic life, in which the male breadwinner household is increasingly becoming an anomaly.

8 Gender and future labour market trends

Gender and future labour supply trends

Gender is arguably the most important variable in any discussion of the future of European labour markets. Not only have women accounted for some 25 million out of the increase of 30 million in the European labour force between 1960 and 1990 (CEC 1994:44) but it is also women who are set to increase further their share of the European labour force. According to projections on future labour supply generated by the IFO Institute for Eurostat (IFO 1995, 1994), even under the most conservative projection for labour supply growth, based on low population growth and low participation rates, women should increase their share of the European labour force (excluding the three new member states) from 40 per cent to 42 per cent by the year 2005 (see Table 8.1). This corresponds to an expansion of the overall labour force by 1 per cent and a female labour force expansion of 6 per cent relative to 1990 Figures. Under these projections women are expected to maintain this share up to 2020, despite a projected overall fall in the labour force of 6 per cent compared to 1990 levels, with the female labour force shrinking by less than 1 per cent even under the conservative scenario. At the other extreme, the IFO Institute has made alternative projections based on high population growth and high participation rates under which women take on an even more significant role in future labour supply growth; overall labour supply growth is projected to be around 17 per cent up to 2005 and 31 per cent up to 2020 relative to 1990 levels, but female labour supply is expected to rise by just under 31 per cent by 2005 and by over 55 per cent by 2020.

Although there is no doubting the future significance of female labour supply to European employment growth, the actual projections produced should be considered with a certain degree of scepticism. For example, the usefulness of the high labour force projections based on both high population growth and high participation rates must be questioned. As we have already noted, one factor associated with changing lifestyles in some countries has been a decline in fertility rates, and it appears somewhat contradictory to base a projection on extreme rates of growth in both fertility and participation.

Table 8.1 Projected changes in female labour force in the European Union, 1990–2020

	Projected female share of labour force		Size of the labour force, males and females (index 1990 = 100)		Size of the labour force, females (index 1990 = 100)	
	Low	*High*	*Low*	*High*	*Low*	*High*
1990	40.1	40.1	100.0	100.0	100.0	100.0
1995	40.8	41.3	101.7	104.3	103.6	107.6
2000	41.5	43.1	101.9	110.1	105.5	118.3
2005	42.0	44.9	101.3	116.6	106.2	130.6
2010	42.3	46.3	99.7	123.1	105.3	142.4
2015	42.4	47.3	97.2	128.5	102.9	151.7
2020	42.3	47.6	93.8	131.0	99.1	155.6

Source: IFO (1995:tables A5 13–14).

The crudeness of the procedure used to project labour supply trends is in fact the consequence of the failure of more sophisticated modelling techniques. The attempts by the projection team to model labour supply behaviour demonstrated that there was no universal relationship between, for example, fertility and participation on the one hand or participation and part-time work on the other (IFO 1995:75). These findings fit with our own analysis of the importance of differences between member states in the structuring of labour supply, so that the relationships between motherhood and workforce commitment on the one hand or between working-time options and labour supply on the other are shaped by societally specific influences, including social norms and structural policies, and cannot be predicted on the basis of gender or family position. Thus while the decision not to adopt a model of labour supply behaviour for cross-national comparisons was appropriate, it might still have been useful to have developed alternative scenarios which quantified, for example, the consequences of a universal move to lower fertility coupled with higher participation rates.

Furthermore, while the projections clearly identify a disproportionate role for women in future labour supply growth, there is a strong case for arguing that the significance of female labour supply has been underestimated, particularly in the high-growth scenario. These projections are based on the rather unrealistic assumption that there will be a rapid growth in participation rates in all age ranges, an assumption which goes against the long-term trend for participation for both younger- and older-age cohorts. There can be few grounds for assuming that youth participation rates will rise significantly, as the fall has been primarily associated with rising participation in education and there is every evidence to suggest that these trends are primarily long-term, not solely cyclical adjustments to falls in demand in the youth labour market. Similarly, for older age workers the long-term trend has been downwards (albeit with very different participation rates prevailing between European countries). There is now a general consensus in Europe over the desirability of curtailing these trends and indeed if possible stimulating a rise in participation rates, but the likelihood of this being achieved must still be questioned. On this basis the role of increased participation of prime-age women in any future labour supply growth takes on even greater strategic importance.

For example, if we are to take seriously the stated objective of the European Commission (CEC 1994) of achieving a significant rise in the average European employment rate, for example from the level of around 60 per cent at the beginning of the 1990s to 70 per cent or above, it is clear that a high share of that increased employment would have to be based on higher participation rates for women.

Figure 8.1 shows the male and female share of the non-employed within the young, prime and older age groups. Women account for just over half of the non-employed among the 15–24 age group at the European level (Figure 8.1a). However, this distribution is relatively even in comparison to the core age group in which women account for 72 per cent (Figure 8.1b). Among the older age group the gender distribution is closer to that for the young, with women accounting for just less than three-fifths of the non-employed (Figure 8.1c). Thus women are likely to dominate any increase in participation, but this effect will be even more pronounced if most of the increase in labour supply comes from the core age group aged between 25 and 49. Women make up more than three-fifths of the total working-age non-employed in the EU and in each member state, except Finland and Sweden where the shares fall to just over half. Moreover, within each country and at the EU level, except Sweden, prime-age women make up the largest share of the non-employed, accounting for 30 per cent at the E15 level. In five countries prime-age women account for more than a third of the non-employed and it is only in Sweden, Finland and Portugal that the share is a quarter or less. In Sweden prime-age women make up over a fifth of the working-age non-employed, just less than for young men and slightly more than for young women. The prime-age male share of the working-age non-employed ranges from just 6 per cent in Luxembourg and Greece to 20 per cent in Finland. In 8 of the 15 countries the share of non-employment made up of men aged 25–54 years was between 10.9 and 12.6 per cent. Given the rather low probabilities of significantly raising participation rates outside these age ranges, the dominance of the potential female labour supply is evident.

Women also provide the largest potential extra supply of skilled labour. While there are marked differences between the educational level of women within the labour market and those outside, with the latter having lower educational qualifications on average, women still constitute the majority of the more educated non-employed (Figure 8.2). For example, among the core-age non-employed (aged 25–49), 46 per cent had medium to high

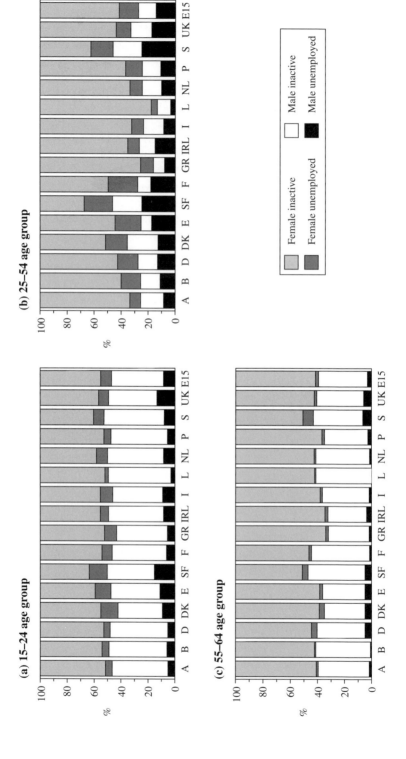

Figure 8.1 Distribution of the non-employed by gender and status, 1995

Source: European Labour Force Survey (1995).

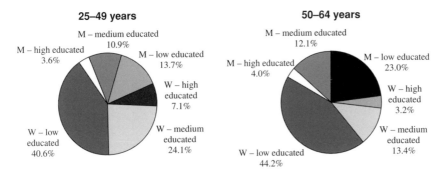

Figure 8.2 Distribution of the non-employed population by educational attainment and gender, E15

Source: European Labour Force Survey (1996).

Notes
M = men
W = women

education, but women accounted for 31 per cent and men for only 15 per cent. Among those aged 50–64 years old, women and men with high or medium education account for 16 per cent each of the total non-employed population, but these people are less likely to be attracted back into work than those of prime age.

Not all the non-employed prime-age population are equally able or likely to enter the labour market, even if job opportunities are plentiful. Male non-employed in this age range tend to include the permanently sick and disabled who are relatively unlikely to provide a major source of additional labour supply. Most of the available prime-age men will thus appear among the unemployed rather than the inactive prime-age population. For women, the situation clearly differs between countries: in societies with a predominant male breadwinner form of household organisation, mothers of young children may not be easily mobilised into the labour market in response to higher demand. In some countries women may also be already relatively permanently involved in informal activities, including homework and work in the family business, which they may be unlikely to give up in response to a short-term change in labour demand. However, the stability of these categories should not be exaggerated; there have been major declines in the share of prime-age women working as unpaid family workers and rapid increases in the participation rate of mothers, even those with very young children. Thus there will be country differences, but also changes over time across countries, in the extent to which these groups remain far outside the wage labour market. It is thus more reasonable, given the recent relatively rapid mobilisation of the prime-age female population, including mothers, into the wage economy, to regard mothers of at least school-age children as a major labour supply source which could be readily mobilised. Indeed, inactive mothers with at least one child under 15 totalled some 12 million in the EU in 1995 and there were in addition some 2.8 million unemployed mothers (Rubery and Smith 1997). If employment targets are to be hit, mothers will need to be mobilised.

To some extent this increased mobilisation of mothers and prime-age women in general into the labour market is assured, through the rising educational levels of younger cohorts of women, and through the evidence of changes in the behaviour and aspirations of younger generations (see Chapter 3 above). Across all countries higher employment rates, whether full- or part-time, for mothers with higher levels of education show how the future, more educated population of mothers will be a key factor pushing up employment rates and labour supply in the EU. Moreover, in some countries a significant rise in female employment rates can be anticipated simply as an effect of the ageing of current labour market cohorts, although in some cases the impact on the average employment rate will be affected by changes in the overall age structure of the population. To estimate these various effects we first of all identify the impact of the changing weight of the female population structure by the year 2010 by holding all female age-specific employment rates constant at 1995 levels. Comparing columns la and 1b of Table 8.2 shows that at the E15 level there is expected to be a slight fall in the overall female employment rate as a result of the changing age structure of the population. Within countries the changing population structure also generally has a negative effect on the employment rate. In Finland and the Netherlands there are falls of over 3 percentage points in the female employment rate, solely as a result of the changing population structure. Only in the four Southern European countries and Germany does the changing structure of the population have a positive effect on the overall female employment rate.

Column 2a of Table 8.2 shows the impact on the 2010 employment rate of the current 35–39 age group moving through the age groups, with the assumption that the employment rates attained by age 35–39 will be at least maintained as these women move through their forties. By age 35–39 most women who are going to have children will have had at least one child, so there is unlikely to be any future negative impact on employment related to motherhood. Where age-specific employment rates were already higher at age 35–39 than for women in their forties, employment rates were left unchanged. Some assumption also had to be made about employment rates among older women. However, whereas in 1995 at the E15 level there was an 8.4 percentage point drop in employment rates (from 61.1 per cent to 52.7 per cent) between women aged 44–49 and those aged 50–54, we would expect the decline in 2010 to be less marked, again as a consequence of the ageing of cohorts with a higher record of continuous employment during prime-age years which could be expected to be carried through into older

Table 8.2 Impact of population and cohort effects on female working-age employment rate, 1995–2010

	(1) Female working-age employment rate		(2) Impact of ageing of the 35–39 cohort on female employment rate in 2010		(3) Impact of ageing of the 30–34 cohort on female employment rate in 2010	
	(a) 1995	(b) 2010 population with 1995 age specific employment rates	(a) Changes to the 35–55 age group	(b) Changes to the 35–59 age group	(a) Changes to the 35–55 age group	(b) Changes to the 35–59 age group
Austria	59.2	57.3	59.3	61.6	59.8	62.3
Belgium	45.4	43.1	47.7	50.7	49.0	52.3
Germany	55.3	55.6	56.9	58.7	56.9	58.7
Denmark	67.0	65.1	66.6	68.3	66.6	68.3
Spain	31.2	33.0	35.3	36.7	36.1	37.6
Finland	58.1	54.8	55.1	56.7	55.1	56.7
France	52.0	51.0	51.9	53.5	51.9	53.5
Greece	38.0	39.8	42.9	44.8	43.1	45.0
Ireland	41.3	39.6	43.1	44.9	46.7	49.3
Italy	35.6	36.2	38.9	41.0	38.9	41.0
Luxembourg	42.2	39.9	42.1	44.1	43.0	45.1
Netherlands	53.2	49.5	51.1	53.0	52.5	54.6
Portugal	54.3	56.5	59.5	61.6	59.5	61.6
Sweden	72.4	69.6	69.8	70.5	69.8	70.5
UK	61.4	60.3	60.7	61.7	60.7	61.7
E15	49.6	49.4	50.6	52.2	50.6	52.2

Sources: European Labour Force Survey (1995) and Eurostat population projections (baseline scenario).

Note
See p. 292 for details of assumptions behind scenarios.

age ranges. Therefore the second assumption in this analysis is that by 2010 the fall in employment rates between age groups in the late forties and early fifties will be half the percentage point fall in 1995, at 4.2 percentage points (64.7 per cent to 60.5 per cent). For the estimate in column 2a the employment rate for those aged 55–59 in 2010 is predicted to be the same as that in 1995, while for column 2b the percentage point decline between the 50–54 and the 55–59 age group in 2010 is assumed to be half the percentage point fall in 1995.

The impact of these assumptions (Table 8.2, column 2a) is that the female employment rate in 2010 would be around a percentage point higher than in 1995 (column 1a) and 1.2 percentage points higher than that predicted in 2010 when only the population structure is assumed to change, assuming no change in the age-specific employment rates (column 1b). The assumption of a higher employment rate for women aged 55–59 (Table 8.2, column 2b) has a bigger impact, with the overall female employment rate at the E15 level rising from 49.6 per cent in 1995 to 52.2 per cent in 2010. This new assumption raises the age-specific employment rates and together with the rising weight of the older working-age population has a much more significant effect on the overall employment rate.

The assumptions in column 2a are sufficient to counteract the negative impact of the changing population structure in 11 countries. There are particularly strong rises in the overall female employment rate in Belgium and the Southern European countries, where there is a clear cohort difference in the level of women's integration into the labour market. In other countries where there is a weaker cohort effect, for example Sweden, Finland and the Netherlands, the predicted change in the employment rates does not offset the effect of the changing population structure. The additional assumption in column 2b has the effect of increasing the employment rate relative to the 1995 level by as much as 5 percentage points in the Southern countries and Belgium and by around 2 percentage points or more in Luxembourg, Germany, Austria and Ireland. However, in Sweden, Finland and the Netherlands the large negative impact of the population structure is still not offset by these assumptions and the employment rate still falls, albeit by less than was previously predicted. In the UK the employment rate remains virtually unchanged under these assumptions.

In some countries in 1995 there was still a large decline of female age-specific employment rates between the 30–34 age group and 35–39 age group. In these countries – Ireland, the Netherlands and Luxembourg – the above assumptions necessarily have a more limited impact, as the difference between the employment rate for those aged 35–39 and those in their forties is less than that between the early and late thirties. Columns 3a and 3b of Table 8.2 thus repeat the analyses with the same assumptions but instead carry through the 30–34 age-specific employment rates rather than those for the 35–39 age group. At the E15 level and within eight countries this change in assumption has no effect on the overall female employment rate in 2010 compared to the assumptions based on the 35–39 group, because the 30–34 and 35–39 employment rates are either the same or similar. In the remaining seven countries there is an effect, particularly in Ireland where the employment rate rises by 8 percentage points with the adjustments to the 55–59 age-specific employment rates as well. In the Netherlands these assumptions are sufficient to more than offset the large negative change predicted as a consequence of the changing population structure. There is also a positive change in the employment rate in Luxembourg, Spain, Belgium and Austria.

These estimates do not include any further adjustment, either for changes in aspirations and behaviour of cohorts younger than 30–34, or for the impact of raising educational levels among these younger cohorts. These latter effects are likely to be very significant. For the population as a whole, that is not broken down by gender, we estimate that the impact of projecting through the 1995 highest educational qualifications of the 30–34 age group, and the 1995 shares of low and very low education among the 20–24 age group, will have the effect of decreasing the share of the EU working-age population with very low education by nearly 40 per cent by the year 2010 (Table 8.3 and Rubery and Smith 1997). All other educational groups rise proportionately as a consequence, but the share for those with low education rises by only 7 per cent compared to a 55 per cent increase in the medium educated and a 25 per cent increase in the more highly educated population. Again, these projections are based on rather simple and crude calculations, but illustrate the significant impact of the changing educational structure on the future European labour supply. This change in the educational profile appears likely to have a very significant impact on women's participation, not only because women's participation is more sensitive to educational level, but also because women dominated the very low and low educational groups in the past (see Chapter 3).

Table 8.3 The educational distribution of the population aged 25–64 as a result of cohort effects, 1995–2010

	Distribution by educational group		Percentage growth of educational group
	1995	*2010*	*1995–2010*
Very low	25.3%	14.7%	−38.7%
Low	42.3%	42.8%	+6.7%
Medium	14.5%	21.3%	+54.9%
High	17.7%	20.9%	+24.5%

Source: Calculations based on European Labour Force Survey data and Eurostat baseline population projections.

Note
Distribution may not sum to 100 per cent as the other general educational group has been excluded. See p. 295, above, for details of assumptions.

Table 8.4 The distribution of usual hours by mothers with at least one child under 15, by educational attainment, 1995

(a) Low level of education

	Short part-time hours (0–19 hrs)	Long part-time hours (20–35 hrs)	Short full-time hours (36–39 hrs)	Long full-time hours (40–42 hrs)	Very long full-time hours (> 42 hrs)
Austria	8.8%	31.1%	15.7%	35.1%	9.3%
Belgium	23.6%	25.9%	33.6%	9.6%	7.4%
Germany(u)	23.3%	31.4%	21.3%	20.0%	3.9%
Spain	10.5%	18.5%	4.4%	47.3%	19.3%
Finland	6.1%	18.7%	50.5%	17.3%	7.3%
France	14.5%	29.1%	42.6%	6.7%	7.0%
Greece	3.3%	15.1%	7.1%	36.2%	38.3%
Ireland	26.1%	31.8%	22.6%	13.6%	(5.9%)
Italy	5.8%	20.5%	20.2%	37.5%	16.0%
Luxembourg	17.4%	32.0%	. .	41.3%	(7.2%)
Netherlands	54.0%	35.8%	2.4%	6.6%	1.1%
Portugal	5.4%	16.0%	3.8%	30.8%	44.1%
UK	38.0%	36.8%	11.0%	6.9%	7.3%
E13	21.3%	29.1%	20.8%	19.0%	9.9%

(b) Medium level of education

	Short part-time hours (0–19 hrs)	Long part-time hours (20–35 hrs)	Short full-time hours (36–39 hrs)	Long full-time hours (40–42 hrs)	Very long full-time hours (> 42 hrs)
Austria	9.3%	25.9%	17.1%	42.9%	4.8%
Belgium	18.8%	28.2%	35.9%	10.7%	6.4%
Germany(u)	25.9%	29.6%	27.7%	13.2%	3.7%
Spain	5.9%	17.2%	15.6%	51.6%	9.7%
Finland	(6.3%)	17.2%	59.5%	10.5%	(6.4%)
France	9.9%	32.6%	45.6%	6.0%	5.9%
Greece	(2.8%)	12.9%	21.6%	42.4%	20.2%
Ireland	15.5%	31.2%	27.7%	19.9%	(5.6%)
Italy	4.8%	28.5%	34.4%	24.0%	8.3%
Luxembourg	(9.6%)	(30.8%)	(8.8%)	47.0%	. .
Netherlands	44.6%	44.6%	(3.4%)	6.2%	. .
Portugal	3.0%	34.5%	12.5%	31.8%	18.3%
UK	33.5%	35.5%	14.3%	7.7%	9.0%
E13	14.8%	29.5%	29.5%	18.2%	8.0%

(c) High level of education

	Short part-time hours (0–19 hrs)	Long part-time hours (20–35 hrs)	Short full-time hours (36–39 hrs)	Long full-time hours (40–42 hrs)	Very long full-time hours (> 42 hrs)
Austria	6.6%	21.4%	10.7%	<u>54.9%</u>	(6.4%)
Belgium	18.3%	<u>35.4%</u>	29.3%	9.6%	7.4%
Germany (u)	16.5%	27.4%	18.3%	<u>32.1%</u>	5.7%
Spain	4.0%	28.1%	24.2%	<u>38.7%</u>	5.0%
Finland	(4.3%)	23.0%	<u>54.8%</u>	12.5%	(5.4%)
France	18.9%	<u>32.6%</u>	28.8%	9.5%	10.1%
Greece	5.8%	<u>40.7%</u>	19.3%	25.6%	8.6%
Ireland	17.2%	<u>40.9%</u>	20.0%	15.6%	(6.3%)
Italy	29.4%	<u>30.3%</u>	21.7%	12.7%	6.0%
Luxembourg	. .	<u>37.8%</u>	. .	(31.4%)	. .
Netherlands	33.1%	<u>51.1%</u>	5.5%	8.7%	1.6%
Portugal	3.8%	<u>64.8%</u>	7.1%	(16.7%)	7.7%
UK	24.5%	<u>32.7%</u>	13.4%	13.1%	16.4%
E13	18.3%	<u>32.8%</u>	20.7%	19.6%	8.7%

Source: European Labour Force Survey (1995).

Note
Modal hours group is underlined for each country and educational gap

Another factor which has not been taken into account here is the issue of working hours. Women are not only under-utilised within the European labour market when they are unemployed or inactive but also when they are confined to short hours working. This effect is greatest for the lower-educated but even among higher-educated women who are mothers, hours of work can be quite short (see Table 8.4). At the E15 level the modal hours of highly educated mothers is in the 20–35 hours category, but 18 per cent of highly educated mothers in employment usually work for fewer than 20 hours. Thus increasing hours of work, through better provision of childcare for example, could further increase the potential for educated women to contribute to the future supply of skilled labour to European labour markets.

The likely contribution of female labour supply to future employment growth varies considerably by country, and also by age range within countries. To provide some more detailed information on the pattern of variation, Appendix Tables 1.1 and 1.2 show the predicted participation rates by age from the IFO projections described earlier (IFO 1994,1995). These projections reflect some of the shortcomings already identified with the projection methodology adopted, but nevertheless serve to illustrate variations between countries. One can here identify those countries – for example the UK – in which the peak increase in participation rates is likely to come for younger women, as the m-shaped participation rate curve disappears further, while in others – for example Belgium – the major increase will be for older-age workers. In the Netherlands the increases will be more evenly spread, as there is both the legacy of an m-shaped curve and that of older generations with relatively low participation rates. Only in the Scandinavian countries are there projected to be relatively even and small changes in participation rates by age group, although there are differences between countries in whether the changes are positive or negative, with Sweden predicted to have negative changes in most age ranges even under the high scenario.

This information underlines the almost universal importance of female labour supply to the forthcoming decade of European labour market developments. The only countries where there are predicted to be limited rises or even falls in female labour supply are those where the participation rates between the sexes have already reached relatively similar levels, and thus where the scope for further female employment growth is limited. On the other hand, they also indicate the wide differences in capacity for female employment growth between member states, calling into question the possibility of discussing labour market trends and developments across Europe as if they were all likely to follow a similar pattern. Thus under the high scenario projection, the range of increases in female participation rates are from 0.9 to 15.9 percentage points, the implied growth rates of the female labour force are from 10 per cent to 68 per cent, and the predicted changes in female shares of the labour force range from 0.7 to 7.6 percentage points (see Table 8.5).

Thus in Ireland, Spain, Luxembourg, Greece and Italy the feminisation of the labour force would increase by 6 percentage points or more, a significant change in the future sex composition of the labour market. In contrast, not only the Scandinavian countries but also the UK, France and Portugal would see much more moderate changes of under 4 percentage points. Moreover, some of the potential increase in participation rates, particularly for older women, may be exaggerated in some of the countries with high female participation rates such as the UK and Denmark, so that the actual scope for differential rates of change in the degree of feminisation may be even greater.

Of course the critical factor will be the way in which employment opportunities interact with this potential scope for broadening the labour force base in countries with currently low female participation rates. Yet rising female participation rates, particularly alongside rising female educational levels, are a key feature of all European member states and appear relatively insensitive to employment opportunities. On this basis, some convergence in participation rates, particularly for prime-age women, can be expected as current and future cohorts move through the age structure, and in this sense the projections provide some indication of the scale of differences between countries in potential female labour supply growth. These projections of labour supply growth reinforce the view that unemployment figures provide a very inadequate indicator of the potential slack in the European labour market. Much female unemployment remains

Table 8.5 Projected changes in female employment, 1990–2005: high scenario

	Projected increase in participation rate (percentage point)	*Projected percentage growth in female labour force*	*Projected female share of labour force, 2005*	*Projected increase on 1990 (percentage point increase)*
Belgium	11.5	36.3	44.6	5.4
Denmark	8.0	16.7	48.0	1.9
Germany	8.7	26.0	45.2	4.8
Greece	10.5	43.6	42.0	6.2
Spain	15.9	55.6	42.2	7.5
France	8.1	28.3	46.9	3.6
Ireland	15.9	68.4	41.3	7.6
Italy	11.5	35.6	42.7	6.1
Luxembourg	12.9	51.6	42.3	7.0
Netherlands	11.7	40.3	44.5	5.7
Austria	9.8	35.1	45.9	4.0
Portugal	11.8	33.8	46.3	3.7
Finland	0.9	10.0	48.4	1.0
Sweden	1.3	10.9	48.4	0.7
UK	7.6	18.8	46.3	3.4
E12	10.2	30.6	44.9	4.8

Source: IFO (1994, 1995).

currently hidden, but the experience of recent decades suggests that this potential female labour reserve will become ever more visible, forcing European economies to find ways of further stimulating the employment rate or face ever rising levels of unemployment or underemployment.

Gender and the restructuring of the European labour market

While women constitute the main potential source of labour supply growth, most experts believe employment growth to be demand- rather than supply-constrained. To the extent that skill shortage could restrict future employment growth, moves towards higher participation among women could considerably relieve the skill shortage, as it is the female labour supply that is currently the more underemployed, in both quantity and skill terms. Increased opportunities to participate on a continuous basis would protect against skill loss and provide women with greater opportunities than at present to participate in lifelong learning. Women's educational levels are rising quickly and women in many countries are exceeding male levels of participation in higher education. Some groups may still be losing out in skill developments, through exclusion from vocational training systems, but the overall effect of raising female employment and providing for more continuous careers would add significantly to the skill base of the European economy.

Thus the more important issues relate to the potential demand for labour than to shortage of labour supply. Gender also plays a major role in the structure of labour demand. Occupational sex segregation is a persistent and even growing feature of European labour markets, a consequence of the increasing feminisation of, for example, clerical and service work, and the rising share of new jobs which are part-time and can often only be taken by those in households with other sources of income, that is mainly students and married women. Sex segregation of employment has in fact been a major contributor to overall female employment growth as the trends over recent years have favoured female-dominated over male-dominated sectors. However, rising female shares of employment within sectors and occupations have made an even greater contribution to female employment growth (Rubery *et al.* 1998a:100–112).

The 1990s recession saw a further deterioration in men's employment relative to women's, but this reflected more a worsening trend for men than good prospects for women. Women's rate of employment growth slowed and in some cases became negative. Moreover, the future prospects appear even more uncertain. Much of the recent growth has come from the expansion of service sector employment, particularly in the public services and in areas such as financial services. Future prospects in the public sector are overshadowed by the general move to reduce public expenditure, while in many countries employment in financial services is already being cut back as a result of rationalisation and adaptation to new methods of banking such as telephone banking.

Male employment was the main victim of the restructuring processes in the 1980s, but the next wave may hit women's employment areas harder. The imposed constraint on growth in public services may have the strongest long-term negative consequences for women and for overall employment rates. For most of the post-war period, advanced economies have been able to match, by and large, increasing labour supply with increasing jobs. Most of these jobs have been in services, both public and private, and to some extent have acted as a direct substitute for domestic labour such as childcare, food preparation or laundry. As women moved out of the home into the wage economy, demand for alternative models of service provision increased, such that changes in the supply of labour have contributed to increased demand for labour in the wage economy. Restrictions on public sector development, particularly in countries with relatively low levels of public sector provision of services, endanger this relationship, preventing the development of a high employment rate to match increased supply. The processes of change in women's behaviour and in family systems may not be so easily reversible, so that the end result may be an increase in the supply of labour relative to demand.

The development of the private service sector may be considered to provide an alternative route to high employment, as in the US economy, but in most cases this results in employment under poor conditions, involving low pay and short-hour part-time jobs. Thus the outcome of a greater supply of female labour not matched by an expansion of the welfare state could be a mixture of higher unemployment or widening dispersion in the labour market as the share of poor jobs increases, taken up by women or by youth labour displaced from other parts of the labour market.

The possibility that the future will not generate sufficient jobs or sufficient good jobs for the large numbers of women who may move into the labour market does not mean that men will necessarily fare any better. Indeed, men may face yet greater employment problems if manufacturing continues to decline in importance within the European economy. Under these conditions women may face increased competition from men at the same time as job prospects in their traditional areas may prove not only insufficient to meet increased female labour supply but could even decline below levels achieved in the mid-1990s.

Women may still fare better than men in the competition for jobs in the service sector, but it is vital for equality that success in the competition is not based upon ever deteriorating terms and conditions of employment. Segregation has in the past acted to protect women's employment prospects, while at the same time in most countries confining women to worse terms and conditions of employment. The experience of Scandinavia reveals that it is possible to make some headway towards equality under conditions of segregation provided the right institutional arrangements, such as compressed wage structures and good employment rights, are in place. However, segregation necessarily increases the risk that future changes will expose women to renewed risks of inequality, such as wider wage dispersion, as either job prospects decline in female areas or as institutions change. It could be argued that only full integration is compatible with the objective of equality, as the risks of any process of restructuring would then be more evenly shared between men and women. However, integration cannot be achieved simply through desegregation of occupations; most research finds a persistent tendency for gender differences to re-emerge even within apparently integrated occupations (Reskin and Roos 1990; Crompton and Sanderson 1990 and Chapter 5 above). Thus gender differentiation in the labour market runs deeper than is recognised in conventional models of labour markets where discrimination is assumed only to affect the allocation of labour within the job structure, and the influence of gender on the structuring of jobs and terms and conditions of employment is not considered.

If gender pervades social and institutional structures, it may be inappropriate to see full integration as a feasible policy objective in the medium term; instead the objective may have to be that of achieving greater equality within segregated labour markets. This involves paying attention, *inter alia*, to wage structures, to promotion ladders within female job areas, and to the creation of links and bridges between female jobs areas and main promotion lines within organisations, as well as to working-time arrangements. Part-time or reduced-hours working may, in some social contexts, help women to reconcile work and family life while maintaining their position in the labour market and on the career ladder; in other contexts the development of part-time work may mainly serve to casualise employment relations and to marginalise women's position within the employment system. Part-time work tends to be concentrated in highly feminised areas in all countries, even when performed by men, and there is thus an urgent need to ensure that the trend towards promoting part-time job growth does not lead to a widening disparity in employment conditions between male and female employment areas. Part-time work is frequently cited as a more acceptable form of work sharing than reduced working hours in European and national policy fora, but the implications for increasing gender inequality within the labour market are not spelt out (Maruani 1995). Recognition of the segregated nature of the labour market – by occupation and by working-time – and thus of the gender dimension to labour market change would help focus attention on the gender aspects of labour market trends and labour market policies.

9   Prospects for equality

Gender equality: a case of uneven progress

Progress towards higher levels of female employment was evident in all
EU member states during the 1990s, except for those countries such as
Sweden and Finland which had already achieved a high level of female
employment by the end of the 1980s. While the direction of change towards
greater integration of women into the wage economy is clear, some important issues remain to be addressed regarding the prospects for integration
with equality. In particular we need to consider whether there is a glass
ceiling to the improvement and advancement of women's position in the
labour market, such that full equality cannot be achieved in the labour
market if there is no change in the traditional gender division of labour in
the home and a low representation of women among decision-makers;
whether there will be a convergence between EU member states in the levels
of gender equality and in particular between less developed and more developed parts of the EU; and whether there will be increasing divisions between
women, between the less and the more educated or between women with
and without children, or whether current differences between women are
more indicative of change in attitudes and aspirations between generations
of women.

We find some evidence of a glass ceiling to gender labour market equality
in the slight declines in employment and activity rates in Scandinavian countries in the first half of the decade, in the rising inactivity rates in the former
East Germany and in the widening pay differentials between the sexes in
countries which had moved furthest towards gender pay equality, such as
Italy. These reversals might be regarded by some as evidence that particular institutional arrangements, such as solidarity wage bargaining, or strong
welfare states, had disguised the extent of continuing differences between
men's and women's orientations and commitment to work, related to their
different roles in the household. The reintroduction of more market-
orientated pay and employment systems therefore tended to widen the gender
gap again, reflecting the continuing differences in productivity between men
and women. For others, however, the reintroduction of more market-based

criteria may simply provide new opportunities to discriminate against women, for example by reducing the wage paid in female-dominated jobs, irrespective of their relative skill level. These arguments represent two opposing interpretations of the role of labour market regulation: one that it distorts the true underlying market values and the other that through regulation some of the discrimination built into labour market systems can be modified and controlled. One of the main arguments of the 1990s has been that it is no longer possible, in the interests of social justice, to buck the market trends and establish greater equality in the labour market at a time when global economic trends are pulling towards greater dispersion (Wood 1994). Countries which in the 1980s moved a long way towards gender equality also tended to have centralised systems of pay determination and a commitment to equality. These structures have been argued to be out of line with market requirements, and hence in the 1990s there has been a near universal call for more flexible wage structures reflecting market trends and individual and firm-level productivity (Marsden 1992). However, the continuing wide variety in pay levels, ranges and practices between countries casts doubts on a simplistic market forces argument and suggests that scope does exist for different social choices, including the choice to promote wage compression and gender pay equality. In the Scandinavian countries the widening pay gap has been in part associated with decreasing relative pay in the public sector, explained more perhaps by public sector deficit targets than by labour market trends and developments. The notion that wage structures are determined by autonomous competitive market forces, rather than by decision-makers in enterprises, trade unions and government, allows those advocating wider wage dispersion to overlook the fact that women are dramatically under-represented in those bodies which shape wage structures and wage policy.

There nevertheless remains the question of whether or not there is likely to be full equality in the labour market, including full convergence towards the participation rates of men, before much more fundamental changes have taken place in the gender division of labour in the household. Where very high participation rates have been measured in the past, this may have arisen in part out of statistical measures which count women as being employed even when they are on full- or part-time leave or temporary absence (Jonung and Persson 1993). Alternatively, in the case of the former East Germany, high participation may have been achieved through some form of compulsion, including economic necessity, and through the linking of the provision of childcare to the place of work. High female participation rates in some countries may perhaps have given a false impression of how far it has been possible to reconcile the demands of work and family life. High and continuous participation rates of men in full-time work imply, to some extent, the withdrawal of opportunities for men to pursue variable and interesting lives, including opportunities for both caring and personal development. Women may well resist pressures to enter a similar straitjacket of full-time continuous

employment for all, and indeed some choice over whether or not to participate should be regarded as part of an equality agenda.

However, it is very easy to slide from that argument to one in which
women's employment is regarded as more contingent than that of men's,
more adjustable downwards in the face of recession, and thus a soft target
for labour market polices designed to reduce labour supply or encourage
work sharing. The debate needs to be more appropriately focused around
how to provide men with both opportunities and incentives to depart from
full-time continuous employment, so that convergence towards equality can
be achieved from both directions. The actual reversals experienced in
Scandinavia have been related to major economic problems, and to some
extent the decline in women's employment reflects the fact that greater
equality in the labour market makes women vulnerable to employment
decline in the recession, alongside men. Nevertheless, there is still the
problem that women's unemployment or enforced inactivity is regarded as
a less serious problem than that of young people or prime-age men.

The second issue, convergence between member states in women's participation rates, rather than convergence between the sexes, depends upon a
number of factors, not least of which is the level of employment opportunities. We have already suggested that the constraints on public sector
employment growth may restrict a process of convergence. There is an acute
awareness in Southern European countries of the need to raise the tax and
social security base of the economy through increasing participation rates;
in the medium to long term some expansion of public services may facilitate a higher employment rate, which would also provide part of the expanded
tax base to fund the development as well as easing economic and social
problems associated with low employment rates (for example reducing pressure on real wage growth in traded sectors as the number of earners per
family increases). There is a real danger that the EU will continue to concentrate on convergence in financial terms without achieving a convergence in
levels of development. The latter would probably require the enhancement
of welfare states in the less developed parts of the region to achieve a higher
employment base.

However, there is also a danger in the argument of convergence of levels
and forms of female employment. It is not self evidently the case that all
women benefit from moves towards more direct wage employment and
away, for example, from forms of self-employment. Low-skilled women in
deregulated labour markets often have to work under poor conditions and
in conditions of greater uncertainty than is the case where women work
within family-based firms on a self-employed basis. Clearly, both types of
systems are open to discrimination and exploitation, as is evident in the
high share of women classified as unpaid family labour, but service sectors
based around small and family firms do not universally provide worse
economic terms and conditions of employment than low-status part-time
work for large multinational chains. A further danger arises in assuming

away all social, cultural and institutional differences between societies which may affect women's employment patterns. Even within the Scandinavian systems there is evidence of different norms with respect to female employment patterns and preferences: Finnish women, for example, have traditionally preferred full-time work combined with full-time absences from the labour market when children are young; Swedish women have tended to take shorter breaks from work but to work reduced hours over longer time periods and Danish women have increasingly rejected short-hours work but taken up options for parental leave. These differences between societies cannot be solely or simply equated to differences in structural arrangements, such as access to childcare, although such factors are clearly important in shaping preferences and choices. Thus a role for societal norms and societally specific institutions and economic arrangements must remain in predictions for the future.

Progress towards equality will obviously depend both on stages of development and on the stage already reached in the emancipation of women. However, alongside these factors will lie political and social choices. Thus, on the one hand, it is no surprise that the countries which experienced the greatest moves forward in terms of equality during the European Commission's third action programme included some of those with furthest to travel; the early 1990s saw a fairly rapid social transformation in favour of women's emancipation in both Spain and Ireland (National reports, Spain: Moltó 1996:90; Ireland: Barry 1996:88). However, the path towards equality is not even. Italy, which started the 1990s with a relatively low female employment rate saw a new law to provide monitoring on equal opportunity and positive action become moribund before it was enacted (National reports, Italy: Bettio and Villa 1996:1) while Sweden, with its already strong commitment to equality, increased the requirements on firms to provide monitoring and action plans for wage equality, requirements which by and large were complied with (National reports, Sweden: Gonäs and Spånt 1996:17). Thus although most positive developments have been found in countries in which there was a real need for a catching-up process to be put in place, the experience of Italy suggests that the path to convergence with Scandinavia will by no means be smooth or inevitable. Despite some backlash against equality, Scandinavian women may still be better placed to withstand the pressures of recession on commitments to equality than those women in countries where the political case for equality has yet to be won.

Polarisation and generational change are both likely to figure as significant features of future European labour markets. As we have identified in discussions of labour supply, there are both significant differences within age cohorts in participation rates, by, for example, level of education, and significant differences in participation rates between cohorts, related both to higher levels of education among younger cohorts and to rising participation rates at all levels of education (Rubery and Smith 1997 and Chapter

8 above). In some countries the differences between cohorts are greater, as women who quit the labour market to have children have not been drawn back in, while in others the high participation rates among older cohorts probably includes a large number who may initially have intended a long or permanent exit from the labour market. A reduction in inter-generational differences may be predicted over time but coupled with a widening, perhaps, of differences between groups of women. The extent of this polarisation will depend on the overall level of female employment: where this rises to a high level the gaps may in fact begin to narrow again. For example, in Scandinavia the high overall participation rate narrows the scope for variations by educational level. It is thus in those countries with low overall participation rates that polarisation in employment-rate terms may increase, thereby leading to convergence in participation behaviour for more educated women across Europe while divergence between countries is concentrated among the less educated.

Where part-time work is a significant part of the employment system and is associated with lower-skilled work, polarisation may emerge around those women in full-time and those in part-time work, with the latter trapped in less skilled and indeed more 'dead-end' jobs. The significance of the polarisation will again depend on country-specific factors such as wage dispersion, so that where there is a wide range of earnings levels the polarisation may result in wide inequalities among women.

One particularly unwelcome form of polarisation which may increasingly emerge within Europe is that between women with and women without children, with only the latter able to pursue a career (Bettio and Villa 1998). This may increasingly apply under two circumstances: first when there are both high expectations surrounding the commitments of motherhood and limited state support in the form of childcare, and second where deregulated labour markets reduce the opportunities to reconcile a career and family life because of pressure to work longer or more variable hours. More women are likely in future to choose voluntarily to remain childless, but the right of women to combine work and family life needs to be not only protected but also promoted. Women will, of course, play a role in shaping these outcomes; the consequence of the greater participation of women in all areas of life is that they cannot be considered as passive victims of circumstance, but also as social actors who will shape their own and their society's future. Nevertheless, power is by no means equally shared and the possibility that policies will continue to reflect male interests must be recognised.

Towards an equal opportunities employment policy in Europe?

One factor which may influence the prospects for equality is the decision in 1997 to include equal opportunities as one of the pillars of European employment policy. The end of the 1990s should in principle see a new beginning and new opportunities for developing a gender equality orientated employment policy in Europe. The Amsterdam Treaty of 1997 enshrined the European Union's commitment to equal opportunities in its set of missions of the European Union and the 1997 Luxembourg Jobs Summit agreed common guidelines on employment policy in which equal opportunities constituted the fourth pillar of employment policy, along with employability, adaptability and entrepreneurship. These developments in employment policy also gave some substance to the commitment by the Commission, following the Beijing Fourth World UN conference on women, of mainstreaming gender into all its policy areas. The equal opportunity guidelines for 1998 proposed three main areas of activity: tackling gender gaps, reconciling work and family life and facilitating a return to work. The member states were asked to translate their commitment to equal opportunities into increased employment opportunities for women; they are required to make efforts to reduce segregation, to reduce the gender gap in unemployment and to seek actively to promote women's employment. Implementation of directives and social partner agreements in the area of parental leave were to be accelerated and monitored and member states have been enjoined to provide for adequate, good quality childcare. Women and men returners were also to receive specific attention and member states were asked to examine ways of eliminating over time any obstacles to their return.

At the Luxembourg Jobs Summit in November 1997 there was some narrowing of the scope of these agreed equal opportunity guidelines in comparison to those proposed by the European Commission. For example, the Commission proposed that member states should be asked to raise childcare provision in line with best practice in member states, and tax and benefit systems were to be reviewed to ensure they did not impede returners re-entering the labour market. These commitments were modified, in the first case, and removed, in the second case, in the agreed guidelines. The final 1998 guidelines also omitted reference to the mainstreaming of gender equality issues into all the other policies enacted under the different pillars, including, for example, women's involvement in entrepreneurship. However, in the 1999 guidelines the commitment to mainstreaming was re-introduced together with a commitment to progress on equal pay. The new employment guidelines do indicate a considerable change in the position of the European Commission with respect to the analysis of gender equality issues and the types of policies that needed to be enacted. This was in comparison to earlier Commission documents such as the 1993 White Paper *Growth, Competitiveness and Employment* (CEC 1994) which initiated the development of a common European employment policy but failed to spell out any specific gender analysis of the labour market (CEC 1995c; Rubery and Maier 1995). This stronger commitment arose out of a clearer recognition of the significance of female employment to the economy, as spelt out again in the Commission's draft guidelines:

As the Commission's Demography Reports have outlined, the working age population is now growing much more slowly than it did during the last 20 years and over the next decade it will start to decline. In the longer term, therefore, the growth in employment necessary to sustain our living standards and the European social model is critically dependent on an increase in participation of women in the labour force.

(Draft employment guidelines, October 1997, submitted by the Commission to the Luxembourg Summit)

The emphases in the employment guidelines also signalled a shift towards an approach to flexibility which emphasised the positive development of productive capacities, rather than a negative flexibility based on low skill and low labour cost. As the latter approach tends to have disproportionately negative impacts on the terms and conditions of women's employment, this shift in policy could be said to be more compatible with equal opportunities. This shift in focus of European employment policy mirrors a softening of the approach to the European employment 'problem' taken by the OECD. In contrast to the 1994 OECD *Jobs Study* (OECD 1994a) that was published at the around the same time as the 1993 EC White Paper (CEC 1994), and which called for more rapid deregulation of the labour market, especially for the removal of minimum wages, more recent documents from the OECD have questioned the policy of low wages and flexibility as the means to sustainable job growth. In this later document the OECD (1997b) recognised that it was not able to provide definitive evidence in favour of removing wage floors, and indeed the document stressed that the emphasis on wage and employment flexibility had been too short term, focusing on getting the unemployed back into work but not on establishing them on a sustainable employment path. More emphasis needed to be placed on increasing the skills of the workforce to meet the minimum wage levels, rather than on lowering the wage levels to whatever level was necessary to clear the labour market. This change of focus must be considered advantageous to women and the data presented in the OECD report provided evidence of some of the gender specific aspects of low pay, including the much higher risk of low pay faced by young people and women, again showing a parallel greater awareness of the gender dimensions of European labour markets than was evident either in the EC's White Paper or the OECD *Jobs Study*.

Overall, therefore, the development in European and international approaches to employment policy during 1997 and 1998 could be considered to signal major progress in the development of an equal opportunities approach to employment. This progress relates both to the greater visibility of equality issues within the employment framework and to the ending of the simplistic 'deregulation and flexibility at all costs' approach to the employment problem, a policy perspective which has potential major negative consequences for equality in general and gender equality in particular. These achievements need to be recognised and perhaps even celebrated.

However, there are reasons for anticipating that the current integration of equal opportunities into EU employment policy will have only limited effects in achieving progress towards equality. In part, the problems lie in the detail of the policy proposals, but perhaps the more substantial barriers to equality lie in the context in which this policy programme is being implemented.

The first problem of context is the macroeconomic environment and macroeconomic policy framework; the second, and perhaps more intractable problem, is the evidence of a lack of political will at the member-states level even to follow the lead provided by the European Commission in the promotion of equal opportunities. Even more fundamental problems exist at a conceptual level. How can an equal opportunities employment policy be developed and carved out without a rethink of the whole organisation

---

Box 9.1 The case for and against mainstreaming

The case for mainstreaming

- Any progress that women have made over recent years has been against a background of rising inequality and reduced employment opportunities. The significance of macroeconomic conditions and the processes of restructuring of economies and organisations for the future of gender equality make plain the need to mainstream gender issues.
- Unless the impact on gender equality is taken into account at the time at which policies are designed and assessed and not after implementation, gender-equality policy will have a primarily defensive role, forced to try to reverse the negative impacts of more general labour market policies designed without a gender assessment.
- Mainstreaming should also improve the quality of labour market policy-formation. Unless the gendered nature of labour markets is taken into account, labour market policy-makers are often surprised by either the ineffectiveness of their policies or their unintended outcomes: for example, when new jobs are taken by the inactive rather than the unemployed, or when the promotion of part-time jobs has little impact on the availability of jobs for unemployed prime-age men (Rubery 1995c; Meulders 1996).

The case against mainstreaming

- There is, first, the danger that mainstreaming will be used to close down specific gender policy bodies or monitoring systems. Yet it is the advocacy from the women's lobby and the existence of such monitoring systems which led to the call for mainstreaming in the first place. The momentum behind mainstreaming may be lost if the new system is used to minimise the role for equal opportunities units and interest groups.
- The second problem relates to the methodology of gender audits of policies. Is it possible, for example, to guard against an outcome in which

of social and economic life? If the outcome of an equal opportunities policy is a move towards dual-earner and dual-career households, what types of policies do we need to ensure that appropriate institutional and social frameworks develop to support the new economic and social order? These conceptual issues lie at the heart of debates over what is meant by mainstreaming: is it indeed possible to mainstream gender issues on a piecemeal, policy-by-policy basis or does mainstreaming require a more radical rethink to policy-making? And how can we take into account differences in the interests and experience of different groups of women and different groups of men within gender audits of policies?

Progress towards equal opportunities is perhaps inevitably dogged by a process of potential major advances being converted and diverted into only

increased gender equality through the downgrading of men's employment conditions is treated as a victory for gender equality; and is it appropriate to look at the average effect on women, when some groups of women may benefit and others lose?
- A third issue relates to the scope of these policy evaluations. Should policy evaluation remain within the framework of existing structures, evaluating returns to policies based, for example, on current wage structures in which discrimination is embedded, or focused on the short-term cost of parental leave policies without identifying the long-term impact on the economy of policies which help women remain in work? Unless a broader and longer-term perspective is taken, the main benefits from equality policy and the main costs of not implementing equality are unlikely to be identified.
- Fourthly, policy-makers always have multiple objectives, and one of the main dangers is that equality policy, even if the gender audits are carried out, will not be given a high priority. Some policy-makers may even seek to reverse the path of gender equality, if women's integration into the economy is considered, for example, to be responsible either for falling fertility or for rising unemployment.
- Many of these issues have yet to be fully thought through and debated even within groups interested in equal opportunity, so that a major educational process is required before a policy of mainstreaming is likely to achieve an integrated and co-ordinated approach to gender equality.

Overview

- While the dangers and problems of mainstreaming must be considered seriously, without this policy development there seems little likelihood of equal opportunities policies being able to make headway against the tidal wave of decentralisation and individualisation in the workplace and macroeconomic restrictions in the economy. Without integrating gender into broader policy discussions, future assessments of progress towards equality in the labour market are likely to be even more pessimistic.

marginal change. High hopes associated with, for example, equal pay legislation were soon dampened by the reality of only marginal gains in women's relative pay; yet history suggests that these small gains are nevertheless significant and not to be undervalued. Perhaps a similar approach has to be taken to both the commitment to mainstreaming (see Box 9.1) and the associated inclusion of equal opportunities within the employment guidelines. The potential of the inclusion of equality issues in employment policy, one of the first manifest signs of mainstreaming, has been constrained and minimised by the commitment by the member states to quantitative targets relating to measures for the unemployed and the rejection of quantitative targets for employment or for equal opportunities, thereby marginalising *de facto* these aspects of employment policy. Moreover, the action points listed under equal opportunities focus primarily on the employment objective and not equality objectives, although the 1998 guidelines have improved the position by making reference to progress on equal pay. Yet these limitations of the guidelines are perhaps more a reflection of the actual political and economic context in which this employment policy is being implemented. The initial omission of mainstreaming and the focus on unemployment reflects the lack of a general political will among member states to place a high priority on equal opportunity, or indeed to focus on issues of employment rather than the more politically sensitive issue of unemployment, particularly male and youth unemployment. Moreover, the narrowness of the conception of equal opportunity employment policy can be considered to reflect the limited scope for employment policy under the tight macroeconomic guidelines agreed for monetary union.

Probably the most promising aspect of the recent developments in European employment policy has been the belated recognition by the Commission of the significance of gender to the operation of the European labour markets. The gender-blind approach evident in the Delors White Paper (CEC 1994) has given way to a recognition not only of the need to counteract gender inequality but also of the fact that women are major players within the emerging European labour market and that to ignore them is seriously to diminish the relevance of labour market analysis.

However, it would be premature to assume that all the conceptual problems of defining an equal opportunities employment policy have been solved. Major progress still needs to be made, not only within policy-makers' fora but also within labour economics, and even within feminist economics debates, in the understanding of the gendered nature of labour market processes and how these may influence the formulation of policy with an equal opportunity objective in mind. The interaction between gender and the labour market phenomenon which is being measured and observed requires much wider recognition and development. For example, policy-makers still refer interchangeably to low-paid and low-skill jobs, without reference to whether either the level of pay or the skill label attached to the job is associated with the gender of the person employed. The debate over working-time and the role of part-time employment is entered into without recognition of the assumption of income dependency that comes from part-time employment, which in almost all cases is insufficient to provide for adult subsistence (Rubery 1998a). The debate over potential skill shortages and the need for widening wage differentials is also not situated within a labour market context in which women tend to be systematically excluded from areas where labour shortage leads to spiralling wage claims rather than simply higher workloads (as, for example, often applies when the shortage is of skilled nurses). Labour economists and policy-makers still conveniently switch their unit of analysis between the household and the individual, depending upon the subject under discussion, instead of recognising the twin influences of household and family position and individual aspirations on all labour market behaviour. The tools for analysis of a gendered and socially constructed labour market have yet to be fully developed, and under these conditions the possibility or likelihood that labour market policy will consistently pursue an equal opportunity objective must be considered slim.

In order to move towards an equal opportunity employment policy, there is a need to situate the issue of employment within a broader perspective, in which participation in wage work is located in a general analysis of the social and economic system. Such an approach looks at the decision whether or not to participate in wage work not solely or mainly in terms of marginal analysis relating to short-term work incentives, but within a broader institutional analysis in which the questions of how social reproduction is secured provide the main focus. In particular, the relationship between paid and unpaid work needs to be understood within the whole framework of the organisation of economic and social activity, highlighting both differences in these arrangements between countries and change over time in these relationships. From this perspective the move towards higher female participation across all European countries can be identified as symbolic of, and related to, a major reorganisation of social as well as economic life.

Family systems and patterns of household formation are changing, with major implications for income transfers outside the state, and at the same time the commitments by government to provide support are being narrowed and redefined. Changes are taking place too in women's and men's division of labour between private care work and wage work. Women have increased their potential access to paid work, while men are experiencing more difficulties in securing jobs offering stable income sufficient to support themselves and dependants. At the same time there is a redrawing of the gender contract, with women questioning their role in the provision of private unpaid caring work, while the state attempts to place more responsibility for care work on the individual or the family. However men, so far, have only made minimal increases in their time input to domestic work (Gershuny *et al.* 1994) All this suggests potentially contradictory but radical changes in the ways in which we organise the fundamentals of our lives, and it is against this background, and not solely that of high levels of unemployment, that European employment policy needs to be constructed. Without recognising the interrelationships between the changing social and economic structure and the labour market, there are very real dangers that those with the least voice in the system – children, the frail elderly or sick, young people not fortunate to be located in stable and affluent households, the divorced or single mothers with limited job opportunities – will be overlooked in the policy of increasing employment without rethinking the responsibilities and commitments to care work and income provision for those outside the labour market.

All these considerations suggest that mainstreaming gender into policy involves much more than a simple identification of gender issues within a narrow policy area, but must also involve a rethink of policy across a wide perspective and a breaking down of traditional barriers between policy-making in, for example, the employment, fiscal and social protection spheres.

Perhaps the most difficult problem of all to address within the debate on an equal opportunities employment policy is that of ascertaining the actual interests of women and ensuring that the policies to be pursued in the name of equal opportunities in fact further these interests. These problems exist at both a nation-state and a European level. At the European level it is clear that women from different European societies express different preferences and objectives and back up those preferences through different patterns of behaviour. Problems exist in interpreting these differences because of the different policy and institutional environments in which the women are located. This approach, that women's expressed preferences reflect available institutions, lies behind, for example, the policy of asking all member states to improve the provision of childcare facilities even though in some countries there are still strong social norms, held by women as well as men, that children should be cared for in the home.

At the nation-state level such problems still exist, as women from different classes and from different stages of the life cycle express different views and preferences, and the identification of a specifically female point of view may be difficult. Major differences can be identified between the interests of different groups of women, both presenting intractable problems in defining what are 'women's interests' and providing ample opportunities for policy-makers to reject the notion of mainstreaming on grounds that gender auditing does not lead to unambiguous results. One such example is that of the individualisation of benefits; while this may promote women's economic independence in the longer term it is likely to redistribute income from women to men in the shorter term. Considerable work needs to be done on how to reconcile and identity these contradictory impacts and effects explicitly and in such a way that policy choices cannot simply be described as in the interests of women or in the interests of men. A more subtle and differentiated analysis is necessary, so that the implications of any policy agenda can be fully assessed. It also needs to be recognised that women's integration into the labour market is having an impact on the extent to which a simple gender story can be told.

However, these developments should be regarded perhaps as much as an opportunity for further development of an equal opportunities policy which may embrace the interests of men as well as women, as a death knell for equal opportunities lobbying. Thus the fact that men are being required to work in low-paid or part-time jobs provides a basis for solidarity between the sexes and a general attack on labour market inequality, rather than evidence of the end of the gender question. The development of an equal opportunities perspective which encompasses the interests of men as well as women and of children as well as adults is the logical outcome of a policy of mainstreaming. However, the current policy framework and agenda of the European Union has not yet evolved to this level. We will need several more stages in the evolution of European employment policy yet before it can really be claimed that equal opportunity has been integrated into the European agenda.

Appendix

Appendix Table 1.1 Female activity rates by detailed age group and the projected change between 1990 and 2005 under the high and low scenarios

		15–19	20–24	25–29	30–34	35–39	40–44	45–49	50–54	55–59	60–64	65–69	70–74	75+
Belgium	1990 activity rate	7.8	58.8	78.5	72.4	68.2	58.8	47.4	30.6	16.8	3.9	1.1	0.4	0.2
	Projected change – low	-2.1	-4.5	2.8	6.1	6.7	7.4	5.5	2.4	-0.1	-0.6	-0.2	-0.1	0.0
	Projected change – high	14.1	4.7	7.4	12.7	14.9	19.4	22.3	23.5	18.6	12.5	4.5	2.0	0.3
Denmark	1990 activity rate	61.3	80.0	86.0	90.8	90.3	89.8	85.8	79.0	62.7	27.5	8.8	3.5	0.1
	Projected change – low	-7.6	-3.8	-1.6	-1.0	-1.0	-1.1	-1.0	1.4	2.2	-0.1	-1.4	-0.7	0.0
	Projected change – high	5.3	5.2	4.6	2.8	3.2	3.5	6.0	9.3	16.4	27.6	18.4	6.6	0.5
France	1990 activity rate	14.1	65.7	77.1	74.1	73.9	74.6	68.9	61.2	41.7	12.7	2.7	1.0	0.5
	Projected change – low	-4.4	-4.8	3.0	5.8	5.8	5.5	4.4	2.6	-0.9	-3.5	-0.9	-0.3	-0.2
	Projected change – high	10.9	5.4	8.3	11.7	12.0	11.5	12.7	12.0	10.1	8.1	5.0	2.1	0.5
Germany	1990 activity rate	33.5	73.2	69.1	63.8	65.6	67.8	64.5	56.0	42.0	11.7	3.4	1.7	0.8
	Projected change – low	-6.8	-4.0	3.7	7.2	7.0	6.5	5.1	5.3	4.7	0.2	-0.5	-0.3	-0.2
	Projected change – high	10.2	3.7	12.1	16.9	16.2	15.0	15.0	16.9	17.3	12.7	4.4	1.9	0.3
Greece	1990 activity rate	18.2	53.7	59.3	57.5	56.1	49.7	44.0	37.1	28.4	18.3	8.1	3.4	1.5
	Projected change – low	-4.6	-2.7	4.6	7.8	7.6	5.5	2.8	0.1	-2.1	-3.1	-2.5	-1.2	-0.5
	Projected change – high	9.7	7.2	14.9	17.9	18.5	19.8	19.7	18.0	14.7	8.6	3.6	1.4	-0.2
Ireland	1990 activity rate	25.3	74.5	68.3	51.7	41.2	36.6	33.5	29.0	23.0	13.9	5.8	2.9	1.3
	Projected change – low	-6.8	-4.2	3.9	8.1	8.2	7.6	5.1	2.4	-0.2	-2.2	-1.1	-0.6	-0.2
	Projected change – high	6.2	2.6	11.2	20.2	24.3	25.7	24.1	21.8	17.8	12.6	6.3	2.8	0.4
Italy	1990 activity rate	23.6	62.1	64.0	61.1	57.9	51.9	43.9	33.9	20.2	10.0	3.8	1.5	0.9
	Projected change – low	-6.1	-4.7	4.1	7.5	7.8	7.8	5.4	2.5	0.2	-0.2	-0.6	-0.1	-0.1
	Projected change – high	7.4	3.7	12.5	16.4	17.9	20.1	21.5	20.9	18.9	12.7	5.4	2.1	0.3
Luxembourg	1990 activity rate	23.0	70.6	67.3	54.5	51.3	48.1	40.1	26.9	18.3	7.8	2.4	0.9	0.2
	Projected change – low	-5.7	-4.3	3.7	7.7	7.9	6.2	5.3	4.6	2.2	0.0	-0.3	0.2	0.0
	Projected change – high	7.9	1.8	11.2	18.9	20.4	20.6	22.4	24.6	17.1	9.4	4.0	2.8	0.4
Netherlands	1990 activity rate	39.6	75.1	69.0	59.1	60.8	57.8	51.4	39.0	23.6	8.2	2.1	1.2	0.8
	Projected change – low	-6.9	-1.5	7.7	12.4	12.1	12.3	10.7	8.0	4.0	0.1	-0.3	-0.1	-0.1
	Projected change – high	7.9	4.1	13.0	19.8	19.1	20.3	21.1	22.6	20.7	12.4	7.1	3.2	0.9

Portugal	1990 activity rate	39.2	68.5	77.0	77.4	74.3	67.6	60.8	50.2	39.7	25.2	14.9	7.5	2.7
	Projected change – low	-11.1	-3.0	3.3	5.3	5.8	6.5	5.1	2.7	-0.3	-3.3	-2.6	-1.4	-0.5
	Projected change – high	5.7	6.0	8.4	10.1	11.7	15.1	16.0	16.7	15.0	11.8	4.6	1.7	-0.2
Spain	1990 activity rate	24.1	61.2	64.6	56.0	48.3	40.5	34.3	29.1	23.2	15.4	3.8	2.0	0.4
	Projected change – low	-7.1	-2.7	9.3	12.8	13.5	13.7	10.5	7.2	4.2	0.0	-0.7	-0.2	-0.1
	Projected change – high	11.7	8.4	17.8	24.5	28.5	32.5	34.6	33.2	27.6	15.6	5.6	1.9	0.2
UK	1990 activity rate	54.1	75.2	70.5	69.2	73.9	77.9	76.3	68.1	54.5	23.1	7.4	3.0	0.9
	Projected change – low	-6.1	-2.2	3.9	6.5	5.8	5.0	3.7	2.3	-0.3	-3.1	-1.4	-0.6	-0.2
	Projected change – high	-1.6	3.8	11.5	14.2	11.9	9.8	9.0	9.6	10.4	13.1	5.6	2.6	0.4
Austria	1990 activity rate	45.6	72.8	67.5	65.2	67.2	67.7	63.4	58.3	25.7	5.3	2.1	1.1	0.3
	Projected change – low	-10.9	-4.7	4.8	7.3	7.0	7.0	5.1	2.7	2.2	0.0	-0.4	-0.2	-0.1
	Projected change – high	2.0	2.5	12.5	15.5	14.6	14.3	13.7	12.9	18.2	11.2	4.0	1.5	0.2
Finland	1990 activity rate	38.0	68.2	80.8	83.6	88.4	89.9	89.9	83.2	60.2	19.6	4.0	1.7	0.4
	Projected change – low	-12.8	-6.8	-1.8	-1.6	-1.2	-2.3	-2.3	0.0	0.0	-3.3	-0.4	-0.1	0.0
	Projected change – high	-2.8	2.1	4.1	3.8	2.1	1.0	-0.1	1.8	5.8	9.0	5.8	2.6	0.3
Sweden	1990 activity rate	50.6	80.6	87.0	90.8	93.0	93.9	93.1	89.0	79.2	53.9	7.5	2.6	0.8
	Projected change – low	-17.2	-11.4	-4.7	-4.6	-3.9	-3.1	-3.4	-3.2	-4.5	-7.4	-1.5	-0.5	-0.2
	Projected change – high	-3.3	-5.7	-1.2	-2.1	-1.4	-1.2	-0.9	0.1	1.5	3.8	13.7	5.5	-0.1

Source: Labour force projections (IFO 1994, 1995).

Appendix Table 1.2 Projected change in female activity rates by broad age group, 1990 base year

	1990 activity rate				Projected low 1990–2005 change				Projected high 1990–2005 change			
	All ages	15–24	25–49	50–64	All ages	15–24	25–49	50–64	All ages	15–24	25–49	50–64
Belgium	36.0	31.3	65.7	16.6	1.3	−0.7	4.4	2.7	11.5	12.1	14.4	20.8
Denmark	60.8	66.2	88.9	57.5	−0.9	−1.7	−1.4	1.5	8.0	9.6	3.7	17.6
France	46.0	38.3	74.0	37.7	1.0	−2.4	4.6	4.5	8.1	10.4	11.0	15.0
Germany	44.9	55.0	67.4	39.0	−0.2	−7.3	4.8	1.1	8.7	5.5	13.9	13.9
Spain	31.9	38.4	49.8	22.5	6.4	2.9	11.1	4.5	15.9	11.9	22.3	20.2
Greece	34.9	32.2	54.3	28.8	0.1	2.7	4.8	−2.1	10.5	14.6	17.3	13.4
Ireland	34.5	41.2	47.3	22.7	2.5	4.9	6.5	0.4	15.9	15.6	21.2	18.1
Italy	34.5	39.6	55.7	21.2	1.5	−1.1	6.7	1.4	11.5	9.9	17.9	18.2
Luxembourg	33.6	43.8	52.4	17.6	1.0	−2.1	5.0	3.6	12.9	8.5	18.3	18.9
Netherlands	43.3	55.7	60.4	24.3	1.7	−2.8	10.0	5.3	10.7	7.7	17.8	20.1
Austria	43.6	60.6	66.2	29.5	1.6	−8.7	6.4	1.7	9.8	1.5	14.3	14.0
Portugal	46.8	49.0	70.6	37.5	3.4	−0.3	6.4	1.7	11.8	12.4	13.4	16.4
Finland	58.0	54.3	86.5	54.5	−3.7	−10.7	−1.5	2.8	0.9	−1.3	2.4	8.8
Sweden	62.9	67.8	91.6	74.0	−4.0	−15.2	−3.9	−4.3	1.3	−5.4	−1.4	2.4
UK	51.7	61.6	73.8	48.8	1.5	−1.5	5.1	1.3	7.6	3.8	11.3	12.4
E12	42.4	46.7	65.1	33.4	1.7	−1.4	5.8	3.0	10.2	9.2	14.6	16.6

Source: IFO (1994, 1995).

Notes

1 Political and economic change

1 The NOW programme was replaced by a special Employment-NOW programme within the employment initiative, one of the structural funds programmes.

2 Organisational and employment change

1 These predicted differences in the nature of research and the research question are reflected in the national reports relating to this section. There appear to be wide differences between countries in the extent of research at the organisational level, and in highly regulated countries changes in regulations or collective agreements are regarded as synonymous with change at the organisational level.

3 Changes in women's labour supply and household composition

1 Ninety per cent of women have their children before the age of 35 (CEC 1995a:65), but the data for the 1960 cohort is likely to be an underestimate.
2 It is motherhood, not marital status which is the most precise delineator of differences in women's labour market engagement. This has replaced the situation which prevailed in many countries in the first half of the twentieth century, when a clear line could be drawn between activity patterns of married and unmarried women. Marriage was commonly accompanied by women leaving the labour market in households where the man's income was sufficient to support this arrangement, often enforced by a 'marriage bar' for women employees in certain workplaces.
3 Women's employment may also be underestimated by activity or employment rates in many countries, particularly where they are working in family businesses, as homeworkers, or in casual or unrecorded employees in certain female-dominated sectors such as textiles, tourism and retail in Greece (Cavouriaris *et al.* 1994:4).
4 The dependency ratio is the proportion of the non-working population relative to the working-age population.

4 Wage work, care work and welfare

1 We are able to combine information from the European Labour Force Survey with data from the national labour force surveys in Sweden and Finland (data for Sweden 1989–1995), but Austria prior to 1995 did not have a labour force survey, so comparable data for Austria are sparse.
2 In 1992, there was a major change in the definition of unemployment used by the Italian statistical office. Changes occurring in the European Labour Force Survey over the period before and after 1992 may be affected by this change in definition and should be treated with caution.
3 This is in contrast to results for 1989 in which Denmark was the only country where having a young child did not increase the risk of unemployment (Eurostat 1993; Rubery *et al.* 1998a:139).

4 In Luxembourg the regulations related to the Guaranteed Minimum Income treat cohabiting couples more favourably than married couples, but this does not apply to the tax system.
5 The Working Family Tax Credit introduced by the UK government's 1998 budget reduces the taper of withdrawal from 70 per cent to 55 per cent.
6 In the public sector in Luxembourg there was a system of parental leave prior to the parental leave agreement.

5 Occupational segregation

1 The index of segregation was also calculated for employees only in 1990, and if we compare the rank order of countries according to the employee-only index between 1994 and 1990 we find a very high degree of similarity, with only Belgium and the Netherlands changing rank by more than one place, the former moving up three ranks to a more segregated position, and the latter moving down two places. (Segregation levels for employees versus non-employees are discussed later in this chapter.)
2 Ireland has over 50 missing occupational categories; in many cases all are classified into the catch-all 'other' category within a 2-digit group instead of being spread across all the 3-digit categories.
3 There are some notable changes in the shares of women employed in either very feminised (80 per cent or more women) or feminised occupations (60 per cent or more women) between the 1990 and the 1994 data. Most of these changes indicate an increase in concentration in feminised areas. The most likely reason for these differences is that the continuing increase in women's employment over this period has increased the female share of some key occupations which previously lay just below either the 80 per cent or the 60 per cent cut off. This explanation is suggested by the fact that in all cases the countries recording large increases had a high concentration of female employment in 1990, in those occupations with a feminisation rate just below the 80 per cent or the 60 per cent cut off. For example, the share of women in France employed in very feminised occupations rises from 17 to 41 per cent between 1990 and 1994, but in 1990 27 per cent of women were employed in occupations with a 70–79 per cent female share. Similarly, the share of women in feminised occupations in Belgium and the Netherlands rises markedly from 36.5 to 49.8 per cent in the case of Belgium and from 38 to 57.8 per cent in the case of the Netherlands, but 42 per cent of women in Belgium and 38 per cent of women in the Netherlands were employed in occupations with a 50–59 per cent female share in 1990. Changes in the classification system, coupled with only slight increases in female shares in some key occupations, thus could account for these apparently starkly different results.
4 The calculation using a standardised index of dissimilarity, which is also reported, shows a slight decline. This index falls from 55.3 to 53.12 but we do not have information on the standardisation procedure used.

7 Gender and working-time

1 An additional temporal dimension is that temporary contracts have an explicit finishing date.
2 The Working Time Directive (93/104/EC) provides for a maximum weekly working-time of 48 hours; a minimum daily rest period of 11 hours in a 24-hour period and 35 hours weekly (24 hours in some cases), in principle including Sunday; 4 weeks' annual leave (3 until 1999) and night work limited

to 8 hours. However, there are several key derogations (see IDS 1995:11–12) which weakens the 48-hour limit and other elements of the Directive.

3   This represented an increase of less than 10 thousand part-time temporary jobs for men in 1991.

Bibliography

NATIONAL REPORTS OF THE EC NETWORK ON THE SITUATION OF WOMEN IN THE LABOUR MARKET

The reports of the European Commission's Network on the Situation of Women in the Labour Market from the Third Action Programme (1991–1995) are available as working papers from the European Work and Employment Research Centre, Manchester School of Management, University of Manchester Institute of Science and Technology, Manchester, M60 1QD UK.

Austria

Pastner, U. (1995) *Women and the Employment Rate: The Causes and Consequences of Variations and Employment Patterns in Austria.*
Pastner, U. (1996) *Trends and Prospects for Women's Employment in the 1990s in Austria.*

Belgium

Meulders, D. and Vander Stricht, V. (1992) *Occupational Segregation in Belgium.*
Meulders, D. and Hecq, C. (1993) *Wage Determination and Sex Segregation in Employment in Belgium.*
Meulders, D., Hecq, C. and Ruz Torres, R. (1994) *Changing Patterns of Work and Working-Time for Men and Women: Towards the Integration or the Segmentation of the Labour Market, Belgium.*
Meulders, D. and Hecq, C. (1996) *Trends and Prospects for Women's Employment in Belgium in the 1990s.*
Meulders, D., Hecq, C. and Ruz Torres, R. (1995) *Women and the European Employment Rate: The Causes and Consequences of Variations in Female Activity and Employment Patterns. National Report for Belgium.*

Denmark

Boje, T. (1994) *Changing Patterns of Work and Working-Time for Men and Women: Towards the Integration or the Segmentation of the Labour Market. National Report for Denmark.*
Boje, T. (1995) *Women and the European Employment Rate: The Causes and Consequences of Variations in Female Activity and Employment Patterns. National Report for Denmark.*
Boje, T. (1996) *Trends and Prospects for Women's Employment in Denmark in the 1990s.*
Knudsen, R. (1992) *Gender Segregation in the Danish Labour Market.*
Knudsen, R. and Pedersen, L. (1993) *Wage Determination and Sex Segregation in Employment in Denmark.*

Finland

Ilmakunnas, S. (1995) *Women and the European Employment Rate: The Causes and Consequences of Variations in Female Activity and Employment Patterns in Finland.*
Keinänen, P. (1996) *Trends and Prospects for Women's Employment in the 1990s in Finland.*

France

Gauvin, A., Silvera, R. and Granie, C. (1992) *La Ségrégation Professionnelle des Femmes: Rapport Français.*
Gauvin, A., Granie, C. and Silvera, R. (1994) *Changing Patterns of Work and Working-Time for Men and Women: Towards the Integration or the Segmentation of the Labour Market.*
Silvera, R., Gauvin, A. and Granie, C. (1993) *Pay Determination and Sex Segregation in Employment in France.*
Silvera, R., Eydoux, A., Gauvin, A. and Granie, C. (1995) *Les Femmes et le Taux de Chomage en France.*
Silvera, R., Granie, C., Gauvin, A. and Eydoux, A. (1996) *Trends and Prospects for Women's Employment in France in the 1990s.*

Germany

Maier, F., Quack, S., Carl, A. and Strunk, S. (1993) *Wage Determination and Sex Segregation in Employment in West Germany.*
Maier, F., Quack, S. and Rapp, Z. (1994) *Changing Patterns of Work and Working-Time for Men and Women: Towards the Integration or the Segmentation of the Labour Market, Germany.*
Maier, F. and Rapp, Z. (1995) *Women and the European Employment Rate: The Causes and Consequences of Variations in Female Activity and Employment Patterns in Germany.*
Maier, F., Quack, S., Martschink, A. and Rapp, Z. (1996) *Trends and Prospects for Women's Employment in Germany in the 1990s.*
Quack, S., Maier, F. and Schuldt, K. (1992) *Occupational Segregation in the Federal Republic of Germany and in the Former German Democratic Republic, 1980–89.*

Greece

Cavouriaris, M. (1992) *Occupational Segregation in Greece.*
Cavouriaris, M. and Karamessini, M. (1993) *Wage Determination and Sex Segregation in Employment in Greece.*
Cavouriaris, M., Karamessini, M. and Symeonidou, H. (1994) *Changing Patterns of Work and Working-Time for Men and Women: Towards the Integration or the Segmentation of the Labour Market. Report for Greece.*
Cavouriaris, M., Karamessini, M. and Symeonidou, H. (1995) *Women and the European Employment Rate: The Causes and Consequences of Variations in Female Activity and Employment Patterns in Greece.*

Cavouriaris, M. and Symeonidou, H. (1996) *Trends and Prospect for Women's Employment in Greece in the 1990s.*

Ireland

Barry, U. (1992) *Occupational Segregation on the Irish Labour Market.*
Barry, U. and Roche, A. (1993) *Pay Determination and Women's Pay in Ireland.*
Barry, U. and Roche, A. (1994) *Female Work Patterns over the Life Cycle.*
Barry, U. (1995) *Women and the European Employment Rate: The Causes and Consequences of Variations in Female Activity and Employment Patterns of Irish Women.*
Barry, U. (1996) *Trends and Prospects for Women's Employment in Ireland in the 1990s.*

Italy

Bettio, F. and Villa, P. (1992) *Occupational Segregation: The Case of Italy.*
Bettio, F. and Villa, P. (1993) *Wage Determination and Sex Segregation in Employment in Italy.*
Bettio, F. and Villa, P. (1994) *Changing Patterns of Work and Working-Time for Men and Women, Italy.*
Bettio, F. and Mazzotta, F. (1995) *Women and the European Employment Rate – Italy.*
Bettio, F. and Villa, P. (1996) *Trends and Prospects for Women's Employment in Italy in the 1990s.*

Luxembourg

Plasman, R. (1992) *Occupational Segregation in Luxembourg.*
Plasman, R. and Adart, F. (1993) *Wage Determination and Sex Segregation in Employment in Luxembourg.*
Plasman, R. and Vanhuynegem, P. (1994) *Changing Patterns of Work and Working-Time for Men and Women: Towards the Integration or the Segmentation of the Labour Market, Luxembourg.*
Plasman, R. (1995) *Women and the European Employment Rate: The Causes and Consequences of Variations in Female Activity and Employment Patterns in Luxembourg.*
Plasman, R. (1996) *Trends and Prospects for Women's Employment in Luxembourg in the 1990s.*

Netherlands

Plantenga, J., Van Der Burg, B. and Van Velzen, S. (1992) *Occupational Segregation in the Netherlands.*
Plantenga, J., and Van Velzen, S. (1993) *Wage Determination and Sex Segregation in Employment: The Case of the Netherlands.*
Plantenga, J. and Van Velzen, S. (1994) *Changing Patterns of Work and Working-Time for Men and Women: Towards the Integration or the Segmentation of the Labour Market, the Netherlands.*

Plantenga, J. and Sloep, M. (1995) *Women and the European Employment Rate: Participation and Non Participation in the Netherlands. The Causes and Consequences of Variations in Female Activity and Employment Patterns.*
Plantenga, J., Koch, E. and Sloep, M. (1996) *Trends and Prospects for Women's Employment in the Netherlands in the 1990s.*

Portugal

Lopes, M., Ferreira, C. and Perista, H. (1992) *Occupational Segregation: Final Portuguese Report.*
Lopes, M. and Perista, H. (1993) *Wage Determination and Sex Segregation in Employment in Portugal.*
Lopes, M. and Perista, H. (1994) *Changing Patterns of Work and Working-Time for Men and Women: Towards the Integration or the Segmentation of the Labour Market, Portugal.*
Lopes, M. and Perista, H. (1995) *Women and the European Employment Rate: The Causes and Consequences of Variations in Female Activity and Employment Patterns in Portugal.*
Lopes, M. and Perista, H. (1996) *Trends and Prospects for Women's Employment in Portugal in the 1990s.*

Spain

Moltó, M.-L. (1992) *Occupational Segregation in Spain.*
Moltó, M.-L. (1993) *Wage Determination and Sex Segregation in Employment in Spain.*
Moltó, M.-L. (1994) *Changing Patterns of Work and Working-Time for Men and Women: Towards the Integration or the Segmentation of the Labour Market.*
Moltó, M.-L.(1995) *Women and the European Employment Rate: The Causes and Consequences of Variations in Female Activity and Employment Patterns. National Report for Spain.*
Moltó, M.-L. (1996) *Trends and Prospects for Women's Employment in Spain in the 1990s.*

Sweden

Gonäs, L. and Spånt, A. (1996) *Trends and Prospects for Women's Employment in the 1990s in Sweden.*
Lofström, A. (1995) *Women and the European Employment Rate: The Causes and Consequences of Variations in Female Activity and Employment Patterns in Sweden.*

United Kingdom

Rubery, J., Fagan, C. and Humphries, J. (1992) *Occupational Segregation in the UK.*
Rubery, J. (1993) *Wage Determination and Sex Segregation in Employment: Report for the UK.*

Rubery, J. (1994) *Changing Patterns of Work and Working-time: Towards the Integration or Segmentation of the Labour Market in the UK.*

Rubery, J. and Smith, M. (1995) *Women and the European Employment Rate: The Causes and Consequences of Variations in Female Activity and Employment Patterns in the UK.*

Rubery, J. (1996) *Trends and Prospects for Women's Employment in the United Kingdom in the 1990s.*

REFERENCES

Acker, J. (1989) *Doing Comparable Work: Gender, Class and Pay Equity.* Philadelphia: Temple University Press.

Anker, R. (1998) *Gender and Jobs: Sex Segregation of Occupations in the World.* Geneva: ILO.

Anxo, D. and Flood, L. (1995) 'Patterns of time use in France and Sweden'. Paper presented to the 7th conference of the European Association of Labour Economists. Lyon, France, September 1995.

Beccalli, B. and Salvati, M. (1995) 'Gender, employment and working time: a long-run view', in *Equal Opportunities for Women and Men: Follow-up to the White Paper on Growth, Competitiveness and Employment.* Report to the European Commission's Employment Task Force (DGV). V/5538/95-EN. Brussels.

Becker, G. (1985) 'Human capital, effort and the sexual division of labour'. *Journal of Labor Economics* 3:S33–S58.

Beechey, V. (1977) 'Some notes on female wage labour in capitalist production': *Capital and Class 3*: 45–66.

Bergmann, B. R. (1974) 'Occupational segregation, wages and profits when employers discriminate by race and sex'. *Eastern Economic Journal* 1: 1–2.

Bettio, F. (1988) *The Sexual Division of Wage Labour: The Italian Case.* Oxford: Oxford University Press.

Bettio, F. and Villa, P. (1993) 'Strutture familiari e mercati del lavoro nei paesi sviluppati: l'emergere di un percorso mediterraneo per l'integrazione delle donne nel mercato del lavaro'. (Family structures and labour markets in the developed countries: the emergence of a Mediterranean route to the integration of women into the labour market). *Economia e Lavoro* 27, 2: 3–30.

Bettio, F. and Villa, P. (1998) 'A Mediterranean perspective on the breakdown of the relationship between participation and fertility'. *Cambridge Journal of Economics* 22, 2: 137–171.

Bettio, F., Rubery, J. and Smith, M. (1996) 'Gender, flexibility and new employment relations'. Paper presented to the European Seminar on Women and Work in Europe; Integration between Labour Policies and Equal Opportunity Policies workshop. Turin, Italy, International Training Centre of the ILO, 18–19 April.

Bettio, F., Del Bono, E. and Smith, M. (1998a) 'Working-time patterns in the European Union: policies and innovations'. European Commission: Employment and Social Affairs (DGV); p. 95.

Bettio, F., Del Bono, E. and Smith, M. (1998b) 'The multi annual employment programmes: a gender perspective'. European Commission: Employment and Social Affairs (DGV); p. 34.

Blackburn, M., Jarman, J. and Siltanen, S. (1993) 'The analysis of occupational gender segregation over time and place: some considerations of measurement and some new evidence'. *Work, Employment and Society* 7, 3: 335–362.

Blau, F. and Kahn, L. (1992) 'The gender earnings gap: learning from international comparison'. *American Economic Journal* 82, 2: 533–538.

Blossfeld, H. and Hakim C. (eds) (1997) *Between Equalization and Marginalization: Women Working Part-time in Europe and the United States.* Oxford: Oxford University Press.

Bosch, G. (1995) 'A Synthesis', in *Flexible Working Time: Collective Bargaining and Government Intervention.* Paris: OECD.

Bosch, G. and Lehndorff, S. (1997) 'The reduction of working time and employment'. Paper presented to the 19th Conference of the International Working Party on Labour Market Segmentation. Porto, Portugal, July 1997.

Bosch, G., Dawkins, P. and Michon, F. (1994) *Times are Changing: Working Time in Fourteen Industrialised Countries.* Geneva: ILO.

Brannen, J. and Moss, P. (1991) *Managing Mothers: Dual Earner Households after Maternity Leave.* London: Unwin Hyman.

Brannen, J., Meszaros, G., Moss, P. and Poland, G. (1994) *Employment and Family Life: A Review of Research in the UK (1980–1994).* Employment Department Research Series no. 41. November.

Burchell, B., Dale, A. and Joshi, H. (1997) 'Part-time work among British women', in H.-P. Blossfeld and C. Hakim (eds) *Between Equalization and Marginalization:Women Working Part-time in Europe and the United States.* Oxford: Oxford University Press.

Casey, B. (1996) 'Exit options from the labour force', in G. Schmid, J. O'Reilly and K. Schömann (eds) *International Handbook of Labour Market Policy and Evaluation.* Cheltenham: Edward Elgar.

Cecchini, P. (1988) *The European Challenge, 1992.* Aldershot: Wildwood House.

CEC (1988) *Men and Women of Europe in 1987: The Evolution of Opinions and Attitudes.* DGX. X/24/88-EN. Brussels: European Commission.

CEC (1992) *Women in the European Community.* Luxembourg: Office for Official Publications of the European Communities.

CEC (1993) *Social Protection in Europe.* Luxembourg: Office for Official Publications of the European Communities.

CEC (1994) *Growth, Competitiveness, Employment: The Challenges and Ways Forward into the 21st Century.* White Paper. Luxembourg: Office for Official Publications of the European Communities.

CEC (1995a) *Women and Men in the European Union: A Statistical Portrait.* Luxembourg: Office for Official Publications of the European Communities.

CEC (1995b) *European Economy* 59, Office for Official Publications of the European Communities.

CEC (1995c) *Equal Opportunities for Women and Men: Follow-up to the White Paper on Growth, Competitiveness and Employment.* Report to the European Commission's Employment Task Force (DGV). V/5338/95-EN. Brussels.

CEC (1996a) Tableau de Bord 1995: *Follow-up to the Conclusions of the Essen European Council on Employment Policies.* Employment Observatory. CE-91–95–657-EN-C. Luxembourg: Directorate-General for Employment, Industrial Relations and Social Affairs.

CEC (1996b) *Employment in Europe, 1996* Luxembourg: Office for Official Publications of the European Communities.

CEC (1997a) '1997 broad economic policy guidelines: the outcome of the Amsterdam European Council on stability, growth and employment'. *European Economy*. Luxembourg: Directorate-General for Economic and Financial Affairs.

CEC (1997b) *Key Data on Vocational Training in the European Union*. Luxembourg: Office for Official Publications of the European Communities.

CEC (1997c) *Employment in Europe, 1997*. Luxembourg: Office for Official Publications of the European Communities.

CEC (1997d) *Equal Opportunities for Women and Men in the European Union: Annual Report 1990*. Luxembourg: Office for Official Publications of the European Communities.

CEC (1998) *Euro 1999, Part 1: Recommendation*. Luxembourg: Office for Official Publications of the European Communities.

CERC (Centre d'Etude des Revenus et des Coûts) (1991) *Les bas salaires dans les pays de la CEE*. V/20024/91-FR. Brussels: Commission of the European Communities.

Chalude, M., de Jong, A. and Laufer, J. (1994) 'Implementing equal opportunity and affirmative action programmes in Belgium, France and the Netherlands', in M. J. Davidson and R. J. Burke (eds) *Women in Management: Current Research Issues*. London: Paul Chapman.

Cockburn, C. (1991) *In the Way of Women: Men's Resistance to Sex Equality in Organisations*. Basingstoke: Macmillan.

Connell, R. W. (1987) *Gender and Power*. Cambridge: Polity Press.

Corti, L., Laurie, H. and Dex, S. (1995) *Highly Qualified Women*. Employment Department Research Series no. 50. London: Department for Education and Employment.

Coyle, A. (1995) *Women and Organisational Change*. Equal Opportunities Commission Research Discussion Series no. 14. Manchester: Equal Opportunities Commission.

Crompton, R. and Harris, F. (1998a) 'Explaining women's employment patterns: "orientations to work" revisited'. *British Journal of Sociology* 49, 1: 118–136.

Crompton, R. and Harris, F. (1998b) 'A reply to Hakim'. *British Journal of Sociology* 49, 1: 144–149.

Crompton, R. and Sanderson, K. (1990) *Gendered Jobs and Social Change*. London: Unwin Hyman.

Crompton, R., Hantrais, L. and Walters, P. (1990) 'Gendered relations and employment'. *British Journal of Sociology* 4, 3: 329–349.

Dale, A. and Egerton, M. (in association with Joshi, H. and Davies, H.) (1995) *Highly Educated Women: Evidence from the National Child Development Study*. University of Manchester: The Cathie Marsh Centre for Census and Survey Research.

Dale, A. and Holdsworth, C. (1998). 'Why don't minority ethnic women in Britain work part-time?', in J. O'Reilly and C. Fagan (eds) *Part-Time Prospects: An International Comparison of Part-Time Work in Europe, North America and the Pacific Rim*. London: Routledge.

De Grip, A., Hoevenberg, J. and Willems, E. (1997) 'Atypical employment in the European Union'. *International Labour Review* 136, 1: 49–71.

de Jong, A. and Bock, B. (1995) 'Positive action in organizations within the European Union', in A. van Doorne-Huiskes, J. van Hoof, and E. Roelofs (eds) *Women and the European Labour Markets*. London: Paul Chapman.

Delacourt, M.-L. and Zhigera, A. J. (1988) *Women's Work and Family Composition: A Comparison of the Countries of the European Economic Community.* DGV. V/1795/88-EN. Brussels: European Commission.

Delsen, L. (1998) 'When do men work part-time?' in J. O'Reilly and C. Fagan (eds) *Part-Time Prospects: An International Comparison of Part-Time Work in Europe, North America and the Pacific Rim.* London: Routledge.

Deven, F., Inglis, S., Moss, P. and Petrie, P. (1997) *State of the Art Review on the Reconciliation of Work and Family Life for Men and Women and the Quality of Care Services.* Final Report for the European Commission, Equal Opportunities Unit (DGV).

Dex, S. (1988) *Women's Attitudes Towards Work.* London: Macmillan.

Devine, F. (1994) 'Segregation and supply: preferences and plans among "self-made" women'. *Gender, Work and Organization* 1, 2: 94–109.

Dickens, L. (1995). 'UK part-time employees and the law'. *Gender, Work and Organization* 2, 4: 207–215.

Duncan, S. (1995) 'Theorizing European gender systems'. *Journal of European Social Policy* 5: 263–284.

Elias, P. (1995) *European Labour Force Survey: Cross-Tabulations, Frequency Distributions of Employment by NACE (Rev .1) and ISCO 88 (COM), Males and Females by Country.* Institute for Employment Research, University of Warwick: Warwick. October.

Elias, P. and Birch, M. (1995) *Implementing a Common Classification of Occupations across Europe.* Institute for Employment Research, University of Warwick: Warwick. September.

Escott, K. and Whitfield, D. (1995) *The Gender Impact of CCT in Local Government.* Equal Opportunities Commission Research Series no. 12. Manchester: Equal Opportunities Commission.

Esping-Andersen, G. (1990) *The Three Worlds of Welfare Capitalism.* Cambridge: Polity Press.

European Childcare Network (1994) *Leave Arrangements for Workers with Children: A Review of Leave Arrangements in the Member States of the European Community and Austria, Finland, Norway and Sweden.* Report prepared for the Equal Opportunities Unit (DGV). Brussels: European Commission.

European Childcare Network (1996) *Review of Children's Services.* Report prepared for the Equal Opportunities Unit, DGV. Brussels: European Commission.

Eurostat (1992) *Labour Force Survey: Methods and Definitions, 1992 Series.* Luxembourg: Office for Official Publications of the European Communities.

Eurostat (1993) *Unemployed Women in the EC.* Luxembourg: Office for Official Publications of the European Communities.

Eurostat (1994a) *Labour Force Survey: Results 1992.* Luxembourg: Office for Official Publications of the European Communities.

Eurostat (1994b) *Demographic Statistics.* Luxembourg: Office for Official Publications of the European Communities.

Eurostat (1994c) *Earnings: Industry and Services.* Luxembourg: Office for Official Publications of the European Communities.

Eurostat (1995) *Demographic Statistics 1995.* Luxembourg: Office for Official Publications of the European Communities.

Eurostat (1996a) *Labour Force Survey: Results 1994.* Luxembourg: Office for Official Publications of the European Communities.

Eurostat (1996b) *Labour Force Survey: Results 1995*. Luxembourg: Office for Official Publications of the European Communities.

Fagan, C. (1996) 'Gendered time schedules: paid work in Great Britain'. *Social Politics: International Studies in Gender, State and Society* 3,1: 72–106.

Fagan, C. (1997) Absent men and juggling women: gender, households and working-time schedules in Britain. Unpublished Ph.D. thesis. University of Manchester, UK.

Fagan, C. (1998) 'Time, money and the gender order: work orientation and working time preferences in Britain'. Paper presented at the Gender, Work and Organisation conference, Manchester, UK, January 1998.

Fagan, C. and Rubery, J. (1996a) 'Transitions between family formation and paid employment in the European Union', in G. Schmid, J. O'Reilly and K. Schömann (eds) *International Handbook of Labour Market Policy and Policy Evaluation*. Cheltenham: Edward Elgar.

Fagan, C. and Rubery, J. (1996b) 'The salience of the part-time divide'. *European Sociological Review*, 12, 3: 227–250.

Fagan, C., Plantenga, J. and Rubery, J. (1995) 'Part-time work and equality? Lessons from the Netherlands and the UK', in J. Lapeyre and R. Hoffman (eds) *A Time for Working – A Time for Living*. Brussels: European Trade Union Institute/Labour Research Department.

Finch, J. (1989) *Family Obligations and Social Change*. Oxford: Polity Press.

Freeman, R. B. (1995) 'Are your wages set in Beijing?'. *Journal of Economic Perspectives* 9, 3: 15–32.

Gallie, D. and Marsh, C. (1994) 'The experience of unemployment', in D. Gallie, C. Marsh and C. Vogler (eds) *Social Change and the Experience of Unemployment*. Oxford: Oxford University Press.

Garnsey, E. and Tarling, R. (1982) *The Measurement of the Concentration of Female Employment*. Working Paper no. 6 on the Role of Women in the Economy, MAS/WP 6 (82). Paris: OECD.

Gershuny, J., Godwin, M. and Jones, S. (1994) 'The domestic labour revolution: a process of lagged adaptation', in Anderson, M., Bechhofer, F. and Gershuny, J. (eds) *The Social and Political Economy of the Household*. Oxford: Oxford University Press.

Ginn, J. and Arber, S. (1994) 'Gender and pensions in Europe: current trends in women's pension acquisition', in P. Brown and R. Crompton (eds) *Economic Restructuring and Social Exclusion. A New Europe?* Series. London: UCL Press.

Ginn, J. and Arber, S. (1998). 'How does part-time work lead to low pension income?', in J. O'Reilly and C. Fagan (eds) *Part-Time Prospects: An International Comparison of Part-Time Work in Europe, North America and the Pacific Rim*. London: Routledge.

Ginn, J., Arber, S., Brannen, J., Dale, A., Dex, S., Elias, P., Moss, P., Pahl, J., Roberts, C., and Rubery, J. (1996). 'Feminist fallacies: a reply to Hakim on women's employment'. *British Journal of Sociology* 47, 1: 167–174.

Glover, J. and Arber, S. (1995) 'Polarization in mothers' employment'. *Gender, Work and Organization* 2: 165–179.

González, P. and Castro, A. (1995) 'The Portuguese labour market: did European integration make a difference? Paper presented at the 17th conference of the International Working Party on Labour Market Segmentation. University of Siena, Italy, July.

Granovetter, M. (1985) 'Economic action and social structure: the problem of embeddedness'. *American Journal of Sociology* 91: 481–510.

Gregg, P. and Wadsworth, J. (1995) 'Gender, households and access to employment', in J. Humphries and J. Rubery (eds) *The Economics of Equal Opportunities*. Manchester: Equal Opportunities Commission.

Gregory, A. (1991) 'Patterns of working hours in large-scale grocery retailing in Britain and France: convergence after 1992?'. *Work, Employment and Society* 5, 4: 515–539.

Gregson, N. and Lowe, M. (1994) *Servicing the Middle Class: Class, Gender and Waged Domestic Labour in Contemporary Britain*. London: Routledge.

Grimshaw, D. and Rubery, J. (1997a) 'Workforce heterogeneity and unemployment benefits: the need for policy reassessment in the European Union'. *Journal of European Social Policy* 7, 4: 291–318.

Grimshaw, D. and Rubery, J. (1997b) '*The concentration of women's employment and relative occupational pay: a statistical framework for comparative analysis*'. Labour Market and Social Policy Occasional Papers no. 26. OCDE/GD(97)186. Paris: OECD.

Hakim, C. (1981) 'Job segregation: trends in the 1970s'. *Employment Gazette* 89: 521–529.

Hakim, C. (1991) 'Grateful slaves and self-made women: fact and fantasy in women's work orientations'. *European Sociological Review* 7, 2: 101–121.

Hakim, C. (1992) 'Explaining trends in occupational segregation: the measurement, causes and consequences of the sexual division of labour'. *European Sociological Review* 8, 2: 127–152.

Hakim, C. (1993a) 'The myth of rising female employment'. *Work, Employment and Society* 7, 1: 97–120.

Hakim, C. (1993b) 'Segregated and integrated occupations: a new framework for analyzing social change'. *European Sociological Review* 9, 3: 289–314.

Hakim, C. (1993c) 'Refocusing research on occupational segregation: reply to Watts'. *European Sociological Review* 9, 3: 321–324.

Hakim, C. (1996) *Key Issues in Women's Work: Female Heterogeneity and the Polarisation of Women's Employment*. London: Athlone Press.

Hakim, C. (1998) 'Developing a sociology for the twenty-first century: preference theory'. *British Journal of Sociology* 49, 1: 137–143.

Hammond, V. (1994) 'Opportunity 2000: good practice in UK organizations', in M. Davidson and R. Burke (eds) *Women in Management: Current Research Issues*. London: Paul Chapman.

Hochschild, A. (1990) *The Second Shift: Working Parents and the Revolution at Home*. London: Piatkus.

Horrell, S. (1991) 'Working-wife households: inside and outside the home'. Unpublished Ph.D. thesis. University of Cambridge, UK.

Horrell, S. (1994) 'Household time allocation and women's labour force participation', in M. Anderson, F. Bechhofer and J. Gershuny (eds) (1994) *The Social and Political Economy of the Household*. Oxford: Oxford University Press.

Humphries, J. and Rubery, J. (1984) 'The reconstitution of the supply side of the labour market: the relative autonomy of social reproduction'. *Cambridge Journal of Economics* 8, 4: 331–346.

Huws, U. (1995) 'Teleworking: follow-up to the White Paper', in *Social Europe Supplement 3/95*: 1–96. Luxembourg: Office for Official Publications of the European Communities.

IDS (Income Data Services) (1995) 'The shifting sands of working time'. *Employment Europe* 407: 11–19.

IDS (1996a) 'Social Security exchange of part-timers not unlawful'. *Employment Europe* 409: 3.

IDS (1996b) 'UK to toe the line on working time limits?'. *Employment Europe* 413: 26–28.

IDS (1998a) 'The 35 hour week unravelled'. *Employment Europe* 436: 2.

IDS (1998b) '40 hour week still disputed'. *Employment Europe* 436: 7.

IFO (Institute for Economic Research) (1994) *Long Term Labour Force Scenarios for the European Free Trade Association.* Munich: IFO.

IFO (1995) *Long Term Labour Force Scenarios for the European Union.* Munich: IFO.

ILO (International Labour Office) (1995) *Yearbook.* Geneva: ILO.

IRS (Industrial Relations Services) (1994) 'Development in job evaluation: shifting the emphasis'. *IRS Employment Trends* 551: 10–16.

Irwin, S. (1995) *Rights of Passage: Social Change and the Transition from Youth to Adulthood.* Cambridge Studies in Work and Social Inequality no. 4. London: UCL Press.

Jacobs, J. A. (1993) 'Theoretical and measurement issues in the study of sex segregation in the workplace: research note'. *European Sociological Review* 9, 3: 325–330.

Jones, B. (1993) *Working Document in connection with the Memorandum on Equal Pay for Work of Equal Value.* V/6108/93-EN. Brussels: Equal Opportunities Unit (DGV), European Commission.

Jonung, C. and Persson, I. (1993) 'Women and market work: the misleading tale of participation rates in international comparisons'. *Work, Employment and Society* 7, 2: 259–274.

Joshi, H. and Andrew-Hinde, P. R. (1993) 'Employment after childbearing in post-war Britain: cohort-study evidence on contrasts within and across generations'. *European Sociological Review* 9, 3: 203–227.

Juster, F. T. and Stafford, E. P. (1991) 'The allocation of time, empirical findings, behavioural models and problems of measurement'. *Journal of Economic Literature* 29, 2: 471–522.

Katz, H. (1993) 'The decentralisation of collective bargaining: a literature review and comparative analysis'. *Industrial Relations and Labour Relations Review* 47: 3–22.

Kempeneers, M. and Lelievre, E. (1991) *Employment and Family within the Twelve.* DGV. V/383/92-EN. Brussels: European Commission.

Kiernan, K. (1991) 'The roles of men and women in tomorrow's Europe'. *Employment Gazette* 99, 10: 491–499.

Laite, J. and Halfpenny, P. (1987) 'Employment, unemployment and the domestic division of labour', in D. Fryer and P. Ullah (eds) *Unemployed People: Social and Psychological Perspectives.* Milton Keynes: Open University Press.

Lane, C. (1993) 'Gender and the labour market in Europe: Britain, Germany and France compared'. *Sociological Review* 41, 2: 274–301.

Le Grand, C. (1993) *Karriär – och utvecklingsmöjligheter på de interna arbetsmarkanderna.* Work-Organization-Economy Working Paper no. 9. Stockholm: Stockholm University, Department of Sociology.

Lewis, J. (1992) 'Gender and the development of welfare regimes'. *Journal of European Social Policy* 2, 3: 159–173.

Low Pay Network (1995) *Priced into Poverty: An Analysis of Pay Rates in Former Wages Council Industries.* London: Low Pay Network.

Maier, F. (1995) *Wage and Non-Wage Labour Costs, Social Security and Public Funds To Combat Unemployment, Equal Opportunities for Women and Men.* Report to the European Commission's Employment Task Force (DGV).

Marsden, D (1992) *Pay and Employment in the New Europe.* Aldershot: Edward Elgar.

Marsh, C. (1986) 'Social class and occupation', in R. G. Burgess (ed.) *Key Variables in Social Investigation.* London: Routledge and Kegan Paul.

Marshall, A. (1989) 'The sequel of unemployment: the changing role of part-time and temporary work in Western Europe', in G. Rodgers and J. Rodgers (eds) *Precarious Jobs in Labour Market Regulation: The Growth of Atypical Employment in Western Europe.* Geneva: International Institute for Labour Studies.

Maruani, M. (1995) 'Inequalities and flexibility', in *Equal Opportunities for Women and Men: Follow-up to the White Paper on Growth, Competitiveness and Employment.* Report to the European Commission's Employment Task Force (DGV). V/5538/95-EN. Brussels.

McLaughlin, E. (1995) 'Gender and egalitarianism in the British welfare state', in J. Humphries and J. Rubery (eds) *The Economics of Equal Opportunities.* Manchester: Equal Opportunities Commission.

McRae, S. (1991a) 'Occupational change over childbirth: evidence from a national survey'. *Sociology* 25, 4: 589–605.

McRae, S. (1991b) *Maternity Rights in Britain: the PSI Report on the Experience of Women and Employers.* London: Policy Studies Institute.

Meager, N. (1996) 'From unemployment to self employment: labour market policies for business start up', in G. Schmid, J. O'Reilly and K. Schömann (eds) *International Handbook of Labour Market Policy and Policy Evaluation.* Cheltenham: Edward Elgar.

Meulders, D. (1996) 'Women and the five Essen priorities'. Paper presented to the European Seminar on Women and Work in Europe. Turin, Italy, International Training Centre of the ILO, 18–19 April.

Meulders, D., Plasman, R. and Vander Stricht, V. (1993) *The Position of Women on the Labour Market in the European Community.* Aldershot: Dartmouth Publishing Company.

Millward, N. and Woodland, S. (1994) *Gender Segregation and Establishment Wage Levels.* Working Paper no. 639. London: Centre for Economic Performance, London School of Economics and Political Science.

Morris, L. (1985) 'Renegotiation of the domestic division of labour', in B. Roberts, R. Finnegan and D. Gallie (eds) *New Approaches to Economic Life*, Manchester: Manchester University Press.

OECD (Organisation for Economic Co-operation and Development) (1980) *Women and Employment.* Paris: OECD.

OECD (1993) 'Earnings inequality: changes in the 1980s', in *Employment Outlook.* Paris: OECD.

OECD (1994a) *The OECD Jobs Study.* Paris: OECD.

OECD (1994b) *Women and Structural Change: New Perspectives.* Paris: OECD.

OECD (1995a) *Flexible Working Time: Collective Bargaining and Government Intervention.* Paris: OECD.

OECD (1995b) *Education at a Glance.* Paris: OECD.

OECD (1995c) *Employment Outlook*. Paris: OECD.

OECD (1996) *Employment Outlook*. Paris: OECD.

OECD (1997a) *Labour Market Policies: New Challenges. Policies for Low-Paid Workers and Unskilled Jobseekers*. Paris: Directorate for Education, Employment, Labour and Social Affairs OECD.

OECD (1997b) *Employment Outlook*. Paris: OECD.

O'Reilly, J. (1994) 'What flexibility do women offer? Comparing the use of, and attitudes to, part-time work in Britain and France in retail banking'. *Gender, Work and Organization* 1, 3: 138–150.

O'Reilly, J. and Fagan, C. (eds) (1998) *Part-Time Prospects: An International Comparison of Part-time work in Europe, North America and the Pacific Rim*. London: Routledge.

PA Cambridge Economic Consultants (1991) *Issues and Policy in the Relationship between Female Activity and Fertility. Study on the Relationship between Female Activity and Fertility*, Volume 1: *Synthesis Report*. V/639/91-EN. Brussels: Commission of the European Communities.

Pahl, R. (1984) *Division of Labour*. Oxford: Blackwell.

Paoli, P. (1995) 'Ageing at work: a European perspective', in J. Snel and R. Cremer (eds) *Work and Aging: A European Perspective*. London: Taylor and Francis.

Phillips, A. and Taylor, B. (1980) 'Sex and skill: notes towards a feminist economics'. *Feminist Review* 6: 76–88.

Plantenga, J. (1997) 'European constants and national particularities: the position of women in the European Union labour market', in A. G. Dijkstra and J. Plantenga (eds) *Gender and Economics – A European Perspective*. London: Routledge.

Pugliese, E. (1995) 'Youth unemployment and the condition of young women in the labour market', in *Equal Opportunities for Women and Men: Follow-up to the White Paper on Growth, Competitiveness and Employment*. Report to the European Commission's Employment Task Force (DGV). V/5538/95-EN. Brussels.

Rees, T. (1992) *Women and the Labour Market*. London: Routledge.

Rees, T. (1995a) 'Women and training policy in the EU'. *Gender, Work and Organization* 2, 1: 34–45.

Rees, T. (1995b) 'Equality into education and training policies', in *Equal Opportunities for Women and Men: Follow-up to the White Paper on Growth, Competitiveness and Employment*. Report to the European Commission's Employment Task Force (DGV). V/5538/95-EN, Brussels.

Rees, T. (1998) *Mainstreaming Equality in the European Union*. London: Routledge.

Reskin, B. and Roos, P. (1990) *Job Queues, Gender Queues: Explaining Women's Inroads into Male Occupations*. Philadelphia: Temple University Press.

Rodgers, G. and Rodgers, J. (eds) (1989) *Precarious Jobs in Labour Market Regulation: The Growth of Atypical Employment in Western Europe*. Geneva: International Institute for Labour Studies.

Rowthorn, R. (1992) 'Centralisation, employment and wage dispersion'. *Economic Journal*. May: 506–523.

Rubery, J. (1988) *Women and Recession*. London: Routledge and Kegan Paul.

Rubery, J. (1995a) 'Performance related pay and the prospects for gender pay equity'. *Journal of Management Studies* 32, 5: 637–654.

Rubery, J. (1995b) 'Internal labour markets and equal opportunities: women's positions in banks in European countries'. *European Journal of Industrial Relations* 1, 2: 203–227.

Rubery, J. (1995c) 'Synthesis', in *Equal Opportunities for Women and Men: Follow-up to the White Paper on Growth, Competitiveness and Employment*. Report to the European Commission's Employment Task Force (DGV). V/5538/95-EN. Brussels.

Rubery, J. (1998a) 'Part-time work: a threat to labour standards?', in J. O'Reilly and C. Fagan (eds) *Part-Time Prospects: An International Comparison of Part-Time Work in Europe, North America and the Pacific Rim*. London: Routledge.

Rubery, J. (with Bettio, F., Carroll, M., Fagan, C., Grimshaw, D., Maier, F., Quack, S. and Villa, P.) (1998b) *Equal Pay in Europe? Closing the Gender Wage Gap*. ILO Series. London/New York: Macmillan/St Martin's Press.

Rubery, J. and Fagan, C. (1993) *Occupational Segregation of Women and Men in the European Community*. Social Europe Supplement 3/93. Luxembourg: Office for Official Publications of the European Communities.

Rubery, J. and Fagan, C. (1994) *Wage Determination and Sex Segregation in Employment in the European Community*. Social Europe Supplement 4/94. Luxembourg: Office for Official Publications of the European Communities.

Rubery, J. and Fagan, C. (1995a) 'Comparative industrial relations research: towards reversing the gender bias'. *British Journal of Industrial Relations* 33, 2: 209–236.

Rubery, J. and Fagan, C. (1995b) 'Gender segregation in societal context'. *Work, Employment and Society* 9, 2: 213–240.

Rubery, J. and Maier, F. (1995) 'Equal opportunity for women and men and the employment policy of the EU: a critical review of the European Union's approach'. *Transfer (European Review of Labour and Research)* 1, 4: 520–532.

Rubery, J. and Smith, M. (1997) *The Future European Labour Supply*. Report to the European Commission's Employment Task Force (DGV). [Available as an Employment and Social Affairs Research Paper, Office for Official Publications of the European Communities, 1999 (ISBN 92–828–6432–4)].

Rubery, J., Smith, M. and Fagan, C. (1994) *Occupational Segregation of Men and Women and Atypical Work in the European Union*. (DGV). V/5619/95-EN, Brussels: European Commission.

Rubery, J., Fagan, C. and Smith, M. (1995) *Changing Patterns of Work and Working-Time in the European Union and the Impact on Gender Divisions*. Report prepared for the Equal Opportunities Unit (DGV). V/6203/95-EN, Brussels: European Commission.

Rubery, J., Fagan, C. and Maier, F. (1996) 'Occupational segregation, discrimination and equal opportunity', in G. Schmid, J. O'Reilly and K. Schömann (eds) *International Handbook of Labour Market Policy and Evaluation*. Cheltenham: Edward Elgar.

Rubery, J., Smith, M. and Fagan, C. (1997a) 'Explaining working-time patterns by gender: societal and sectoral effects', in D. Meulders, G. Bosch and F. Michon (eds) *Working Time: New Issues, New Norms, New Measures*. Brussels: Editions du Dulbea.

Rubery, J., Bettio, F., Fagan, C., Maier, F., Quack, S. and Villa, P. (1997b) 'Payment structures and gender pay differentials: some societal effects'. *International Journal of Human Resource Management* 8, 3: 131–149.

Rubery, J., Smith, M., Fagan, C. and Grimshaw, D. (1998a) *Women and European Employment*. London: Routledge.

Rubery, J., Smith, M. and Fagan, C. (1998b) 'National working-time regimes and equal opportunities'. *Feminist Economics* 4, 1: 71–101.

Ryan, P. and Büchtemann, C. (1996) 'The school-to-work transition', in G. Schmid, J. O'Reilly and K. Schömann (eds) *International Handbook of Labour Market Policy and Evaluation*. Cheltenham: Edward Elgar.

Seymour, J. (1988) *The Division of Domestic Labour: A Review*. Working Papers in Applied Social Research no. 13, Manchester: Faculty of Economic and Social Studies, University of Manchester.

Siltanen, J. (1990a) 'Social change and the measurement of occupational sex segregation by sex: an assessment of the sex ratio index'. *Work, Employment and Society* 4, 1: 1–29.

Siltanen, J. (1990b) 'Further comment on the sex ratio index'. *Work, Employment and Society* 4, 4: 599–603.

Siltanen, J. (1994) *Locating Gender: Occupational Segregation, Wages and Domestic Responsibilities*. UCL Press: London.

Siltanen, J., Jarman, J. and Blackburn, R. M. (1993) *Gender Inequality in the Labour Market: Occupational Concentration and Segregation. A Manual on Methodology*. Geneva: ILO.

Smith, M. (1998) 'Lost youth? The changing nature of the school to wwork transition in the European Union'. Paper prepared for the Labour Process conference. University of Manchester Institute of Science and Technology, Manchester, UK, April 1998.

Smith, M., Fagan, C., and Rubery, J. (1998) 'When and why is part-time work growing in Europe?', in J. O'Reilly and C. Fagan (eds) *Part-Time Prospects: An International Comparison of Part-Time Work in Europe, North America and the Pacific Rim*. London: Routledge.

Spain, D. and Bianchi, S. M. (1996) *Balancing Act: Motherhood, Marriage and Employment among American Women*. New York: Russell Sage Foundation.

Toharia, L. (1997) *Labour Market Studies: Spain*. Luxembourg: Office for Official Publications of the European Communities.

Traxler, F. (1996) 'Collective bargaining and industrial change'. *European Sociological Review*, 12: 271–287.

Trends-Tendances (1995) 'Femmes-entreprise: Où faire carrière'. 15 June, 24: 22–27.

Tuijman, A. C. and Schömann, K. (1996) 'Life-long learning and skill formation', in G. Schmid, J. O'Reilly and K. Schömann (eds) *International Handbook of Labour Market Policy and Evaluation*. Cheltenham: Edward Elgar.

Tzannatos, Z. (1990) 'Employment segregation: can we measure it and what does it mean?'. *British Journal of Industrial Relations*. 28: 105–111.

Van der Lippe, T. and Roelofs, E. (1995) 'Sharing domestic work', in A. Van Doorne-Huiskes, J. Van Hoof and E. Roelofs (eds) *Women and the European Labour Markets*. London: Paul Chapman.

Vogler, C. (1994) 'Money in the household', in M. Anderson, F. Bechhofer and J. Gershuny (eds) *The Social and Political Economy of the Household*. Oxford: Oxford University Press.

Walby, S. (1998) *Gender Transformations*. London: Routledge.

Warde, A. (1990) 'Household work strategies and forms of labour: conceptual and empirical issues'. *Work, Employment and Society* 4, 4: 495–515.

Watson, G. (1992a) 'Hours of work in Great Britain and Europe: evidence from the UK and European Labour Force Surveys'. *Employment Gazette* 100, 11: 539–557.

Watson, G. (1992b) 'Working arrangements and patterns of working hours in Britain'. *Employment Gazette* 100, 3: 88–100.

Watson, G. (1993) 'Working time and holidays in the EC: how the UK compares'. *Employment Gazette* 101, 9: 395–403.

Watts, M. (1990) 'The sex ratio revisited'. *Work, Employment and Society* 4, 4: 595–598.

Watts, M. (1992) 'How should occupational segregation be measured?'. *Work, Employment and Society* 6, 3: 475–487.

Watts, M. (1993) 'Explaining trends in occupational segregation: some comments'. *European Sociological Review* 9, 3: 315–319.

Watts, M. and Rich, J. (1993) 'Occupational sex segregation in Britain 1979–89: the persistence of sexual stereotyping'. *Cambridge Journal of Economics* 17: 159–177.

Wood, A. (1994) *North–South Trade, Employment and Inequality: Changing Fortunes in a Skill-Driven World*. IDS Development Studies Series. Oxford: Clarendon Press.

Index

Acker, J. 220
Almond, P. 8
Alphametrics (UK) Ltd 8
Amsterdam Treaty (1997) 1, 18, 54, 308
Anker, R. 168, 170
Anxo, D. 251
Arber, S. 108, 112, 155
Austria: access to training 73; bonus payments 229; children and maternal employment 106; collective bargaining 241–2, 252; data sources 8; deferred families 101; devolution of responsibility 71; equal opportunity policies 77; female employment rate 294–5; gender discrimination 77, 78; gender and employment rates 57; gender pay gap 227–8, 230; graduate mothers 93; impact of Eastern European economies 33; labour market continuity 83; Law of Equal Opportunity (1993) 74; marginal workers 256; marriage 94; maternal employment rates 105–6; maternity leave 42; minimum wage 236, 238, 239; occupational segregation measurement 176–80, 208, 210; organisational structures 71; overtime payments 229; parental leave 43, 164; part-time employment 201, 254; pension reforms 40; performance-related pay 243; population change/migration flow 32; positive action policies 74; public sector employment 45; qualifications 89, 220; science and engineering qualifications 89; single mothers 164; taxation systems 158; temporary work 252; unemployment benefits 153; unemployment and educational attainment 143; unpaid domestic work 276; vocational training 50, 91, 125, 139; working hours 257–9, 260; working hours, gender preferences 266; working hours, mothers 105; working mothers 100; youth education 127; youth employment 124, 125

Barry, U. 36, 39, 41, 43, 47, 67, 86–9, 91–2, 107, 136, 212, 217, 240, 253, 274, 276, 306
Beccalli, B. 263
Becker, G. 109
Beechey, V. 168
Beijing Fourth World UN Conference on Women (1995) 1, 18, 308
Belgium: career breaks 43; childcare facilities 163; children and maternal employment 106, 108; clerical work 192; core age group employment 129; educational attainment and employment 130; employment rates 120; equal opportunities policies 53, 221; female employment rate 294–5; fertility rates 96; gender and employment rates 57; gender pay gap 224; Global Plan (1993) 43, 47, 48; graduate women 92; hours worked by mothers 105; labour market flexibility 47; labour market trends 297; minimum wage 236; non-wage labour costs 48–9; occupational segregation measurement 172–80, 208; older-age employment 132, 133; parental leave 162, 164; part-time employment 201, 253, 255; positive action policies 75; professional jobs 186; short working hours 47; status prior to unemployment 139; taxation systems 158; unemployed mothers 143; unemployment benefits 146; unemployment and educational attainment 143; unemployment gender gap 131; wage moderation policies 35, 36; welfare benefit reforms 40, 41; working hours 67, 259, 261; youth employment 126, 144
Bergmann, B.R. 169
Bettio, F. 18, 23, 36, 39, 46, 48, 52, 59, 64, 67, 74, 86, 89, 99, 110, 112, 137, 139, 151, 154, 162, 164, 208, 214–15, 220, 227, 240–42, 244, 248–9, 260, 263, 270–71, 274, 277, 281, 306–7
Bianchi, S.M. 165, 166
Birch, M. 9, 170

Blackburn, M. 168, 170, 171
Blau, F. 22, 248
Blossfeld, H. 252
Bock, B. 53, 62, 74, 75
Boje, T. 36, 42, 45, 67, 73, 91–2, 105, 151, 208, 214, 220, 229, 240, 242, 244, 248, 253–4, 265, 271
bonus payments 229
Bosch, G. 22, 66, 68, 256, 263, 265, 274
Brannen, J. 86, 87, 166
Bremen laws on positive action 54
Büchtermann, C. 125

care work 119, 165–6
Casey, B. 132, 271
Castro, A. 63, 278
catering workers 193
Cavouriaris, M. 45, 76
Cecchini, P. 17
Chalude, M. 53
child benefits 42–4
child homecare allowances 41–4, 106
childbearing decisions 101
childcare facilities 163
childless women 80, 97, 99–100
clerical work 183, 192–3, 211, 213
Cockburn, C. 169
cohabitation 94, 98
collective bargaining 232–3, 237–42, 252
compulsory competitive tendering (CCT) 244
computer professionals 191–2
Connell, R.W. 2, 116
contracting out 259
contractual status 256–64
core-age population 128–31; employment 128–30; inactivity 131–2; non-employed 289–92
Corti, L. 87, 165
Coyle, A. 70, 71
Crompton, R. 2, 80, 88, 101, 127, 168, 169, 217, 301

Dale, A. 87, 101, 108, 165
de Grip, A. 277
de Jong, A. 53, 62, 74, 75
decentralisation 69–70, 240–41
Delacourt, M.-L. 106
Delsen, L. 254, 260
demographic shift 112
Denmark: access to training 73; bonuses/overtime payments 229; catering workers 193; children and maternal employment 106, 107; clerical work 193; collective bargaining 240; computer professionals 191–2; core age group employment 129; decentralisation of wage bargaining 69; drivers 191; employment performance 29; employment rates 120; equal opportunities policies 52; female

inactivity 132; gender and employment rates 57; gender pay gap 224; gendered job queue 91; graduate mothers 93; graduate women 92; household data 9; jobs for women 214; labour market activity 82; labour market continuity 83; labour market trends 298; long-term unemployment 144; marriage 94; maternal employment rates 104–5; maternity leave 42; occupational segregation measurement 172–80, 208; parental leave 82, 161, 162, 164; part-time employment 201, 253, 254, 255, 270–71; pay dispersion 248; pension entitlements 156; professional jobs 186; public sector employment 45; public sector pay 244; qualifications 220; status prior to unemployment 139; taxation systems 159; teaching 192; unemployed mothers 105, 143; unemployment insurance schemes 151; vocational training 50, 91; wage moderation policies 36; working hours 67, 105, 259, 260; working mothers 98–9, 100, 105; work-time preferences 265, 306; youth education 127; youth employment 124, 125
Deven, F. 165
Devine, F. 101
devolution of responsibility 70–71
Dex, S. 102
Dickens, L. 54
discrimination by employers 53, 91, 102, 168; *see also* occupational segregation
dismissal 63–4, 78
divorce 94, 98
domestic labour, gender division 81, 87, 120, 165–6, 168
drivers 191
Duncan, S. 2

Earnings in Industry and Services (Eurostat) 223
East Germany (former): childcare facilities 163; children and maternal employment 108; collective bargaining 240–41; competition from men for jobs 216; core age group employment 128, 129, 130; dismissal 65, 78; educational attainment and employment 130, 132; employment rates 120; female employment rates 121–2; fertility rates 96–7; full-time graduate mothers 109; gender pay gap 227; graduate mothers 93; labour market activity 82; maternal employment rates 104; new mothers' employment 106; occupational segregation measurement 172–80; older-age employment 133; participation rates 304; part-time temporary work 279; part-time work 253,